Praise for Mick Wall

'[A] flaming juggernaut of heavy-metal biog . . . the author writes a deceptively casual-looking, sincere but half-amused prose'

Guardian

'*Enter Night*, Mick Wall's biography of Metallica, confirms this grizzled veteran to be as engaged and waspishly authoritative a chronicler of metal's most hirsute behemoths as Barry Miles has been for the Beats' *Independent on Sunday*

'It takes a writer of Mick Wall's pedigree and calibre . . . to present the whole wild, wonderful and emotionally draining tale all over again and make it as consistently fascinating and momentous as *Enter Night*' *Classic Rock*

'As well as being the most complete account yet of a great British rock band, *When Giants Walked the Earth* is, as its name implies, a document of a bygone age . . . Wall has done his subject proud'

Sunday Times

'So this is the big one: a fat, juicy biography of the biggest band ever . . . Mick Wall, the veteran rock journalist, lays it all bare in a book that can only be described as definitive' *Daily Telegraph*

Mick Wall is Britain's best-known rock writer and broadcaster, and is the author of numerous critically acclaimed books, including definitive, bestselling titles on Led Zeppelin (*When Giants Walked the Earth*) and Metallica (*Enter Night*).

By Mick Wall

Diary of a Madman – The Official Biography of Ozzy Osbourne
Guns N' Roses: The Most Dangerous Band in the World
Pearl Jam
Run to the Hills: The Authorised Biography of Iron Maiden
Paranoid: Black Days with Sabbath & Other Horror Stories
Mr Big: Ozzy, Sharon and My Life as the Godfather of Rock,
by Don Arden
XS All Areas: The Autobiography of Status Quo
John Peel – A Tribute to the Much-Loved DJ and Broadcaster
Bono – In the Name of Love
W.A.R.: The Unauthorised Biography of W. Axl Rose
When Giants Walked the Earth – A Biography of Led Zeppelin
Appetite for Destruction
Enter Night: Metallica – The Biography
AC/DC – Hell Ain't a Bad Place to Be

HELL AIN'T A BAD
PLACE TO BE

MICK WALL

PHOENIX

A PHOENIX PAPERBACK

First published in Great Britain in 2012
by Weidenfeld & Nicolson
This paperback edition published in 2013
by Phoenix,
an imprint of Orion Books Ltd,
Orion House, 5 Upper St Martin's Lane,
London WC2H 9EA

An Hachette UK company

1 3 5 7 9 10 8 6 4 2

A CIP catalogue record for this book
is available from the British Library.

ISBN 978-1-4091-3525-8

Typeset by Input Data Services Ltd, Bridgwater, Somerset

Printed and bound by CPI Group (UK) Ltd, Croydon, CR0 4YY

The Orion Publishing Group's policy is to use papers that
are natural, renewable and recyclable products and
made from wood grown in sustainable forests. The logging
and manufacturing processes are expected to conform to
the environmental regulations of the country of origin.

www.orionbooks.co.uk

For Malcolm Edwards

CONTENTS

Author's Note   viii

Acknowledgements   x

Prologue: Highway to Heaven   1

1. The Clansmen   3

2. Bonnie Boy   20

3. Young Blood   41

4. A Groovy Old Man   67

5. Got Balls   89

6. Bon the Likeable   114

7. Not a Nice Band   142

8. All in the Name of Liberty   168

9. A Giant Dose   195

10. A Wolf in Wolf's Clothing   226

11. Blood on the Rocks   252

12. The Place Down Under   284

13. What Did You Do for the Money, Honey?   313

14. Two-Fingered Salute   340

15. The Master Switch   360

16. Last Chance to See   391

Epilogue   418

Notes and Sources   419

Index   423

AUTHOR'S NOTE

When writing a biography of this nature, it's important to both seek the truth, whatever that might be, and to give a good sense of balance; allow readers to see things from all sides – or as many as the author may be able to muster – so that they may make up their own minds about the characters and stories depicted. For that reason, I endeavoured to make contact with AC/DC and their management when writing this book, to a) let them know what I was doing and, b) to allow them the opportunity to put their side of things and respond however they saw fit.

AC/DC, though, as this book makes clear, do not engage easily – or much at all – with those they perceive to be outsiders. As I was told time and time again, while interviewing various managers, record company executives, musicians, producers and friends that have worked with the band at various junctures throughout their 40-year career, as far as the Young brothers who run the group's affairs are concerned, you are either part of the AC/DC clan – privy to the inner sanctum and all that entails – or you basically don't exist. Having also dealt with the band and their entourage, in my guise as music journalist and broadcaster, on numerous other occasions over the years, I already knew this to be true. Therefore it came as no surprise when none of my enquiries to their current management, in regards to this book, were met with any response at all. Or as one of the few current insiders told me off the record, 'You won't even be on their radar'.

It is for this reason that, in some cases, there is no recorded response to some of the views held by others that were close to them that are now represented in this book. Fortunately, having interviewed and met various AC/DC members – including Malcolm Young, Brian Johnson, Angus Young and Bon Scott – on various occasions stretching back from the late-Seventies, up to present times, plus the dozens of people close to them that were interviewed specifically for this book, as well as taking careful note of other interviews they have all given to various media throughout their career, I feel the band's own views are as fairly and accurately represented as could possibly be expected. Indeed, the fact that none of the leading present members – i.e. the Young brothers – have had any direct involvement in this book meant that I was beholden to no one in my telling of their story. I know from my own bitter experience working with many of the biggest names in rock these past 35 years that full cooperation almost always means full compromise. And there are enough of those bloody-good-bloke fan books out there already. Instead, what you have here is the closest anyone has ever been to discovering just what the real story of AC/DC actually is, and told without fear of being expelled from the brotherhood.

I hope both you and they will appreciate the honest, blood-spilling endeavour involved.

ACKNOWLEDGEMENTS

The author wishes to give his utmost thanks to the following people, absolutely without whom ...

Linda, Evie, Mollie, Michael Wall; Malcolm Edwards; Robert Kirby; and Vanessa McMinn, Charlotte Knee, Ian Preece, Jane Sturrock, Jillian Young, Nicola Crossley, Craig Fraser, Dave Everley, Mary Hooton, Joe Bonamassa, Roy Weisman, Dee Hembury-Eaton, Nicola Musgrove, Peter Makowski, Ross Halfin, Joel McIver, Ian Clark, Colin Gilbey, Diana and Colin Cartwright, Anna Dorogi, Mark Handsley, Duncan Calow and Elizabeth Beier.

PROLOGUE

Highway to Heaven

The Queen Elizabeth Hospital, South Australia, February 1974. It is the morning after the night before. When Bon awakes it only takes a moment to realise this is not the usual Sunday morning trouble he is in. There's the hangover, but that's normal. A bump on the head and a few aches and pains elsewhere are also par for the course. Bon's a drinker and a scrapper. So what, mate?

But this is different. His eyes can't focus. His body can't move. His mouth can't breathe. He twists in and out of consciousness before finally a face he doesn't recognise hovers over him, telling him the score. 'You've been in an accident,' the voice says. 'You've been very badly injured.' This is doctor-speak for 'You fucked up, mate. Looks like you're a goner.'

The quack gives it some more lip but Bon has blacked out again. A goner, gone again ...

Later ... the next day, the next moment ... he overhears Irene talking it through with Vince, crying ... broken leg, broken arm, broken nose, broken teeth, broken jaw ... broken fucking everything by the sound of it, why didn't she just come out and say it? Broken dreams, that was the real cause of the pain. Twenty-eight years old, married, just about, but going nowhere, already been everywhere, what it felt like. He'd had his chance. He knew it, everyone knew it. Nobody was supposed to talk about it but you could see it in their eyes, the way they tried not to look at you but couldn't help it.

What was left? Pop star, been there done it. Rock star, been there couldn't quite manage it. Jail, ha, ha, ha. Women? There were always women. You didn't have to be the jolly fucking swagman to find a woman. Money ... ah, what was the fucking use? Everything you'd ever nearly had they'd taken away. Wouldn't even let you give it to them, they just wanted to take it all then watch you wonder why.

Then Irene over the bed ... 'Don't die, Bon, don't die ...'

Then Vince ... 'Come on, mate, you can do it ...'

Then the whine of the machine as it flat-lined; God looking down at him, saying, 'It's time, Bon ...'

Fuck it, so what? I was already dead before they brung me in here, said Bon to himself.

God shook his head sadly. Bon looked at him square like he was going to give it to him then changed his mind. For the first time he felt ... scared. No, not scared. That was for poofters. More just ... worried. Seeing his mistake. Feeling sorry for Irene and Vince and his poor mum and dad.

Bon told God: 'I don't care about dying. You know that. I just care about ... you know.'

'I know,' said God, infinitely patient yet not willing to stall.

'I'll tell you what. Give me back five years and I'll fix things, alright, God?'

God, who had heard it all before, began to tune out.

'Listen, you old fuck, five years, that's all I'm asking for. What's that to you? Fuck all!'

God paused. God could do what he liked.

'Five years, right, to sort things out, then you can have me back, all right, God?'

Silence. Deep, forever deep, silence ...

'Five years, you cunt! To do things properly this time, learn to keep my big mouth shut and look the other way when things get a touch too much. Five years, that's all, fuck's sake. Then I'm your man. What do you say, mate?'

CHAPTER ONE

The Clansmen

'**W**e are going to be huge, mate. Bloody huge ...'

That's what the Young brothers would tell anyone in Sydney that listened. Nobody did though. Who the hell did they think they were anyway? A couple of arse-hanging-out larrikins from the shit end of the stick. Pretty boy Malcolm with his long hooligan hair and Angus, his nutty little skinhead brother; neither of them barely more than five feet tall; aggressive little fuckers stick one on you quick as look at you.

They didn't even look Australian; didn't even sound it. Instead they looked and sounded like what they were: jocks from 'up the road'. Scotland, where the sun never shined, and the wind and rain lashed the gritty black smoke right into your poor, squinty eyes.

Born into the woebegotten schemes of Cranhill, runt of the litter to the Big Four east Glasgow schemes of Easterhouse, Pollok, Castlemilk and Drumchapel – the high-rise estates the government replaced the violent black-brick tenements with after the war, the Young brothers were rough-and-tumble snot-noses, playing in the shadow of Cranhill's water tower with all the other waifs and strays. Proddies, paying lip-service to the Union, but part of a larger clan; respecters of no man outside it. Some said it was the lead in the pipes that made the Young brothers so short. Others said it was down to sheer bloody-mindedness. They didn't want to grow up and be part of your world. They were happy where they were, thanks pal, down here close to the gutter.

As fellow Glaswegian and musician Derek Shulman, who as an

American record company executive would help drag AC/DC's career from the doldrums in the early Nineties, says now: 'A clan is exactly what they are. Despite all the success that would come their way, they never stopped looking at the world as us against them. It was all about family, about blood. And you were either totally one hundred per cent in that incredibly tight circle, or you were completely out.'

Accessed from the M8, to the east of Glasgow, visiting Cranhill now, it's still a bleak place, the skyline dominated by three tower blocks that loom over the rest of the scheme. With a population of less than 5,000, it is a place of poverty, mass unemployment and deprivation. It bears no relation to the dreams of its post-war planners, when all its newly built streets were named after proud Scots lighthouses like Gantrock and Bellrock. All except for Longstone Road – named after an English lighthouse – which is where local residents agree the Youngs lived 50 years ago. One resident, Malcolm Robertson, says the house they lived in is still standing as all the houses on the street are the original post-war structures, but no one can agree on which specific number.

A mixture of maisonettes and traditional stone-built council houses, Cranhill is over three miles from the nearest shopping centre so most don't bother. Front gardens are strewn with rubbish and although, in keeping with similar schemes, the area is surrounded by greenery, it only serves to add to the sense of isolation about the place. According to another former resident of the Glasgow schemes, Billy Sleath, it's still an improvement, however, on the world the Youngs grew up in. 'People go to places like Cranhill now and think it's a pretty grim place. But you should have seen it in the Fifties and Sixties. Smoke from the factories and shipyards, smoke from coal fires and cigarettes, the air was thick and black. And it affected everything. The walls were all black; the windows tarred. It was positively satanic.'

William Young and his wife Margaret already had six children before Malcolm (6 January 1953) and Angus (31 March 1955) were born. William had been a ground mechanic for the RAF during the Second World War. After it he'd found work as a spray painter; one of thousands of tiny cogs in the steel and shipping industries until, in his forties, he found himself on the dole, one of the many discarded and suddenly unemployable middle-aged men in a city where poverty and joblessness were becoming its defining features.

Thankfully, by then the first five of William and Margaret's kids – Steven (1933), Margaret (1936), John (1938), Alex (1939) and William (1941) – were old enough to fend for themselves, though they all still lived at Longstone Road. Outside the pub, music and football were the chief distractions. The only sister among the seven brothers, Margaret, 17 at the time Malcolm was born, had a record box containing such scratchy illicit confections as Fats Domino, Little Richard and Chuck Berry. The boys could all play a bit too; Stevie knew how to squeeze a tune out of a piano accordion; John was a wizard on the guitar. Alex was thought to be the most musically gifted, though, a jack-of-all-trades on guitar and, later, saxophone, clarinet and bass. By the time wee Malcolm and even more wee Angus had started at Milncroft primary school – where the school song began, 'School that is set on a hill, *we salute you!*' – Alex looked to be on his way as a professional musician, working at US Air Force bases in West Germany, playing with Tony Sheridan, whose 1962 hit 'My Bonnie' was huge in Scotland (and who later found more lasting fame for once having used The Beatles as his backing group, during their Star Club days in Hamburg).

Though it wasn't yet apparent, the real musical talent in the family, however, was George, seven years older than Malcolm, but whose dreams initially focused more on his football skills; he was thought at one stage to be good enough maybe for a trial with his beloved Glasgow Rangers. But it wasn't to be, George's dreams of soccer stardom finally laid to rest when the family emigrated to Australia when he was 16. At which point, inspired by Alex's example, George also began to learn guitar.

Born contrary, neither Malcolm nor Angus showed any signs early on of following in their big brothers' footsteps, most of their earliest memories centring on their shared experiences of school playground brawls, habits that would stay with them throughout their adult lives.

George was good with his fists too but Malcolm and Angus were killers. 'Cos of their size people would get the wrong idea and take them on,' recalls former AC/DC tour manager Ian Jeffery. 'But let me tell you they never lost a fight. Didn't matter how big you were, the brothers were fucking scary. They would go in, do their business, and leave you on the floor.' Even after they'd moved to Australia, whenever the brothers had 'a blue' with someone, it was their Cranhill blood that took over. Angus would later laugh and say he wanted to go back and rename it Angusland. 'I might drive up to the water tower and put my flag up' – emblazoned with the now famous AC/DC lightning bolt logo. 'It would be just like the Hollywood sign.' Note the sarcasm masquerading as irony. The fact was you had to be tough to get by in Cranhill, and Malcolm and Angus, as Ian Jeffery notes, 'weren't just tough – they were *fucking* tough'.

Nevertheless, life was hard, relentless. Prospects, such as they were, were limited to the shipyards, the factories and the dole. When Angus got knocked over by a car after school one day, his father decided enough was enough and began to talk seriously about taking advantage of the Australian Government's £10 immigration package, known as the Ten Pound Pom scheme (£10 per adult; kids for free). It was the winter of 1963, the worst on record, given its own rotten name, the Great Freeze, snow up to the top of the front door, ice causing all the pipes to burst. The idea of swapping such heart-stopping drudgery for a life on the beach, as the Youngs thought of Oz, suddenly seemed like a bloody good one. The only one of the family who didn't fancy it and eventually stayed behind was Alex, who, at 23, was on his way to pop stardom, he felt sure. The rest of the Youngs had no idea what lay in store for them when they landed at Sydney Airport, though eight-year-old Angus would make an immediate impression on fellow passengers by throwing up all over the baggage-claim area.

Arriving just as Australia was sliding into its own version of winter, whatever sun-filled visions the Youngs had of their new home before they got there were soon overtaken by the reality. It rained for six weeks solid after they arrived, causing them to joke they'd brought the weather with them. Not that anybody was laughing too hard. Obliged to spend those first months shacked up with other immigrant families in sparse, barrack-like living conditions at the Villawood Migrant Hostel (now the Villawood Detention Centre), in Sydney's poorer western suburbs, they would awake each morning to find snakes and lizards sharing their warm, dry bedding, or the biggest blackest spiders they'd ever seen making their own purpose-built homes among their few belongings. 'They had us in these tin huts, and it rained, relentlessly,' said Malcolm. 'When you got up in the morning, there was two inches of water in the hut and black worms swimming through it.'

William and Margaret began to feel they had made a terrible mistake, as did everyone huddled there waiting for the rain to stop and the new life they'd been promised to begin. One night they could take it no more and burst into tears, holding on to the bairns to stop them shaking. What had they done? Why had they allowed themselves to be dragged from one hellhole into another? But then the morning came and the clannish spirit began to assert itself again. No good crying over spilt milk. It was too late to go back now, said elder sister Margaret, fierce in her determination to hold the family together and force them to make a go of it.

While the older members of the family wondered what had hit them, George, for one, was already finding his feet. Nearly 18 and impatient to explore his new horizons, he made friends easily in the communal dining hall. It was in the basement laundry room, however, that he met the people who were going to help shape his destiny – and eventually that of his younger brothers. Two Dutch immigrants named Dingeman Vandersluys and Johannes Vandenberg. Like George, both played guitars – Johannes, the more adept of the two, could already play rudimentary solos, while Dingeman, less adept but good at keeping time, thrummed away at the bass strings. For handiness, George, who struggled to pronounce their names, called them Dick and Harry. Noting how everyone tripped over their names they soon settled on being known as Dick Diamonde (sic) and Harry Vanda.

Comfortable with the gang mentality that had dominated his Cranhill upbringing, George began bringing Dick and Harry with him everywhere he went as they began to explore the wider environs of Villawood, strolling up to nearby Leightonfield railway station, watching the trains coming and going and imagining themselves going too. When they began bringing their guitars out with them they would attract a crowd, especially of girls. One local lad, himself a recent arrival from England, another little tough nut named Stevie Wright, didn't like the idea of these strangely accented new boys getting so much attention and wasn't slow to show his feelings towards George, accusing him of being the brother of another local hard case he'd recently had 'a tumble' with. Unmoved, George refrained from headbutting him – his usual rebuke to anybody foolish enough to try it on – and simply laughed. As fiery as his younger siblings but with a cooler head on his shoulders, George was already thinking several moves ahead and before long Stevie had begun joining in, singing with him and Dick and Harry.

They got good at doing rudimentary versions of Beatles songs and other Top 40 stuff. Australia may still have been regarded by the rest of the world as a cultural backwater – literally, the ends of the earth – but it had radio and TV like any other civilised country and the cornerstone rock'n'roll artists of the Fifties and early Sixties had had the same impact there as in Britain and America. When the hostel began to organise 'Wogs and Rockers' nights – in reflection of the multi-ethnic backgrounds of its inhabitants, they cheerfully explained – George and his new best mates offered to perform too. Only snag: they needed a drummer. Enter yet another Ten Pound Pom: Gordon 'Snowy' Fleet. Already in his mid-twenties, Snowy wasn't hired for his looks but the fact he could actually hold down a beat – and hit the drums really bloody hard.

When the Young family were finally able to move into a small house of their own – at 4 Burleigh Street, near the police station – in the better-off Sydney suburb of Burwood, Stevie Wright moved in with them. 'Getting lost in amongst the clan of the Youngs,' he later recalled. 'I loved it and they shared their love.'

By then the group had a name – The Easybeats, inspired by Merseybeat, but with their own sun-baked twist on it. They had also begun to make a name for themselves on Sydney's nascent live pub and club scene and in 1964 they signed a management deal. The man who talent-spotted them, Mike Vaughan, was an ambitious young former estate agent with one priceless connection in the music business: that of producer Ted Albert.

Ted was the 27-year-old son of Alexis Albert, titular head of J. Albert and Son, one of the oldest, most powerful music business companies in Australia.

Typically of the Albert family's trailblazing history, Ted hit pay-dirt with practically his first signing, Billy Thorpe & The Aztecs, who gave the company its first nationwide Australian hit in the summer of 1964 with their cover of Leiber and Stoller's 'Poison Ivy' – famously keeping The Beatles from the No. 1 slot on the Sydney charts just as the group was touring Australia for its first and only time. It was a feat that briefly made Thorpe into a national hero of Ned Kelly-size proportions and over the following years he and his group enjoyed a handful of further hits – until they were left to choke in the fumes of Ted's next big signing: The Easybeats.

Ted was happy to allow his pal Mike Vaughan's new group to audition for him at the Alberts-owned 2UW Theatre. Surprised by how well they did, he offered to produce a single for them, a recording of a song George and Stevie had written together called 'For My Woman'. A mid-paced sub-Stones blues number, most memorable for George's skin-tight rhythm guitar and Harry's proto-psychedelic guitar solo, covering up for decidedly undercooked drums and over-laid by a distressingly repetitive three-line verse-cum-chorus, 'For My Woman' was released in March 1965, to great excitement at Burleigh Street. But instead of becoming the instant hit George and the family fantasised it would, the first Easybeats single was a stone-cold flop.

Showing that Cranhill us-against-the-world spirit though, George and Stevie simply went to Ted with another song they had written, 'She's So Fine'. Not dissimilar to its predecessor – bare-minimum lyrics laid over a semi-catchy tune, except more up-tempo and featuring the kind of snub-nosed staccato opening AC/DC would later develop into monster riffs like 'Whole Lotta Rosie' – Ted, whose own never-say-die attitude had also been inherited from his self-made family, gamely recorded it and put it out, in May 1965. Three weeks later it was No. 1 all over Australia. A month later it was still there and the legend of The Easybeats had begun in earnest.

Over the next two years, The Easybeats became to Australia what The Beatles were to Britain: the first home-grown talent to equal the success and popularity of overseas superstars like Elvis and, of course, The Beatles themselves. Though as a producer Ted was no George Martin, he had great 'ears', the most valuable possession in the record business, and an almost intuitive gift for sifting out material with commercial appeal, then honing and capturing that sound on record. As such, The Easybeats came with an instantly recognisable musical identity, which helped build a fan-base more quickly. Also similarly to The Beatles, all their important hits were originals, written initially by George and Stevie, with Harry becoming more involved as time went by. Between 1965 and 1966, George and Stevie provided The Easybeats with four No. 1 hit singles, three Top 10 hits and several other chart singles. They were so prolific the Oz press started writing of 'Easyfever' and began referring to Wright and Young as 'the Australian Lennon and McCartney'. And just like Lennon and McCartney, they had enough material to provide hits for other artists too, notably 'Step Back', another No. 1, this time for Johnny Young (no relation) in 1966.

Despite their success, George never lost his Glasgow edge. When, during an outdoor radio promotional appearance one afternoon in Sydney, a crowd of nearby labourers began shouting insults, calling them poofters, George's initial reaction was to play it cool, ignore them. When one of them then aimed a punch at Stevie's back, however, George decided to have a wee word. The singer watched in petrified glee as George strolled over and kicked the ringleader in the balls then dropped his nearest mate with one punch.

Easyfever came with the same unsettling side-effects as its British counterpart Merseybeat. At a show before 5,000 mainly female fans at Brisbane's Festival Hall in December 1965, the set had to be abandoned after 15 minutes when police began to panic at the outlandish crowd scenes. With the band bundled into a taxi, hundreds of Easyfever-stricken fans set about demolishing the car, as the freaked-out band members huddled inside, shielding themselves from broken glass. Facing off with a gang of hard nuts was one thing, learning how to survive a tsunami of hormonal teenage girls quite another – and much more frightening.

While the rest of the family revelled in George's good fortune, Malcolm and Angus were still too young to fully appreciate how things had changed for their older brother. The first inkling Angus had of the very different new life George was suddenly leading occurred when he came home from school one day to find hundreds of screaming girls on the street outside the house. A teen magazine had given George's home address out and now the police had to be called to try and control the huge and very excited crowd that had descended like locusts. Never one to be outgunned, Angus skipped round the back and over the garden wall. What he hadn't bargained for was the tenacity of George's fans, a great cluster of which followed him round the back and over the wall, then crashed as one through the backdoor, knocking him over in their rush to … do what exactly? He had no idea. It was his first close-up experience of pop fandom and he watched fascinated as the police fought to clear the house.

Malcolm, now in his teens, had already made up his mind what he could do about it and began taking his guitar practice more seriously. With George hardly around any more, though, it was his older brother John that Malcolm got most of his early encouragement from. 'Those were great days,' he would later say, 'I was just going into puberty and we were getting all these screaming girls, a couple of hundred of them, hanging outside our house for a glimpse of The Easybeats.' He added: 'Me and Angus used to hang out there with them thinking, "This is the way to go!" That planted the seed for us …'

Just like school in Cranhill, Burwood public school was a washout, Malcolm picking up where he'd left off, fighting anyone who got in his way, inside and outside of class. Other pupils ran scared of him.

Teachers gave up on him. When Angus followed him into Ashfield Boys High School, in 1966, he recalled, 'I was caned the first day. The guy said, "What's your name?" "Young." "Come out here, I'm going to make an example of you."'

Unlike his good-looking brother, Angus was gawky in school photos, wearing glasses and an ugly sneer, He was not a popular student; his best friend at Burwood, Jeff Cureton, says they were 'larrikins': getting up to mischief, buying fireworks at an old fruit shop in Stratfield and letting them off in the street while hiding behind bushes. Once they bought a box of cigars but got so sick trying to smoke them Angus vowed he would never smoke again. Which he didn't, until the next day when he was back on the cigs, bought singly in those days. No matter what antics he got up to, Angus was always forgiven though, the baby of the family, indulged by his mother, who Cureton recalls as 'a really nice lady'. As long as you didn't get on the wrong side of her fiery Scottish temper, that is. When the headmaster reprimanded Angus for having long hair, ordering him to get it cut, mother Margaret went in to see him the very next day, telling him exactly what he could do with his orders. No one told the Youngs what to do, least of all some jumped-up bookworm with a bald head.

It was also at Ashfield Boys High that they met Steve Armstrong. Malcolm was 'the pretty boy of the two', remembers Armstrong. 'I got the impression that [Angus] was always in the shadow of Malcolm, especially where the girls were concerned. None of us had a hope in hell of getting a girl when Malcolm was around. He had them all and I mean all of them. [But] Angus had that real attitude and was not frightened to display it to anyone.'

Angus had also beaten Malcolm to the punch when it came to wanting to play guitar. He'd begun back in Cranhill by getting older brother Alex to show him a basic 12-bar blues, based on what he'd heard from his sister Margaret's Chuck Berry records. From there he was up and running. Indeed, it would be the only lesson he ever had. Now in Burwood, he began plucking away at a customised banjo that found its way into the Burleigh Street house, unwittingly forging a style that would become the signature of his style in AC/DC, from the wheel-spinning motif he lays over the top of early cross-burners like 'Let There Be Rock', to the spurs-jangling riff of later street-corner classics like 'Thunderstruck'. When Angus did finally talk his mother into getting him a cheap acoustic guitar, to his disgust he was told he'd have to share it with Malcolm. 'When we were kids we fought like cats and dogs,' said Angus, 'and then when we started playing guitar it was even worse. He wouldn't let me in his bedroom because he'd say, "Angus has got a photographic memory. Play a lick and he steals it." Whenever I'd walk in the room he'd say, "Get out!"'

Unlike his younger brother, Malcolm (who also never had a lesson) took his cue as a budding guitarist initially from the surf hits that had swamped the Australian charts in the mid-Sixties. 'Hangin' Five' by The Delltones had been a favourite but it was the instrumental hit 'Bombora' by The Atlantics that he found easiest to learn, and that inspired him to keep practising in the early days when his little hands could barely grasp the guitar neck let alone hold down the strings. Malcolm loved the primitive drums and the flash way Jim Skiathitis played the guitar with his teeth. The Atlantics were a group of teen-agers from Sydney's eastern suburbs, and if they could do it . . .

Malcolm's and Angus's guitar-sharing quarrels were finally solved – and Malcolm's determination to master the instrument was given an extra boost – when, in 1968, the year he left high school, Harry Vanda gave the older Young brother, now 15, the electric Gretsch Jet Firebird that he'd actually been playing onstage on tour with The Easybeats. Forced to play with an open tuning until his hands grew large enough to manage more, like a lot of short teenagers, Malcolm was aggressively self-conscious about his lack of height. At a time when most of his mates were having mid-teen growth spurts, Malcolm's body seemed unchanged. It meant he didn't need to shave yet and couldn't get served in the pubs his mates were now becoming frequent visitors to. So he simply stopped going, and spent most nights at home in his room, fiddling away at the Gretsch.

Angus, still smaller than Malcolm, though he would catch up eventually, came at the guitar from a different angle. He hated surf music. 'When I was young and first heard harmonies, I thought,

"That's too nice". The Beach Boys always reminded me of the nice kids in school.' Good at art and music, but utterly uninterested in sports, Angus had had it with school anyway and, like Malcolm before him, left as soon as he was legally allowed. 'I left just turned fifteen because school's school and I was a bit of a truant,' he later explained. The teachers would 'cane you on the hand because you didn't have the ability [even] if you genuinely didn't know answers. Art and history were okay, but all the other stuff ... ah, you didn't need it.'

Maybe not. But as far as William, their father, was concerned, and despite the evidence to the contrary presented by George and even Alex (now living in London and working for The Beatles' newly formed Apple record company), he remained as convinced as ever that music was not a career option for his two youngest sons. Putting his foot down, he demanded they take up an honest trade and both Malcolm and Angus drifted through a succession of short-lived jobs, purely to keep the 'auld man' off their backs. Malcolm actually got a job in a bra factory, while Angus worked briefly in a print shop. But with some money of their own in their pockets at last, and freed from what they saw as the tyranny of school, neither boy felt hard done by. Their Cranhill roots still showing, they understood the value of a hard day's work – an attitude they would carry over eventually into AC/DC, which to this day they continue to refer to – at least in public – in working-man's terms. 'I've never felt like a pop star,' Malcolm was insisting as recently as 2008. 'This is a nine-to-five sort of gig. It comes from working in the factories, that world. You don't forget it.'

Not that they gave up on their playing. Through the week both boys would spend their evenings at home, playing their guitars and dreaming. In both instances, they received huge encouragement from their brother George. As Dave Evans, another young face on the Sydney scene with one eye on becoming a singer would recall: 'To have people like Stevie Wright coming round to the house, and all the other members of The Easybeats, was probably just a normal way of life.' Adding, 'It wouldn't have been foreign to them to have great ambitions because they'd already seen it demonstrated with George.'

*

George also kept his brothers' interests going with regular packages home of records and music magazines, stuff that he'd come across on his travels. With The Easybeats now based full-time in London but regularly touring America and Europe, he was able to provide his brothers with what, for Australia then, were ahead-of-the-curve insights into music and artists that had barely been heard of back home. The brothers would spend days and weeks pouring over such treasures, adding them to the sum of knowledge they were also now gathering from Sydney's own radio and television pop shows. Saturday mornings the whole family would gather round the TV, giving their opinions on the latest chart hits over endless cigarettes and pots of tea. When George was home on a visit he would join in, then encouraging Malcolm and Angus by playing along on bass as the two younger lads thrashed away on their guitars. He would shout out chord changes, to see how easily they could switch. But the noise was so loud sometimes they didn't hear him – or pretended not to, unwilling to take instruction even from their pop star big brother.

What they did listen carefully to was the practical advice George was able to give them on things like which guitar strings to use, how best to use pick-ups, how to change the tuning if you wanted, which amps to use. Or not, depending on how the younger two saw it. George was especially useful in pointing them in the right direction in terms of who the really cool new gunslingers were in Britain and America. Names alien then to most Australian ears like Eric Clapton, whose *Beano* album with John Mayall's Bluesbreakers he forced them to pay close attention to; Peter Green and Jeremy Spencer from Fleetwood Mac, another band no one in Sydney yet knew anything about; and from America Mike Bloomfield, the dazzling young hotshot guitarist who'd enabled the Paul Butterfield Blues Band to become an internationally renowned act, then helped Dylan metamorphose into an electric rock artist. George also reminded them constantly to keep listening for the best that the old school in America still had to offer, like their beloved Chuck Berry and Little Richard. Lessons the boys took to heart: 'You can't forget Chuck Berry,' said Malcolm, 'I mean, just about everything he did back then was great.'

Malcolm and Angus were quick to make their own discoveries too. 'The first time I heard "My Generation" by The Who that was something,' Malcolm told Australian writer Murray Engleheart. 'The Beatles and the Stones were the big thing and then all of a sudden this thing sounded heavier. That changed my whole thing. Later on I guess "Jumpin' Jack Flash", and I'll give you two more, "Honky Tonk Women" – and then "Get Back" by The Beatles. That's just pure rock'n'roll as it evolved, I reckon.'

The next logical step was to play in a band. Soon the brothers had gone from slowing down records on their record player to learn the chord changes of various songs, to actually playing those same numbers live. Supporting himself with a string of dead-end jobs – sewing machine repairman, apprentice fitter-and-turner, warehouseman – Malcolm began with the amusingly aptly named Beelzebub Blues, aka Red House and/or Rubberband, depending on the sort of gig they had wangled. The five-man band, fronted by Malcolm's pal, singer Ed Golab, featured the same drums, bass, two guitars line-up that AC/DC would later adopt, but with Malcolm on lead guitar.

'Malcolm was a great lead player,' recalls Ian Jeffery now, 'maybe even better than Angus at that stage. In the early days when I began working for them you'd see him do a brilliant solo or guitar-break sometimes. But he was an even better rhythm player – probably one of the best ever – and his genius was to spot that – and the fact that Angus was a better frontman as a guitarist.'

That was all for the near future, however. In the meantime, Malcolm very quickly made a name for himself as the pint-sized guitar-killer who could rip through songs by everybody from purist blues-rockers like Blodwyn Pig, Savoy Brown and Clapton in his Bluesbreakers guise, to more self-consciously progressive new blues-rock gods like Black Sabbath, Clapton in his psychedelic Cream phase, even Jimi Hendrix in his all-guns-blazing *Are You Experienced* showman phase. Even at that incredibly early stage, as a teenager barely out of school, there were to be no concessions to Top 40 familiarity. If the audiences had never heard of Blodwyn Pig or Savoy Brown more fool them. Malcolm's only concession: a heavy rock version of 'Come

Together' by The Beatles. By then, recalled Golab, Malcolm Young 'was *the* guitarist' on the scene.

Rehearsing at an old scout hall which they'd broken into and now slept in when they were too drunk to go home, fun though blasting out cover versions was, Malcolm already had bigger ideas. He and Golab would drink beer and talk into the small hours about making their own original music, not like The Easybeats or any of the other copycat Australian groups. But something with an identity of its own, something different. By the time Malcolm was 18, they were writing their own songs, taking inspiration from the new album-oriented songs of Stevie Wonder and the burbling sounds of innovative new American groups like Santana, whose Latin-influenced sound Malcolm saw as another expression of the R&B grooves he loved best in rock music. Rock was becoming pretentious, groups like Led Zeppelin and Deep Purple relying on virtuoso techniques over simple grooves. Stevie Wonder and Santana had all that *and* the ability to make you move your feet and jump in the air. For a while, he even tinkered with jazz chords, working out how songs were written by playing them on a keyboard. For someone who would later make a virtue out of jettisoning such above-their-station ideas, young Malcolm was incredibly studious about music. People thought he only played rock'n'roll because that's all he knew. But he never rejected groups or songs before understanding intimately what it was they were actually doing.

At the same time, Malcolm wanted to be taken seriously, couldn't stand it when he was still mistaken for a schoolboy. Ed Golab recalled how even in their late teens Malcolm was still 'looking like he was twelve, thirteen, just because of his height. And it was something that I guess he always had a hard time with, cos all his girlfriends were sort of really young girls who thought that he was a very young boy. And that was always a problem for him.'

By contrast, nothing ever seemed to be a problem for the apparently charmed seventh son of the family. Unlike Malcolm, Angus seemed utterly unconcerned about what people thought of him. While Malcolm grew his hair, bought tight-fitting flared trousers and was fond of a tinny, Angus had become a skinhead, replete with shaved head, bovver boots and who-gives-a-fuck attitude. Malcolm used to joke and say the reason Angus got in fewer fights than him was because no one wanted to fight him. He certainly had an air of intimidation about him. Unlike Malcolm, though, the only brew Angus liked was tea, and if that wasn't handy, milkshakes – and, of course, cigarettes. Everyone in the Young family smoked heavily, didn't know anyone that didn't.

By the time he'd left school and begun putting his own bands together Angus had also inherited a smart new electric guitar, care of George's connections: a Gibson SG, as used by everybody from Chuck Berry to Jeff Beck. (He adored the latter's hit 'Hi Ho Silver Lining', a song the musically-snobbish Beck himself abhorred.) Unlike Malcolm, who liked to practise the guitar alone, Angus was happy to invite pals into his bedroom to see him rock. No meticulously learning chords for Angus, either. He just plain wailed away and that was it. Recalled one astonished visitor, Herm Kovac, 'He's on the dressing table, he's kicking his legs up, he's jumping on the bed, he's just all over the place.' At the end of which Angus grinned at Herm and said, 'What do ya reckon?' Herm looked at him and said, 'Do you know any chords?'

Angus also had a battered old Hofner guitar which he'd plug into a 60-watt amp and turn up to maximum volume and crash-bang-wallop on until his parents threatened him with his life if he didn't stop. By the time he was 11, he could replicate Hendrix solos and blast out the chugging riff to 'I'm A Man' by the Yardbirds. He wasn't fussy, as long as it was loud and he could jump around while playing it, Angus was happy. Not choosy, he loved – and played along to – Australian bands like The Missing Links and The Loved Ones as much as he did The Animals and Chuck Berry. He became obsessed with Little Richard's 1957 classic 'Keep A-Knockin'', replicating the feverishly honking sax break on his guitar and repeating it over and over until his mother Margaret again had to physically threaten him. The riff in various forms would eventually become the backbone to some of AC/DC's greatest moments. (Interestingly, 'Keep A-Knockin'' would also become the song that later 'inspired' Led Zeppelin to knock out

'Rock And Roll'.) One thing Angus did share as a musician with his brother was a mature appreciation of music that went way beyond his years – or the popular later perception of them in AC/DC as uncouth rock'n'rollers who'd never got past 'Go' in their musical education. When his sister Margaret took Angus to see Louis Armstrong perform at Sydney Stadium, he was in a deep swoon for days afterwards.

Known as 'The Banker', for his knack of saving every dollar he could, Angus had no qualms about spending his pocket money on records, taking the bus into town to buy imports. He also became a frequent visitor to the local library where a kindly librarian helped him order music books and magazines from overseas. He would sit in the library for hours at a time, pouring over yellowed copies of *Downbeat* magazine, cooing over articles and pictures of blues guitar heroes like Muddy Waters and Buddy Guy. Not that he was a solitary kid. Another pal from those times, an American immigrant a year older than Angus named Larry Van Kriedt, who could also wield an electric guitar with an impressive swagger, recalls always seeing Angus with 'a gang of friends around him'. They were 'tough guys' and, although Angus was the smallest, he was 'the ring leader'.

A quietly spoken newcomer, when Van Kriedt found himself being picked on by bullies, Angus, half their size, would ward them off with the words: 'If you touch him I'll see you in the ground!' Angus was, his new friend deduced, 'a pretty assertive sort of guy. He got into trouble quite a lot and he attracted a "gang" culture around him … But I always felt he was very honourable and loyal.'

Honour. Loyalty. Toughness. And an ability to pick things up quickly as you went along while following no one's rules but the ones you made for yourself. Cranhill may have seemed like an increasingly distant memory to Malcolm, Angus and George Young as they began to find their way on the sun-baked streets of Sydney in the Sixties, but its shadow would continue to cloak their souls every step of the way.

CHAPTER TWO

Bonnie Boy

In the early days of AC/DC when people in the Sydney pubs would get smart and ask Bon Scott if he was AC or DC, rather than punch them in the mouth, as he would have done once upon a time, and might do again if they persisted in such folly, he would simply smile his gap-toothed smile and tell them: 'Neither. I'm the flash in the middle.'

And so he was, on so many different levels it's difficult to think of a better description for the role Bon Scott played to the hilt in AC/DC, once he was finally allowed to join. The meat in the sandwich between the riffs and yet more riffs of the Young brothers, Malcolm and Angus, Bon Scott didn't just provide the perfect artful dodger voice to their crafty rhythms and devil-may-care bluster, it was Bon that came up with the lyrics, the front, the sheer cheek. And of course the tattoos and blood that made them. Bon would later boast, 'It keeps you fit, the alcohol, nasty women, sweat onstage, bad food – it's all very good for you!' Except of course it wasn't. Good for the ego, maybe, no good at all though for body and soul, as Bon would eventually be the first of the band to find out. Nevertheless, as Angus later confirmed, if it hadn't been for Bon, 'I don't think there would have been an AC/DC ... Bon moulded the character and flavour of AC/DC. He was one of the dirtiest fuckers I know. When I first met him he couldn't even speak English – it was all 'fuck', 'cunt', 'piss', 'shit'. Everything became more down-to-earth and straight-ahead.' A man's man in the old school sense, there was nothing ironic about Bon Scott. He really could out-drink, out-fight and out-fuck anyone who stood in his road. He also had a great sense of humour, which meant he was good company. The whole world was Bon's friend – until suddenly it wasn't. Then you'd see the other side of him, the gloomy, depressive side that would tell the world to fuck off and leave him alone. Or else.

Being a Scott from Scotland, Bon came from a long – long – line of bad motherfucker 'heid-the-baws', as they say in Scotland. Unlike the Youngs, who acted like a clan but were in fact more like a sept (pronounced 'set') – smaller families, of non-noble lineage, but who pledged allegiance to and behaved like a proper clan – the Scotts were a one-time powerful lowland clan, derived from the clan that invaded Argyll from Ireland centuries before the advent of Catholicism. Their motto was 'Amo', which means 'I Love'. Held in high esteem among nationalists as being staunch supporters of Robert the Bruce, fighting alongside him at Bannockburn and many other of the set-piece battles of the Wars of Independence, when The Bruce was excommunicated by the Pope, so too were the Scotts, who were also threatened with death for following him. Grievances that stand through the centuries for clans as steeped in blood as the Scotts.

Charles Scott – 'Chick' to his pals – was born in 1918, in the small market town of Kirriemuir. Situated five miles north-west of Forfar, a climbing, single-lane road, the A928, takes you into Kirriemuir, in the county of Angus. Surrounded by countryside, Kirriemuir sits atop a hill at the gateway to Glen Clova and Glen Prosen, facing south towards Glamis, the castle where Queen Elizabeth the Queen Mother was born. A town of two distinct halves, on the one hand, its ancient market town past is still evident in the narrow lanes and alleyways winding between and behind its traditional red sandstone buildings. You can easily picture the gas-lamps that once would have illuminated its narrow streets and closes. On the other hand, its modern facelift speaks of the tourist industry it now embraces and the once-cobbled streets are now neatly paved with bricks; the museums and gift shops a testament to how vital tourism is to the town that once thrived on a now-defunct weaving industry.

Kirriemuir's most famous former son, J. M. Barrie, is commemorated by both a statue of his famous creation Peter Pan and a plaque marking the house in which Barrie lived on Brechin Street. The statue stands on the town square, at the junction to Bank Street, just opposite Cumberland Close, where Chick and his family lived, and in front of the 'tollbooth' – an ancient clock tower that over the centuries has seen service as a tollbooth, magistrates' court, police station and now as part of the museum. Several older buildings boast a 'witch stane': a hard, grey stone set into the traditional red sandstone, there to ward off witches – a remnant of the history of witch-hunting and the accompanying hysteria that briefly consumed the area in the 16th century.

Bank Street is a short street, just a few hundred yards in length with a Co-op cashpoint and a Royal Bank of Scotland on one side, along with a three-star hotel and bar called The Thrums. At one end, it leads off from the town square and at the opposite sits at the junction between Mary Well Brae and Schoolwynd. This is where it is alleged the Scott family had their bakery. However, there is no trace remaining now and several older residents can recall no bakery ever being there. Rather, it is suggested, the bakery had been behind Bank Street on Reform Street. There is a bakery in the area, very close to Bank Street, but as another resident confidently explains, it had been 'Aw sort ae hings' (all sorts of things) over the years. More certain is that the Scott menfolk would have drunk at Bellie's Brae Inn, extant since 1857, which sits on the corner of Cumberland Close, where the Scotts lived at No. 2. The actual house that the Scotts lived in was demolished, along with the rest of Cumberland Close, in the early Nineties, to be replaced by a gift shop and tourist centre, and more modern dwellings.

Wherever it was, there's no denying the Scott family business centred on their own bakery, opened in 1920 by Chick's father, Alexander. Just like his own son would do later in life, Chick sought adventure with a pal named Angus, the two teenagers dreaming of running away to sea before Alec put a stop to such foolishness. Instead, Chick worked in the family bakery with his older brother, George. Always up for a drink and a singsong after work – Alec loved to sing with his sons, and their mother, Jayne, encouraged George to play piano – Chick had tried his hand at piano and fiddle but mainly he liked to sing or keep you amused with his jokes and stories. Known as a character, with hard-man tattoos on his arms and a face that never turned the cheek, as he would tell Australian writer Clinton Walker, 'I just liked to get out and have a good time, be a bit of a delinquent.' Already a member of the local territorial Citizen Military Forces (CMF), when the Second World War started 22-year-old Chick Scott finally got to see some of the big wide world, joining up with the British army, where he served as a baker, stationed first in France, then Ireland, North Africa and Italy.

It was during his basic training at the coastal town of Kirkcaldy that Chick met Isobelle Cunningham Mitchell – 'Isa' – at a Saturday night dance. A dark-haired, slender girl with a fierce intelligence which belied her sweet, pretty face, Isa had grown up as one of four daughters and didn't miss a trick. Like Chick, she loved music and came from a musical family. Her mother played piano, as did her father, as well as organ. '[He] had a lovely operatic voice,' she told Walker. When, in 1941, during one of Chick's army leaves, he and Isa married, Jayne Scott was aghast. As bakers owning their own family business, the Scotts saw themselves as 'respectable folk' – middle-class – and Jayne was 'black affronted' (offended, shocked) at the prospect of her son marrying beneath himself, as she saw it, to a family of 'plain working folk'. But Chick was 23, a soldier now and no longer prepared to be told what he could or could not do. Two years later, Isa gave birth to their first child, a boy named Sandy. But the baby died just nine months later before Chick even had the chance to see him.

When Chick was demobbed, in December 1945, Isa was already pregnant with another son and she and Chick settled back in Kirriemuir, into a modest terraced house in the Roods bought for them by Alec. With Chick back working with his father and brother in the bakery, married life was sweet at last. Isa liked to go to church every Sunday, Chick joined an amateur light-opera company, singing Gilbert and Sullivan. He also finally found an instrument he could stick with, playing drums in the Kirriemuir Pipe Band. When their son, named Ronald Belford (his grandmother's middle name) Scott, was born on 9 July 1946, the picture seemed complete. But though young Ronnie had his mother's dark, sensitive eyes, he also had his father's wolfish features, and it was Chick's roving ways he took most after, even as a toddler, learning to walk and 'getting into everything' at a very early age. Once he started school, 'He never used to come home,' Isa told Walker. 'He'd just go off with some of his little mates ... I used to have to go chase him. So it started young!'

Like his father, Ronald loved to play drums, hitting a biscuit tin with his mother's knitting needles, or banging on the bread board with forks and spoons. Whenever his father's pipe band would come marching by the house, which they did most Saturday evenings, freckle-faced little Ronnie, as his mother always called him, would march up and down with them. He was three when Isa gave birth to a little brother for him, Derek, and seven when she had another, Graeme. As big brother to the younger waens little Ronnie ruled the roost but he was 'more mischievous than naughty', said Isa.

His father, however, was getting decidedly itchy feet. Six years in the army living largely abroad had given him a taste for what lay beyond the safe but confining environs of wee Kirriemuir. Now with a wife and three small children to consider, 34-year-old Chick Scott began to rail against the notion that this would be his lot till the end of his days. Like Ireland, Scotland had long got used to so many of its sons and daughters seeking a better life away from home, travelling down to England and beyond. Now in the post-war years of austerity, people were flocking further afield to newer, younger countries much further away but whose economies were booming. Places like Canada and the United States, New Zealand and Australia.

Attracted by the same 'assisted passages', begun in 1947, that would later allow the Young family to make a new life for itself in Australia, Chick and Isa began to talk seriously about the prospect of starting a new, more exciting life on the other side of the world. Isa already had a sister who'd emigrated to Melbourne in 1951, and would read her letters home, telling of her new life in the ever-present sun, with growing envy and agitation. Australia, whose pre-war population had been under seven million, had attracted more than a million migrants since it had begun its immigration programme five years before. Not all were as welcome as others, though. 'Wogs' and 'spics' were almost as badly treated as 'Aboes'. The English would forever remain 'whinging Poms', and even the Irish, with whom the country was now flooded, were looked down on, especially the Catholics, who were viewed with outright suspicion and contempt. The Scots, however – and with them the Scotts, who much against the advice of Chick's mother took the plunge and got the boat to Melbourne in 1952 – were welcomed with open arms. Seen as brothers in arms, survivors of centuries of English disdain and oppression, working-class Australians identified more easily with hard-working, hard-playing Scottish Protestants than they did any other race.

Staying initially with Isa's sister, in the aptly named Melbourne suburb of Sunshine, before finding a place of their own further down the same street, Chick left behind his former trade and found work instead as a window-framer. Little Ronnie was enrolled in Sunshine primary school, where his skills as a marching drummer made him popular with the other kids, who would fall into line behind him as they marched to school every morning. He also took up playing a recorder and liked to plonk away on the family piano. Isa tried encouraging him but, like his father, he simply couldn't sit still long enough to take lessons. When, however, he started pestering his parents for an accordion, promising faithfully he would definitely turn up for lessons on that, they took the bold step of selling the piano and buying the seven-year-old an accordion. A good lad, he went to his lessons dutifully, then just as determinedly stopped. What he *really* wanted, he said, was to play drums. Like his dad. So they sold the accordion and bought little Ronnie his first proper drum kit. 'You never had to tell him to do that,' Isa smiled. 'It was just natural to him.'

He was also a natural athlete and loved swimming, becoming a regular at nearby Footscray Baths, where he liked to show off by diving from the highest board at the top of a tower, as other children, his age and older, gasped in wonder. He would wait until the lifeguards became perturbed by the commotion and warn him not to jump – then leap, half-flying, half-falling, hitting the water with an almighty belly-flop. These were little Ronnie's first high-dives before an awestruck audience. They would not be his last.

When, in 1956, baby Graeme was diagnosed with asthma, the Scott family were advised by their doctor to move to the dryer, hotter climes of Western Australia, which they did, settling in Fremantle, a small but busy port town 12 miles south of Perth. For over a hundred years, Fremantle had been the bustling home-from-home for the usual seedy docklands mix of hustlers, two-way sailors, brothel keepers and pimps, and the rough, tough clientele they attracted. By the mid-Fifties, however, the newly erected presence of the Kwinana industrial site 15 miles to the south had begun to change the cultural complexion of Fremantle's residents. As men flocked to find jobs in Kwinana, suddenly newly arrived families outnumbered the vagabonds. Into this rapidly changing social melee arrived Chick Scott, who'd been offered a job at the western branch of the same place he worked for in Melbourne, eventually buying a house on the north side of the river, where Isa and the boys joined him. Good mixers – Chick joined the local Caledonian Society while Isa became an active member of her own 'Scottish club' – it wasn't long before Chick had also signed on with a Scots pipe band, taking little Ronnie with him, as a side-drummer. Whenever the band put on a show, the whole family would put their kilts on and go.

It was at North Fremantle primary school that Ronnie, now ten, got his nickname: Bonnie. Making fun of his by now mangled Scots-Australian accent, and picking up as only kids can on the handy congruity of his surname, little Ronnie Scott suddenly became little Bonnie Scotland. He hated it and would scrap with anyone who taunted him with it in the playground but the name would just not go away. 'I didn't take any notice,' he would shrug. 'No one railroads over me.' But by the time he was a teenager, even his best friends were now calling him Bonnie – or just Bon, for short.

It was also around this time he gave his first public performance as a musician: playing recorder in a school concert at North Fremantle

Town Hall. Revelling in the feeling it gave him, he began to take the marching drums more seriously, eventually becoming the Under-17 champion five years running. A good-natured, happy-go-lucky kid with big freckles and a broad smile, Bonnie was a popular boy and 'A credit to your parents', as he got used to being told. When he started secondary school at John Curtin High, however, that image changed. No longer a boy but a growing man with a taste for high jinks and pranks, Bon, like every other teenager in the world at that time, had discovered rock'n'roll and suddenly there was no looking back.

As well as all the usual suspects, from Chuck Berry and Little Richard to Elvis and eventually The Beatles, young Bon Scott was equally fascinated with home-grown Australian rockers like Johnny O'Keefe, whose original co-composition 'Wild One' Bon would sing in the shower (and a song that would later be covered in various forms by Jerry Lee Lewis, Iggy Pop and Lou Reed, to name just a few). Bon later recalled Isa yelling at him to stop. 'My mum used to say, "Ron, if you can't sing proper songs, shut up! Don't sing this rock'n'roll garbage."' And then there were girls, the attention of which, he discovered to his everlasting delight, dovetailed neatly with his own love of rock'n'roll. His brother Graeme recalled: 'He loved the attention from the girls. He was in the paper one time, in the Scottish get-up, with two highland dancers, about the same age as him, twelve or thirteen, and he had this big smile on his face.'

With the newfound obsession with rock music and girls, however, came the accoutrements of cigarettes and alcohol – and, as he got older, blues (speed) and dope (marijuana). And with those interests came Bon's involvement in local 'mobs' – street gangs of teenage boys, who liked to fight, then fight' some more. Hanging out with older kids down by the river, Bon earned his stripes smoking and fighting and getting off with girls as often as he could. By the time he was 15 he was running his own mob, with his best friends, Terry and Moe. Bon was the leader because Bon could put them all down with his fists. He would knock down anybody that 'stood in his road'. Having your own mob gave you the kind of deep-held respect not even being good at drums could. It certainly beat hell out of school lessons and, in 1961, first chance he legally could, Bon left school and got a job, driving a tractor on a farm. He chucked it in though when Terry wangled him a gig on one of the local crayfishing boats. But if Bon envisaged a life of derring-do on the high seas, that fantasy soon came crashing down. A sea fisherman worked hard, getting up and going out on the boat while it was still dark and not returning until his arms felt like they were dropping off and his legs could no longer hold him upright. The only good that came of this brief foray into the blood-slipping shoes of a fisherman was that he got his ear pierced; an almost unheard of accessory for a young man who wasn't a sailor to have. But by now he'd found himself a less wearisome number as an apprentice weighing-machine mechanic. Young Bon didn't care what he did as long as he came away at the end of the week with a few dollars, and the job didn't interfere too much with his real mission, to be a rocker.

One of Bon's girlfriends from this time was Maureen Henderson, sister to his mate Terry. She and Bon would dress up at the weekend and go rock'n'roll jiving. Or they would go to the drive-in to see rocker movies like *The Girl Can't Help It* and *Jailhouse Rock*. Bon would arrive in the full bad-boy regalia. You were either a rocker or a bodgie. Bon, in long, Brylcreemed and quaffed hair, black leather jacket and skin-tight jeans, was most definitely a rocker. Bodgies purportedly liked the same music but whereas Bon and his mates lived high on a diet of Elvis and Little Richard, bodgies preferred Buddy Holly and the Everly Brothers – girls' music. They dressed like girls too, in preppy cardigans and slacks and sharp crew-cut hair. Bon would rather die than be thought of as a bodgie. As soon as he'd passed his test, he was into cars too. Preferably big, fast, flash American models, anything that looked – and sounded – the part. 'Tanks' they called them in Fremantle. Woe betide anybody that tried to overtake Bon in his, literally or figuratively. No longer a boy scrapping with other boys, Bon was developing a vicious streak, and would lay it on the line until he or his opponent lay bloodied on the ground, the bigger the better. Bon may have been short, but he never backed down from a fight. Bon didn't believe in turning the other cheek. Something else he had in common with his father and the rest of the Scott clan.

He began to get a reputation locally as the one boy you didn't mess with; an image he deliberately set out to reinforce by getting what would be the first of his many tattoos. There was always a funny side to such shenanigans too, though, a twinkle in those bright, dark eyes that always allowed for the joke to be on him as well. When he and Terry went down to East Perth to get tattooed that first time, Terry came back with Death Before Dishonour on his arm. Bon had the same but had to go one better so had the tattoo done on the lower part of his belly, just above his pubic hair. The tears ran down his face as the tattooist's needle dug in but Bon wouldn't give in, wouldn't allow himself to admit he might have gone too far this time. He couldn't pull his trousers up properly for weeks afterwards, the pain was so great.

Not yet the alcoholic he would become in his twenties, Bon gobbled down blues, smoked anything he could roll between his fingers, and never had to go far looking for trouble. Hanging out on a Saturday night with Terry and Maureen and the rest of the gang at the Cafe de Wheels, outside there would be an impressive array of Chevrolets, Dodge Customs, even Mustangs. And just like they'd seen James Dean do in *Rebel Without A Cause*, they would race each other, playing chicken on the main drag or driving down to Port Beach to race each other. Terry had a Ford, single-spinner. Bon would just steal a car he fancied for the night. Once they were on the beach and Bon crashed into a van, practically sliced it in half. Inevitably the police got involved. Soon they had Bon and Terry's number every time something got stolen or broken in the town. 'They used to go out and knock fuel off,' Maureen later recalled. 'I would have to go look-out while they siphoned it.' When the boys just laughed in the cops' faces things turned nasty. One night they gave Terry a severe beating. Bon got his own back, beating another copper half to death. Nothing was ever proved though and so things went on, going from bad to worse. Deeply troubled by the way their son was turning out, Chick rowed with him time and again. Until one day Bon just walked out, sleeping on the couch over at Terry's parents' place.

*

It's a thin line between taking things to the limit and actually going too far. Bon Scott finally crossed that line for the first time when he was 16. One Saturday night, attending a dance on Port Beach where he had got into the habit of climbing up with the house band and singing a song or two, Bon 'took a walk' along the beach with a pretty teenage girl he'd just met. When he returned, however, some of the other lads, seeing what had just gone down, decided they wanted their 'turn' too. Bon may have been a hoodlum and a chancer but he was still, to his mind, a gentleman, at least when it came to the ladies. It was a matter of barely a moment's thought for him to decide a lesson in manners was called for. He lit into the gang, a one-man army, sending all before him scattering. Tables were broken, glasses were smashed. The police were called and a blood-spattered Bon fled in Terry's car. But of course the cops knew full well who he was and eventually caught up with him later the same night – trying to make off with 12 gallons of stolen petrol. Arrested and kept in jail until Monday morning, when he appeared at the Fremantle Children's Court, Bon pleaded guilty to charges of giving a false name and address, fleeing legal custody, having unlawful carnal knowledge with a girl under the age of consent and, lastly, for having made off with those 12 gallons of gas. Chick and Isa, who both attended the hearing, were rightly appalled, and Bon was 'committed to the care' of the Child Welfare Department until he was 18, with the additional 'recommendation' that he be kept housed in a maximum-security facility. He was also placed on bond for two years, for additional sentencing should he at some point be called up on the unlawful carnal knowledge charge. (Fortunately for him, he never was.)

It was a terrible blow for Bon and his family. It had been coming for some time, but that did not lessen the effects for any of them. It did, however, put the brakes on Bon's budding career as a full-time crim-inal. Had it come five years later it might have been seen as merely a blip in his downward trajectory. Coming at 16, though, just as he was beginning to fancy his chances as a singer, it became something Bon Scott would spend the rest of his life trying to live down. Run by local singing star Johnny Young, the Saturday night Port Beach dances had made Bon nearly famous for something other than being leader of the gang. Johnny Young would sing a song or two but rarely got any further as the crowd, led by Maureen, would start shouting, 'We want Bonnie! We want Bonnie!', at which point an utterly unabashed Bon would board the stage, taking the mike from Young, and belt out 'Long Tall Sally' and 'Blue Suede Shoes'. Maureen recalled how 'all the girls used to go wild over him … Johnny Young used to get pretty upset'.

There would be no more nights making the girls go wild for Bon now. Although he refused to dwell on the details in later life, bits and pieces of the back story eventually emerged. The main thread being that, as ill-luck would have it, Alec and Jayne, Bon's grandparents from Kirriemuir, had chosen just that moment to visit Chick and Isa and their grandkids in Australia for the first time. Despite his wayward behaviour Bon still saw himself as 'a pretty good guy'. At the same time he was drag racing, stealing cars and fighting, he'd also recently won Avery's Best First Year Apprenticeship Award. He'd been looking forward to meeting his grandparents properly for the first time since the family had moved to Australia. How could he face them now? Speaking years later to Clinton Walker, Silver Smith, a later Bon girlfriend, explained how Bon 'had a choice of either being remanded into his parents' custody, and it all being forgotten, or going through the legal process'. Because he couldn't bear to face his grandparents under such circumstances, 'He made the choice of going through the legal process. By the time he got out, the grandparents had gone home, and of course, they subsequently died. So he always wanted to do something to rectify that.'

Riverbank was no ordinary borstal. It was a purpose-built prison for the worst of the convicted boys. There were no open dormitories; only locked cells. It was meant to be hard and it was. Bigger boys preyed on the younger ones and sexual assault was rife. Bon eventually served nine months there. In jail, suddenly, being a hard nut didn't seem like such a handy thing to be. Up at six every morning lining up for the freezing-cold showers. Bed again by dark, lying there smoking in his bunk, unable to stop thinking. The rest of the day passed in a tedious round of odd jobs in the craft shops and kitchen, or the laundry, hours spent on hands and knees, scrubbing cold dirty floors that never quite got clean, fingers pink and numb, head all over the place. Then in the evening, after the usual grotty meal, shoved into the common room, where most of the boys played cards or just hung about listening to the radio. The screws pushed the boys to read a book, or play a musical instrument, but there were few takers. Sometimes there would be half-hearted singsongs. Bon joined in but not often. He was too concerned with watching his back. Boredom ruled and fights were daily, sometimes hourly. Punishment: being put 'in the box' – solitary confinement, the hardest thing of all for a sociable lad like Bon to take. The only respite came on Sundays, when after lunch the boys were allowed visitors. Occasionally, they were encouraged to put on concerts for their visiting families. Because of his drumming skills, Bon always featured. That's when he really got it into his head he wanted to be in a band. Like The Beatles, who he had heard about for the first time on the radio at Riverbank. Soon he was telling his parents how he was going to knuckle down when he got out, join a proper band and become famous. They just hoped he didn't end up back inside again. You only had to look at the faces of some of the boys Bon was hanging around with to tell that this was just the start of their journey to a life where prison quickly became home.

Released from Riverbank just before Christmas 1963, Bon moved home and was encouraged by his parole officer to join the Citizen Military Forces (CMF). But at the interview, accompanied by his parole officer, he was told he didn't have what it took to become a soldier, not even as a member of the reserves. That he didn't have the right character. His card had been permanently marked, it seemed. Sure enough, when Australia's involvement in the Vietnam War escalated over the next two years and Bon had to register for National Service, he was never called up. He would later boast how he had been 'rejected by the army, because they said I was socially maladjusted'.

This was one rejection Bon secretly welcomed, though, as it meant he could concentrate instead on making his new teenage dream come true: being the drummer in a rock'n'roll band. Working in the storehouses of the Western Australian Egg Board, he practised drums each night on a kit he'd put up in the bay window of the family sitting room. Would-be singers and guitarists were ten-a-penny, but decent drummers were hard to come by and it wasn't long before Bon did finally find himself in a working band: the Spektors, named after producer Phil Spector. Comprising two lads he'd met that worked at the nearby Kwinana oil refinery – Wyn Milson, who played guitar, and John Collins, who sang – with Bon on drums and another mate, Brian Gannon, who agreed to twang the bass, the Spektors became a covers band playing the same dances Bon had been going to as a fan. Places like The Big Beat Centre, in downtown Perth. Not satisfied with being stuck at the back for too long, Bon decided it would be a good gimmick for the drummer to step out and sing a couple of songs each night. The others didn't necessarily feel the same way but nobody was going to argue with the little hard nut just out of the slammer, and Bon's raucous version of The Kinks' 'You Really Got Me' became a highlight of the set. Bon certainly thought so.

It was 1965 and Australia was as in thrall to The Beatles, the Rolling Stones and their various copycat offshoots as the rest of the increasingly pop-conscious world. The Spektors milked it for all they were worth, bashing out one-size-fits-all versions of the Stones' 'It's All Over Now', Them's 'Gloria', even at one point 'Yesterday' by The Beatles. Bon had sweet-talked his father into letting him borrow Chick's shiny new Falcon station wagon to drive his drums to the gigs in, on the solemn promise that he wouldn't treat it the way he had the dragsters he had once raced along the beach. He kept the promise but it wasn't speed that was his undoing this time but fatigue. Falling asleep at the wheel on his way home one Saturday night, he smashed the car into a street lamp on Stirling Highway and ended up in hospital with cuts to his face and hands.

It was during another Spektors gig at the Medina Youth Club that year that Bon had another, different kind of an accident, falling in love for the first time, when he met a stunningly beautiful 17-year-old blonde named Maria Van Vlijman. Bon had got used to having girls at gigs fussing over him. He'd been chasing them, or been chased by them, since he was at school. There had never been a girl in his life before quite like Maria, though. For a start, she was a good Catholic girl with strict rules of courtship, who, in the perception of young larrikins like Bon, would kiss but wouldn't fuck. Suddenly it wasn't enough being a rogue, or a drummer, or even a twinkle-eyed mixture of both. Bon had to remember the good manners he'd been brought up with by Isa, become a gentleman. A girl like Maria demanded wooing and Bon gave it all he'd got.

Maria later claimed Bon asked her to marry him – 'He wanted to marry a virgin' – and that she would have let him too, were it not for the fact she knew darn well that if he wasn't getting his rocks off with her it was with someone else, some other 'scrag' from the gig. Around her, though, he was always on his best behaviour, never swearing, never drinking. Coming from a country riven by sectarianism, Protestant Isa found herself placed on the back foot again by her son's apparently insatiable desire to ignore other people's rules. Not only was Maria a 'pape', she was a stuck-up one at that, according to Isa. Maria's parents had a similar problem, in reverse, with their daughter dating this scruffy larrikin from up the road. Surely she could do a lot better for herself? But parental disapproval was nothing new to Bon, and, besides, he couldn't keep away from Maria. When Maria showed that she, too, had enough about her to ignore the barrage of abuse from her parents by taking a job at the Fremantle docks, moving in with her brother Joe to an apartment of their own in order to be nearer to where Bon's folks lived, Bon began to spend all his free time with her. As she was still unwilling to consent to sex before marriage, Bon simply redoubled his efforts to win Maria over, dressing up smart to take her for lunch, even going to church with her – a Catholic church at that! – on Sundays. Anything to prove his love, and finally get in her pants …

The great rivals to the Spektors on the local Perth scene were the Winztons, fronted by singer Vince Lovegrove. Vince had been singing and playing guitar in various pop outfits since he was 14, beginning with a Shadows-style instrumental surf group called the Dynells, before moving on to front the Dimensions and, latterly, the Winztons. He and Bon's paths had crossed several times already over the years. He later recalled: 'Bon was the cute little drummer with cute little eyes, pixie-like ears, a cute, turned-up nose, a cute little Scottish accent, and about four very obvious cute little tattoos.' He added: 'You just knew if you hung out with him you were going to have a good time.'

When original Perth kingpin Johnny Young finally had a No. 1 national hit with the single Stevie Wright and George Young had written for him, 'Step Back', in June 1966, he did what every aspiring pop artist did in Australia in those days and relocated to Melbourne – then the centre of the Australian music scene, such as it was. With Johnny gone, that left the Spektors and the Winztons to fight it out for top spot. Vince Lovegrove, however, had a better idea. Why didn't the two groups combine, forming one almighty supergroup, mopping up all the local bookings for themselves? With Bon's own group starting to look shaky – Bon and Wyn wanted to keep going, but for the others the novelty of working every weekend was starting to wear off as they found girls they wanted to marry and settle down with – there were no objections from the Spektors. When a local DJ named Alan Robinson, of Radio 6KA in Perth, came up with a name for this new group – The Valentines – it seemed there was no turning back.

Specialising initially in pop-soul covers of hits by the likes of Wilson Pickett and Sam and Dave, the group's gimmick was that it boasted two singers: Vince Lovegrove and Bon Scott, with Vince in the lead role as the handsome hunk who delivered the songs straight-faced, and Bon his less conventionally good-looking, cheeky chappie sidekick. According to Vince, neither of them was yet confident enough to work alone. 'We worked off each other a lot. We had a pretty wild stage act for the time. We'd jump up on the amps; have fire bombs going off ... We'd work stuff out beforehand, what we'd do and what we wouldn't do.' The Perth scene was largely a cabaret scene, where they would have corkage fees, bring your own bottle, as a way around not having a drinks licence. The clubs stayed open until 3 a.m. though and the pay was decent enough. More lucrative, if more dangerous, were the clubs that catered for the moneyed-up workers that came down from the mining towns in north Australia. Places like Mount Tom Price, where the miners would work for six months then have three months off, and ride into Perth to spend all their dough in licensed discos like the Top Hat, North Side and Trend Setter. What they wanted to hear was Top 40 stuff and The Valentines were happy to give it to them for pay. The Valentines would wear puff sleeves, blue sharkskin suits and big smiles as they delivered 'Build Me Up Buttercup', Bon clutching his breast on the word 'heart' while Vince simmered and swayed. Bon had proved he had a voice, belting out 'Gloria' with the Spektors. But it was Vince who encouraged him to think more about his singing. The only places they tried out their own original material, usually written by Vince and Bon, were the surf clubs along the west coast, which regularly held 'stomps'. One they played regularly was Swanbourne, on the beach. But they didn't pay as well as the city centre gaffs and the band soon left them behind, as they did all the little clubs eventually, as their star rapidly rose and with it their ambitions.

As Vince wrote in an article in 2008: 'When he sang, Bon took off into charisma-land; his eyes would twinkle, his brows would slightly raise, his lips would purse into an impish grin, his swagger demanding attention. Bon had a raw, unique voice which would be perfect as an offset to my rather flimsy pop voice.' Together they would take on the world. 'We were very poor, almost starving, driving down the highways, absorbed with rock'n'roll, stealing people's front-door milk money to survive, living on boiled potatoes, the dreams of success our mantra.' Bon chucked in his job at the Egg Board and became a postman, delivering the mail each morning on his bicycle. He'd come to work often still wearing his stage gear from the night before, still awake and sweating bullets. Vince worked at Pellew's Menswear, in Fremantle, and Bon would drop in on him on his rounds. He and Vince would go round the corner from the shop and have a snort of speed or a drink, or both. 'We'd dream our dream of what we were gonna do next,' said Vince.

When, in October, P. J. Proby arrived for a concert in Perth, there could be only one support act: The Valentines. By the New Year they'd been offered their own record deal with Clarion Records, the same label that had taken Johnny Young to the top. Run by local Perth businessman Martin Clarke, Clarion had begun just the year before, part of the first wave of Australian independent labels dedicated to domestic talent. As such, money was tight. The first Valentines recording session took place in a tiny basement studio off Hay Street in Perth's city centre. Recording through the night, when studio rates were virtually free, they left blinking into the sunlight the following morning with the two tracks that would constitute their first single: a rough-and-ready cover of an Arthur Alexander country-soul number called 'Every Day I Have To Cry' (a catchy ditty that would later provide hits for Ike and Tina Turner, The McCoys, Dusty Springfield and others), backed with their one-take version of an obscure Small Faces track, 'I Can't Dance With You'. Released in May 1967, and backed by heavy rotation on Alan Robinson's Radio 6KA show, it actually made the Top 5 of the Western Australian charts. Not a national hit but proof – real, solid, hold-it-in-your-hand-and-taste-it proof at last – that Bon's dreams had actually become more than that now. That he was proper, at last: a proper singer in a proper group. Second banana still, maybe, but a singer nonetheless, with a record to show for it and a bloody good one at that.

When the Vallies, as they became known to their growing band of fans, then opened for the biggest act in Australia, The Easybeats, for two shows at His Majesty's Theatre in June 1967, it was the closest they'd ever come to the real thing. Already superstars in Oz, the Easys had just returned from the UK, where 'Friday On My Mind' had turned them into a stellar international success too. Like every other aspiring young Australian pop act, the Vallies took their cues directly from the Easys. Bon in particular, who bore more than a passing resemblance to their singer, even began aping many of the streetwise stage moves of 'Little' Stevie Wright. The Vallies couldn't believe their luck when the headliners invited their callow support act to come back to their hotel afterwards and party with them. The Easybeats were the real thing, surrounded by screaming teenage girls wherever they went, onstage or off, night and day. Vince and Bon got high simply trailing in their fumes. When at the end George Young and Stevie Wright insisted on both bands swapping shirts like a pair of opposing football teams at the end of a great match, Bon was made up. When George and Harry Vanda then flippantly offered to throw a song together for them, making it up virtually on the spot, Bon looked at Vince and for the first time in his life didn't know what to say.

The song itself, 'She Said', was as inconsequential a ditty as any-thing George and Harry would ever put their names to, replete with Bon wittering away on cringe-inducingly awful recorder. But it was another hit, giving them their second Top 10 Western Australian single, again backed by Robinson at 6KA. When that same summer The Valentines won the Western Australian Hoadley's Battle of the Bands competition and qualified to appear in the finals in Melbourne, Vince and Bon convinced themselves that The Valentines were ready to become a national presence. One able to follow in the footsteps of other recent domestic success stories like Johnny Young, Ray Brown and the Whispers, Billy Thorpe & The Aztecs and, not least, their beloved new best mates, The Easybeats. 'She Said' had carried all that promise in its flimsy, clichéd chords and wispy choruses; feelings hugely amplified by this talent contest win and with it the chance of a lifetime to travel cross-country to Melbourne, Australia's music Mecca. More important, it would become just the first of three hit songs The Easybeats would write for the Vallies over the next couple of years, all of them hits. And though neither man knew it then, it was also the start of what would become one of the most significant and successful relationships Bon Scott and George Young would ever have.

Jetted into Melbourne for the televised finals, both Vince and Bon fully expected to win – their luck had been so good lately. The show itself was held before 5,000 overexcited teenagers. There were 12 bands in all, from all over Australia, each playing two songs. First prize: an all-expenses-paid trip to London. The Vallies took to the stage brimming with confidence and put on a good show. Yet they did not win, narrowly missing out to an outfit called, non-ironically, The Groop. Deflated and disappointed but refusing to show it, Vince and Bon simply went out into the hall and did everything they could to impress upon people the mistake they had made in not voting them the winners. Second prize did have some comforts though: they got to spend four days in Melbourne checking out all the hip music clubs that Melbourne was then famous for, so very different from the provincial beer-and-skirt joints they were used to playing back home. While Bon made dozens of new best friends in every bar he got drunk in, Vince networked furiously, hanging out with local scene-setters like Ian 'Molly' Meldrum of the influential *Go-Set* magazine, and well-known Melbourne radio jock Stan 'The Man' Rofe, both of whom had caught the show and told Vince how much they'd liked what they'd seen, encouraging him to bring the band out to stay, promising him they had what it took to make it in the big city. By the time they were sat next to each other on the flight back to Perth, Vince and Bon and the rest of the group were agreed: they would be going back to Melbourne just as soon as they could. And this time they would not be coming back until they were stars. Not some talent show winners like The Groop, but proper actual stars in their own right.

Vince was the one with all the ambition at that point; the leader of the group determined to make the most of this golden opportunity, willing to sacrifice anything to do so. Bon, who shared those dreams, but still saw them more as just that – dreams – had more pressing reasons for wanting to get down to Melbourne. Maria had already moved out there some months before. Tired of Bon's philandering, sick of waiting for him to come back from his endless one-night stands on the road with The Valentines, a bright girl who'd decided there was more to life than working in a small pay office in Fremantle, waiting for someone to marry her who didn't even have a proper job anymore, she'd set out to make her own dreams come true in Melbourne, beating Bon to it by more than six months.

Now, just a week before he and Vince would set out on the long train ride back to Melbourne, Bon wrote to Maria, telling her of his big plans. How he and Vince were selling everything they owned in order to raise the money for the trip. Plaintively, he told her how much he hoped 'we can both have a good time together when I arrive' and that 'it works out this time' or he would be 'so flippin' lonely'. Maria, for her part, was hoping Bon would keep to his word this time and join her in her new home town. No one else, though, wanted him to go, could see the sense of it. 'No one in Perth could understand why we wanted to leave,' moaned Vince. Clinton Walker would later write how the scene at the station the morning they all set off for Melbourne 'was like something out of Exodus. Mothers were sobbing, fathers stoic. The boys were beside themselves. They felt like explorers or crusaders ...' The journey across the Nullarbor Plain lasted for four long days and nights, all sense of expectancy quashed as the bedraggled gang sat huddled with their suitcases and equipment in the cheap seats. They bought some beer to help pass the time but they didn't seem to feel it, no matter how many tinnies they downed. Eventually they all just sat there, staring out the window and smoking, wondering what the fuck. They had told everyone they would not be back until they had made it. They had meant it when they said it, perhaps. Now sitting there fretting over their future, they did not feel so brave or confident. Who did they think they were kidding, thinking they were going to return home stars? What a load of bullshit, mate.

Yet that's exactly what they did.

CHAPTER THREE

Young Blood

When his great adventure with The Easybeats finally ended, prematurely, at the end of 1969, after their inability to follow up 'Friday On My Mind' with anything remotely as successful internationally, George Young was still only 23 and in no mood to call it a day. Angry, frustrated, this was one Aussie not content to go travelling around the Old Country for a few years then return home to spend the rest of his days regaling the folks back home with what a shithouse England was. For the shrewd, thick-skinned and bloody-minded George, if anything his experiences with The Easybeats, who had found fame but never really come within touching distance of real fortune, left him more determined than ever to prove his worth, both inside and, most especially, outside of Australia.

Fortunately for him, in the slightly older, more laconic Harry Vanda, George had a musical and business partner willing to hang on in there with him and lend support. The two had started the group five years before and it was the two of them that saw it through to the bitter end, closer than ever; a bond deepened by the fact that it was George and Harry that had come up with the Easys' biggest hit, 'Friday On My Mind'. Recorded during their first overseas sessions, at Abbey Road Studios in London, in the summer of 1966 – originally overseen by Ted Albert, until in a weird future echo of what would happen to George and Harry as producers of AC/DC, Ted was replaced by a record company impatient for a sound that would translate onto British and American radio, installing Shel Talmy of Who and Kinks fame – 'Friday On My Mind' was an infectious little pop-powerhouse built upon two similar but opposing riffs, and spiced with clucking backing vocals inspired by the French vocal a cappella group The Swingle Singers. It gave The Easybeats another Australian No. 1 and, more significantly, their first – and only – major chart hit in Britain and America.

From here on in, George never wrote with anyone other than Harry, a situation that left singer Stevie Wright, George's former songwriting partner, feeling increasingly alienated within the group. By then, however, Stevie, always a volatile character, as good frontmen tend to be, was on the road to booze and drug addiction, his previously charming wayward behaviour slowly but surely dwindling down to being unreliable, indifferent and, eventually, impossible. Though George and Harry continued to write great songs, they never did find a way to replicate the success of 'Friday On My Mind'. Not with The Easybeats anyway, where they tried every different type of style to find a follow-up, including syrupy orchestrated ballads. 'It was a classic mistake from our point of view,' George later recalled. 'We were a rock'n'roll band and what was a rock band doing with this cornball schmaltzy shit?' A hard-learned lesson they would later pass on to their little brothers.

There were some last hurrahs – a rollicking single, 'Good Times', which became a more modest international hit in 1968, and featured Small Faces vocalist Steve Marriott on raspy backing vocals, and was said to be a favourite of Paul McCartney, who had phoned Radio One personally to request they play it. (Around the same time, McCartney had also signed George's elder brother Alex – the Young who'd stayed behind when the rest of the family relocated to Australia five years before – as a songwriter for The Beatles' newly established Apple publishing company, making him part of Grapefruit, a new group named after a Yoko Ono book and art exhibit. Alex was renamed by John Lennon for the group as George Alexander. An extraordinary situation that found both Lennon and McCartney co-credited as producers of tracks on the band's debut album, *around*. The group, however, lasted just two years and had little commercial success, and interest quickly waned.)

Already looking beyond The Easybeats, by the start of 1969 George and Harry were sharing a flat in Bayswater, which till then had been a small studio for recording jingles for pirate radio stations. They turned it into their own four-track recording facility, working on their own together, knocking out demos ostensibly intended for the Easys but, in truth, for anybody else that was interested too. Among them, the song 'Peculiar Hole In The Sky', written with their young mates in The Valentines in mind, and, interestingly, the song that would become the final Easybeats single, a back-to-basics rock number called 'St Louis', a direct precursor for the kind of upbeat song – and raucous sound – George and Harry would encourage the fledgling AC/DC to develop.

When, after one last tour of Australia at the end of the year intended to mop up a significant chunk of the $85,000 debt The Easybeats were now in, George and Harry decided to become full-time songwriters and producers for other artists, it seemed like a typically smart move. But the new Vanda–Young imprimatur got off to a less than encouraging start when they arrived back in London at the start of 1970 and found themselves having to start from scratch again. Yet they wouldn't give in. Or rather, George wouldn't give in. Easygoing Harry didn't seem to care where he laid his hat, but for George going back to Oz was still seen as failure, making it in London the ultimate goal, on the ladder to making it in New York.

None of their efforts were a success though and finally, in 1973, under the aegis of a face-saving deal with Ted Albert, George Young and Harry Vanda returned to Sydney. Shrewd as ever, the deal Ted offered amounted to an offer George and Harry couldn't refuse – or would have been extremely foolish to have turned down. Essentially a three-way partnership in Albert Productions, with regular cash advances set against future royalty earnings, it was the kind of deal that all sides could see as an investment. Ted would be the boss: the one ultimately to decide who should be signed and what records they would release. But it would be up to George and Harry to find the acts and produce – and often write – their records.

By the start of 1974, the deal – unofficially known between the three as the Albert Hendrick Redburn venture (a combo of Ted's surname and Harry and George's middle names), aka the AHR agreement – was ready to be signed. However, as the company secretary at the time, Brian Byrne, would later recall to Jane Albert, 'We did go to see a solicitor to draw up a draft contract but it all became so complicated we said "forget it" and it remained a gentleman's agreement, done on a handshake.' After the meeting they all returned to the King Street office 'and everybody pledged a note of trust in each other and we decided to give it a go'. The AHR agreement would be renegotiated periodically, reflecting the increasing success of the partnership, and would remain the template for all George and Harry's business with Alberts right up until 2001. Harry would later describe it 'like falling into a bloody goldmine'. When their very first record under the new agreement – Steve Wright's 'Evie', released on the newly minted Albert Productions record label – went to No. 1, it seemed everybody's faith was justified. Over the next few years the names Vanda and Young, always said in tandem, became the gold standard for guaranteed success in the Australian music business, notching up 20 Top 10 singles and 18 Top 20 albums between 1973 and 1980.

Crucial to this eventual success was the faith Ted Albert showed in the struggling young team. They may not have reached the heights of the record business in London, but they had amassed a staggering collection of top-drawer demos of potential hit songs, and they had also had an unrepeatable opportunity to hone their skills as producers and sound-recordists, singers and multi-instrumentalists. When Ted opened up Alberts' new studios, at Boomerang House, he shrewdly judged that if he had his own in-house production team already making hit singles, it would bring in business from outside labels and artists, making Alberts the leading studio in Sydney, which till then had always sent its artists – including those signed with Alberts – to studios in Melbourne. He also wanted names that would be well-known to the domestic music scene and who better than the Australian Lennon and McCartney? Equally important, he wanted guys he could trust; that were already part of the extended Alberts family. That they were now having hard times didn't hurt either. It was always good to bring guys in when they really needed to prove something – to themselves and to everybody else.

For George's part, there were also family reasons why a move back to Sydney was suddenly more appealing. His wife Sandra pointed out that their six-year-old Yvette would surely be better off growing up in the sunny climes of Australia, where they would own a large, open-plan house, than in the cramped terraced abode they shared in grey old London. Ultimately, though, the deal was just too sweet to resist. As Vanda later told Ted's niece, the writer Jane Albert, 'Ted … thought, what's the point in having George and Harry over there [in London] when they could be over here doing what I'm doing? So when our saviour asked us to help out with the production company, he didn't have to ask twice. He made us an offer we couldn't refuse. We'd had a gutful of London anyway.' Just before they left, their luck appeared to be turning anyway, when former Jimi Hendrix manager Chas Chandler declared an interest in managing their careers. 'But it didn't appeal any more.'

As in London, where they had worked only with a few close friends and family members to make their music, back in Sydney George and Harry began by sticking with what – and who – they knew. It was a tried-and-trusted method that paid immediate dividends with the first single they wrote and produced together at Alberts: an ambitious three-part rock 'anthem', with erstwhile Easybeats singer Stevie Wright, entitled 'Evie Parts I, II And III'. Combining elements of Vanda and Young's rediscovered love of stripped down rock'n'roll, and the current taste for album-length progressive rock songs, overlaid with their irrepressible talent for simply making catchy pop tunes, 'Evie' was essentially three songs (up-tempo rocker; dry-eyed ballad; cathartic, soul-inflected climax) delivered as one, credibility-reinforcing 11-minute opus. It went to No. 1 in Australia in May 1974 and became the benchmark by which everything George and Harry did next would be judged. Fortunately for them and Alberts – and soon after AC/DC – they were more than able to match it.

*

Even closer to home and more to George's surprise was the rapid progress his two little brothers had made on their instruments since he'd been away in London. Now aged 20 and 18, respectively, Malcolm and Angus had begun playing in their own outfits, cadging gigs wherever they could. George, who could see at once how 'extraordinarily good' they had become 'in the style they had latched on to', realised though that it was best for the time being to 'stand back because they were my brothers'. Nevertheless, he kept a close eye on them, offering encouragement whenever it was sought, which was not often, the brothers having big enough heads to think they already knew it all.

When George received word, though, that one of his and Harry's shit-at-the-wall ideas – the Marcus Hook Roll Band – had astonishingly gained some retrospective traction in North America with the track 'Natural Man', and that the EMI label execs in charge of the track were now keen to finance more 'Marcus Hook' material, he and Harry hastily reassembled the same team, albeit in Sydney. A mixture of blues and boogie, mixed with the usual astute Vanda and Young pop nous, Hook had originally been the brainchild of the former Pretty Things bassist, Alan 'Wally' Waller (aka Wally Allen). When it was decided they needed a second guitarist George phoned home and pulled in Malcolm for what would become his first ever recording session. Working at EMI's Sydney studios with English engineer Richard Lush, whose previous claim to fame was engineering at Abbey Road on The Beatles' *Sgt. Pepper*, Angus tagged along too and would also get to play on some of the finished tracks.

A decent enough album was eventually cobbled together, entitled *Tales Of Old Granddaddy*. Listening now to tracks like the steady-building 'Power And The People' or the self-consciously crazy 'Ape', you can already hear the wire-taut rhythm guitars and tail-lashing lead breaks that would come to characterise the early AC/DC sound – and how much they were given direction by George's mature songwriter's instincts to keep things crisp if not always clean. You needed a formula, a map to follow, but you also needed atmosphere and charm, and the *Granddaddy* album exuded both. Looking back, Lush's main memory is of how 'stunned' he was by 'the skills of Malcolm and

Angus. I was amazed because they were like little kids. I thought, wow! This is amazing! Especially Angus.' Nevertheless, the album, though paid for by American label money, would not be released in the United States for another five years, by which time the Marcus Hook concept was dead and buried. It was another lesson in corporate record company tomfoolery that George was determined his younger brothers would never be subjected to – not while George had anything to do with it anyway.

Malcolm had been the first of the youngest Young brothers to get into a band when, in 1971, he joined the unpromisingly named Beelzebub Blues, bashing out livewire versions of songs like Joe Cocker's 'The Letter' and jamming on regular 12-bar blues standards. He bailed out though when Easybeats singer Stevie Wright recommended him for a gig with a new band in town with the equally unlikely name of The Velvet Underground – not to be confused with the already far more famous Velvet Underground in New York. The only thing the Sydney VU had in common with their better-known US counterparts was an eerie ambience derived from their keyboards, itself highly derivative of Ray Manzarek's tremulous sound in The Doors. Live, however, they'd built a reputation for themselves in Newcastle, NSW, where they came from, though more for the destructive stage antics copied from The Who, led by their self-styled 'wild man' singer, Steve Phillipson. In Sydney, however, they opted for a more considered approach, replacing Phillipson with the less provocative but more vocally gifted Andy Imlah (later to find fame in Australia as part of the John Paul Young group), and were also on the lookout for a second guitarist to flesh out the sound.

Put in touch by Wright, VU drummer Herm Kovac and guitarist Les Hall turned up at the Burwood homestead to meet Malcolm. Two obstacles immediately presented themselves. First, the all but impenetrable Scots accent the Youngs spoke in when at home, and – to the joint horror of both men – the T. Rex posters on Malcolm's bedroom walls. Kovac put his new young friend straight: 'That's shit, Malcolm! All those singles sound the same!' But Malcolm remained unperturbed. Just sat there drinking his tea and chain-smoking his cigarettes. When it was suggested he might like to turn up at the band's next rehearsal for an informal jam, he merely shrugged. How about he simply grab his Gretsch guitar and take off with them right now? One all-night session back at the band's house in nearby Mona Vale and Malcolm was in, though there was some concern initially over their prospective new member's age, which they guessed – given his height and weight – to be around 12. Something a scrunch-faced Malcolm also put them straight about in record time.

The new band cultivated a bad-boy image, though musically they remained as promiscuous as every other band pushing to make an impression on the pub and club audiences of Sydney in those days, bashing out Deep Purple's 'Black Night' one moment, followed by George Harrison's 'My Sweet Lord' the next. A particular favourite of Malcolm's at this time was *Extraction*, the 1971 debut solo album from Spooky Tooth vocalist Gary Wright, and he pushed for the band to include as many of the tracks from the album in their set as he could get away with. Even though he was the youngest and newest member, Malcolm spoke his mind – as Kovac discovered during a discussion about the Australian singer and songwriter Richard Clapton. 'Look at this fucking tosser Richard Clapton!' Malcolm told Kovac. 'Fuck me dead! He ain't gonna get anywhere trying to copy Eric Clapton's name!' He may have looked only 12 but when it came to music Malcolm had the cold heart of a convict and the old grey head of a hanging judge. And he plainly didn't care who knew it.

But he could be fun too. He shared a room on the road with Kovac, and the pair would often bring back girls who they would fuck lying side by side on the twin beds. It was Imlah though who became Malcolm's new best buddy when he discovered the joys of dope smoking. The two would hire a fishing boat and take it out to Palm Beach, north Sydney. Kovac: 'I said, "Fucking hell, Malcolm, you're a fucking hippy!"' The joke wore thin though when the pair began smoking before gigs, causing the set to slow down and become appreciably heavier. In response, Kovac started taping the gigs, 'so whenever they were stoned I'd point it out to them'.

When he wasn't 'fishing' with Andy, Malcolm spent most weekends over at Kovac's place, where the two would spend afternoons jamming together, spacing out on improvised jazz-rock fusions. 'What a lot of people don't realise is that Malcolm loved jazz,' Kovac recalled. 'From midday until six on Saturday and the same on Sunday, Malcolm would play nonstop jazz – all these jazz licks and jazz chords.' Live, the less crowd-pleasing aspects of Malcolm's love of jazz began to show itself in the band's increasingly down-tuned sound. Though they were no longer smoking weed before shows, the band's sound continued nonetheless to morph into a slower, beefier melange of blues and stoner rock. And to go with it, a name change to Pony – in homage to one of the heavy blues tunes by Free they were now including in their set, the long-striding 'Ride On A Pony'. It didn't last. They had built up a name for themselves as The Velvet Underground. Becoming Pony was like starting again. Within weeks they had switched back again. Things began to get more complicated, though, when the band began backing a middle-of-the-road Australian singer-guitarist named Ted Mulry. With Kovac now also drumming in Mulry's live band, the Ted Mulry Gang, The Velvet Underground began opening the set for him too. Malcolm drew a line as to what he would – and wouldn't – do. Happy to play along whenever Ted bashed out one of his rock'n'roll numbers, Malcolm would walk off when it came to performing either of the saccharine pop ballads that Ted had actually had national hits with, his composition 'Julia' or, which made Malcolm even more red-faced, 'Falling In Love Again', Ted's version of one of George and Harry's syrupy numbers from their lost London days.

Watching all this was 15-year-old Angus, whose mother Margaret gave him permission to go to the shows on strict condition that he had his own seat at the front where his big brother could keep an eye on him from the stage. 'We'd have to drop Angus home and Angus used to make us all Ovaltine,' Kovac recalled. A few months later Angus had also formed his first semi-professional band, Kentuckee. Angus had toyed with calling the band The Clan, but instead plumped for naming it after the first Kentucky Fried Chicken to open in Sydney the year before, of which he had become inordinately fond. Once again, the key man for the Young brother was Herm Kovac, who'd been giving lessons to the band's drummer, Trevor James, and introduced him to Angus. It had seemed an unlikely alliance: Angus was a well-known member of what were known locally as the Town Hall Sharps, a gang of teenagers heavily influenced by British skinheads, while Trevor was part of the Long Hairs, an opposing tribe of kids more influenced by American hippiedom. The two sides were not supposed to mix but drummers were hard to come by and Angus made do. The singer was a closer mate of Angus's named Bob McGlynn, whose main memory of Angus now is of a moany little guy with pinched facial features and a rotten smile. 'He had green teeth [and] didn't have a lot of confidence in himself' – not yet the attention-grabbing ball of energy he would become in AC/DC. McGlynn was the one who 'did all the moving'.

Still only five feet tall, Angus could barely reach the knobs on his giant Marshall stack amp. Yet he was clearly the leader of the group, picking all their material, drawing from his own collection, most of it bought from a small import record shop in Burwood, the more obscure – by Australian standards – the better. As such, Kentuckee's live set revolved around a hard core of material taken from albums by Deep Purple, Cactus, Mountain and Argent, propped up by better-known numbers from Jimi Hendrix, the Rolling Stones and The Who. Rehearsals would take place at the same Scout Hall Malcolm's band used or, just as often, in Angus's bedroom at home, where his mum kept the band supplied with endless pots of tea and plates of biscuits. When Angus wasn't rehearsing with his band he would sit in his room and practise alone, for hours at a time every day.

As a guitarist, even at that stage, says McGlynn, 'His speed was incredible.' Another, slightly older guitarist on the scene back then, Kim Humphreys, who played in Hot Cottage, remembers the teenage Angus as even 'more flashy then than he is now, because of the sort of things he was listening to. He really liked Jeff Beck and he also liked Paul Kossoff from Free.' Humphreys also cites Mountain's Leslie West as a key influence: 'That's where I think he got that really distinctive vibrato from.' But while the playing side was coming together at an astonishing rate of progress, Angus was still some way from the duck-walking, school uniform-clad, crazy fish onstage persona he would adopt in AC/DC. Mark Sneddon, who later joined Kentuckee as a second guitarist, recalled how 'He used to stand there and just pose and move a bit, like shake his leg. But he didn't do a lot of jumping around.'

The album that influenced the live performances of Kentuckee most of all though was *Ot 'N' Sweaty*, the final half-live, half-studio album, in 1972, from short-lived American rockers Cactus. Formed around the bulldozing talents of bassist Tim Bogert and drummer Carmine Appice, musically Cactus became everything Angus Young and, later, Malcolm would aspire to. Fast, furious, no frills, just straight down the line, good time rock'n'boogie; if you want to hear proto-AC/DC look no further. So much so that Kentuckee played practically all of *Ot 'N' Sweaty* live, most notably the towering 'Bad Mother Boogie', itself a live recording, and its swaggeringly evil twin, 'Bedroom Mazurka' ('about loose women everywhere', leers vocalist Peter French to a whooping audience). Occasionally, Angus's band would try its hand at an 'original' like 'The Kentuckee Stomp', musical muscle built to be played live that could have been lifted wholesale from any Mountain or Cactus album. All of which went down a storm with rowdy audiences at venues like Chequers, where Kentuckee found themselves playing four sets a night on Fridays.

Once Sneddon, who could also sing, joined, however, McGlynn began to feel left behind. It was no surprise when he left. His would-be replacement, Dave Evans, was a big, burly guy's guy who Angus had seen singing with The Velvet Underground, which Malcolm had finally left, just before the new singer joined. Evans, who had been building a reputation as a frontman with a voice to go with his big, brash stage presence, saw himself as a cut above the average pub singer. He didn't realise, however, that in Angus he would be rubbing shoulders with genuine Australian rock royalty. Or so Angus would have liked him to believe, anyway.

Evans, who was born in Carmarthen, in South Wales, in 1953, before arriving with his family in Australia five years later on the same Ten Pound Pom scheme as the Youngs and the Scotts, recalls being at home one day when there was a knock on his door. It was 1973, towards the end of the year, and Dave had recently bailed out of The Velvet Underground, his interest waning along with their pulling power and increasing lack of gigs.

'I answered it and there was this fat guy standing there [Trevor White], and this really little guy with hair right down to his arse, and this funny little voice. He said, "I'm Angus Young, brother of George Young from The Easybeats." I didn't know George at the time but I'd heard of The Easybeats so I was like, yeah? He said, "And Malcolm Young", who I had heard of. So I was like, yeah, and what do you want? He said, "I've got a band and we want you as our new singer." So we went inside and he played me some of his records, really heavy guitary stuff. I wasn't really into it so I just said I'd let him know. I never did though. I was really looking for something a bit more professional and this guy looked like a little kid.'

Nonplussed by Dave Evans's lack of interest in his offer, Angus simply reverted to using Mark Sneddon as his vocalist, though by now they'd agreed on a change of name to the more double-syllabic, Cactus- and Mountain-sounding Tantrum. All the while, both Malcolm and George were keeping their eyes on what was happening with their little brother. Malcolm, who had finally walked out on The Velvet Underground and was now looking to put his own outfit together, begrudgingly described Tantrum as 'not a bad band' and would occasionally get up and jam with them at rehearsals. Even he had to admit though that Angus was now 'making a big noise on that stage'. George went one step further and brought a big reel-to-reel tape recorder down to rehearsals to record them. 'Holy shit!' said Sneddon, 'It sounds huge!' In their new capacity as Alberts' leading production lights, George then took Angus and Tantrum in to record with him and Harry at the controls, the band knocking out a rough and ready version of 'Evie'. No more came of it though until, towards the tail end of 1973, Angus began to fall out with Trevor. Increasingly at odds with Angus's leadership of the band – the drummer wanted to stretch his abilities and play, Angus insisted he simply keep a tight beat, something that would become a recurring theme throughout the career of AC/DC – Trevor finally lost his place in the band after a fistfight with the guitarist at rehearsals one day. Angus issued an ultimatum: 'Kick him out!' The others reluctantly agreed but getting in another drummer even half as good as Trevor wasn't easy. Early in 1974, Tantrum juddered to a halt.

Sneddon found himself, instead, gravitating more towards Malcolm Young. With Angus left out in the cold, George stepped in and suggested his brothers simply form a new band together. Angus was aghast. 'We can't do that,' he told Sneddon, 'we'll kill each other.' This was almost certainly disingenuous. Kim Humphreys later claimed that Angus had been openly discussing forming a band with Malcolm for months. 'He said that was his ultimate aim.' Although George Young did later tell Jane Albert that he 'didn't know how it would work out because they are different personalities, and brothers in bands are notorious for beating the hell out of each other, which in my brothers' case would be no exception'.

The major difference with the new line-up was that this was no longer Angus's sole property: quite the reverse, in fact. With his older brother already having recruited Larry Van Kriedt, who'd played guitar with Malcolm in Beelzebub Blues but now switched to bass, plus former Masters Apprentices drummer Colin Burgess, as if to rub it in the singer of Malcolm's new band was none other than Dave Evans. 'It was definitely strange,' says Evans with a chuckle. 'I'd answered this ad in the Sydney *Morning Herald*, and when I called the number Malcolm Young was on the other end of the line. There was Malcolm, Larry and Colin and they were looking to get a singer to get the band ready to work. So I went over there and auditioned and we all shook hands and we had a band.'

Dave goes on: 'A week or two later Malcolm said his younger brother Angus's band Kentuckee had split up and could he come and audition too? All of the decisions at that time were democratic. We hadn't named the band at that stage [but] it was the original four guys that got the concept going. So, yeah, Angus came down and jammed with us. He had to audition, same as me. [But] it was a foregone conclusion, really. So he joined, we all shook hands and there was five of us.' He adds: 'Angus never forgot the fact that I turned him down though – and he had to audition for us, to join the band that I was in. He never, ever forgot that.' Something that the forthright Evans felt was to have lasting repercussions.

George, who Malcolm asked to come down and size up the singer, thought they had an ace in the tall, burly frontman. Evans, though, nearly put his foot in it before he'd even played a gig with them. Speaking years later, Malcolm recalled how the rest of the fledgling band 'loved it' when Angus plugged in and let rip. But that Evans had told him afterwards: 'We can't have this guy. He doesn't look like a rock star.' While it was true that Angus, this tiny troll-like figure with waist-length hair and scrunched-up face, hardly looked like Keith Richards or Jimmy Page, this was the singer's first big mistake. Blood being thicker than any other substance in the known Young world, Malcolm told him: 'If you don't like it you can move on.' Evans stayed: for now, anyway.

As far back as 1971 Malcolm had been boasting of his younger brother's talents to Kim Humphreys. He knew he had what it took. He just wanted to make sure Angus knew who was boss. Laying down the law from day one so that everyone, including his brother, knew who was in charge – no argument allowed. Dave had already heard about Malcolm before he met him, from the other guys in The Velvet Underground. 'They used to talk about "the little fella". And believe me, I'm not that tall myself, five nine and a half, something like that. And the other boys in the Velvet Underground were shorter than me. I used to laugh. "What do you mean, the little fella?" They'd go, "No, we mean, the *real* little fella." In a nice way, they weren't bagging on him or anything. They mentioned him because of his famous brother, you know?'

Only six months younger than Malcolm, 'We were friendly first up. We were all friendly. We'd just put a band together, for goodness sakes! We were in it because we all liked the same music too, so we had all that in common. When we first started doing gigs Malcolm used to bunk with me, in my room. We used to hang together, go out for a few drinks together and stuff like that in between shows. So we were friendly. I got on well with Malcolm. I liked him, too. It was just later on when the jealousies started happening.'

If Angus did not quickly forgive his older brother for putting him through what he saw as the humiliation of an audition for his new band, he understood that this was a far more serious proposition than any band either brother had been in previously. Auditions had been overseen by well-known Sydney scene-maker Allan Kissick, who'd spent the previous decade working, variously, as an agent, talent spotter, artist manager and record company link man. He'd been there when The Easybeats began to take off, handling their early business dealings before Alberts got more fully involved. It was Allan who had the Masters Apprentices connection, too, introducing Malcolm to Colin. And it was now Allan and his partner and experienced roadie, Ray Arnold, that effectively became AC/DC's managers, albeit ones that worked on trust and without a contract.

There would also be a clear direction to the new outfit Malcolm put together. His jazz affectations aside, in the context of a live rock band guaranteed to survive the nitty-gritty of Sydney publand audiences, Malcolm understandably gravitated towards a sound and ideal far removed from the musical 'experiments' of contemporary rock giants like the Pink Floyd or even David Bowie. He may have loved T. Rex but that was for the instant buzz of hits like 'Get It On' and 'Ride A White Swan', themselves barely more than modern pop pastiches of Chuck Berry and Eddie Cochran licks and riffs. Seeing them play at Sydney's Hordern Pavilion in 1973, Malcolm wanted to taste the same raw excitement from an audience that T. Rex singer Marc Bolan got from his. Malcolm was less taken with more self-consciously 'album-oriented' acts that, as he saw it, obfuscated their obvious attractions with stodgy dollops of meaningfulness. In this he was encouraged in his views by his brother George, who had returned from England with tales of new, no-bullshit outfits like Rod Stewart's Faces and Paul Rodgers and Paul Kossoff's Free. They had both also noted how even The Beatles – at whose door could be laid almost all the blame, as the Youngs saw it, for turning rock into a more introspective, 'arty-farty' activity fit only for star-gazing hippies – appeared to throw off the shackles of so-called pop artistry towards the end of their career, in favour of no-shit, back-to-the-garden rockers like 'Get Back' and 'The Ballad Of John And Yoko'. Predictably, the Rolling Stones had followed suit, retreating from the cod psychedelia of 1967 to bring the world what remain their quintessential albums, the blood-and-guts of *Sticky Fingers, Let It Bleed* and, their zenith, the double *Exile On Main Street*. That was the stuff that got Malcolm going. That was the kind of thing he saw his new band doing. Cut the crap, no-bullshit rock'n'roll, no arguments allowed, mate.

And there was something else. The element that George now identified as the biggest mistake The Easybeats ever made: trying to please all of the people all of the time. Instead of maintaining the strong musical identity that had reached its apotheosis with 'Friday On My Mind', they had allowed their hunger to maintain that success lead them down the blind alleys of ballads, of esoteric novelty songs, of trying anything and everything to get another hit instead of simply staying strong and letting the world come to them. There would be many lessons George would impart to his younger brothers over the coming years, as AC/DC fell prey to the same temptations in their own long search for a level of success that somehow made all the angst and heartache worthwhile. But this was the most important lesson and the one he most consistently hammered home to them time and again. Find your groove, own it, and stick with it, come what may. Don't go wandering off down rock's lost and lonely highways. Above all 'don't disappear up your own arse'. You would come to regret it, as even The Beatles and the Stones did. Or as Malcolm would later put it in an interview with Australia's *Juke* magazine: 'You're gonna come back there anyway, so why leave in the first place?'

George's influence on Malcolm manifested itself in other ways too. As Mark Evans, who would later join on bass, says now, 'Right from the word go it was made clear to me that becoming big in Australia was not the whole deal. Because of the success of their brother, I think Malcolm and Angus saw success there as a given, just something that would definitely happen for them. The big thing was to get overseas and succeed where even The Easybeats hadn't. Right from my first rehearsal with them, I was told: "This time next year we'll be in England." I didn't believe them. But I was wrong.' Dave Evans recalls Malcolm telling him, too: 'I don't give a fuck about Australia! We're gonna make it fucking big, man! The world!'

The new band's first official gig was in December 1973, sandwiched into the middle of a three-band bill at a club called The Last Picture Show, on Sydney's Southside. Only snag: they didn't have a name for the band yet. They decided to draw names from a hat at rehearsal, except they didn't have a hat handy. Instead they plumped for AC/DC: a name that not even the band can now recall definitively how they came by. Received wisdom passed down through countless magazine and newspaper articles has always had it that it came from a suggestion by the brothers' older sister, Margaret, who got it from the sticker on her vacuum cleaner. According to Dave Evans though, speaking now, it came from George Young's wife, Sandra, who got the idea from the label stuck to the side of her sewing machine.

For a while it looked like they might call themselves The Night Hawks – Dave's suggestion. 'But we couldn't agree. Then at one of the rehearsals Malcolm said that Sandra had come up with a name and just tossed it in – AC/DC – and what did we think of it? So we all thought about it and said, yeah, it's catchy: AC/DC. It was easy to remember, short and snappy. Also it meant power and it was on the side of a lot of appliances in those days,' he chuckles. 'So we all agreed, said, "Yeah!" and all shook hands. That's how it was – democratic, in the beginning. We all felt that it was our band, yeah.'

Dave denies that there was any awareness of the name AC/DC being slang for bisexual. 'No, not at all. AC/DC was power. It was on the side of record players and that type of thing. I'd never heard anyone described as AC/DC. And if I had I wouldn't have known what that meant. I've always been a heterosexual person. I don't understand anything else. I never hung around with that crowd so I never heard the term.'

A lot has since been made of the use of the name as a metaphor for the electrical currents in rock'n'roll. One of the reasons it may have appealed to Malcolm Young was that the term 'AC/DC' was then one of the *noms du jour* in the glam rock-dominated environment of the early-Seventies British music scene. 'AC/DC was shorthand for bisexual and if you were in a band and weren't bisexual in the early Seventies – or at least, dressed like you were bisexual – you weren't considered cutting edge', as the rock writer Peter Makowski, then working for *Sounds* magazine, explains.

Although they always played it down subsequently – arguing that they had not been aware of the connotations of their new name – many of AC/DC's early bookings were in gay bars and strip shows. Sometimes it worked in their favour, as when they were surprisingly offered the opening spot on Lou Reed's first Australian tour in 1974, in the wake of the success of his *Transformer* album and attendant hit single, 'Walk On The Wild Side'. Sometimes it was a drag, as when future vocalist Bon Scott was propositioned by the head of a music publishing firm in the gents' toilets at a gig. Bon, though, left no one in any doubt over the true nature of his sexuality. 'You can hit with both sides of the bat, it doesn't affect me,' grinned Bon. 'Just don't expect me to join in with you.' The words 'or else' left hanging in the air.

Early shows featured the two Young brothers alternating on lead guitar. It was Malcolm – ironically, the more technically adept of the two – who called a halt to that, announcing that from now on he would stick to providing the solid slabs of rhythm guitar with Angus free to come up with the lightning-fast breaks and freeform soloing. 'Malcolm said, "You do it – it gets in the way of my drinking",' Angus would later laughingly recall. 'He used to always push me out in front of the stage, saying, 'People want to see a show, and that's what you do so well'.' It wasn't only Malcolm, though, that could see the potential in Angus, who according to Harry Vanda 'was just so bloody vibrant and violent, you could see he was a guitar hero in the making'. Yet it was a decision that would prove more significant than anyone could have known at the time. 'Malcolm was a bit of a visionary,' declared Larry Van Kriedt. 'He didn't just think of the guitar. I remember hearing him say that he would like to be like the guy that plays guitar who's organised.' Gordon 'Buzz' Bidstrup, who would later become the drummer in another Vanda and Young-sponsored group signed to Alberts called The Angels, remembers how 'George would always tell me and tell anyone really at the time that Malcolm was a much better guitar player than Angus. And they would produce lots of other sessions and Malcolm would play on those, more than Angus. Malcolm was a very good rhythm player but he was also a jazz player and a blues player. He had more of a repertoire of guitar techniques than Angus did. And Malcolm didn't make mistakes.'

The official unveiling of the newly named, newly organised group came on New Year's Eve 1973 at Chequers, then Sydney's premier rock club and general hangout for the Oz music business. They got the gig because of George and because Colin was also in the band, the Masters having appeared there too in their hit-making days. 'There were obviously great expectations that the band was gonna be great,' recalls Dave Evans, 'and we were.' They had played there before, filling in at short notice when other acts pulled out at the last minute or were suddenly deemed inadequate. This though was the start of their own week-long residency and the band were 'nervous as shit'. That all got forgotten in the sweat and blood of ploughing their way through four sets spread over four or five hours a night. With only a handful of their own songs to call on – sketchy early numbers included such never-heard-of-again originals as 'The Old Bay Road' and 'Midnight Rock' – they relied almost entirely on cover versions. They would take a three-minute Stones hit like 'Jumpin' Jack Flash' and batter it into a monolithic 12-minute jam. For an encore, they would do the same to an old blues like 'Baby, Please Don't Go' (ostensibly learned from Them), with Malcolm singing, bouncing vocal lines off Angus's madly improvised guitar responses. Even then they often had to improvise to make up the time, Malcolm switching to bass while Larry pulled out the saxophone.

This is where the fledgling AC/DC really learned the ropes, laying down the foundations of a work ethic that would carry them over the highs and lows of the rest of their career. Sometimes they simply didn't have enough numbers and Malcolm would turn to the band and growl, 'We're doing this in E.' Or G, whatever. Dave could sing in any key so it didn't matter. 'Just follow me.' And he'd start riffing, pulling stuff out of the bag spontaneously: anything that moved, Dave making up lyrics on the spot. When they were really stuck towards the end of the night they would even resort to telling a dirty joke or two.

It was part of Oz rock scene tradition that you had to hit the ground running, grab the audience's attention from the get-go and maintain it throughout. One false move and you were dead. Dave: 'Towards the end of the set you've actually got to crank it up, kind of like a blitz-krieg.' Booked to play at the Greek wedding of a friend of Dave Evans', they happily obliged, when asked, by knocking out a passable version of 'Zorba The Greek'. When faced by a roomful of drunken bikers at another early show they simply ramped up the volume still higher and played a selection of Fifties rock'n'roll classics, then legged it off the stage as the bottles started to fly – in appreciation.

The band rarely played anywhere in Sydney without either or both George and Harry being there, taking mental notes. Within weeks of their Chequers residency George had taken them into a small room at the same EMI studios he had recorded the Marcus Hook album in, to work on original material. Coming up with riffs was never much of a problem for Malcolm or Angus, who when stuck for ideas merely purloined their favourite licks from their favourite Chuck Berry and Little Richard songs. For words, though, they initially looked to George for assistance. An accomplished songsmith apparently without ego – at least when it came to lyrics – George was adept at rewriting anything singer Dave Evans didn't like or couldn't manage to sing convincingly enough, often changing the words on the spot, scribbling corrections down on any scrap of paper handy. Early tunes included typically first-draft rock-by-numbers stuff like 'Can I Sit Next To You, Girl', destined to become their first single; 'Rockin' In The Parlour', which would become the B-side; 'Sunset Strip' (later repurposed as 'Show Business' and destined for the Oz version of *High Voltage* with Bon); 'Soul Stripper' (from the *Jailbreak*

EP with Bon) and 'Rock 'N' Roll Singer', the only really top-drawer number of the bunch (and later to become a highlight of both the Oz and international versions of *High Voltage*).

Within days of that first session, though, the band underwent the first of several line-up changes when Colin Burgess got the boot, after collapsing onstage at Chequers. According to Burgess, his drink had been spiked, causing him to fall flat on his face in the middle of a number. He admits he'd 'had a couple of drinks' before going on that night but insists he wasn't drunk. He'd bought a drink arriving at the gig then left it for half an hour to go and check his drums and get ready. When he returned he simply picked up the glass and drank it down in one. Once he got onstage, 'my head was going whooh-ooh-ooh-ooh. It flipped me out. I thought I was turning to jelly. I did this drum roll and kept it going till I'd rolled off the floor.' He had to be carried off the stage. According to Dave Evans, 'Ten minutes later or so Malcolm walked up to me and informed me he'd sacked him.' But then, according to Dave, Malcolm and Angus already had the arse with him. Colin had been a pop star in the Sixties 'and would arrive at a gig with a girl on either arm. I thought it was great but Angus and Malcolm would talk behind his back. Call him rock star, pop star.' They were, he said, simply 'very, very jealous of Col'. As Burgess would later recount, 'I'd played in a band that had had quite a few hits – lots of hits – and I thought, here we go again. I knew they were going to be big.' Then came the bombshell. Malcolm, who had already rung George, who was now on his way over to the club to fill in on drums, went straight to Colin and told him: 'Obviously you're so drunk you can't play – you're sacked.'

According to Dave Evans though: 'He'd been in one of the biggest bands in Australia and he was always surrounded by girls. He'd been a pop star. And behind his back they were always calling him "Rock star!", always bagging him. I thought it was great that Colin had chicks hanging off him. I thought, well, something to look forward to, you know? But they sacked Colin then I got it after that, all this "rock star, pop star" bullshit.'

Next out the door was Van Kriedt, after Malcolm returned from a recording session organised by **Allan** Kissick, with a much better idea for a rhythm section. Hired to play on a track by the Sydney band Jasper – whose frontman, Johnny Cave, Malcolm also later thought about bringing into AC/DC, but who soon after topped the Australian charts under the name William Shakespeare, with a brace of cheerfully rote Vanda–Young songs, 'Can't Stop Myself' and 'My Little Angel' – Malcolm had been so impressed by the tightness of the band's rhythm section, bassist Neil Smith and drummer Noel Taylor, he'd talked them into throwing in their lot with him instead. For Neil and Noel this was an offer impossible to turn down, given the fact that Malcolm was George Young's brother. For Malcolm, there was the bonus that the pair came with their own van and PA system.

This was the beginning in a long line of sackings, nearly all of which the Youngs have always steered away from commenting on. The new line-up convened professionally for the first time in late February 1974, with a month-long residency at the Hampton Court Hotel. Similar to Chequers, if far less hip, the schedule ran to three sets a night, with 30-minute breaks between. Both brothers still had day-jobs and the late finish played havoc with their work shifts. During the breaks, Angus could often be found curled up in a corner of the dressing room, fast asleep. There was never much complaining from them though: at least, not about playing. Their self-belief was such that even their own band mates were often staggered. Angus once told an astonished Neil Smith that it was 'a shame Hendrix died cos we could've blown him off stage!' More common were the endless boasts that 'We're gonna be one of the greatest bands in the world.'

Dave, who'd been shocked and upset by the sudden sackings of Chris and Larry, worried that he might be next, but did his best to hang on. When Malcolm made his next 'suggestion' – that the band should all wear their own individual costumes onstage – Dave, normally wary of compromising his butch jack-the-lad image, bit his tongue and reluctantly agreed. Unlike Angus, who accused his brother of trying to turn them into a cabaret act. Malcolm wasn't listening though. Until then AC/DC, despite their name, had appeared onstage in that most rudimentary of rock uniforms: faded blue jeans and scraggly old T-shirts. But glam rock, now at its peak in Britain, was just starting to impact on the Australian music scene and Malcolm was determined that AC/DC not get left behind.

The band had been booked to appear that April at a big outdoor festival in Sydney's Victoria Park. Malcolm decided that would be the perfect platform from which to launch the band's new look. It was the first – and last – time AC/DC would give such minute consideration to things like image. But it was to have lasting repercussions for their entire career.

'Malcolm said, "We've got to do something different",' Evans recalls. '"So Angus is gonna wear his school uniform and we're gonna drop his age from nineteen down to sixteen, so people can relate and think he's a school kid." And Malcolm said, "I'm gonna wear like an airman's outfit, like a satin airman's outfit with boots" – a jumpsuit-type thing. This is before Village People. And he said he wanted the other three boys to think of something. So the drummer at the time, Noel, came up with the top hat and the Harlequin outfit, like a joker in a pack of cards. And the bass player had the idea to look like a New York cop with a crash helmet, jodhpurs and dark glasses. I thought, well, I'll come up with the ultimate rock star look and went for the Slade bottom half, with the tights and platform boots, and a top half like Rod Stewart, with a striped jacket and scarf. I stuck those together and of course it worked. Everybody thought we were English!'

Evans remembers how 'You heard the crowd gasp', when AC/DC hit the stage that day. The most striking arrival, however, onstage that day – and all the days and nights that have followed – was that of Angus himself, dressed in what was in fact his old school uniform, including school cap and satchel swinging from his back. 'The reaction was quite amazing.' What's more, 'The schoolboy uniform did something to Angus. He really ripped up the stage. He just went berserk. I'd never seen him like that before.'

It nearly didn't happen. When his sister Margaret first suggested he wear the same uniform he'd been in such a hurry to leave behind at 15 – inspired by her memories of seeing him playing guitar in uniform, having raced home from school and immediately picked up his guitar – Angus was appalled. Malcolm and George, though, thought it an inspired idea. Angus just thought they were taking the piss. But the alternative suggestions – that he wear a gorilla suit, or a superman costume (cringingly restyled as Super Ang), both of which he actually did at some of their earliest shows – were even more seemingly ridiculous. At one point he had even affected a Zorro look, replete with mask and cape, drawing a plastic sword across his guitar strings in pantomime emulation of Jimmy Page's use of a violin bow in parts of Led Zeppelin's show. So why not a school uniform? Perhaps because that was the one costume that really cut to the heart of who Angus Young was in those days: symbolic of the spoiled brat that never had to grow up, Peter Pan in reverse, with Malcolm loitering next to him as the ruthlessly conniving Captain Hook.

In the end, Angus very reluctantly agreed to put on a version of his old school uniform remodelled by his sister Margaret. His brothers were still laughing at the sight of him as he got ready to walk onstage in it for the very first time at Victoria Park; Angus determined that this would be his one and only appearance in the embarrassing get-up. Looking back almost 35 years later, however, Angus confessed to *Rolling Stone* how, without that suit, 'I would never have made the effort to get out there and have a presence. I was a lot more shy before that. I would stand back and play. But the suit pulls me.'

'Up to that point he'd just stand there and play, like the rest of us,' recalled Malcolm. 'But as soon as he put on that school uniform he became a monster. Of course, they jeered and whistled when he walked on – these places you're playing to men's men – but as soon as he struck up, the looks on their faces changed.' Once it became an established part of their act, said Malcolm, and Angus began jumping offstage and spinning on his back on the floor, or leaping up onto tables, 'drinks would be going over and more drinks being bought so the club owner loved us'.

'I was always a bit shy, but when I put the suit on I thought, well, you'd better do something in case you're a target for a missile!' Angus recalled. When his sister's hastily put-together costume began to wear out he actually dusted down his old Ashfield High uniform, 'borrowing' the blazer from his nephew, Sam Horsburgh, as blazers were only allowed for Year 11 students and Angus had never made it that far.

Other soon-to-be-signature AC/DC stage moments also date back to this time. The earlier Zorro experiment, though thankfully short-lived, had led to Angus having a sword fight with Dave onstage, usually during an extended 'Baby, Please Don't Go', the singer using his mike stand to fend off Angus's plastic rapier. A dual that would climax each night with Evans hoisting the guitarist onto his shoulders as he kept furiously chugging away on his guitar – a part of the act that would remain, in only slightly altered form, throughout their career.

The Victoria Park show was to be a turning point in the AC/DC story in other ways too. Just six weeks after being hired, and after just one appearance in their new stage gear, both Neil Smith and Noel Taylor were summarily dismissed. The former feels the pair might have kept their gigs had they taken Malcolm's endless claims that AC/DC were on their way to being 'the biggest band in the world' more seriously. 'We'd go, "Yeah, yeah, yeah", and have another beer,' said Smith. 'I can just imagine how frustrating it must have been for Malcolm.' The increasingly canny guitarist, however, had already lined up their replacements: bassist Rob Bailey, who Malcolm had clocked at Victoria Park, playing with Flake, and drummer Peter Clack, both then playing regularly in a local power-trio called Train, fronted by show-off guitarist Dennis James. Having been invited to audition for AC/DC after a phone call from Ray Arnold, James tagged along. 'Those two, plus my singer, Wayne Green, were asked to join,' James recalled. 'Wayne unfortunately [for him] declined.'

As James's remark reveals, though he didn't know it for sure yet, Dave Evans's position in AC/DC was also now being called into question by the brothers. No longer the focal point onstage, now that Angus and his new stage outfit and attendant high jinks had usurped him, Dave was being excluded from offstage discussions too: another harbinger for the way the band did business that endures to this day. As if to underline his growing unease, Evans came into rehearsal one day to be told both Kissick and Arnold had also now been fired.

This time, Dave let his feelings be known to Malcolm, and a nagging argument ensued that would drag on for weeks. Dave wasn't just up against Malcolm and Angus but George, too, who he now calls 'the unofficial manager'. Evans wasn't in disagreement about every decision, just that he wasn't even 'sitting at the table' when they were made. He adds with a sigh: 'They expected everybody to toe the line.'

Correction: the Young brothers didn't just *expect* the other band members to toe the line. As Dave Evans was about to find out to his cost, they demanded it.

CHAPTER FOUR

A Groovy Old Man

The train carrying Bon Scott and The Valentines arrived into Flinders Street Station, in Melbourne, early on the morning of Friday 13 October 1967. With the Australian spring in full bloom, Melbourne – culturally the most European, if any can really be considered that way, of all Australian cities – was bright and welcoming and the future suddenly looked good again. The present, however, was somewhat more arduous for a group of young wannabes new in town.

Hooking up almost immediately with former Loved Ones singer Gerry Humphries, who had recently gone into management with his fellow former musician partner, Don Pryor, ex-drummer with Johnny Young, the good news was they had plenty of live work on offer almost straight away. The bad news was they weren't exactly the kind of gigs their singer-leader, Vince Lovegrove, and his vocal sidekick, Bon Scott, had in mind when they persuaded the rest of the group to leave family and friends behind in Perth.

Melbourne was then the centre of the nascent Australian music business. *Go-Set*, Australia's top teen magazine – and the first to include a national Australian pop chart – was there and national TV shows like *Commotion* were made there. If The Valentines could make it in Melbourne, they could make it anywhere. That was the thinking. And so it almost proved. With its thriving pub and club circuit, its cheap rehearsal spaces and professional recording studios, Melbourne had everything that Perth did not, as well as a budding film and fashion industry. Relocating to Melbourne was supposed to have provided a leg-up on the greasy music biz pole. Instead The Valentines found themselves starting practically from the bottom again, their most frequent gigs the Saturday morning shows for kids that most big department stores put on.

To keep the much younger audience they were now playing to happy they quickly ditched their former reliance on American soul and Motown covers and began bashing out their own less sturdy versions of hits of the day from now fashionable British rock stars like the Rolling Stones and The Who. Bon, for one, was much more at home with this idea. Vince and the others, though, began to wonder where all this was leading? Would they ever work properly in adult-age nightclubs again? They needn't have worried. By the end of 1967 they were playing up to four times a night, zipping from one overcrowded smoky bar to another that might be almost empty. It could be soul-destroying, knowing none of the audience were there specifically to see you, whether they turned up or not. Money was tight and they got used to cadging drinks where they could, and living off the goodwill of anyone willing to spring for the price of a Coke and burger. Renting a cramped two-up-two-down in the poor eastern suburb of Burwood, they would loiter in supermarket aisles, eating biscuits taken straight from packets on the shelves. On their way home from gigs in the early hours, they would push Bon out of the car to sneak up to houses and filch milk money from the doorsteps.

The only one apparently unaffected by this grim existence was Bon himself, who treated the whole experience like one big jape – outwardly, anyway. But then he also had his old girlfriend from Fremantle, Maria, to stay with sometimes. Now living in a flat in the upmarket Melbourne suburb of South Yarra, Maria had been thrilled when Bon first pitched up leering into her intercom. She became less so, though, as it became clear that, far from settling down, or even finding his fortune, Bon seemed to be at more of a loose end than ever. As one of Bon's new best friends from this time, singer-songwriter Brian Cadd, then of The Groop, says, 'He wasn't a guy that was anything other than ultra-social, so all the times we ever spent with him we spent out drinking and hanging out and rocking, you know?'

Maria knew the group invited as many female fans as they could to the dump in Burwood – apart from anything else they relied on them to bring food and drink and occasionally cook – and she knew that Bon, with Vince, was the principal attraction for these so-called fans. And she hated it. Every time Bon stayed with Maria it seemed to end with her throwing him out again. But despite his unwillingness to keep away from groupies, or indeed any other woman that crossed his path in those days, he always maintained his love for Maria, writing her lengthy letters, full of the usual promises, every time he was too far away to drive over. Maria told Clinton Walker how Bon would paint rosy pictures of a time when the Vallies would be famous and their tour bus would have 'a little caravan attached' at the back especially for him and Maria. Nevertheless, says Maria, 'Bon and I split up when we were in Melbourne a number of times.' Then after yet another breakup – 'for good' this time – near Christmas, Maria came home late on Christmas Eve to find Bon had let himself into her flat and left her a present under the Christmas tree. 'This fantastic picture of this girl with long blonde hair which was supposed to be me. Bon had broken into the flat, left me a Christmas present, then just disappeared.'

The really hard work was left, as ever, to Vince. With his film star looks and easy charm, Vince made the kind of friends Bon wouldn't have been able to – music biz types who could offer real help and advice. The kind of people you wouldn't find getting legless every night in some downtown Melbourne bar. The type of people Bon saw as out of his league. Bon had 'a lot of bravado', as Vince put it, but not one-on-one where it really counted. Bon was a people-pleaser: an excellent quality in a frontman; irksome and unhelpful when trying to get outsiders to take the group seriously from a business point of view. So while Bon flitted between rows with Maria and cavorting onstage with the Vallies, Vince engineered an ambitious move from their present booking agents, over to Ivan Dayman, a Brisbane-based promoter with an interest in Sunshine Records, the label that had launched Normie Rowe, one of Australia's biggest pop sensations in the late Sixties. Dayman had first dibs on a vast circuit of live venues all over Australia, notably the Cloudland Ballroom in Brisbane, the Bowl Soundlounger in Sydney and the Op Pop disco chain. Getting signed by him signified another meaningful step up the ladder for The Valentines.

Emboldened, in February 1968 The Valentines released their first single of original material, a psychedelic waltz-time bit of puff called 'Why Me?' backed with an equally insubstantial chimer called 'I Can Hear The Raindrops'. Still popular with the folks back home, 'Why Me?' made the Top 30 in Perth, but failed to trouble any other regional chart in Australia, including, gallingly, that of their adopted hometown of Melbourne. Still they carried gobbling up as many gigs as Dayman could muster for them and by June they found themselves in Sydney recording a rousing cover of Soft Machine's 'Love Makes Sweet Music', replete with distorted guitar effects, backed this time with their join-the-dots version of the old Vanda–Young composition for The Easybeats, 'Peculiar Hole In The Sky'. This fared only marginally better than its predecessor, making the Top 20 in both Perth and Adelaide, but still no cigar in Melbourne, let alone nationally. As Vince Lovegrove would write on his MySpace page over three decades later: 'We suffered near-malnutrition just to experience that hour or so onstage, our adrenalin-rush audience-feedback addiction satisfied once more in a fix of rock'n'roll performance. Our main charter, sadly at the start anyway, wasn't to achieve the brilliance of musicianship, but to live the life; we had many experiences, were run out of a couple of towns, had a few run-ins with the law; our charter was sex, drugs and rock'n'roll. I say this as a matter of fact, not a matter of pride, necessarily.'

It was time for another change of music and image, this time away from the hard-line rock they had been peddling since arriving in Melbourne, towards an unashamed pop stance. Brightly coloured band uniforms with see-through puff sleeves were suddenly the norm, a bopping Bon in his new page boy hairdo. Something which distressed Bon, initially, as you could still see the tattoos on his arms – not the greatest look for a frontman trying to appeal to a female teen audience. He tried covering them with pancake makeup but it would start to run as soon as he got sweaty. Brian Cadd recalls seeing them at this time. 'On they came onstage and they were wearing these absolutely brilliant yellow band uniforms. They looked like fluffy ducks.'

Finally, in March 1969, The Valentines were rewarded with a national hit in the Australian charts, with yet another Vanda–Young number, this one penned especially for them, 'My Old Man's A Groovy Old Man'. They had planned to release it on Valentine's Day but the record was so low on the list of priorities at the pressing plant it didn't come out until three weeks later. No matter, 'My Old Man', backed with the jaunty, almost folksy 'Ebeneezer', one of the only Valentines recordings to feature a pure lead vocal from Bon, changed everything for the group. Suddenly they had so many bookings coming in, they grew used to playing two sets a day: an early show for underage fans; a late show for the older, fully licensed crowd. They even began to be mobbed. Best of all, they began to make money. Not enough to retire on to their mansions in the hills, but enough to make the difference between eking it out together in one rented house and each having their own – for a little while anyway.

Interviewed in *Go-Set*, Vince was quoted as saying the secret of The Valentines' success was basically the interaction onstage between him and Bon. 'I'm more popular than Bon,' he explained straight-faced. 'But he's a far better singer than I'll ever be. In fact, I think he's the most under-rated singer in Australia.' The group had developed a split personality to go with its double-headed frontage. Playing early-evening, cabaret-style shows, designed to please their growing pop audience, where they would mingle their syrupy hits with equally eye-winking covers of others' hits like 'Build Me Up Buttercup', they would then re-emerge, often later the same night, in some of Melbourne's less salubrious rock clubs, stripped of their puff-sleeved glad-rags and belting out covers of Led Zeppelin and Stones tunes. Hooking up with another newly arrived old mate from the Perth scene, Billy Thorpe, now fronting his own rock'n'roll outfit, The Aztecs, Bon got to let his hair down – figuratively and metaphorically – with a band that seemed closer to the heart of what he was really all about. Or at least that part of him that still wanted to play rough with the big boys. Describing the Bon he knew in those days as 'a fucking madman', Thorpe recalled for Clinton Walker a young tearaway high on speed and dope and anything else he could get into his system, swigging from bottles of whisky and ready to 'have a blue' with whoever stood in his road. There was 'Bon the cabaret singer ... making a living in a tuxedo with a bow tie' and there was the Bon who sat backstage with Billy and his boys, 'smoking dope and drinking booze [and] jumping up onstage and having a wail whenever he could get a look in'. Thorpe recalled Bon telling him one night when he was high: 'You know I'm going to make it, I'm going to fucking make it.'

The dichotomy in both Bon and The Valentines reached its apotheosis with their next hit, a trite but undeniably catchy riff on the children's rhyme 'Nick Nack Paddy Whack'. The B-side, however, was 'Getting Better', written by guitarist Wyn Milson, with lyrics by Bon. By far the best thing The Valentines had ever recorded, it featured a speedy riff and genuinely soulful vocal from Bon and, in the hands of a more recognised hit-making outfit like the Spencer Davis Group might have made a handsome addition to their catalogue. Still, a hit is a hit and it kept The Valentines on the cover of *Go-Set* and on the radio all winter. The good, clean fun The Valentines expounded, though, at least publicly, was about to come to a bitter end, when, in September, they were busted for possession of marijuana. The cops had been tipped off – the suspicion, though never proven, was by another rival band, envious of the Vallies' growing success – turning up at the band's new rehearsal base, a former surf house on the beach in Melbourne, and arresting them all en masse, although it was only really Vince and Bon who were heavy weed smokers. Indeed, the others rather disapproved of their fondness for 'the old wacky baccy', as Bon called it.

The first time the two singers got stoned in front of the band they were threatened with the sack. That had been at the Crest Hotel in Sydney during another one-nighter. 'It was the first time either of us had ever had a joint,' Vince later recalled. 'This band that we knew, the keyboard player invited us back to his place to smoke some dope.'

They ended up 'shit scared in the corner of the room, giggling'. They tried to counteract the effects by staggering to a nearby bar and getting drunk, 'But were still stoned the next morning.' The rest of The Valentines reared up on them about it, which only made them giggle more. The result of their bust, however, was to put the band all in the same boat, whether they smoked or not. At the subsequent court case in Geelong, all five pleaded guilty to possession of and smoking marijuana, and each received a $150 'good behaviour bond' – a suspended sentence. More immediately troubling, though, was the ban then imposed by ABC TV's *GTK* programme. The band tried to make light of the situation, parlaying the embarrassment of the bust into a hastily arranged Legalise Marijuana campaign. It even seemed at one stage as though the headlines might help ease their transition towards a more credible proposition: finally ditching the matching stage costumes in favour of the jeans and T-shirts of their late-night appearances.

They left Melbourne and – symbolically – the past behind and relocated to Sydney. When they performed in the guest slot on an ABC TV special for The Easybeats – celebrating their return to Oz following their much trumpeted success in the UK with 'Friday On My Mind' – Bon was hopping with delight. He and Vince gave it their all onstage that night at Sydney's prestigious Caesar's Palace and the band received a huge ovation as they walked off the stage. Almost as good, Stevie Wright gave them his own personal thumbs-up after seeing them rip into Led Zeppelin's 'Whole Lotta Love' at one of their late-night rock spots.

But although swathes of the record-buying public appeared unfazed – the Vallies were hardly the only group in the late Sixties to call for the legalisation of 'soft' drugs – their teeny audience was wrong-footed. Optimism remained high, however, into the New Year. There was always a next time and the next Valentines single would be another original – only this time written and sung almost entirely by Bon and titled 'Juliette'. Unlike anything The Valentines had ever considered for an A-side, 'Juliette' is a slow, groove-paced, acoustic pop ballad augmented by an orchestral string arrangement that would not have sounded out of place on a Bee Gees album. It could and should have placed The Valentines ahead of every other domestic Australian act – including The Easybeats – when it was released in February 1970. Instead it became a kind of swan song for The Valentines, when it was denied radio exposure due to an industrial dispute over copyright payments to home-grown Australian acts. With all domestic content removed overnight from playlists across the country, 'Juliette' failed to make any impression at all on local or national charts. Neither fish nor fowl in terms of their schizophrenic pop-rock shows, it was dead in the water almost from the start and represented the biggest disappointment so far of Bon's career. He became angry, bitter, alienated from the whole ethos of the group. What was the point of trying if your best records couldn't even get played on the radio? Bon had had enough. Vince also began to think seriously about life after the band. By that point, he said, 'We were only being kept alive by publicity about pot, not by what we were doing [musically] … We got lost, basically.'

There was one last unofficial hurrah in July 1970 when The Valentines performed together for the last time at a well-attended show at Bertie's in Melbourne. They had just been voted the sixth best Australian group in *Go-Set* magazine's annual readers' poll (up from ninth the previous year) but by then Vince and Bon had already told the others they were throwing in the towel. The Valentines ceased trading as such on 1 August 1970. As Ted Holloway reflected, 'We reached, not the top of Australian music obviously, but we got fairly close. We did some major tours and we recorded some music and I thought we did pretty well at the time.' For Bon Scott, though, 'pretty well' was nowhere near enough. He was 24 and worried that time was already running out for him. And he was tired of living a lie, as he saw it. Bon would carry on singing, he'd already decided, but this time in a band that embraced the manners of the age in the same way they did in their real lives. In short, he was sick of trying to make it as a pop star. He wanted to rock'n'roll. He'd never wanted to do anything else.

On his way home to Perth, Vince had stopped off in Adelaide, where a very different domestic music scene had been evolving away from the chart-driven imperatives of the competing Melbourne and Sydney circuits. Many such as future Australian Hall Of Fame inductees The Masters Apprentices, The Twilights (featuring future Little River Band vocalist Glenn Shorrock), and The Vibrants (two national hits) were aimed as squarely at the Oz charts as anything in Melbourne. There were many other artists though, like folk singer Doug Ashdown, singer-songwriter Peter Tilbrook and the James Taylor Move (who played the kind of intelligent pop-rock the Vallies could only dream of), pitched at the rapidly growing album-oriented audience. When *Go-Set*'s hip young publisher, Phillip Frazer, who Vince had become friends with, suggested he set up and run an Adelaide branch of the *Go-Set* editorial team, Vince jumped at the chance. By 1971, Vince had become such an influential mover on the Adelaide scene he was presenting his own Saturday morning TV music show called *Move*, and was writing a weekly music column in the *South Australian News*.

Bon, who would soon join Vince in Adelaide, had meanwhile opted to stay in Sydney, where he'd finagled himself into an offshoot of another locally popular outfit, Levi Smith's The Clefs. The Clefs had been going since the mid-Sixties and had their roots in people-pleasing soul and R&B, a belting live outfit that had become almost a franchise, with dozens of different singers and musicians flitting through its ranks as it took on year-long residencies at Sydney hot-spots like the Whisky Au Go Go, in King's Cross, and Chequers. Bon had become mates with their bass player, Bruce Howe, hanging out together whenever The Clefs came down to Melbourne. When the nucleus of the latest Clefs line-up, in an echo of the singer's own recent exit from The Valentines, announced they had grown frustrated by the lack of forward movement in the band's career – there had been occasional singles and one-off local hits but the emphasis was firmly on entertaining the folks from the stage, not on their shiny new stereo record players – Bon looked on enviously as Bruce Howe along with guitarist Mick Jurd, keyboardist John Bisset and drummer Tony Buettel (soon to be replaced by John Freeman) struck out on their own with a new line-up, to be called Fraternity.

The band had already recorded a single as Fraternity, a rambling goodtime lope-along called 'Why Did It Have To Be Me?', when Bon was invited by Howe to become their new frontman, the one component they still lacked. A self-conscious late-comer to the party, aware that certain members of the group were 'a little sceptical at first' about his appointment, Bon was determined to make his mark from the very first gig. This he did in memorable fashion, his voice so loud it all but drowned out the guitars. Suitably impressed, Howe proposed that their new singer move in with the band at the two-storey terraced house in Jersey Road, east Sydney, that same night. Bon was 'made up', he told Vince. Formed initially in emulation of musicianly new heavyweight groups like Vanilla Fudge and Deep Purple, who took the blues and twisted it into something much more cathedral-like, Fraternity soon left those ideas behind, as did some of the behemoths themselves like Zeppelin, in favour of the latest wave of American roots-influenced rock and blues heralded by the arrival of Bob Dylan's former backing group, The Band, as recording artists in their own right.

For Bon, Fraternity was much more typical of the rapidly changing times than The Valentines had ever been: a newly bearded, extravagantly long-haired post-hippy conglomeration whose extra-musical rituals centred exclusively on free love and drugs. Especially drugs. As John Bisset – known to the others simply as 'JB' – explained nearly 35 years later, one cannot talk about Fraternity 'without talking about subjects like excessive alcohol consumption, marijuana smoking and the use of drugs like LSD and mescaline'. In an effort to try and fit in with what he saw as the more cerebral surroundings he now found himself in, JB recalls Bon as 'a little Pan-like in those days, often sitting in his room playing his recorder'. Other times he was more himself. 'Bon was a great one for dispelling myths about acid culture, like the vegetarianism that many hippies embraced. I remember him wandering around gleefully chomping on a large leg of roast lamb at one very acid-soaked party in Jersey Road.'

JB, who years later would renounce drink and drugs and find peace through Christianity, observed how many people, including him, would have 'a Jekyll and Hyde' change of personality when drunk but that 'Bon was always Bon – straight Bon, stoned Bon, tripping Bon, legless drunk Bon'. He added: 'Some commentators saw us as a bunch of clean-living hippies into lentils and sandals. Nothing could be further from the truth.' He recalled how at a gig at the Whisky one night Bon shared some Mandrax pills – 'Mandies' – he had with him. 'I fell asleep during a set and flopped onto the Hammond keyboard with my foot right down on the volume control. The band initially thought I was doing a wild improvisation. Later on it was Bon who fell asleep, slouched in a seat in the club. They were closing the club and we couldn't wake him so I dragged him out with his arm over my shoulder and took him home in a cab.'

On another occasion, the band all dropped 'Windowpane acid' – aka 'Clearlight': small, thin gelatine squares containing liquid LSD – on a train journey to a gig in Perth, which resulted in Bon being unable to remember a thing about what should have been a triumphant homecoming gig. The next time they played there they flew. But the outcome was even worse when their harmonica player, 'Uncle' John Eyers, began passing around lit joints. When the in-flight crew intervened he told them the smell was patchouli oil. They got away with that but were so drunk and stoned by the time they landed a local radio interview had to be cancelled.

Even Bon Scott's unusually robust constitution would be tested to its limit, though, when Fraternity found themselves opening for Jerry Lee Lewis at Sydney's White City Stadium. He later boasted of how Jerry Lee – a boyhood hero, whose double-entendre lyrics would become a big influence on Bon in his later career with AC/DC – regarded him as his 'drinking partner'. Bon would relate how Jerry Lee's manager would try to hide the bottles of booze from the pair, but that Jerry Lee outfoxed him by hiding bottles of bourbon in his cowboy boots. He would constantly remind his assistant: 'Don't forget my boots!', then later, backstage at the show, Bon was beckoned into Lewis's dressing room with the words 'In here! In here!' before Jerry Lee pulled out two bottles of bourbon, which the singers would share between them before they went on.

And of course there were groupies – though that was something Bon, whose stage attire now regularly included his new Super Screw T-shirt, had going for him long before he joined Fraternity – among them, 'a very beautiful, dark-haired, very pregnant lady friend' he introduced to JB once in Melbourne; a member of what the band called the Baby Brigade, because they all had babies to rock stars or up-and-coming rock stars. This particular girl, whose name he can no longer remember, JB recalls Bon introducing to him as, 'this beautiful chick – about eight months pregnant'. Taken aback at the admission, JB exclaimed, 'Oh, you're gonna get married?' At which Bon and the girl both simply laughed.

After Fraternity opened for Jerry Lee Lewis at White City in Sydney, there was talk of the band relocating to the US, where it was said MCA Records were interested in signing them to make an album. Excited but clueless as to what to do next, the band went ahead and recorded an album's worth of tracks during one marathon 14-hour session that December in Sydney. Around the same time, Bon picked up a few dollars for helping out on sessions for the debut album by rival band Blackfeather, whose *At The Mountains Of Madness* collection he can be heard playing recorder on, on a track called 'Seasons Of Change', and timbales and tambourine on 'The Rat (Suite)'. At the time, it seemed like no biggie but the sessions would come back to haunt him soon after.

When Fraternity's so-called deal with MCA never materialised, Sweet Peach, a small independent label based in Adelaide, came to the rescue and offered to release it. This in turn led to the band's decision to relocate, in January 1971, to Adelaide, where Bon was reunited with his old mate Vince Lovegrove. 'Fraternity were excellent musicians,' Lovegrove recalled in 2008. Bruce Howe, who he characterised as 'a dogmatic, hard taskmaster', was the one, reckoned Vince, that 'weaved his mentor magic on Bon' forcing him 'to push the envelope [in Bon's] approach to singing'.

In this they were aided by the attentions of local tycoon Hamish Henry, who offered the band a communal home on a seven-acre farm – which they dubbed 'Hemming's Farm' – 13 miles to the south-east of Adelaide just outside the bushy hills of the small town of Aldgate. The son of a wealthy family in North Adelaide, Henry was a millionaire, entrepreneur, son of an automobile wheeler-dealer, and budding patron of the arts who desperately fancied getting into the music business. By the time he took Fraternity under his wing, he was already overseeing the careers of several other local acts, including W. G. Berg (aka War Machine) and Headband, fronted by pianist and singer-songwriter Peter Head, who also became close to Bon during this period. Aside from bringing the band down to start a new life in the Adelaide Hills, the first major move Henry made on their behalf was to get them on the bill of the Myponga festival, which he helped stage and promote through his recently formed Music Power company. Staged in the steaming hot Australian summer of 1971, in the quiet dairy-farming town from which it took its name, about 35 miles south of Adelaide, Myponga was Australia's first major outdoor rock festival. Sold as 'the Australian Woodstock' and held over a long weekend, the bill featured a mix of domestic acts, including new dicks on the block Daddy Cool and Bon's mates Billy Thorpe & The Aztecs, and was headed by Fraternity, along with major British artists such as Cat Stevens and headliners Black Sabbath. Stevens pulled out at the last minute but that didn't deter more than 15,000 people paying A$6 each to attend, with thousands more jumping the temporarily erected fences to join in the fun.

Media attention focused inevitably on what it saw as the more salacious details of the event – naked young men and women dancing while drinking and taking drugs. A typical headline read: 'Bye Bye Bra', the story explaining how 'Myponga has turned into the biggest expose of the "no bra" look yet seen in South Australia.' The *Sunday Mail* complained about the amount of unlicensed alcohol being sold and consumed onsite. 'Ten thousand heavy rock fans at the Myponga pop festival tonight settled themselves firmly in their garbage-strewn pop paddock for a night of love, peace, banshee rock music and booze, booze and more booze,' it reported, adding: 'There are about 2,500 girls at the festival and there does not seem to be a bra between them.'

Naked chicks, free drink and drugs, and the chance to appear second on a large festival bill to huge rock stars like Black Sabbath, for Bon Scott, this was the life. 'I got sick of doing bopper audiences with The Valentines and I wanted to become a musician, to be recognised in the Australian rock scene as more than just an arse shaker', as he later put it. When Henry then got Fraternity to open the show for Deep Purple and Free, he didn't care that Howe had the band practising six hours a day, or that Henry sometimes expected him to mow his lawns or wash his cars. Henry was also a friend and patron to the award-winning artist and photographer Vytas Serelis: like the guys in Fraternity, a handsome young hippy, whose passions for art and photography mingled with a fondness for playing sitar. Introduced by Henry, Bon would take Vince and his new friend Peter Head with him to Serelis's own 17-acre property in nearby Carey Gully, where the artist's paintings, sculptures and other works of the imagination were scattered about the place, along with an apparently endless collection of cars and even buses. Head later recalled Sunday evening campfire scenes, with singing and guitar playing while Vytas jammed along on sitar, everyone 'getting stoned on marijuana, magic mushrooms, acid, booze'.

With the addition of new recruits 'Uncle' Eyers on harmonica and Sam See on guitar and keyboards, Fraternity did what The Valentines had not managed to and, in July, came first in the Hoadley Battle Of The Sounds. First prize: an all-expenses-paid trip to Los Angeles, A$2000 in cash and A$300 recording time at studios in Melbourne. Deciding against the trip to America until they were able at least to get a record out there, they leapt at the chance to record in a professional studio in Melbourne, recording the 10 tracks that would become their second album, *Flaming Galah*, released the following year.

Life was good, onstage and off. JB recalls how happily Bon, 'a natural-born daredevil', took to his new circumstances. 'He entertained the local kids in one town by jumping off a high point on a pier into a swarm of jellyfish in the ocean below. He would ride a trolley down an embankment at the Adelaide Hills property into a small lake at the bottom. When the trolley hit the bottom he would be projected into the lake.' He was always crashing on his trail bike too 'but never lost his spirit'. While Bon was more naturally drawn to Uncle – like him, still seen as the newbie of the band – he always felt strangely attracted to Bisset. Prone to mood swings hardly helped by suffering the continual highs and lows of acid, dope and, most depressingly for the already gloomy keyboardist, his excessive drinking, even by the louche standards of Fraternity, JB could go into his shell for days at a time. Bon was intrigued. Beneath his own Wizard of Oz-like front, obliged to keep up the cheeky-chappie facade 24 hours a day, Bon fought his own black moods and growing insecurities. Like all people-pleasers, his sense of self-esteem remained buried beneath the conviction that he was only really faking his way through life, even as things seemed to be going his way. When he saw JB retreating into yet another barely concealed depression, his first thought often was to follow him down there, to see if he could bring him back – and so, too, maybe find a way to bring himself back.

On one memorable occasion, according to Bisset, he had dropped some acid while sitting alone on the beach, hoping for a 'spiritual awakening' to bring him out of his depression. But the LSD was of an inferior batch and JB was left feeling 'miserable and paranoid'. Enter, uninvited, his new singer friend. 'Bon had gone off down the beach on his trail bike. When he returned he beckoned me on to the back of the bike. I objected that I had to mind the dog. "The dog will be all right" said Bon and insisted I get on. So I did. He took off down the long deserted beach at great speed. The eastern end of the beach was blocked by massive sand hills, and a wide stream of water flowed down across the beach from inland to the water, just prior to the sand hills. I expected Bon to slow down but he went even faster. We rocketed through the stream and I was drenched with water as though by a fire hose. The bike then ploughed into the base of the sand hills at great speed and Bon and I were both thrown about 10 metres from where the bike stopped dead. When I regained my senses I was covered in water and sand but seemingly uninjured. I looked up the sand hill and there was Bon smiling and laughing at me. That's what it took to "awaken" my sanity on that day – I immediately saw the funny side of it and laughed too. Bon said "I knew you would either laugh or hit me". He also said later, "I knew there was a normal happy bloke in there somewhere."'

Gordon 'Buzz' Bidstrup also first met Bon during this time. 'I was a bit younger than him but I used to watch The Valentines on this TV show called *Uptight*,' he remembers now. 'I'd been playing in bands in Adelaide since I was fourteen so we knew Fraternity.' Far from the tattooed hard man he would become famous as just a few short years later, the Bon Scott Buzz Bidstrup met in 1972 was, he says, 'a long-haired recorder-playing hippy. He lived up in the hills and took magic mushrooms and smoked pot.' He goes on: 'I don't ever remember him as being a hell-raiser, fighter guy. Almost everyone was peaceful by then. I reckon Bon and John Lennon had a lot in common. Like he was probably a bit of a rougher guy but when I met him he was this hippy dude, as we all were. Long robes and all this stuff …'

It was an idyll into which trouble would soon find its way again. To help launch the band's debut album, *Livestock* – one of only ten albums eventually released on the short-lived Sweet Peach label – it was decided to release a single from it, Bon's first with the band. The obvious choice was 'Seasons Of Change', the very same song Bon had helped Blackfeather record the previous December. When Fraternity recorded their own version, overseen by Henry, in March 1971, it sounded so good with Bon singing they were convinced they had a hit. They did, but only locally in South Australia, where it reached No. 1. It might have happened nationally too if Blackfeather's 'original' wasn't then hurriedly released in April. Bon was apoplectic, not least as he had been assured, verbally, he said, that Blackfeather's version would not be released in competition with Fraternity's. No one, though, had expected the Fraternity single to do so well and Blackfeather's label, Infinity/Festival, had understandably decided to cash in while they still could. As a result, while Fraternity's 'Seasons Of Change' reached No. 51 on the national chart, Blackfeather's 'original' actually cracked the Top 20.

Bon was so outraged – rage fuelled by the fact he now felt extremely foolish for having agreed to take part in the Blackfeather session – he went on national television and accused his former friends in Blackfeather of having 'stolen' *his* song. Never mind that the song had actually been written by Blackfeather guitarist John Robinson and vocalist Neale Johns. A scene, bizarrely, watched at home in Sydney by the teenage Angus Young, and recalled in interview more than 30 years later. 'First time I ever saw Bon Scott was on a talk show on Australian television,' said Angus, 'something to do with some pop bloke nicking one of his songs, and the interviewer was being totally condescending thinking he was this stupid rock and roller. All of a sudden Bon was yelling, 'Fucking cunt!' and leapt across the studio diving on top of the pop bloke. I thought, Hmm, pretty lively ...'

Despite another local hit in September with 'If You Got It', which went to No. 2 on the South Australian chart, the release, at the end of 1971, of *Livestock* fell considerably short of the band's commercial expectations, barely registering locally and doing nothing at all nationally. Partly, this was due to the lack of clout a tiny indie like Sweet Peach had in the fast-growing Oz music biz. Partly it was because of an image problem the band had developed – one that would continue to dog them into their eventual commercial grave. Despite *Livestock* being a lively collection of loose-limbed rock'n'blues, Fraternity flew the freak flag so high over everything they did they would go down in history as being an out-and-out 'hippy' or even folk group. Listening to their few recordings now, though, far from being folksy, on straight-ahead numbers like 'The Race Pt 1' they sound like so many other bands of the era, from the Faces to Free, while on the portentous 'Raglan's Folly' and the eight-minute 'It' they bordered on what was now becoming known in Britain as progressive rock. 'Cool Spot' finds them actually hovering somewhere in that previously unsourced musical zone between Santana and Led Zeppelin. Beards, shades and hanging loose were the order of the day; Bon even had the long, curly hair of a young Robert Plant. And his voice, while never in Plant's stratospheric league, is stretched to a far fuller – and impressive – vocal range than anything he would later achieve with

AC/DC. His fluid recorder playing is also a feature, something that would have had the Youngs spitting in disgust.

People just weren't getting it though and Christmas 1971 was a miserable one for the boys down on the farm. The New Year brought fresh resolve, however, and with the arrogance that only rock bands with just one unsuccessful album under their belts can muster, Fraternity decided they were simply too good for the 'backward' Australian scene. Groups with their talents and ambitions got treated a lot better in Britain and America, where they understood what musicians of their calibre were trying to do. Hamish Henry, who had the money to support such ideas if not the hands-on experience, agreed to back them in their plans and in March 1972, as the Australian summer waned and the British spring shivered into view, Fraternity set off on the journey that, they decided, would be either the making of them, or the breaking.

They didn't even wait for the release of their next single, 'Welfare Boogie' (co-written by Bon), or second album, *Flaming Galah* – its title taken not from the well-known cocktail but a reference to an old Australian slang term for a fool, or in this case, as intended by the band, an idiot savant. There was nothing particularly visionary about the second Fraternity album though. Retaining a handful of the same tracks – including, as if to prove a point, 'Seasons Of Change' – the new numbers comprised mainly rock'n'blues shufflers like 'Annabelle' and 'Hemming's Farm', all co-written by Bon, all intended to beef up their sometimes soporific live performances but instead moving the band's sound closer to Status Quo than Pink Floyd.

There was one last showpiece occasion for Fraternity when they were invited to appear in the Adelaide production of Peter Sculthorpe's musical, *Love 200*, written to commemorate the Captain Cook bicentennial, also featuring jazz singer Jeanie Lewis and the Melbourne Symphony Orchestra: a performance that was about as far from the sound on 'Welfare Boogie' as it is possible to imagine.

Thanks to Henry's continued largesse, and with nothing left to tie them to Australia, as they saw it, Fraternity departed for London en masse, taking with them wives, girlfriends, two roadies (Rob and

Bob), a tour manager, Bruce King, and, in JB's case, a young son and a dog – a party of 17, in all. Bon, who'd never been short of girlfriends but had little luck in securing a long-term relationship, had recently become close to a pretty blonde local girl from Adelaide named Irene Thornton. Using the flight to London as the perfect excuse to seal the deal, he talked Irene into going with him – as his wife. The two were married on 24 January 1972, in Adelaide. The trip to London with Fraternity was to be their honeymoon: the start of a new life that would last barely 18 months.

Swapping an Oz autumn for a Pom spring, Fraternity had expected, at least, that there would be warm weather to greet them, if little else. As with every other preconceived idea they'd had of what life in 'the old country' might have to offer, they were sorely mistaken. The weather was cold, the rain apparently never-ending. Moving into a large, three-storey house in Finchley that, in common with most London houses then, had no central heating and was therefore expensive to keep warm, as JB recalled: 'It was very cramped and communal and there was a lot of bickering.' To ease their passage, Henry had also paid to have their tour bus shipped to England. Not over-thrilled at the prospect of a house packed with fresh-off-the-plane Aussies moving into their street, local residents also had to get used to a large greyhound bus taking up most of the narrow London street it was parked on. Worst of all was the 'noise' that came from the house as the band rehearsed for hours each afternoon and evening. Gigs were hard to come by, though: paying gigs almost non-existent. And without the exposure they would bring, the band's chances of landing a record deal with a prestigious London-based record company grew more slender by the day.

Money was so tight Bon took a part-time job behind the bar in a local pub. Worse still, a supply of good dope – so plentiful back in the Adelaide Hills – was hard to come by, the band unused to the sticky resin prevalent then in Britain, as opposed to the lush green weed they were used to back home. Not that they were over-choosy, either. Bon was given the nickname Road Test Ronnie as he always volunteered to be first to sample any new drugs that came their way in Finchley.

'He seemed able to cope with any drug that science or nature could come up with,' recalled JB. The only time he came a serious cropper was when he 'road-tested' some datura, a hallucinogen, aka Angel's Trumpets and/or Moonflowers. 'He had a bad couple of days and the rest of us avoided it.'

Fraternity's first UK show was opening for Status Quo. The audience had been 'appreciative and kind', according to JB, but the band saw just how far off the pace they were when Quo came on and with their much bigger and better PA system blew Fraternity and their not-so-hidden hopes and dreams clear off the stage and out the door. 'The whole mood of the band went downhill in London – harsh reality began to set in. The party was over.' There was one bright spot – a week-long visit to West Germany, late in '72, playing small club shows in West Berlin, Frankfurt and Wiesbaden. Bon got the hang of introducing songs in German and the band upped the ante in terms of their set, focusing on up-tempo rockers and ditching the perambulatory 'It' and others. When they returned to London, however, things were still the same, but getting worse, the thought of winter at the drafty house in Finchley enough to make them all wonder what on Earth they had got themselves into.

By the start of 1973, both guitarist Sam See and John Bisset had left the band, to return to Oz. Feeling less fraternal by the minute, in a last-ditch attempt to salvage the situation, the band changed its name to Fang – in line, as they saw it, with then hot UK bands like Slade, Free and a previously little-known band from the North-East then having their first chart hit, 'All Because Of You', called Geordie. With the change of name came an attempt to update their image: gone were the days when receding hairlines and beards signified good musical standing. To be replaced by the spangles and lights of glam rock. Even Geordie and Slade, who looked like they were peopled by bricklayers, knew how to put on a show. Briefly, it looked like the new band might click. Opening for Geordie at Torquay Town Hall, on 23 April, and Plymouth the following day, Bon was particularly taken by the band's rough-and-ready singer, Brian Johnson. He particularly liked it when the singer threw himself to the floor at the end of Geordie's last gig with Fang supporting and began screaming blue murder. Not realising the singer's agony was real – he was rushed to hospital that same night with a burst appendix – when Johnson was then carried off, as if at death's door, leaving the band to bring the set to a premature end without him, Bon thought he was magnificent.

Looking back now, Johnson's long-ago memories of his one and only meeting with Bon are of 'a completely different fellow' to the one he would have to one day try and find a way to replace in AC/DC. 'Short hair, tooth missing. He was the funniest man and we had a lovely time. But it was all too brief. It was, "See ya, mate".' Fraternity was simply 'a different kind of band', Bon a very different kind of singer. 'He wasn't half as good as he was when he joined AC/DC. They brought something out in him, as they did with me.'

In their new, glammed-up guise, what was left of Fraternity continued to score upscale support slots throughout the summer of 1973 – Amon Duul II in May, the Pink Fairies in June – but after one final show of their own, before an uninterested pub crowd in August, Fang lost its bite. Bon, aggrieved to still be regarded as something of a junior member of a band he was second-last to join, yet one of its fiercest protectors since its change to Fang, had already made up his mind, though he kept his thoughts to himself for the time being, until he could afford the plane tickets home. He knew there had actually been talk of trying to replace him during the last days of Fraternity, and felt little loyalty to whatever cause the others may have still deluded themselves they were fighting for. Finally, with the prospect of seeing out another drear English autumn and winter, Bon decided he'd had more than enough and booked a ticket home for Irene and him. They arrived back in Perth, en route to Adelaide, in time for Christmas 1973, where they spent the next three days with Isa and Chick, before catching the train back to Irene's tiny apartment in Adelaide.

Although his dreams of making it as a musician were far from over, the reality was that at 27 years old Bon Scott was now all but over the hill – certainly by 1973 standards, when the average age of a pop star was 21 and his expected career lifespan less than five years. Not yet officially a has-been, but with no record deal, no band and absolutely zero offers on the table to improve that situation, he had no option but to find himself a 'proper' job.

Even Irene seemed to be having her doubts about his chances of ever making it as a singer. They began to row and he began to drink more and care less. Or so it seemed. In the meantime, he began 1974 as a casual labourer working cash-in-hand scraping the barnacles from the underside of docked fishing boats. Never one to stand still, though, within weeks he'd managed to find himself something steadier and better paid: working at the Wallaroo fertiliser plant. 'Shit shovelling', as he joked to his few remaining musician mates, that permanent grin on his suddenly much older face growing thinner and meaner by the minute.

CHAPTER FIVE

Got Balls

Malcolm Young knew exactly what he wanted for the band. Or thought he did. One thing was for sure. He didn't need anyone else telling him what to do. With one exception: his older brother George. The only person Malcolm ever met that he genuinely believed did actually know more about AC/DC than he did. But then Malcolm owed George a lot. Growing up in the shadow of his older brother's international success had afforded Malcolm privileged insights into a world no other aspiring Australian musician his age had the faintest idea even existed. The Easybeats had had hits, lots of them, not just in Australia but around the world. They wrote their own songs, produced their own records – yet still came back from London not just broke but heavily in debt. They had the fame, had learned the game, but that's all they had. As Buzz Bidstrup reflects now, 'George's whole thing was he wasn't gonna let his brothers have the same experience as he had in The Easybeats, where they got so close to superstardom but it didn't quite get there. He was gonna make sure that his little brothers didn't have that problem – in the sense of musically and in business and within the record company. George was a very integral part of Alberts Records and they were the kings, you know?' The only person more determined than George that that would not happen to Malcolm and his band was Malcolm himself.

In this way, the Youngs and AC/DC were more fortunate than The Easybeats. By 1973 the music business in Australia had begun to establish itself as more than just an international backwater. It would take the rest of the world some years yet to grasp this – its major concerns still focused primarily on the still booming British and American music industries – but the record-buying public in Oz now got all the same music papers that the Brits and Yanks did, albeit some weeks later, and were buying most of the same records. Touring traffic to and from Oz was also now a more firmly established part of most major bands' touring cycles. In the Sixties, when The Beatles arrived for their first and only Australian tour, it was a one-off in every sense. The only previous occasion when 'foreign' rock'n'roll stars had toured Australia had been in 1957, when Gene Vincent, Eddie Cochran and Little Richard all arrived on a package tour. Even when groups like The Who, the Yardbirds and the Small Faces followed The Beatles, their visits were still treated as a novelty. By the early Seventies, however, Elton John, Rod Stewart and the Faces, Led Zeppelin, Deep Purple, Slade, Black Sabbath, T. Rex and others now routinely included dates in Australia and New Zealand on their tour itineraries. With them came not just the sound but the look, the smell, the feel of what rock what was like at its best outside Australia in the early Seventies. In this way, Malcolm, who looked to George for guidance in almost every other respect when it came to steering his career, felt he had the edge.

Unlike George and his partner, Harry Vanda, who worshipped The Beatles and the Stones but looked down on Johnny-come-latelys like T. Rex and Slade, 20-year-old Malcolm was a fan who looked around in dismay at the scene he was already too familiar with in Sydney, seeing nothing to match what was coming out of Britain. So while George imbued him with the commendable idea that you shouldn't chase fashion, or fall prey to the temptation of easy hits through novelty – ideals that hardened into the character traits that would see AC/DC remain steadfast to their core sound and audience, come what may, throughout their career – it was Malcolm who was convinced that they still needed an edge; something to make them stand out from the herd, certainly in terms of the domestic Australian rock and pop scene. Something that showed they had more going for them than the others. Not just through their blood ties to George (and Harry) and the legacy of The Easybeats, but through their very real connection with modern Seventies rock. It would be this latter quality, first fostered by Malcolm and fed by Angus Young's own drive and personal ambitions that would prove equally important in AC/DC's almost overnight rise to the top – in Australia, at least.

It first manifested itself in Malcolm's command that the group take note of the prevailing trend in what had become known as glam rock and begin dressing up for gigs, beginning with the Victoria Park show in April 1974. It may have looked like an attention-grabbing stunt. It was. But even when, just weeks later, Malcolm decreed that the band should go back to its jeans-and-T-shirts stage look – in unspoken recognition of the fact that another rapidly becoming successful Melbourne act called Skyhooks were doing the whole glam thing so much better – he insisted that Angus keep wearing the school uniform, thereby retaining and building on the best gimmick in rock since Pete Townshend began ending every Who set by smashing his guitar, or David Bowie became reborn as a bisexual alien named Ziggy Stardust.

Not everybody got it. According to Bob Daisley, a Sydney-born bassist who would later find fame in first Rainbow then Ozzy Osbourne's band, the first time he saw AC/DC perform with Angus in his school uniform rolling around on the stage, 'You could see that they had something but to be honest with you I thought the Angus thing was always a little bit gimmicky. I kind of thought, what are they gonna do when he gets older?' Those sorts of opinions, though not uncommon in the band's earliest days, were based on the old Sixties paradigm of rock music: that 'serious' artists should eschew any suggestion that what they did was in any way related to outmoded ideas of entertainment. That, above all, they should carry a message and that it should be conveyed with utter seriousness and utmost originality. But where the best Sixties rock had been innovative and forward-thinking, its Seventies descendant, even at its best, would be derivative, self-reflecting, nostalgic for a perceived 'golden age' that had only just passed. No longer over-concerned with social 'issues', apparently ignorant of personal politics, the music of Bowie, Bolan, Alice Cooper and Rod Stewart was first and foremost about escapism

– just as it had been in the days of Chuck Berry and Elvis Presley, before foot-tapping rock'n'roll had metamorphosed into furrow-browed rock with a capital 'R'.

Malcolm and Angus Young's AC/DC would fit into this new pop landscape all too easily, helping define the new decade – with its distinctly second-hand feel – more stringently than almost any other act, narrowing their focus to almost a pinprick as they sought a means to relay the simple spirit of rock'n'roll in ways that, four decades on, their current roadie, Geoff Banks, only half jokingly now describes as 'almost borderline Asperger's'. Certainly they were taking few chances with the Dave Evans-fronted line-up of 1974. Within days of their Victoria Park appearance, AC/DC would begin a run of 12 shows at Chequers – interspersed with one-offs like the Police Citizens Boys Club in Hornsby, on 25 May – that would take them up to June. The set was comprised almost totally of covers: of Chuck Berry songs 'No Particular Place To Go', 'Carol', 'School Days' and 'Bye Bye Johnny'; Rolling Stones numbers 'Jumpin' Jack Flash', 'Honky Tonk Women' and their version of 'It's All Over Now'; both 'Tutti Frutti' and 'Lucille' by Little Richard and various other rock'n'roll standards like 'Blue Suede Shoes' and 'Shake, Rattle And Roll', and more recent hits like Free's 'All Right Now'. By the summer of 1974 they were able to include a small handful of 'original' material – like the ashtray-chugging set-opener 'Soul Stripper', and the song that would soon become their first single, 'Can I Sit Next To You, Girl' – but these were entirely redolent of the covers they were inspired by; purpose-built not to stick out from the rest of their crowd-pleasing live set. The logic was simple, as Angus would explain: 'When we first started what was going down in the clubs was any band that bashed out a good rock'n'roll tune. These people were interested in "Johnny B Goode" at a hundred miles an hour so they could all get on the dance floor and yell and scream.'

Recorded in January, while Burgess and Van Kriedt were still in the band, the first AC/DC single – backed with 'Rockin' In The Parlour', a sub-Faces good-time tune that sounded exactly like what it was: a B-side – was released on the Albert Productions label on 22 July 1974 and almost immediately became a local, then national Australian hit. The band's profile had already been lifted by their appearance on the bill, a month before, opening for Stevie Wright at the then still relatively new Sydney Opera House. Wright's mammoth, Vanda and Young-written-and-produced hit, 'Evie', released in May, was on its way to becoming the biggest-selling single of the year in Australia. With the album it came from, *Hard Road*, also sitting at No. 2 in the charts, an estimated crowd of more than 10,000 turned up for what was billed as a special free show. With the Opera House capacity tagged at just 2,690, it left the streets surrounding the venue thronged with thousands of cheerful, if disappointed, people, a fact which made headlines across the country. Meanwhile, onstage, AC/DC received the kind of exposure none of the 35 shows they had done so far had come close to matching – augmented by the guest appearance for Wright's encores of Malcolm on second guitar and Dave on backing vocals (along with both George and Harry on bass and guitar, respectively). They even picked up their first national press notice when *Go-Set* noted in its subsequent review that 'AC/DC look great and sound great' and were fast becoming 'a force to be reckoned with'.

Under the tutelage of George and Harry, AC/DC were formally signed to Albert Productions the same month; followed by the rush-release of 'Can I Sit Next To You, Girl'. Although the song would later be re-recorded with Bon Scott at the mike, the germ of what was to become the classic AC/DC sound can be detected here. With George and Harry at the production controls and, though uncredited, helping shape the songwriting process too, 'Can I Sit Next To You, Girl' sounded a bit like a cross between The Easybeats, on the jaunty intro and verses, and what AC/DC quickly became on the chanted chorus and swaggering good-geezer riff.

An almost as significant event, certainly a more image-defining moment, occurred in August when the band turned up for a gig at The Last Picture Show in Cronulla and noticed a striking new aspect to the logo on the poster for the show: notably the way the AC and DC were now separated by a diagonal lightning bolt: the brainwave of Alberts' new marketing and promotions guru, Chris Gilbey. Angus saw it as a cool artistic flourish the company had cleverly added; Malcolm saw it as emphasising the power and attack of the band's name and music. George remained unconcerned either way. As long as the boys were happy ...

It was also at the 30 June gig at The Last Picture Show – a reconditioned movie theatre – that the first AC/DC promotional film was shot. In it, Evans comes across as the archetypal cock-rocker, mike stand thrusting phallus-like from between his legs, his feet squeezed into calf-high stack-heeled boots, his voice clearly based on Slade singer Noddy Holder's window-rattling growl, his hairy chest bursting from a white and red blouson. Years later Malcolm would scoff and say he thought Dave was too 'conscious of his image'. That he was, in fact, 'totally ridiculous'. Certainly no more 'ridiculous' though than Malcolm looks in the same clip, in his dark blue jodhpurs, knee-length Bowie boots and yellow-and-black silk top with – double-cringe! – matching Tam O'Shanter, replete with bobble on top. Meanwhile, bassist Rob Hale looks like a fugitive from the Glitter Band, in silver foil bell-bottoms and matching wide-lapelled jacket; drummer Peter Clack bouncing on his stool at the back in sparkly dark waistcoat, no shirt. It says something that the only one of the band who wouldn't look horribly dated even a year after the clip was shot is Angus, looking decidedly cool next to the clown-costumed others in his schoolboy uniform with big white A on his school cap, and too-big satchel bouncing off his back. No matter. As Evans points out, 'The record was released and they saw the film clip [of the glam look] on TV and they all thought we were an English band! And it helped us to get a hit record, so it worked!'

Well, to a degree. 'Can I Sit Next To You, Girl' did eventually reach the Top 5 in the local Sydney-based charts and parts of Western Australia, but it fluttered around for a few weeks in the Top 20 in other states and did not register nationally. What it did do though was give the band enormous exposure on local radio stations and, even more so, on TV. Directed on the morning of the Last Picture

Show gig by Bernie Cannon, producer of ABC TV's daily *GTK* (*Get to Know*) slot – broadcast Mondays to Thursdays for 10 minutes from 6.30 p.m. – Cannon took the unilateral decision to shoot the clip using colour film, even though colour TV transmission was still some months away in Australia. Colour or black-and-white, what really counted in their favour was timing, the first *GTK* broadcast of the clip coming in August, just as the band began their most high-profile dates yet, opening for the then reigning king of sleaze rock, Lou Reed, on what was his first Australian tour: nine shows, including three at Sydney's Hordern Pavilion (capacity 5,300), four at Melbourne's Festival Hall (5,400), and one apiece at the Adelaide (2,000) and Brisbane (4,000) versions of the Festival Hall. There had been problems early on, when at the first Melbourne show Reed's American crew informed AC/DC's locally hired crew that their use of the venue's sound equipment would be drastically lower than the woozy headliner's. Outraged, Malcolm phoned home to complain, and big brother George caught the next flight down from Sydney. According to Dave Evans, 'George flew at them. "You give these boys whatever they fucking need!" Then he stood by the mixer during the show to make sure we got it, the full rig.' There was a simple reason for the Reed crew's attempted sabotage, adds Evans: 'We blew him off the stage! [Reed] was so screwed up he had to get people to help him onto the stage and help him off. I thought; "That's his stage act" But I saw him at breakfast the next morning and he had two people help-ing him for breakfast as well! It wasn't a stage act, mate ...'

By then, however, Dave had more to worry about than the recalcitrant behaviour of Lou Reed and his miscreant road crew. He felt he had Malcolm on his back. It began with what seemed like snide remarks disguised as friendly jokes. Dave couldn't understand why. They had been mates from the start, sharing a room together on the road. That ended during the Lou Reed tour, when Malcolm moved in with Angus. Finally, as things got worse, the singer twigged. It all stemmed from a return gig at The Last Picture Show, in Cronulla, on 14 July.

'There was a bunch of girls hanging out the front,' Evans says, 'we were going in the back way but Malcolm said, "Why don't you go and talk to them?" But I was a bit shy, really, just to go over to a bunch of girls and say hi. But Malcolm said, "They're fans, go over and talk to them. They'll love it".' Doing as he was told, Evans approached the fans and, sure enough, as Malcolm had predicted, 'the chicks loved it'. He goes on: 'The thing was it worked really well. And I became surrounded by them all of the time. It was one of the reasons Malcolm wanted to bunk with me. But in the end he got so bloody jealous.' At another show, 'There was some girl all over me and someone was pulling my hair at the back. I turned around, thinking it was a joke, but no. It was Malcolm. He said, "What are you gonna do about it?" I thought, what the fucking hell's this crap, you know? I said, "What's up with you?" He said, "You don't like it, let's go outside and sort it out!" I mean, Malcolm's five foot two or something. I could have broken him in half. But he's a plucky bastard, I'll give him that. And I realised he was serious. I thought, what is this, we're all in the band together, you know? But that was the start of it ...'

Dave was now on the outside, definitely not the place to be when it came to AC/DC and especially not the Young brothers. He had never been at ease with Angus and he'd never really got on with Bailey or Clack – 'they were all right but they were older, and they'd been hired without me being involved, which was totally against how the band started' – but he'd always seen Malcolm as a friend. Not any more. 'They wouldn't back down, that was for sure,' he says. At an early show at the Town Hall, in Newcastle, NSW, in March: 'Angus came at me one time in Newcastle. We weren't getting on that well [and] Angus suddenly came flying at me backstage, fists flying. And it was the old cliché, I put my hand on his forehead and pushed him away so he couldn't reach me. I'm thinking, I could kill this guy! It didn't stop him. I thought: he's mad! Then I think Malcolm grabbed him and pulled him away.'

During one of their Hordern Pavilion shows with Lou Reed, in Melbourne, Evans recalls Angus pulling the same stunt on Reed's tour manager. 'He was a big blond guy, about six foot three. And Angus for some reason didn't like something that was going on, this was at soundcheck, and he stood behind him yelling abuse. This bloke turned around to see where it was coming from and it was this little bloke. The guy didn't know what to do. Angus was just "Grrr!" but the guy could have just blown him off the stage cos he was so small. He's yelling out, "Will someone get rid of this guy"! You can't win, mate. That was half the problem with Angus. He knew he could scream and carry on because who's gonna beat him up? Especially if you're in the band cos you'd get the sack.' He chuckles darkly. 'The guy that was the producer was his brother, and the A&R guy that signed him to the record label was his older brother, right? So he was over-indulged. He knew he was untouchable and could have whatever attitude he liked. No one was gonna bash him cos he's got protection from his brothers. But take away his brothers, right, and what's he got?'

The brothers would even fight each other sometimes. 'We picked them up for a gig one time and before they even got in the car they were having a go at each other. The next thing Angus flew into Malcolm and it was on! Fists going everywhere! We didn't touch them, just let them sort themselves out. But yeah, they'd have a go at you. Same when Malcolm pulled my hair. Fair dinkum, he was gonna have a go. But I couldn't win. If I bashed them up, how could I win? I'm too big. And I can fight, don't worry about that, mate. I grew up pretty tough …' Not quite tough enough though to force his way back into the Young clan. 'I felt very, very isolated and very lonely. Then I had a big falling out with Dennis too.'

Dennis Laughlin was the third manager the band had employed in less than six months. The original singer of Sherbet, who would also go on to become stars in the mid-Seventies after he left, Laughlin was 'more of a friend' than a manager: fine at keeping their eyes on the road, but less good at knowing just where and how far that road could potentially take a band like AC/DC. As he would later tell Clinton Walker, he saw his main job as 'keeping everyone happy. There's a few dope smokers in the band, right? Instead of giving everyone fifty bucks a week, it's like, all right, whatever you need, we'll get it. Thirty bucks a week plus a bag of dope, a bottle of Scotch. Well, Angus was a pain in the arse, because he says, "Fuck ya, I don't drink booze, or fucking take drugs." I'd give him a bag of fish and chips, a Kit Kat, a packet of Benson and Hedges and a bottle of Coke.'

Now the band had a chart single that was no longer a workable solution to their day-to-day management, they felt. 'We were flat broke,' says Evans, 'yet we're doing all the top shows. We had a hit record, Top 5 in some states. We're working our asses off but no money whatsoever. And Dennis was flying around the country, sitting around in new clothes and having his hair permed. He seemed to be doing pretty good. And I had rent to pay back in Sydney and I didn't have any money. And I've worked my arse off all tour! And he was the manager and so it came to a head one night in Adelaide. We'd all had a few drinks – and everybody was pissed off, by the way, including Malcolm and Angus – and I spoke up and [Dennis] said something smartarse back and – bang! – I'd stuck one on him. The boys grabbed me off him and stopped the fight, but I said, "Fuck you, I'm leaving the band!" and that was it, I left the band.'

The next morning, however, 'in the cold light of being sober', Dave agreed to carry on for the next already booked gigs, rather than leave them in the lurch, hoping this latest outburst would act as the catalyst that would bring all his problems to a head. It did, but not in the way he had hoped.

The first time Bon Scott heard 'Can I Sit Next To You, Girl' was on the radio in Adelaide. Loud, catchy, blokey: he dug it – until the DJ back-announced the name of the band and he changed his mind. He didn't mind poofters but he was fucked if he was going to sing along to a gay rock band. But then, he wasn't in the best of moods, at the time. Home from London with Fraternity nearly a year and still nothing going on, he felt washed-up, done for. Twenty-eight years old and less than nothing to show for it, except the scars, mental and physical, the two locked within him like dog teeth round a bone. As Vince Lovegrove would say, Bon was a lovely bloke but one that 'could turn very quickly, into a really bad mood, very aggressive'.

When Bon first got back to Adelaide, he told Irene it would only be a matter of time before he was 'back in the saddle again'. In fact, it would take almost a year, and then only by chance. By which time he'd fallen off the horse completely.

Things had started well when he hooked up with his old mate Peter Head, whose own outfit, Headband, had also recently split. Neither man had much money, so Bon took the first job that came along, as a casual labourer at the Wallaroo fertiliser plant, at the Port Adelaide docks. It was backbreaking work, loading up the trucks, unloading others. 'Shit shovelling', as he so succinctly put it. Apart from the money, which was miserable but much needed, the best thing about the job was that he didn't have to think. And so he spent his days up to his neck in shit at the Wallaroo plant, dreaming up lyrics and melodies for songs he would take to Peter in the evenings, when the two would brighten their days by putting them to music, most supplied by Pete, but with increasingly adept input from Bon, who Head was now showing how to make barre chords in order to construct his own riffs and melodies.

Peter had his own ideas, too. In keeping with his avant-garde musical background and his hippy ideals, Head busied himself putting together 'a musical collective' he called the Mount Lofty Rangers. As he explained, 'The purpose of the band was for songwriters to relate to each other and experiment with songs so it was a hotbed of creativity.' Over the next three years, the Rangers would eventually incorporate nearly 200 different musicians, mixing familiar names from the Adelaide scene like Bon's old mystic mucker, Vytas Serelis, a welder named Barry Smith, and various local Adelaide muso-heads like future Little River Band singer Glenn Shorrock and musical stage singer-actor Robyn Archer. The 'band' would have its own theme song, 'The Mount Lofty Rangers Theme', but essentially became a vehicle for Head's own material. It was those early, impromptu evening sessions with Bon, though, that kept the spark alive for both during the early weeks of 1974.

Several Scott-and-Head originals emerged from this period. Notably, the lilting 'Carey Gully', a gentle blend of Gram Parsons-inspired country and Celtic roots folk, based on the small town of the same name in the Adelaide Hills where Bon now lived. As lyrically autobiographical as anything he would later write for AC/DC, yet of an entirely different emotional hue, its opening verse gives a wonderful glimpse of how life had changed for Bon since his return from London: *'You go on down Piggy Lane through the flowers / That paint the hills as far as you can see / And that's where I while away my hours / Hours of eternity / In a little tin shed on the hillside / Where we sit and drink our peppermint tea ...'* There was also the moving ballad 'Clarissa': Bon's pen-sketch of a petite local Adelaide ballet dancer. Closest to the kind of bawdy, wink-and-a-nudge tune he would pen for AC/DC was the almost wincingly autobiographical 'Been Up In The Hills Too Long', which describes his frustrations at finding himself suddenly sidelined with a wife and a day-job: *'Well, I feel like an egg that ain't been laid / I feel like a bill that ain't been paid / I feel like a giant that ain't been slayed / I feel like a saying that ain't been said / Well, I don't think things can get much worse / I feel my life is in reverse ... I been up in the hills too long ...'*

This was the Bon that 'could turn very quickly' from the joy at the simple things of 'Carey Gully' to the spitting venom of 'Been Up In The Hills Too Long'. Bitterness disguised as tongue-in-cheek. Bon had lately taken to carrying a school exercise book around with him, in which he would jot down lines that came to him; a habit that would stay with him for the rest of his life. He had taken to carrying a bottle of whisky around with him too; another habit that would carry through to the end of his days. As Vince Lovegrove, still one of Bon's closest friends in his Adelaide days, would later recall: 'Bon was desperate for success, almost twenty-eight, and had not reached the fame and fortune he desired. The pressure was on and he felt trapped, frustrated, almost too old, and without direction.'

He began taking out his frustrations on those around him, starting with Irene, who he was now fighting with almost every night, and even Peter Head, who he secretly envied for his social poise and classical music education. Peter seemed happy with his lot, brimming with self-confidence and apparently unmotivated by dreams of fame and success. Bon saw things differently. Having rebelled against his middleclass Scots and Australian background, and having found himself repeatedly on the wrong end of failure, including jail, serial relationship breakdowns and now two unfulfilled careers with two distinctly different kinds of close-but-no-cigar pop groups – having seen his youth all but thrown away on what he now considered one fuck-up after another going all the way back to the Spektors in 1964 – he was desperately conscious of time slipping by, of lost opportunities he could no longer afford to miss.

Bon was in a downward spiral that finally hit rock bottom on the night of Friday, 22 February 1974. The night he died, then came back. Earlier that evening he'd turned up already drunk for another Mount Lofty Rangers session at the Lion Hotel in North Adelaide. As usual he had his exercise book of words and rhymes, and as usual he had a bottle of Jack Daniels with him too. The others were not surprised to see that he had ridden over on his Suzuki 550 motorcycle. Bon could drink and drive better than most and there was never a lot of traffic on the backwoods roads. What concerned them more was the mood he was in. He'd had another 'blue' with Irene, he told them. This one worse than usual, though. There had been raised fists, curses and oaths. Not for the first time, the others got the feeling the problem wasn't so much whatever lay between husband and wife but what seemed to be going on in Bon's head. It wasn't just Irene. He was ready to pick a fight with anybody and everybody – the Jack, rather than mellowing him out as it had once done only firing him up and making him even more foul-tempered.

Suddenly he got into it with them. Called one of them a cunt. Then another. Offered to bash their brains in. Then smashed through the door and out onto his bike again, hurling his now empty bottle of Jack onto the ground where it shattered, sending glass flying. Then he roared off, without looking back. Peter and the others had tried to stop him. They didn't care if he stayed; they just didn't want him riding the bike in that state afraid he might have an accident.

Vince Lovegrove got the phone call from Irene at about 2 a.m. She was calling from the reception area of the Queen Elizabeth Hospital. It was serious. Bon had run his bike straight into an oncoming car. Now he was in a coma and near death. The police had fetched Irene and now she was hysterical. She didn't know who else to call. Lovegrove later wrote of how he drove straight to the hospital, ' ... and there was Bon as I had never seen him; limp, smashed to smithereens, his jaw wired, most of his teeth knocked out, a broken collar bone, several cracked and broken ribs, deep cuts across his throat.'

Bon would stay in a coma for three days. Doctors told Irene to prepare for the worst. Would she like a priest to come and give her husband the last rites? One of the nurses informed her that before he blacked out, Bon had been hallucinating, talking gibberish. 'He said he's a singer,' she told Irene, rolling her eyes.

Eighteen days later, Bon Scott was discharged from hospital. Much to his doctors' surprise, he was alive, though far from well. It would be some time before he would be able to walk unaided, longer before he was able to sing again. And he had lost his job at Wallaroo. And his marriage too. Irene had had enough. It was hard enough trying to look after a fit and well Bon, such were his bad tempers and mood swings. Putting up with the angry shell that staggered out on crutches from Queen Elizabeth, already looking for a drink and a joint, was quite another. She admitted to Vince that she could no longer cope. They agreed to 'share' the responsibility of looking after him. Bon, for his part, was in no hurry to return home either and over the next six months he lived less and less with Irene, and more and more at Vince's place, where he lived with his wife, Helen.

Though still hobbling around on crutches, sometimes a walking stick, living with Vince, Bon could at least feel a tangential part of the music biz. The Lovegroves ran their own booking and management agency called Jovan, acting for upcoming Australian acts like Cold Chisel (featuring an 18-year-old Jimmy Barnes, who would go on to enjoy a string of multi-platinum solo albums in Australia), Skyhooks (who would enjoy their first No. 1 album later that same year with *Living In The 70s*), Buster Brown (featuring future Rose Tattoo frontman Angry Anderson) and several others. As Bon's strength returned, he made himself useful, putting up posters for Vince and Helen, painting the office for them, helping chaperone some of the visiting bands they were booking for local gigs. All in exchange for a

few dollars in his pocket and a roof over his head – and, more importantly, a growing sense of self-esteem.

When, in August, Vince booked what he later described as 'a young,
dinky little glam band from Sydney' called AC/DC, Bon again offered
to help. Both he and Vince knew George Young, of course, from
their days in The Valentines. Vince had always admired George and
Harry's ability to craft a commercial pop tune; Bon had worshipped
at the feet of Stevie Wright, the kind of take-no-prisoners frontman
he wished to see himself as. This time there was an extra twist to the
booking: the day before the first Adelaide show, George had phoned
Vince to tell him they were a) looking for a new singer, and b) not to
give the fee for the show to Dennis Laughlin, who was also now officially on the Youngs' shit list. George told Vince to make sure he gave
the money for the gig to Malcolm instead.

Vince didn't mind who he gave the money to, as long as George
was happy. He wasn't there when Evans attacked Laughlin, before
melodramatically announcing he was quitting, but with less than 24
hours before the Adelaide show, Vince had an instant answer to their
problems, if they needed a singer. 'I immediately told him that the
best guy for the job was Bon,' Vince later wrote. 'George responded
by saying Bon's accident would not allow him to perform, and that
maybe he was too old.' Undeterred, Vince took it upon himself to
mention his idea to Malcolm and Angus. 'I told them that Bon could
rock them into the ground and leave them for dead.' But the brothers
had already got their own ideas about Bon, when he ferried them
around on a sightseeing trip in his old 1954 FJ Holden sedan. Sitting
there in his faded red overalls, explaining how he'd recently got out
of hospital after writing off his motorbike, clutching the steering
wheel of the bumpy old car with one hand while lighting a succession of enormous joints with the other, which he passed around the
back, neither Malcolm nor Angus could see how this broken-down
'old hippy' could possibly fit the bill as the replacement for Evans.
Nevertheless, they told Vince to bring him down to their show that
night at the Parooka Hotel. He'd be a laugh, if nothing else.

For Bon's part, he liked what he saw that night – the band were young, full of energy and attitude, and seemed to have one or two decent originals in with the standard rock'n'roll covers they were doing. What impressed him most was how Angus, the smallest guy in the room, dealt with the endless heckling he received from a drunken group of locals who thought it hilariously poofterish to have a guitarist dressed as a schoolboy. When Angus finally lost it, stopping the show to call them out, one by one, waiting with his guitar poised to whomp it across the heads of anyone who dared come forward Bon couldn't believe what he called 'the big balls' on such a little guy. There was still one snag though as far as Bon was concerned. Backstage after the show, Vince looked on in wonder as Bon told them straight: he wasn't sure they were experienced enough or would be 'able to rock' enough for him to sing with them. The brothers scoffed and told him they thought he was way 'too old to rock' anyway. But if he wanted to give it a go they'd let him 'have a blow' with them later that night, at a little after-show gathering to which Dave Evans was pointedly not invited. Never one to duck a challenge and, in reality, desperately wanting to show these whippersnappers what he could do, Bon talked Bruce Howe – who was also there, among most of the leading lights of the Adelaide music community – into letting them set up in the base-ment of his suburban home. At first Bon tried to show them what a good drummer he was, afraid that they were right and he was too old to actually front the group. But the brothers weren't having it. Finally, a drunker-by-the-minute Bon was pushed towards the mike and told to sing, while former Fraternity drummer John Freeman took over the drum stool, Bruce Howe plugged in his bass and Malcolm and Angus let rip on their guitars. They were still there jamming away amid the empty cans and bottles and overflowing ashtrays as the sun came up the following morning, riffing on old Chuck Berry tunes and various 12-bar blues standards. At which point Bon's old mate Dennis Laughlin stepped over and, having had a quick, not-so secret confab with the brothers, offered Bon the job. Contrary to the end, Bon, now on the point of collapse, told them he would think it over, before cadging a ride back to his spot on Vince Lovegrove's couch ...

*

Dave Evans's memories of meeting Bon in Adelaide are not dissimilar to those of the brothers, though it never crossed his mind that this was the bloke that would take his place in AC/DC. 'Bon hung around with us and helped set up with the roadies. He was never one of our roadies though – I helped the roadies too whenever we were late. But he used to hang around with us. The other boys went out with him for a couple of nights but he was never our chauffeur either. Anybody who drove a car I was in was never a chauffeur. So all that stuff people write now is bullshit. It makes for good reading, you know what I mean? But I met him there and he was a nice enough bloke, always have a laugh and crack a joke.'

Dave had not been invited down to the basement session with Bon. After the show at the Parooka, 'I went out with a couple of girls. And the [brothers] were like, "We're gonna have a jam with Bon Scott and a couple of the guys from Fraternity." I was like, yeah, cool, and just took off. The next day I was like, "How's the jam?" They were like, "Oh yeah, pretty good." Looking back now of course they were auditioning him.' Although as far as Dave was concerned, 'I'd already left the band by that stage', he wasn't yet aware that AC/DC were already actively looking for someone to replace him. If anything, his announcement about quitting, after his fight with Dennis Laughlin, was more a cry for help. For someone – ideally, Malcolm – to come forward and beg him to stay, to reassure him his role in the band was still crucial, despite being increasingly sidelined in all their offstage decisions. When it didn't happen, he felt 'completely isolated from everybody. I was still in the band and I would still be in the band if things had been reconciled. But they just got worse.'

Having agreed to effectively work out a period of notice, while still hoping against hope that the situation would somehow resolve itself and that the rest of the band would decide they couldn't do without him, he now faced almost two months of shows in an atmosphere of, as he puts it, 'pretty bad feeling'. They'd been hired for a three-week residency in Perth at Beethoven's Disco – opening for the star of the notorious Sydney cabaret show *Les Girls*, Carlotta, aka Richard Byron, a transgender 'showgirl' who would later become one of the chief inspirations behind the Australian hit move *Priscilla, Queen of the Desert*. Having booked the band purely on the basis of their name, assuming any act called AC/DC would be perfect casting for support to Carlotta, the owners of Beethoven's were appalled at their mistake the first time they saw the band blasting through their rough-and-ready, clearly hetero-heavy set. If the two-day drive across 1,700 miles of Nullabor Plain, from Adelaide to Perth, hadn't increased the tension among band and crew, 19 consecutive shows opening for Carlotta's camp and almost wholly uninterested in rock crowd nearly finished them off. It certainly proved too much for Dave Evans, who began 'calling in sick'. He had vocal problems, he said, and so Dennis Laughlin would step in and replace him whenever he had to.

According to Dave now, those last shows he did with the band 'were fantastic. We were killing everywhere, playing to packed houses. But I wasn't talking to anybody, really. I did interviews and stuff like that, but it was just to keep it together until that final meeting in Melbourne. By that stage it was irreparable though, mate. Nobody was talking to anybody. I was happy with the band getting big, but by the time all that was happening I was absolutely miserable. I was by myself. I had pretty girls hanging round me, so that was still good. But to go back to wherever we were staying and walk in to complete silence, it was unbearable.' Dave suggests a pattern was beginning to emerge. 'By the time I finished with the band we were onto our third bass player, third drummer, third manager. By that stage, Malcolm, Angus and George were making all the decisions. I particularly felt left out and miffed, because at the beginning we were making the decisions ourselves and we all felt part of the band. But by the time we had [Peter Clack and Rob Bailey], who I didn't particularly get on with, I was sort of isolated. You sort of felt like you were just there and it wasn't a good feeling.'

The problem, he is now convinced, was less about personality clashes, as he felt initially, or any disagreements over image, as Malcolm would later claim, but about money. 'Once all the original members were gone they could own the name AC/DC, all the merchandising, you name it. And they could have guys on a wage ... After I left the band the only two original members that were there were Angus and Malcolm. And with George they could run the whole thing.' When, on the long, arduous drive back east, they stopped off once again in Adelaide for a further two shows – the first a return visit to the even more packed this time Parooka, the second the following night at the Countdown Disco, a larger-capacity room at the Mediterranean Hotel – Evans was at his wits' end, and so was the band. The intervening weeks since that first Adelaide show, when Bon, one moment so desperate to be involved, the next apparently playing it cool, had seen them on the phone to George back home in Sydney, pushing him to find a new singer. At one stage George had asked Stevie Wright if he'd be interested. But Stevie had the biggest-selling song of the year with 'Evie' and a smash hit album with *Hard Road*. In England, Rod Stewart had even recorded a cover of the title track to put on his own album, *Smiler*. Though he was too smart to say so – offering instead the polite excuse that Malcolm and Angus didn't need any help from him – there was no way the singer was going to take a 'step down' by joining George's little brothers' band. It had taken him nearly five years to recover from The Easybeats' split, he wasn't going to fuck it up now, he decided. (In fact, Wright needed no help ruining his career. Already in thrall to heroin as he was, it was, in retrospect, a lucky escape for the band that he did not take their offer seriously.)

Next on the list was the cringingly stage-named William Shakespeare, a 26-year-old Sydney singer, real name John Stanley Cave, who had also had a big hit that summer with a Vanda and Young-written-and-produced composition, 'Can't Stop Myself From Loving You'. George and Harry had been searching for a copycat singer who could fulfil the role of Australia's own Gary Glitter and found him in Cave, who they promptly renamed and remodelled as a glam icon for the extremely gullible. The advantage of having Shakespeare front the band was that he could sing – he had a growl to match Evans's but a falsetto few other singers could reach – and he knew his place and how much his success depended on others, specifically George and

Harry. In short, he could sing and would do what he was told. The disadvantage, as Malcolm and Angus made abundantly clear, was that he was a joke. In their minds, they were ditching one problem, why would they hire an even bigger one to replace him?

Then there was John Paul Young, another Glasgow-born immigrant to Sydney who'd also had a Top 20 hit in 1972 with a Vanda and Young composition called 'Pasadena'. But there had been no follow-up and Young spent the next two years playing the high priest Annus in the Australian production of *Jesus Christ Superstar*. When the show came to the end of its run in February 1974 he re-signed to Alberts and began working with George and Harry again. So far, though, neither of the two singles he'd released with them had gained any traction. JPY, as he was known, could certainly sing. But his image was a little vanilla for bands like AC/DC and his vocal style was better suited to pop ballads – as would be demonstrated in spectacular fashion four years later when he had a massive international hit with another George and Harry song, 'Love Is In The Air'.

On the list of runners and riders then for the job of vocalist in AC/DC in September 1974, there was just one name left: that of the 'old man' they had encountered in Adelaide, the one who'd only recently thrown away his crutches and walking stick, but had the voice and attitude they were looking for: old Bonnie Boy Scott. But he hadn't exactly jumped at the chance of joining when they'd given him the thumbs-up. In the weeks since then, however, Bon had begun to rue his indecision. He'd been stockpiling cheap demo recordings of his songs with Peter Head and the Lofty Rangers, and had retained hopes of it leading somewhere useful. As Head recalled, 'The tracks were recorded for 40 dollars which was all the studio time we could afford then. Bon and I used to help each other out. I'd write music and he'd sing lyrics ... They were recorded at the first eight-track studio in Adelaide.' But when Vince told him the AC/DC boys were coming back for two more shows, he decided not to hang around any longer. For all Bon knew they had fixed the situation with their singer, or already found a new one. For all the band knew, Bon was off his rocker and wouldn't even be around this time.

Thankfully for both sides, the truth was something else. Still feigning indifference, Bon allowed himself to be talked into getting up the first night at the Parooka and singing a couple of songs, looning around drunk onstage like someone's dad at the office Christmas party. When the following night, however, at the Countdown Disco, Evans threw another wobbly and at first refused to go on, the band turned to Bon. This time they weren't joking; this was no jam or quick cameo, this was the real thing. What do you reckon, mate? 'We knew he had a good voice,' Malcolm later told the writer Sylvie Simmons. But he was plainly nervous. 'He said, "What do you want me to sound like?" because he'd been in these bands who wanted him to copy whatever was hip at the time. He couldn't believe it when we said, "Just sound like you sound." He downed two bottles of bourbon with some coke and speed and says, "Right, I'm ready." Next thing we knew he was running around with his wife's knickers on and yelling at the audience.'

Needless to say, the party continued at the hotel long after the disco had closed its dance-floor. When Bon returned to Vince's place the next morning, drunk and stoned and completely elated, he immediately began packing his few clothes and possessions into the same old suitcase he'd taken to London and back with him with Fraternity; that had journeyed with him from Perth to Melbourne three years before, and then back up into the Adelaide Hills.

Dave Evans's last show singing for AC/DC came at the Esplanade Hotel, in St Kilda, the red-light district of Melbourne, just days after Bon had sung for the first time with the band at the Countdown. 'I remember walking up the street by myself in St Kilda,' Dave says, 'and I met two girls. And I told them, "That's it. I'm leaving the band." They were begging me not to leave, saying the band was fantastic. I said, "I have to."' The day after the show there was a final meeting. 'The first thing Malcolm said was, "Right, Dave, you're out." I said, "Fine." Then he said to the bass player and drummer, who were always grumbling too that they didn't have any money, he said to Rob, "You got any problems?" "No!" Then: "You got any problems,

Peter?" "No!" They just backed down straight off because they saw me get sacked. Didn't do them any good anyway, mate, because they got sacked too shortly afterwards. At least I left with my head held high. I didn't eat humble pie or any shit like that. And also the manager got sacked not long after too.'

After Dave left the meeting that day, he went back to Sydney and immediately joined Rabbit – a no-holds-barred rock band who, interestingly, had been having problems with their original singer, Greg Douglas, and sacked him to make way for their own new guy. Dave never heard from any of AC/DC again. 'I saw them around a couple of times – at one of these festivals where they were playing at a different time of day from [Rabbit]. Just to say hi and have a bit of chitchat. [But] I've sacked guys too and never spoken to them again.'

Incredibly he says he didn't know Bon was their new singer until 'I was back in Sydney and I heard they were doing a show at Victoria Park. I didn't know he was the singer. I didn't take any notice. I was too busy with what I was doing. So I thought I'd go and see it, see who the singer is. When Bon came out I got the shock of my life! Cos he was so old and he was still wearing the bloody overalls and stuff, still really hippy-ish. And they didn't go over well. The Sydney crowd were expecting me! It wasn't that long after I'd split from the band, only two months [and] the Sydney crowd expected AC/DC, the one that they knew with me. When they came out with Bon and he starts singing "Can I Sit Next To You, Girl" they were like, "What?" Then Bon started getting stuck into the crowd, started abusing them a bit. He was like, "Clap, go on, clap!" But they weren't clapping. "Well, you've probably all got it!" he said. I'll never forget it. It didn't turn the crowd on at all. I thought, naw, they're fucked.'

Evans's departure from AC/DC left both sides with a wound that would never quite heal. While Evans maintains that he played a crucial role in their story, the Young brothers were still being rude about him nearly 30 years later. In a 2003 interview with the British rock writer Dave Ling, Malcolm showed just how deep that wound remained for him. 'Every time we go back to Australia there's something in the local paper [from Evans] about, "I made the band AC/DC into what they are." He laughed sarcastically. "The day we fuckin' got rid of him, that's the day the band started." He went on, giving a new spin to the story of why Evans was eventually let go. "We were playing at this pub in Melbourne. Dave was almost like Gary Glitter in the gear he'd insist on wearing, it was ridiculous. All these hard-nosed, beer-drinking Aussies were after him, so we told him to go for a walk for 10 minutes, we'd play a boogie number. But it went on for half an hour and the place was rocking. After that we realised that we didn't need a singer." At which point, Angus chimed in: "No, we realised we didn't need *that* singer! Actually, to call him a singer was being a bit polite."'

That said, there's no doubt the better man got the job singing in AC/DC. Fifa Riccobono, then label manager at Alberts, who also saw Bon for the first time with AC/DC at the Victoria Park show, came away with a markedly different impression to the one the still understandably shell-shocked Evans had. 'This guy came out in red satin bib-and-brace, tooth missing and a shark tooth around his neck and I just looked and thought, "Oh my god!" Anyway he started to sing and he was just incredible. He didn't know the words to most of the songs so he ad-libbed quite a bit. But by the end of the night there was no doubt that he very much suited the band. It really felt like there was a magic element there that really created the band as a unit. The [rest of] the guys, in typical AC/DC fashion, just gave it their all and put on a great show.'

Bon had made his official debut with the band at the Rockdale Masonic Hall, in the southern suburbs of Sydney, on Saturday, 5 October 1974. Hair down to his arse, worn-out red dungarees in place, barefoot – an affectation he would not give up until the band finally began touring outside Australia, and then only grudgingly – making up his own lyrics when he couldn't remember the real ones, which was almost every song, the crowd, expecting to see Dave Evans, were agog. Having smoked his way through a quarter-ounce of weed and worked his way onto his second bottle of bourbon before he'd even walked onstage, Bon was in no mood to be toyed with. As he hit the stage ahead of the band, who were only slightly less awestruck than the audience, he snatched the mike and told the crowd: 'Anyone that's come to see Dave Evans sing with AC/DC ain't gonna see it tonight – the band have fired him because he got married!' In the dressing room, Malcolm, who was regularly downing his own bottle of Stone's Green Ginger Wine before going on, had been unperturbed by the singer's antics. Now gazing from the wings as Bon made his gauntlet-chucking announcement, he gasped: 'Fucking hell! What's this guy done!'

According to Angus, who had wondered whether Bon would be able to stand up straight onstage, 'My fucking feet lifted off the fucking ground' when Bon opened his mouth to sing. Leaving nothing in his locker, he got straight into it, giving it all he'd got, literally roaring through the set. Where Evans had tried to show what a capable frontman and vocalist he was, Bon just roared, flame fully on from start to finish. When he introduced a new song that he'd literally just finished writing with the band, called 'She's Got Balls' – inspired, he told the uncomprehending crowd gleefully, by his estranged wife – they didn't know whether to laugh or be offended. In the end they just stared – then erupted into thunderous applause when the song juddered to an end.

According to George Young, speaking more than 30 years later, 'When I saw [Bon's] first gig with the guys, I thought, "He is it, what they need." He was Captain Jack Sparrow.' Nevertheless, the jury on whether 'old man' Bon Scott was a good choice to replace young Dave Evans would remain out for some time. Looking in from the outside at least, it didn't make much sense. The band with Dave had had a hit record; they had already routined material for their first album. And they had a deal with the biggest company in the Oz music biz, Alberts, and the full backing of the Aussie Lennon and McCartney, Vanda and Young. Why would they gamble all that on a future with a has-been like Bon Scott? All of which was not lost on Bon, who would remain insecure about his role in the band throughout most of his time in it.

Fortunately for him, George and Harry, who remembered him as the hop-skip-and-a-jump second banana vocalist in The Valentines, could see the potential. From their point of view, his desire to make the most of what they realised he must have seen as his last chance was a bonus. It meant he'd do what he was told. But he also had a voice, full of the kind of knowing expression you could only find in someone his age, someone who'd been there, bought the T-shirt and then lost it – twice. And there was something appealing about his character. A genuinely funny man, as depressives often can be, there was certainly plenty to work with. He'd already mentioned that he wrote his own lyrics. Which may or may not be a bonus, they'd have to see. The most important thing was that Malcolm and Angus liked him. They seemed to get a kick out of his old-school larrikin ways. He may have still dressed like a hippy but there was very little about 'the old man', as they had taken to calling him behind his back that relied on peace and love. A born dope smoker, he was also a diehard drinker, up and shouting one minute, sunk deep into his swampy thoughts the next. This was his yin and yang, and this was what added interest for them. Even more than George, they sensed his neediness. When, within weeks of pitching up in Sydney, Malcolm commanded Bon to cut his waist-length hair short and lose the overalls, he complied immediately.

This was in stark contrast to Dave Evans, who Malcolm had also told to cut his hair during their stint in Perth. 'Malcolm said, "Oh, we've got a new image for you." I said, "What?" He said, "Cut your hair short and wear dark glasses." I said, "Get fucked, I'm not cutting my hair for anyone." I left home at sixteen because I had long hair, do you think I'm gonna cut my hair for some band? I said, no way, I'm not doing it.'

Bon would never dream of speaking to Malcolm, or indeed any of the Young brothers, like that. Pushing 30, he knew where his bread was now buttered. A fact he would never forget. Or never for too long, anyway ...

CHAPTER SIX

Bon the Likeable

Leaving Adelaide and his old life behind, the one that ended the night he crashed his motorcycle and cracked open his head, meant Bon Scott leaving his wife Irene behind too. Within weeks, though, he was boasting to a reporter: 'I dug the band more than I dug the chick, so I joined the band and left her.' He claimed he bought a huge batch of speed and simply hightailed it to Sydney before the group could change its mind about offering him the gig. All of which was true but did not give the whole story. Bon still had feelings for Irene, writing 'She's Got Balls', his first song for AC/DC, about her. And there would be plenty of times over the coming months and years when, on the road, he would ponder the path he had taken, the choices he had made, and compare them not always favourably to the ones others close to him had made. Things he would never discuss with Malcolm or Angus, who were young enough still to be thrilled at the prospect of spending Christmas on the road, as they did for the first time in December 1974. As if to rub salt into the wound, by then Bon's brother Graeme had begun a serious relationship with Irene's sister Faye, while his other brother, Derek, was married with a couple of kids. Sitting on his own in his hotel room, Bon would find little solace in the endless beers and whiskies, the nonstop parade of joints and nose candy; the endless supply of willing young groupies whose names and faces had already blurred into one session, long before he ever became properly famous. He would sit there drunk and stoned, and write long melancholy letters to Irene, as though she were still by his side, at least in spirit, as though really she understood everything.

But she did not and he was on his own and on the inside he knew that.

The rest of the band only ever saw the funny side of their new singer, the one that Angus Young would later joke he'd at least taught some manners to, getting him to refine his usual gutter mouth, exclaiming, 'Excuse me, cunt' or, 'Get fucked, if you don't mind.' Soon 'the old man' had a new nickname: Bon the Likeable, after Simon the Likeable, a character on the old American TV comedy show *Get Smart*, whose secret weapon is that he is impossible to dislike. Angus, in particular, benefited in other ways too, as Bon passed on old singles and LPs that somehow said what he felt he could not yet in song. Many, like Jerry Lee Lewis's 'Great Balls Of Fire', were already familiar to the young guitarist. But he revelled in the way Bon explained them to him anew, delighting in the wordplay which would become such a signature of Bon's own best lyrics in the years to come. Happy just to see Bon happy, getting over-excited about Scots pipes bands in a way he hadn't witnessed since the days o' sittin' at the feet o' his auld yin in Glasgee. Even Malcolm Young – never one to give praise freely – would later describe Bon as 'the biggest single influence' on the way AC/DC would develop in the Seventies, from bar band dodging flying beer bottles to arena headliners all over the world. 'When Bon came in it pulled us all together,' he said. 'He had the stick-it-to-'em attitude. We all had it in us, but it took Bon to bring it out.'

Not everyone took so kindly to Bon's unforeseen arrival on the scene, however. According to Dave Evans, 'He saw me with my shirt off. He saw my stage act. He saw what was required – the rock star, the bare chest. That was my image that he acquired.' There was also one other person at the end of 1974 that still needed convincing that Bon Scott was the right man to front AC/DC: their new manager, Michael Browning.

Already a successful music biz figure, based in Melbourne, Browning had begun his career in the mid-Sixties with the opening of one of Australia's first discotheques: Sebastian's Penthouse, on Beaconsfield Parade, near St Kilda Beach. Decked out in what is now regarded as classic Sixties, Austin Powers-style kitsch, Sebastian's was intended as the cultural equivalent of Tramp in London. But with a far more accommodating non-members door-policy and far fewer celebrities to entertain, it became one of several Melbourne night-spots that reflected the new, anything-goes atmosphere of the late Sixties. Working with his business partner, Arthur Knight, scion of Melbourne's wealthy Knight family, Browning was soon overseeing the complementary charms of other locally famous discos like The Thumpin Tum and Catcher's. The jewel in the Knight family crown, however, was Bertie's, at No. 1 Spring St, which also became the first venue Michael was encouraged to book pop groups into.

Soon all the fashionable Melbourne discos and clubs were look-ing to up their bar-take with regular live band bookings, and Michael shrewdly seized the opportunity to establish his own booking agency, which he named the Australian Entertainment Exchange. Almost inevitably, this led to him becoming actively involved in the day-to-day management of the best of these acts: notably, Python Lee Jackson, Doug Parkinson In Focus, and last, and most usefully, in terms of his later involvement with AC/DC, Billy Thorpe & The Aztecs, all of which Browning would take into the charts at home and, even more impressive in the larger scheme of things, as far afield as London, still the holy grail for domestic Oz acts then as now. Python Lee Jackson had been around in various line-up forms since the early Sixties, enjoying minor domestic hits, but would be best remem-bered posthumously for an opportunistic hit, 'In A Broken Dream', taken from a session with a then little-known session vocalist named Rod Stewart, during the band's brief spell in London in 1969. The track was never intended for release, but eventually slipped out in 1972 after Stewart became famous in his own right.

It was his other acts that really introduced Browning to the big time, though, at least domestically. Doug Parkinson In Focus, though completely unknown internationally, had become one of the biggest chart acts in Australia in 1969, with singles like 'Dear Prudence' and 'Hair'. Billy Thorpe & The Aztecs, however, were an even bigger deal. They had been around since the Sixties, specialising in feelgood covers like 'Poison Ivy' and 'Love Letters'. Now in the early Seventies they had metamorphosed into a wild rock'n'roll band with hit tracks like 'Most People I Know Think That I'm Crazy' and 'Cigarettes And Whiskey'. Their show-stealing appearance at the 1972 Sunbury festival in Melbourne had resulted in the hit double album *Live at Sunbury*, which had vied for top position in the Australian national charts with such landmark classics as *Exile On Main Street* and *Led Zeppelin IV*. 'Billy and The Aztecs were a four-to-the-floor, full-on heavy rock band that I eventually managed for about five years,' Browning says now. No surprise then that Thorpe himself had been mates with Bon since the latter's Valentines days. They were also the first act that Browning would travel with to London, where he stayed for six months. The closest they got to lasting success 'in the old country' though was when Radio One play-listed their single, 'Most People I Know Think That I'm Crazy', released on Mickie Most's RAK label. 'Mickie and his brother Dave Most worked their arses off on it but it just didn't resonate. But it was a good dry run for when I returned with AC/DC, just a few years later. London then was pretty much the destination of choice for an Australian band trying to do something at that point.'

By then Browning was one of the leading lights of the newly formed Consolidated Rock talent agency, along with Michael Gudinski (whose later label, Mushroom Records, would rival Alberts as Australia's premier outlet for domestic rock talent). When CR absorbed Philip Jacobsen's rival Let It Be, Browning found himself at the forefront of the only national Australian talent agency, handling huge domestic stars of the era like Daddy Cool and Spectrum. Indeed, their grip on the nascent Australian live-music scene was such that it constituted a virtual monopoly. (Another of CR's upcoming young agents, Roger Davies, would go on to take Tina Turner to her reinvigorated Eighties supremacy, and these days also manages Pink.)

When, however, Consolidated Rock ran aground in 1973, in the wake of Browning and Gudinski's joint attempt to create 'a credible Rolling Stone-type weekly publication', *The Daily Planet*, which failed in its bid to overhaul the success of *Go-Set* magazine, the agency hastily reconfigured into what became the Premier/Harbour Agency and its international tour promotion offshoot, Frontier Touring Co. The upshot was that both Browning and Gudinski bailed out: the latter to form Mushroom, the former to become the manager – and talent booker – for Melbourne's Hard Rock Cafe. It was here that Browning first saw the Dave Evans-fronted line-up of AC/DC. 'I thought they were pretty amazing,' he remembers. Though he didn't think Evans 'was anything too thrilling. The thing I really loved was the Angus schoolboy routine and just the general playing of the brothers. That's what really got my attention. The rhythm section was almost non-existent then. It was just Angus, this skinny little kid with a snotty nose running around the stage, I just loved it!' Talking to them after the show, 'They said they were going to Perth and I said when they got back we'd maybe book some dates.'

Good as his word, Browning booked the band in for further shows at the Hard Rock in late October. In the intervening weeks, however, they had fired Evans and brought Bon in. There had also been another significant loss: that of manager Dennis Laughlin, who 'got the shits with them one night' during a three-night booking at the Larg Piers Hotel in Adelaide. If Laughlin had been hoping for the constant bitching about his style of management to die down now Evans was no longer there to dish it, he was sorely mistaken. Instead, the source of the attacks now switched to the brothers. In particular, Angus, who as the only teetotal, non-dope-smoking member of the band was not so easily appeased by Laughlin's jam-tomorrow promises. Angus lived on a strict diet of cigarettes, tea, chocolate milk and candy bars and he didn't need Laughlin to obtain them for him. (The only drug Angus has ever taken regularly is aspirin, which he claims his mother would grind up and stir into milk for him, whenever he had 'an earache, a toothache' or anything else that might keep him from a school day. A habit he would keep up throughout his adult life.) Fed up with the constant carping – and feeling the strain of having what he thought of as the spoiled brat of the family now almost permanently on his case – Dennis finally flipped. 'I said, "Fuck ya, I'm not working my arse off any more, here's your books, you've got to be in Melbourne by one o'clock tomorrow, I'm going home, see ya later."'

Put out, Malcolm – after all, he did drink and did enjoy the largesse of Laughlin's dope-first stewardship – instead of phoning big brother George, as he had always done before whenever there was trouble brewing, took it upon himself in his sudden and unsought for new capacity as band manager to call Michael Browning, ostensibly to let him know the band wouldn't be able to make the show in Melbourne, but no doubt hoping the experienced Browning would come up with a more useful suggestion to save the day. Malcolm's instincts proved correct. Browning recalls: 'He said, "We don't have any money. You booked us for one of our gigs in Melbourne, well, we can't get back there." So I actually said, "I'll wire you the money, it'll get you into town then you can do my gig and whatever else you've got to do." When [the band] got to Melbourne, Malcolm came to see me and said, "I really appreciated that, you really helped us out." And we started chatting. I don't think at the time he realised I actually had a history in the management business. So the conversation just led to, "you guys need a manager …"'

When the band showed up though with Bon Scott as their new front-man, Browning admits he had his doubts. 'I'd known Bon for many, many years, from his Valentines days. They were pretty much a teeny-bopper band, akin to the Bay City Rollers or something. So my perception of Bon was that he'd been in this teenybopper group. Then after that he was in this progressive Hawkwind type of group. So when they told me he was joining as the singer I was a little bit taken aback.' His fears were allayed, however, the first time he saw them perform together in front of the noisome Hard Rock regulars. 'Bon morphed into the role pretty quickly. He went from being the kind of long-haired hippy guy in Fraternity into a rock and roller. He adapted to the role until the role seemed quite normal, and you sort of didn't question it again. Bon had definitely been around but somehow the chemistry between him and Malcolm and Angus kind of worked and as soon as he started writing lyrics for the tunes, I think that's when they really realised they had something special.'

As with every important decision of their career, no deal could be made between AC/DC and their prospective new manager until George Young – who flew down to Melbourne the very next day –

had rubberstamped it. Michael Browning immediately felt the hot breath of the clan leader on his neck. 'Look, as a manager you're under constant suspicion from those guys. See George in his group The Easybeats had sort of a fairly good shot of success internationally and then it all turned sour and he came back to Australia and blamed the manager, Mike [Vaughan].' As a result, neither George nor the younger brothers he had schooled 'were very manager-friendly, let's put it that way. All artists blame the manager when things go wrong, but I think that attitude was probably exaggerated in the case of the Youngs. When I proposed my management contract to them I really had to put my money where my mouth was. They had no financial resources whatsoever. In my opinion, they were about to disband almost just out of lack of finance.' Even though a deal had already been done by then with Alberts, says Browning, 'that didn't imply that Alberts were about to put any money on the table to keep them alive. They had signed to Alberts to make records but that's where it left off.'

The recording deal they signed – to which Bon was added, once Fraternity's former manager, Hamish Henry, had agreed to sell his rights to Bon's publishing to Alberts for A$4,000 – was for an equal share of the royalty rate, as one of three equal members of the band. 'It was what they used to call the "standard deal",' Browning recalls now. 'Alberts also owned the publishing on original AC/DC material. Again, under the standard deal, ownership of copyright, fifty-fifty [plus] half of the revenues from overseas ... God bless them, but it wasn't just them that was doing the standard deal in those days. I think a lot of American and British record companies were doing the same thing. But Alberts were definitely at the tail end of the standard deal, and continued it for a lot longer than a lot of other record labels did.' A throwback to the Wild West days of the music biz when labels and managers virtually owned their artists in perpetuity – that is, their song publishing, their live performance fees, the master tapes to all their recordings, quite literally often the very shirts on their backs – by the mid-Seventies, standard practice in the British and American music businesses had reached a stage of maturity where major artists at least, though still treated essentially as serfs, were in a stronger bargaining position than ever before. After The Beatles and the Stones had shown there was a potentially highly lucrative long-term career to be made out of being in a rock band, artists were not only commanding ever higher fees for their shows, they were on escalating royalty rates, depending on their levels of success, with the very highest earners even owning their own labels – and hence their own masters, the green kryptonite of any artist willing to take on the superpowers of the major record labels.

Such practices had apparently yet to reach down under, however, and with Alberts then the biggest game in town, their take-it-or-leave-it attitude paid huge dividends. As Browning points out, 'The good part of their recording deal with Alberts was that there were no recording costs, because they had the studio. I think there was a small [fee], about a hundred bucks a track, something like that.' In terms of royalties on retail sales, Browning has said that the deal was weighted far more heavily in Alberts' favour: 3.4 per cent, compared to the 5 per cent that was then the norm. (Within a decade that had risen to an average rate of 10 or even 12 per cent, though not, again, at Alberts.) Whatever the going rate for the times was percieved to be, however, what Alberts were doing was likely no different to what every other significant record company of the era considered fair and normal. Browning remains philosophical. 'There [are] a lot of other managers and other record companies that have always been aware of the Alberts deal and used to be fairly critical of it. But in hindsight when you look at how many groups spend enormous amounts of money on recording, on the basis that they'll get 12 per cent instead of five per cent but never end up seeing a penny and end up owing the record company a million bucks and then the only thing to do is to break up, the Alberts deal actually wasn't too bad – initially. Sure, the percentage was low but you didn't have to pay back recording costs and there was actually right from day one a flow of royalties.'

All well and good, perhaps, assuming you sold enough records. With AC/DC still months away from being able to look forward to royalties from record sales, however, Browning 'put together a plan' whereby he paid them all a weekly wage of A$60, plus all their out-of-pocket travel expenses, even bought them a new tour bus – a huge, unwieldy second-hand tank originally owned by Ansett Airlines – paid all their road crew, and found them and paid for rented accommodation. 'I paid for everything for six months. The deal was that I could keep all of the revenue [from live shows] for six months. It was kind of like a stabilising situation for them, then after six months that deal would just revert to a normal manager–artist twenty per cent cut situation.'

Browning's only other condition was that the band move base from Sydney down to Melbourne, where his new management company, Trans-Pacific Artists, was based. 'I was there and that's where I knew I could work it. I had a partner at that stage, a guy called Bill Joseph. He owned half of Melbourne's pubs and clubs, and I owned a couple. So I was able to offer them a deal where they were all on a wage and the rest of it, knowing I could utilise them in our venues to generate the revenue to pay for all of that. It created an incredible incentive for us to make them as famous as possible as quickly as possible, because if I was able to really make them popular within that six months, it was a big windfall for me. We had them playing everywhere. Before long they became probably one of the biggest attractions in that Melbourne pub and club scene. So it worked out well for both parties.' The brothers were certainly happy. 'We thought this is it! Don't have to work,' recalled Malcolm. 'We can make fifty bucks a week each here. We can survive, without a day-job!'

The hub around which this newly generated activity would take place would be the band's first album, which George arranged to be recorded during downtime at Alberts' newly installed Studio One room, at their 139 King Street office, during the final weeks of 1974. A comparatively small room with bare brick walls, the new studio had been designed and built for Ted Albert by an old buddy named Bruce Brown, an engineer and 'very creative electrical guy' who had previously overseen ATA, one of the oldest studios in Sydney. Chris Gilbey, an English musician who had begun working at Alberts as the label's head of A&R in January 1974, but had graduated to marketing and promotions by the time AC/DC were signed, and would, in his own words, 'eventually basically run the label', recalls how the studio would be occupied by Brown during the normal working day, 'recording things that were contracted, studio-for-hire stuff, and George and Harry would go in on the weekends and night times' with their own projects, beginning with AC/DC. Their own production deal with Alberts meant that George and Harry went fifty–fifty on everything they brought to Alberts: 'George and Harry on the one side,' says Gilbey, 'Ted on the other. That was the deal, including with AC/DC.' Gilbey remembers how George and Harry 'used to get very cranky about the ones that Ted or I would sign independently [and that they didn't get a stake in].' For example, 'they hated Ted Mulry being on the label. They tried to get Ted Mulry off the label but they couldn't because Ted Mulry had signed during the days when George and Harry were pissing around in London and Ted Mulry was in Sydney working gigs at hole-in-the-wall, flea-bite pubs. So Ted Albert was very loyal to the people that were loyal to him – including George and Harry.'

Gilbey had proved his own worth to AC/DC early on by adding the lightning flash to their logo which they still use today. It was also Gilbey who suggested the title of their first album before they had even finished recording it: *High Voltage* – again, inspired by their name and 'flash' logo. More importantly, Gilbey became Michael Browning's most useful ally at Alberts; the only one he could really relate to on a day-to-day basis at what Gilbey describes as 'the closed shop' of Alberts. 'Chris's involvement was very important in those early days, especially,' says Browning. 'But again, like everyone that's ever been involved with AC/DC and Alberts, you get written out of history. But he was certainly very, very important to Alberts throughout that period. As evidenced by the fact that when he did leave, their record label in Australia just fell in a heap.'

For Gilbey, though, there was no doubt who really ran the show, as far as AC/DC were concerned. 'The character of AC/DC that is most interesting to me is that which was architected by George. He really is the central *éminence grise* in AC/DC.' Certainly it was George that ran things on that first album. With the band still picking up gigs in Sydney and thereabouts whenever they could before making the move to Melbourne, they would often arrive at Studio One straight from a show and simply plug in, bashing away until dawn while George and Harry operated the machinery. Buzz Bidstrup, whose band The Angels became another Vanda and Young production deal for Alberts shortly after, recalls the pair's modus operandi in the studio. 'Harry was pretty relaxed and kind of sitting at the back of the room kind of nodding his head and looking around the place. George was the guy sitting at the desk with the engineer, with his hands on the knobs [and] faders and saying [mimes Scottish accent] "I think that's a bad take. I think take two's better." They were definitely a team, though.' Even someone as opinionated as George Young needed someone to check in with. 'Harry was his sounding board.'

To keep the atmosphere going, the room would be stocked with booze and dope and cigarettes – and milkshakes for Angus – and anything else they felt would help re-create the atmosphere of a live club show. In future, once Bon had consolidated his position in the band as lyricist and they finally settled on a long-term rhythm section, more care would be given to the construction of the original material, with George, Malcolm and Angus occupying the same stool at the piano as George broke the songs down to their component parts then built them up again, minus extraneous licks and spits but with added melody and rhythmic punch. For the *High Voltage* sessions, though, it was about getting the basic live set down on tape then getting on with the move to Melbourne. With the nucleus of the recording entity now established as Bon and the brothers, Rob Bailey and Peter Clack weren't involved as much as they would have liked; George supplied most of the bass parts, while a succession of different drummers were brought in, depending on who was available, including Tony Currenti from The 69ers and John Proud, who George and Harry had used on the earlier Marcus Roll sessions. (Clack would eventually appear on just one track, 'She's Got Balls'.) When all else failed, the ever versa-tile George would provide the drums. (Bailey was outraged when the album would appear without a credit for him, bitterly disputing the suggestion that he barely played on it. According to Clinton Walker, Bailey 'certainly has never seen any money from Alberts'.)

Instead of sounding bitty and out of sync, as might have been expected from such ad hoc arrangements, the final result, gleaned from less than a dozen sessions, would became the belt-studded template from which all other AC/DC albums in the Bon era would eventually be made. It opened with 'Baby, Please Don't Go', its shuffling beat made more lapel-grabbing by George's astute decision to speed the tape up (an old production trick that rarely fails to yield dividends and is still much in use today). Then followed the first original track the brothers had worked up with Bon – the ode to Irene, 'She's Got Balls' – this was AC/DC in a nutshell: Bon in full storytelling mode, taking the details directly from his own true-life experiences, as Malcolm and Angus extrapolate around him with boot-stompin', wide-boy riffs and lead breaks as devilishly attention-seeking as the tattoos on Bon's hairy arms.

The next track, a low-riding, lascivious groover called 'Little Lover', another of Bon's first attempts at adding lyrics to a Malcolm and Angus riff which he later laughed off as being about Angus ('The most prominent littlest lover that I know'), was another actually inspired by Irene. Yet the story the lyrics tell of a young female fan Bon first espies at one of the band's shows, who leaves a damp patch on her seat that Bon is sure *'wasn't Coca-Cola'*, seems more attuned to the new lease of life he was suddenly, unexpectedly enjoying in AC/DC. What separates it from the uncomfortable misogyny of any number of similarly slanted rock numbers of the time – lifting it out of the teeth-sucking darkness of, say, Zeppelin's 'Whole Lotta Love' or the abrupt sexual pounce of the Stones' 'Stray Cat Blues' – is the deliberately mocking way Bon seems to send the whole thing up. More *Carry On* humour than depraved Seventies chic, Bon simply can't keep a straight face as he delivers his *bon-mots*. Even the music is more carnivalesque than the musical mores of most 'serious' rock bands of the time would allow.

The only equivalent in rock at the time was the Sensational Alex

Harvey Band, another self-consciously hell-for-leather rock band whose Scottish storytelling roots and unabashed musical farce had the same kind of cartoon gang mentality as the one AC/DC with Bon was now fostering (if not quite the same clannish mentality) – except that the SAHB was operating 10,000 miles away, back in the homeland Bon and the brothers had left behind. Indeed, the parallels are too close to be written off as coincidence. Led by an older Scottish guy whose Celtic roots and Glaswegian attitude would put the fear of god into the 'southern softie' rock critics who clamoured to praise him in the mid-Seventies, the SAHB also featured a bizarrely attired guitarist, Zal Cleminson, a loner who kept his own counsel offstage, then, emboldened by, in his case, *Clockwork Orange*-inspired Pierrot makeup and costume, turned into a pantomime maniac onstage, becoming the perfect foil to the singer's leader-of-the-pack persona while the rest of the band played the straight men dressed in the more musicianly post-hippy tees-and-flares of the era. While there's nothing to suggest that either of the Young brothers had been particularly enamoured of Harvey's exquisitely off-kilter takes on rock, Bon Scott certainly was a big fan, inspired by the older Glaswegian to add his own, much more knowing vantage point to the mix, not just in his bawdy lyrics, but in his own, similarly splendid way of delivering them; louche, lairy, not so much a twinkle in the eye as a glint of something more painful than punning. Certainly the links between the early AC/DC and the classic period of Alex Harvey and his more advanced band of brothers – the bloodlines, cultural conclusions and musical outcomes – are fascinatingly similar. Not least, too, when one considers that both singers would die young, in the small hours of a forlorn February morning less than two years apart. As Rose Tattoo singer Angry Anderson once recalled: 'One of my fondest memories of Bon was when he introduced me to the music of Alex Harvey. He gave me a cassette of Alex's and it was like an epiphany. Everyone talks about the clichéd stuff of women, drugs and booze with Bon, but he really loved good music. Bon was the rock poet of the era.' Or put another way, perhaps, a sensational Australian version of Alex Harvey.

Of the *High Voltage* album's remaining five tracks, most had originally come from the Dave Evans era. He now claims they had already recorded several of the songs in the studio with George and Harry, including the show-stopping 'Soul Stripper' (one of the few AC/DC tracks to feature Malcolm and Angus actually trading lead guitar licks, and re-recorded now with Bon on vocals), plus one track, 'Rock'n'Roll Singer', that would be re-purposed for their next album, and two more he had 'written the lyrics and melody for' called 'Fell In Love' and 'Sunset Strip'. 'But Bon joined the band and changed the lyrics. So "Fell In Love" became "Love Song (Oh Jene)" and "Sunset Strip" became "Show Business". So Bon didn't have any problems with rewriting lyrics of two songs that I was already performing in public and that he heard me perform.' It wasn't the only thing Evans feels Bon had co-opted from his own stage act, citing the bit where Bon would hoist Angus onto his shoulders and walk him around the stage while still playing guitar during 'Baby, Please Don't Go'. 'I didn't mind that so much. It's a form of flattery really. But I did resent him changing the lyrics to two of the songs I'd [written and] performed live.'

By then, however, it no longer mattered how Dave felt. The AC/DC the world would first be introduced to on the *High Voltage* album was already of a very different character: the addition of Bon Scott had seen to that. He hadn't quite got into his stride yet, as substandard fare like the plodding, sub-Stones-alike 'Stick Around' (about Bon's problems holding on to women for longer than it took to have sex with them: 'I got a good song out of it,' he joked. 'They still leave [but] now I sing it every night in bed') and the uninspired if irritatingly catchy 'You Ain't Got A Hold On Me' demonstrated (the latter also featuring a rare but eloquent Malcolm guitar solo). As for the two tracks Evans claims to have written but which the band with Bon now reshuffled, the first, 'Love Song (Oh Jene)' – due to a spelling mistake: it was supposed to have been 'Oh Jean' – sounds like a leftover from Fraternity: a dreadfully self-conscious pop-opera ditty that would have been cringe-making in the flower-power era and here is merely excruciating. Nevertheless, this was the track that George and Harry, usually so faultless in their ability to pick winners, earmarked as the first single from the album, seeing it in the same potentially groundbreaking mould as Stevie Wright's 'Evie' of a year before. That, though, had been a genuinely stirring Big Pop moment, written and tailor-made for Wright by George and Harry frustrated by their failure to make it as producers in the UK and determined to prove themselves all over again back home; 'Love Song (Oh Jene)' was a patchwork of ambitious ideas that never quite got off the drawing board. The second rewritten Evans song was album closer 'Show Business'. Despite being worked over with a typically tongue-in-cheek Bon lyric and suitably gurning Chuck Berry guitars from the brothers, it would have been better left in whatever whisky bottle it first spilled out of onto the floor. The sort of balls-out live number that simply doesn't stand repeated listens on vinyl.

Though their working practices would soon evolve, in their search for American success, towards a completely different, far more considered attempt at the summit of technical excellence, the studio was not yet the place to go searching for perfection. For now, the onus was still on fine-tuning the line-up of the band in order to make the most of the arduous schedule Michael Browning was busy putting in place for them, starting with a prestige show opening for Black Sabbath at the Hordern Pavilion on 5 November. Sabbath were coming to the end of their world tour, following the release the year before of their last great album of the Seventies, *Sabbath Bloody Sabbath*, and Bon used it as an opportunity to rekindle what would become a life-long friendship with singer Ozzy Osbourne, then at the height of his own vicious alcohol- and drug-abusing circle. 'I liked Bon as soon as I met him,' Ozzy would later tell me. 'He made me laugh. A very nice, easygoing bloke. That is, until he'd got stuck into the booze and whatnot. Then he was a fuckin' animal. A bit like me,' he smiled sadly.

Once sessions for the album had been completed, Browning had AC/DC back at the Hordern Pavillion for the second time in as many months, this time supporting Skyhooks, who had recently broken through into the national Australian charts with their single 'Living In

The 70s'. Within a year, their album of the same name would become the biggest-selling Australian album of the time. None of which persuaded Malcolm that he'd been wrong to try and push AC/DC as far out of their glam-conscious orbit as he could, while still retaining Angus's unbeatably demented schoolboy-from-hell gimmick. He knew Skyhooks had beaten them to the glam-punch and he wasn't about to settle for coming second. AC/DC would have to be different again. As soon as that was taken care of, Browning put them on the bus to Melbourne and their new life at the forefront of the liveliest music scene in Australia, beginning with regular spots at his Hard Rock Cafe, where they even appeared at the club's weekly Gay Nights. Malcolm and Angus may have looked at such crowds as 'a bit funny' but Bon entered into the spirit of things with his usual mad gusto, wielding specially bought props like zinging vibrators and whizzing whips, and strutting around with his shirt off and his short skinny legs squeezed into the tightest-fitting jeans he could find. 'He'd wear those shirts with the sleeves cut off,' recalls Browning, 'buying them a size too small to show off his muscles.'

Mainly, though, it was the gigs performed to a largely straight audience that the band began to build their reputation on. Years later, Angus would reflect on how much the arduous Australian pub and club circuit moulded AC/DC's ability to maintain a level of performance, no matter where they were or what the obstacles were they faced. 'Starting from there, we had an edge that possibly no other band would ever have. In those days, the [Australian] circuit was relatively limited – you had to be willing to play anywhere.' It wasn't just onstage that their reputation now grew. 'They fell straight into that whole sex, drugs and rock'n'roll thing,' says Browning. 'They pretty much became the centre of gravity of that whole scene. Not so much the drugs thing – although Bon had his moments – but definitely the sex and rock'n'roll and the booze.' For their initial move to Melbourne, Browning rented them rooms at the Freeway Gardens, a motel off the main freeway that runs from the airport into the city. 'Then that became the hotel where all the bands stayed. Other bands would come and go but AC/DC were always there and they became like the hosts of parties, just about every night. It was all happening at the Freeway Gardens motel. That was the centre of it all.'

It all carried on even when Michael found them a house to share, a single-storey dwelling in Lansdowne Road, in East St Kilda – worth a fortune today but back then notoriously part of Melbourne's red-light district. 'There weren't any other groups staying there but it was just the party house,' says Browning. It became the place for waiters finishing shifts but not yet ready to crash, for girls looking for a place where they could hang out past the 10 p.m. pub closing time – even for local gangsters and, just to balance out the yang with some yin, various Hare Krishna sect members. Inevitably, the local police would also regularly feel required to show up. But even they got taken in by the atmosphere – and the band's offer to let them play the instruments that lay about the place, and have a drink or two with some of the girls. 'There would be something happening there every night. That's where they picked up the nickname The Seedies. The groupie scene was beyond anything I'd ever seen before in my life. I can remember instances where they were almost queuing up. It wasn't just Bon [that was into groupies] they all were. They were young and could have whatever they wanted.'

Meanwhile, the musical side of the band was finally taking a more permanent shape with the arrival, in the first days of January 1975, of the man who was to become as crucial a part of the archetypal AC/DC sound as that of the brothers' interlocked guitars: drummer Phil Rudd. Born in Surrey Hills, Melbourne, on 19 May 1954, Phillip Hugh Norman Witschke Rudzevecuis had been drumming since he was 15, when he left school to become an apprentice electrician and used his first wages to buy a cheap second-hand drum kit. Impatient to learn he booked himself a course with a drum teacher but never went back after the first lesson. Phil wasn't interested in textbooks, not even the ones with pictures; curled his lip at theory. He preferred to learn from close listening to the work of favourite drummers like Free's Simon Kirke and Mountain's Corky Laing. That's where he got his much lauded 'feel'. His acute ability to keep time came from sitting in his bedroom playing along to Ringo Starr on Beatles records.

His dynamism from one record: 'Tin Soldier' by the Small Faces. It wasn't their drummer Kenney Jones's signature percussive style so much as the way he simply brought down the house on the bridge.

A series of stints 'whacking hell' out of his drums in short-lived local outfits followed: weekend heroes like Krayne, who specialised in Zeppelin and Deep Purple covers (and featured Phil's old pal from school and future Rose Tattoo bassist Geordie Leach), and Charlemagne, who leaned more towards the Humble Pie and Free end of the Seventies spectrum. Phil had just entered the final year of his apprenticeship in the summer of 1973 when he got involved in his first professional outfit, the horribly named Smack – so named not because any of the members were habitual heroin users, but simply because they actually thought it sounded 'cool'. Fortunately, the arrival of a ball-of-energy singer named Gary 'Angry' Anderson (another future Rose Tattoo founder) signalled a change of name to the more crowd-friendly Buster Brown, and from there they never looked back. With Anderson's irrepressible stage presence and gravelly voice, the band quickly became popular on the same pub and club circuit AC/DC would start to make their own a year later. Nevertheless, walking out on his day-job before he'd fully qualified seemed a rash decision for the 19-year-old to make but by then the car-mad teenager was earning enough scratch from Buster Brown to afford his first serious wheels: an old yellow HK Monaro four-speed coupe, picked up via his dad's garage.

Signed to Michael Gudinski's fledgling Mushroom Records label in the summer of 1974, they had begun work on the first – and only – Buster Brown album, *Something To Say*, around the same time AC/DC were beginning work in the studio for the first time with Bon Scott. Produced by another local Melbourne star, Lobby Loyde, of proto punk-metallists Coloured Balls, in one intense as-live 12-hour session, and released in December 1974, Buster Brown looked like serious rivals to AC/DC, maybe even one step ahead of them. Their future appeared fatally holed beneath the waterline, however, when Rudd – who called a spade a spade and asked perhaps one question too many – was sacked within weeks of the album appearing in the shops. That was when the Young brothers, uncomfortably aware of Buster Brown's already well-established rep in Melbourne, pounced.

Phil was helping out washing cars at his dad's garage when fellow drummer Trevor Young – no relation to the brothers – from Coloured Balls stopped by to chat. Trevor had heard that the new band in town, AC/DC, who had a deal with Alberts, were looking for a new rhythm section. There had been half a dozen club shows during the first week of January, with Russell Coleman – who'd played on Stevie Wright's album – on drums and George Young filling in on bass. Coleman was a good player but was not seen as a long-term prospect. The brothers wanted someone they could control, who hadn't done more than they had already, and who wasn't the worldly Coleman. So word was out, which was how Trevor heard about it. It was he who suggested that Phil should give the band a call, maybe even bring his mate Geordie Leach, also now out of Buster Brown, with him to see about being the bass player. Phil, still upset about getting the boot and desperate to get back in the swing with another band before the car-washing gig with his dad became permanent, thought that was a great idea. Leach, though, had other ideas. (Within months he and Anderson would form Rose Tattoo.)

Getting in touch with AC/DC was not difficult in 1975. The house in Lansdowne Road was already becoming a well-known drop-off point for every degenerate in town and all the young musicians on the scene knew Michael Browning. Two phone calls later – to and from Mike – and Phil had an afternoon appointment at the house. When he arrived, there were only the brothers there to meet him. Cue: uncomfortable silence. Having got back late the night before from a gig, they were still in their underwear. Not that they bothered to explain that to Phil. They simply indicated the drum kit set up in the hallway, which Phil sat down at while Angus plugged in his guitar and Malcolm picked up a bass. Then they both lit cigarettes and began playing. Not anything the new boy might know either but stuff from the as yet unreleased *High Voltage* album. When Phil seemed to handle that well enough, they lit into a couple of rock'n'roll standards, just to see what the new boy could do when really given the chance. Phil charged into them and the brothers, though saying little, were impressed. 'Come back tomorrow,' Malcolm told him when they'd stopped. 'Meet George ...'

A week later, Rudd having been given an unequivocal thumbs-up from the elder Young brother, the AC/DC clan had itself a new blood-brother to take into battle; his first gig – still with George on bass – at the El Toro club in Liverpool, NSW. They were still playing six covers a night – three by Elvis, two by the Stones and the obligatory 'School Days' by Chuck Berry – sprinkled among the seven tracks about to appear on the album, plus 'Can I Sit Next To You, Girl' and, later, 'Rock'n'Roll Singer', but the signature AC/DC sound – lowdown shuffle boogie with a beery leer strapped to it like a dildo – was now solidifying around them, and with it the camaraderie that would take them to the top of the Australian music biz as 1975 opened up and increasingly became their year. 'They were a proper gang after Phil joined,' Browning remembers. 'He was one of them: short arse but a tough little cookie. And he didn't fuck around. Musically, he was on the money from the word go.' Or as Lobby Loyde put it when he was producing Phil in Buster Brown: 'He syncopated like a dunny door. He was a rocker.'

In terms of the latter, this was something Malcolm ensured from the word go, insisting during their first rehearsals at Lansdowne Road that Rudd 'cut the crap' and stick almost monotonously to the beat no matter what. The flash would all come from Angus; the sly wit from Bon. The propulsive, 'tighter than a duck's arse under water' rhythm needed to showcase those dynamics though would all come from the work Malcolm and Phil did together, as one; neither showing off, nor letting up. Phil wasn't entirely sure he liked this new arrangement, but he knew who was boss and as the gigs piled up and the under-standing between the two grew ever tighter, he began to grasp better than anyone, even Angus, where Malcolm was coming from, music-ally. Where he would always live, come what may. 'One thing about Malcolm,' Browning observes, 'you always knew where you stood. He did all the thinking for them. They just had to get on with it.'

In terms of becoming part of the gang, Phil had even less problem there, as he soon demonstrated. His eighth gig with AC/DC was to have been at the fourth annual Sunbury Pop Festival. Held over the last weekend of January with around 15,000 people at a 620-acre farm halfway between Sunbury and Diggers Rest on the outskirts of Melbourne, Sunbury held fond memories for Michael Browning. It was at the first Sunbury in 1972 that Billy Thorpe & The Aztecs had reinvented themselves as a credible rock band. Since then it had become the biggest annual gathering of domestic Australian rock talent. Each year there had been a breakout act. To kill at Sunbury was to create a buzz that could transform your fortunes. The previous year it had been Skyhooks. When a last-minute offer was made to have AC/DC on the Saturday night bill Michael was determined to make the most of it. If things went well, 1975 would be the year AC/DC became the band everybody talked about for weeks and months afterwards. He almost got his wish, too, though not in the way he had anticipated.

1975 was also supposed to have been the second time a huge international act had been brought in to headline on the Saturday: Deep Purple. The problem was nobody was sure until the very last minute whether the band was really coming. After the release of their *Stormbringer* album just weeks before – the last to feature co-founder and star of the band, guitarist Ritchie Blackmore – things were not running smoothly in the Purple camp. The organisers were nervous too. A year before, they had brought Queen in as headliners and seen the band booed off to cries of 'Go back to Pommyland ya pooftahs!' When word reached them just days before the show that Purple almost certainly would not be showing up, they put in a call to Michael, to see if AC/DC could be brought in to close the Saturday night bill. He was elated. However, when he arrived at the site with the band, it appeared Deep Purple had shown up – along with mountains of PA and lighting equipment and a platoon of roadies unwilling to cooperate with locally hired stage staff.

Forced to struggle through the crowd to get to the backstage dressing rooms, the brothers – all three, with George still filling in on bass – were already in the wrong mood when they were then told

The Easybeats, left to right: Stevie Wright, Harry Vanda, Dick Diamonde, Henry 'Snowy' Fleet and George Young. Germany, 1967

(Getty Images)

Fraternity, the Adelaide hills, circa 1971   *(Fraternity)*

First professional photo shoot, including original singer Dave Evans
(second right), Sydney, 1974   *(Philip Morris)*

One of AC/DC's earliest shows at Chequers nightclub, circa 1974   *(Philip Morris)*

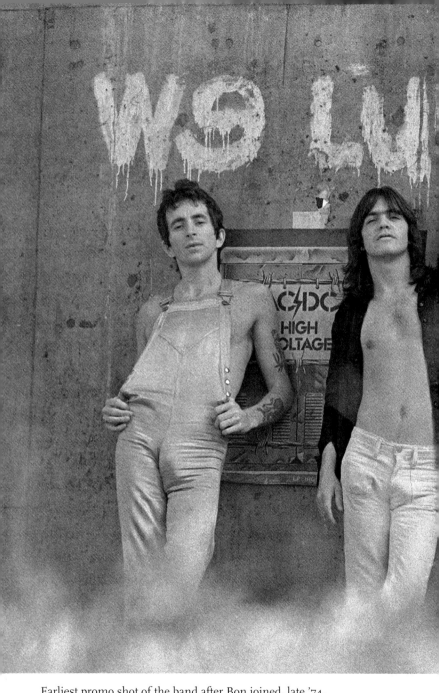

Earliest promo shot of the band after Bon joined, late '74.
Note Bon in newly shorn hair and dungarees   *(Philip Morris)*

Visiting the London offices of Atlantic Records, May 1976. Bon wore dark glasses to hide the scars form a recent pub brawl. Phil Carson in schoolboy uniform

(Getty Images)

A touch too much.
Angus Young,
Copenhagen, 1976
(Getty Images)

The clan, backstage, London, circa 1977. Coral and Michael Browning centre-back
(Michael Browning)

Backstage, on the highway to hell, California, 1978.
Ian Jeffery (left), Bon (middle)   *(Ian Jeffrey)*

they'd be going on after Purple finished their headline set. 'We just about got past that,' says Browning, 'but when Purple finished we're all standing at the side of the stage watching the riggers pulling down the gear. They were gonna completely strip the stage, which meant we wouldn't have gone on till about four in the morning.' At which point Browning gave the order to his own crew to begin setting up the AC/DC gear. 'I was gonna send them on straight away regardless,' he laughs. Instead, when the Purple crew who had never heard of AC/DC took offence and threatened to pummel the noisy incomers if they didn't leave the stage immediately, Michael found himself, along with the band, George and their crew in a huge fight right there on the stage before 15,000 astonished punters. When it was over – a draw declared by frantic organisers desperate to try and clear the stage without upsetting their illustrious overseas visitors – Browning, a giant among pygmies, ordered his crew to pack up and the band to retreat. They could fuck their festival. AC/DC were out of there. They had proved their point without playing a note. The mostly drunk and stoned crowd stood and cheered as they walked back through them to their waiting jalopy of a tour bus. The next morning Michael received another phone call from the organisers, apologising for the debacle and inviting the band back to play on the Sunday night. Michael told them what they could do with their offer, as Malcolm and Angus looked on and smirked. 'It was after that,' says Browning now, 'that I really started thinking seriously about getting them out of Australia. Home-grown acts just didn't get the same respect as the overseas stars. I thought, we'll see about that ...'

The clan was growing stronger, the bonds between them ever deeper. They were learning to love if not entirely understand each other. Bon, a serial drinker and drug-taker, couldn't understand how Angus was able to summon up his ferocious onstage energy from an offstage diet consisting solely of endless cups of tea and packs of cigarettes, crisps, candy bars and milkshakes. Yet Angus was always the centre of attention at every show, even with a frontman as canny as Bon doing his best to upstage him. There was the ludicrous school uniform, of course, to help keep all eyes on him, but more than that there was the sheer frenzy he was able to summon each night. Incorporating Chuck Berry's duck walk into a stiff-legged version of his own, he added a demented head-banging motion that literally never stopped, not even when taking a guitar solo. There was also the moment now when he clambered onto Bon's shoulders, still wildly thrashing away at his guitar, often getting tangled in the dozens of yards of lead wire needed to keep the guitar attached to his amp. To round off the set, Angus would dive off the stage, take his extra-long lead – and whatever poor roadie was responsible for keeping it connected to the PA – out for a duck walk among the crowd, standing on tables, jumping up and running along the bar, before finally coming to a kind of autistic whirl on the dance floor, where he lay on his side, still playing like a champion, his little legs running on an invisible hamster wheel as his body whirled round and round in circles. Angus would do anything to get the required over-the-top reaction from any crowd, big or small. 'I'll shit and piss on people if need be,' he declared in one interview. Meantime, watching from the side, George Young was again directing operations, telling his youngest brother: 'If you trip and fall over the stage in the middle of a tune, make it look like you intended to fall, that it's all part of your show.'

Bon had his own attention-seeking ways. When one local town council made Browning post an insurance bond worth more than they were actually getting paid for the gig, declaring there would be no foul language or 'incitement to misbehaviour' at the show, Bon stepped onstage and told the audience: 'Let's get this over with quick – fuck, shit, piss!' Angus shook his head: 'That was it – our money gone.' And if others gagged at the sight of Angus coming offstage stinking of sweat and cigarette smoke, covered in his own saliva and snot, what no one outside the band and their roadies saw was how much his own performance took out of Bon. Still in chronic pain from his accident eight months before, towards the end of those early sets he would whirl around to the side of the stage, pretending not to know where he was going, then collapse onto his knees fighting for breath. Bon would joke and blame his hard-living ways and the heaviness of the previous night's party – as when he collapsed side-stage mid-gig at the Hard Rock one night and Malcolm and Angus were forced to share the vocals to the end of the set – and in a meta-phorical sense that's exactly what it was. The doctors that had pro-nounced him dead knew better though. As time went by and his health recovered and his stagecraft increased, he learned how to pace himself through a whole 90-minute show, allowing Angus to be the one throwing himself about the stage. But for now Bon's stage show relied on a lot of bluff and bluster. The funny man who dare not stop laughing for fear of bursting into tears ...

As the band were beginning to learn, Bon could be the life and soul of the party one minute then simply disappear the next. Living back in Melbourne for the first time since 1968, Bon reacquainted himself with another old friend from those days, Mary Walton, whose fashion boutique was blossoming but whose marriage, like Bon's, had recently hit the rocks. Mary was witness to Bon's inculcation into the Young clan. They were 'very, very tight initially', she recalled. As far as Mary could tell, Malcolm and Angus were just kids that missed their home comforts. 'They would go and buy a roast, a leg of lamb, and they'd bring it around and ask me to cook it.' Bon was not slow either to take advantage of the homely atmosphere at Mary's Carlton apartment. As Angus observed, 'Bon gets the women with flats who cook him dinners.' To which Bon mischievously added, 'I like to put my feet up. Not to mention other parts of my body.'

That snug scene got cancelled out though when Bon became infat-uated with a teenage fan named Judy. Blonde, breathtakingly pretty and just 17, Judy had been a promising sprinter at school, for whom great things were predicted in track and field events. Having seen AC/DC at yet another Chequers show in February, and encouraged by the full-on attentions of Bon, who 'did his balls over her', as his friend and former roadie John Darcy put it, Judy had hitchhiked to Melbourne to be with the singer. She shacked up with her older sister, Christine, then working in one of the many massage parlours that lined Fitzroy Street in St Kilda, turning tricks to support her heroin habit, shooting smack to help blot out the tricks – the usual dead-end trip. There were other girls then hanging around Lansdowne Road that would top up their purses by working shifts in massage parlours, and others that liked to zonk out on smack. Judy, though, was different, as far as Bon was concerned. She wasn't beaten up yet by life. She still looked like a princess – even when she too found herself shooting smack and turning tricks. She was soon causing Bon all sorts of trouble – with drugs, with the law, even the band if he wasn't careful.

Bon had been on the wrong side of the law many times before of course, with or without women. But in Melbourne he seemed unable to keep out of its way. One of his antics even made the headlines in *Truth*, Melbourne's notoriously tacky tabloid: 'POP STAR, BRUNETTE AND A BED: THEN HER DAD TURNED UP!' Bon was quoted telling the story of being in bed with a teenage groupie when her father turned up at the house. 'Eventually I went to the door ... Suddenly, he started punching me in the head and body. He knocked me into a rose bush and dragged me through it ...' The band laughed it off as just another of Bon's increasingly high-profile misadventures, deciding it did their collective image no harm at all. But the dental plate that Bon had worn since his bike accident had been smashed and the resulting trip to the dentist to get it fixed set him back A$500 – two months' wages.

The fling with Judy was something else though. First there was the bust for pornography. 'One morning,' Bon later told *RAM*, Australia's newest and most hip music magazine, 'I was in bed – completely out of it – and the chick who was living with me at the time [Judy] was trying to hitch to work – also completely out of it – well, she got picked up by the police and she's so gone she can't speak. The police were familiar with the house. So they drive her back and run through the place ... and what happens but they bust me for pornography!'

Worse – much worse – was to follow. When Bon got back one night from another double-header in the Melbourne suburbs, he asked to be dropped off at the flat Judy shared with Christine. When he got there they were both out of it on smack. Rolling himself a joint, Bon was looking to kickback in his usual weed-and-whisky fashion. But the girls started taunting him, daring him to have a hit of their gear. This had happened before and Bon usually resisted, certainly from injecting himself, even if he would allow himself the occasional line. This night, however, the old Road Test Ronnie resurfaced and, using his studded biker belt as a tourniquet, Bon tied up his left arm and allowed Judy to probe for a vein. She found one immediately, and drawing the blood back into the syringe of the chamber, smiled glassily into his eyes as she pressed it down again and the smack hit home. Instead of getting higher than he'd ever been, as the girls had promised, Bon plunged right down to the bottom of the sea and stayed there, passing out and turned a frightening shade of blue. He was gone. Judy freaked out but Christine who'd seen it before told her to cool it while she checked his breathing – still there but very faint. Checked his eyes – rolled back into his head. Judy screamed and Christine filled up another syringe, this time with speed, hoping it would counteract the smack and bring him back around. She stuck it into his upper arm and pressed the trigger, a skin pop straight into the muscle: nothing. Now both girls hit the panic button. Christine reached for the phone and dialled the emergency services. The two girls sat stoned out of their gourds, taking turns to keep Bon's inert figure propped up while they waited for the ambulance to arrive. By now, he appeared to have stopped breathing so Christine tried to give him mouth-to-mouth resuscitation. Again, nothing. They waited and waited ...

'I remember him ending up in hospital,' says Michael Browning now, 'but it's news to me that it was heroin. I was always under the impression that it was amphetamines of some kind. But it could well be. I stayed away from that side of it, really. I went to visit Bon in hospital but I don't think anyone would have confided or mentioned anything to me exactly what it would have been, because they may have felt it would have a negative impact of some kind.'

Bon – who'd sat bolt upright, his whole body in shock, after the paramedics revived him – had no intention of telling Michael or any of the boys – especially not the boys – that he'd nearly done himself over letting some love-sick junkie chick shoot him up with smack. This wasn't Fraternity any more, whose largesse with drugs was seen as a crucial part of their creative trip. This was the Young brothers, and for all Malcolm's dope-smoking and boozing, Bon was not foolish enough to believe he would look kindly on his new singer dabbling with heroin. He'd seen what happened to Dave Evans, whose crimes were far less serious. He'd already said goodbye to one manager and two other musicians, whose crimes he still wasn't entirely sure of. He wasn't going to put his own head in a noose. Not now when things were looking so good. 'That definitely would have been frowned upon,' says Browning, 'Because the brothers experienced the fall of Stevie Wright who got addicted to heroin, so it was a huge no-no. Heroin pretty much amounted to self-destruction and end of band, you know?' None of the Young brothers were going to allow that. Bon was back gigging with the band the same week.

High Voltage and the 'Love Song (Oh Jene)' single had been released simultaneously in Australia, on the Alberts label, on 17 February 1975. It wasn't long, though, before it became plain how little anyone thought of the nominal A-side and began playing the flip side of the single, 'Baby, Please Don't Go'. In this case, the people were right. 'Baby, Please Don't Go' told you everything you needed to know about AC/DC: hard, fast, not taking itself too seriously though, mostly it spelt f-u-n; a commodity in woefully short supply in the self-regarding world of mid-Seventies rock. A message reinforced by the front of the album sleeve: a large, rusting electrical substation, cordoned off behind barbed wire, at the base of which can be seen crushed empty beer cans and a small dog lifting his leg and urinating. Chris Gilbey, who came up with the concept, laughs now at the simple 'controversy' it engendered when he first showed it to his sales force. 'It was all, "You can't do that! Show a dog pissing on the cover! It's disgusting!" I mean, looking back at it now it all seems so innocent. But it definitely got the message across that this was a down and dirty rock'n'roll band, and of course the kids loved it.' Within weeks the single had reached the national Top 10, with *High Voltage* looking similarly good in the albums chart. Suddenly AC/DC were the hot new band of the moment.

To celebrate the release, Michael Browning organised a one-off show at the Hard Rock. Billed as a 'Special AC/DC Performance, New Album', with admission set at just A$1.00 – or free with 'an AC/DC eyeshade'. A similar reception was also held in Sydney, followed by four 'homecoming' shows at Chequers, the first of what would be 25 shows back-to-back, constituting the first leg of the official *High Voltage* tour. By then they had recruited Paul Matters on bass, the good-looking blond from Armageddon, a blues-rock trio from Newcastle, NSW, that George rated but who never quite made it. Brought into the fold at George's suggestion, the brothers put up with him for a while – Matters could certainly play – but it wasn't long before they took against his easygoing charm and tendency to remind one and all that he had, of course, already been there and done that in Armageddon. For Malcolm, it was Dave Evans all over again. Matters lasted exactly 11 gigs.

CHAPTER SEVEN

Not a Nice Band

In March 1975, Bon Scott gave an interview to *RAM* magazine in which he spoke about the difficulty in finding a suitable bass player for AC/DC. 'It's a pretty rare type of bloke who'll fit into our band. He has to be under five feet six. And he has to be able to play bass pretty well too.' He was joking but it was true. With George Young weary of filling in – and left even wearier by his little brothers' inability to settle on anyone else as a permanent bassist – the band were forced to continue either with Malcolm taking over on bass, leaving Angus as the sole guitarist, something they had reluctantly begun doing when George flew back to Sydney, or finding someone – anyone – that could play the bass that they could be in the same room as for longer than five minutes. George denies he was ever tempted to simply throw in his lot with his brothers. Staying at a house 'overrun by girls' may have brought back memories of what he called 'the old rock'n'roll days all over again' but George, despite being the same age as Bon, already felt too old for all that. Besides, he'd already been there, done that. His goals now lay elsewhere. 'It wouldn't have been right,' he said. 'They were doing their own thing and I would have been too interfering with their music.' Here, though, he was perhaps being disingenuous. Arguably George had full control over AC/DC's music without the need to put up with actually being in the band.

Instead, the answer to the band's problems lay practically on their doorstep. Nineteen-year-old Mark Whitmore Evans had started out as a guitarist then switched to bass – 'less strings' – and found he had a talent for rock steady rhythm and blues, drawing his influences in a direct line from Rory Gallagher and Johnny Winter back to Freddy King, the Stones and Howlin' Wolf, the latter being 'the greatest of them all'. But if his enthusiasm was real, his experience was limited, extending only as far as senior school groups and semi-pro pub outfits. By the time his old mate Steve McGrath – recently hired as an occasional gear-humper for new dicks on the block AC/DC – told him about the band's search for a bassist, encouraging him over several beers and games of pool to throw his hat into the ring, Mark had 'nothing better to do', working as a clerk at the offices of the Postmaster-General's Department of the local civil service. 'So I thought: why not? I was living in a cheap hotel sharing my room with my giant bass rig, bored out of my head and feeling guilty about not being in a proper band.'

Steve gave him the address of the Lansdowne Road house – as chance would have it, Mark's older sister, Judy, lived in an apartment in the building directly opposite – and the following Saturday afternoon, Evans caught the tram down and simply knocked on the door. To his delight, a 'very attractive young lady' answered. Introducing herself as Angus's girlfriend, she explained that the band were playing a gig that afternoon at the Matthew Flinders Hotel in Chadstone, a nearby Melbourne suburb, but that he was welcome to wait for them to return, if he liked. Evans wandered in past the bedrooms that led off the hall and through the single lounge and out the back towards what he assumed was 'a family room sort of arrangement' – until he was told that it was Bon's domain and that it would not be a good idea to be there when 'the old man' returned. He slunk back into the lounge and made himself at home while trying not to stare at his 'cute as a button' host.

He didn't have to wait long. Malcolm was first through the door, followed by Phil and Angus. Seeing Phil, who he recognised from Buster Brown, caused Evans to realise this was no mere bar band. But there was no Bon and no explanation as to why. (There never would be.) Evans would later recall in his memoir, *Dirty Deeds*, that the first thing he noticed about the brothers was how short they were. 'I'm only five-six on a good day, but these guys made me feel tall – I couldn't recall meeting anyone smaller than Angus.' At which point, 'the whole school uniform fell into place'. The other thing he noticed was 'a coldness about [the brothers] that I hadn't experienced before'. Asked now what he meant by that, he says: 'I think that's just the way they were. They were like a lot of pals that I grew up with that are Scottish, who were part of that immigration to Australia in the late Fifties and early Sixties. Once you're welcomed into that circle, you're all part of the deal. Of course there are limits to that. Blood's thicker than water. But they could be, personality-wise, a little standoffish.'

But while the brothers affected not to notice their unexpected guest, they were taking in every word he said, sizing him up from the corners of their hard little eyes. Told to come back the following day for 'a blow' – on the strength, he thinks now, of his having mentioned his admiration for the no-frills approach of Rory Gallagher bassist Gerry McAvoy – when Evans returned that Sunday afternoon, he was blown away by the contrast between what his eyes were seeing and his ears were hearing. Angus 'reminded me of a little old man' – until he started playing. 'I was completely unprepared for the Angus and Malcolm show. I wasn't that experienced but I knew this was something else.' They ran through most of the songs from *High Voltage* then took a tea and ciggie break, during which conversation was desultory and non-committal. When, after an hour, Angus laid down his guitar and wandered off Evans assumed that was the end of the audition. Fearing he'd failed, he was cheered when Malcolm invited him, at least, to come and see the band play two nights later at the Station Hotel in nearby Prahran – Mark's hometown.

Confused, he accepted the offer of a lift back to his digs by Ralph, one of the two roadies that also lived at Lansdowne Road. His spirits lifted when Ralph told him he was sure he'd got the gig. Though there were caveats. 'He basically said, "There's two things you've got to remember: number one, it's Malcolm's band; and number two, we're gonna be in the UK in twelve months." And that was after not even playing a gig with the band. So it was put on the table from the start that this thing was moving ahead. He may as well have said to me, "Remember that it's Malcolm's band, and we're gonna be playing on the moon in twelve months." I just took it with a grain of salt. But it didn't take me very long to realise these guys were deadly serious – particularly Angus and Malcolm – and that they intended to pick up all the marbles. You got infected by it. It became apparent to me very early on that along with George the band expected to be big. It wasn't expected to fail, it was going to work – that world domination was the only option.'

It was this latter quality that Evans now recalls best from his time with the band. 'Once you're inside, you're *very* inside and once you're outside, you're pretty much on the outside, let me tell you.' He laughs. With AC/DC, he says, 'that's just the way it works, man, and that's always the way it's gonna be. The circle was very, very limited – a siege mentality. That's the way we operated. It wasn't us against them; it was us against *all of them*. There was a confidence and arrogance. We weren't competing just against other bands, we were competing against everyone.' He adds: 'Sometimes it could be a bit stifling. I knew that Bon struggled at times with the constrictions that they put on him socially, but you know, that's just the way it was.'

Less than a week later the new-look AC/DC gave their first performance on the country's newest weekly TV pop show, *Countdown*. Recently launched on Sunday evenings and hosted by Ian 'Molly' Meldrum, previously of *Go-Set* magazine, *Countdown* was unashamedly based on the same chart-driven format as the UK's *Top of the Pops*: the week's highest-placed chart acts invited to mime to their hits before a studiously attentive audience of young dancers. Plumping for 'Baby, Please Don't Go' over 'Love Song (Oh Jene)' as a sure-fire crowd-pleaser, which the band was happy to mime to while Bon provided a live vocal, most bands in their position – making their show debut as a relatively new outfit – would have been delighted merely to have got through the song and milk the canned applause. As a veteran of several earlier incarnations of the same thing with first The Valentines and then Fraternity, Bon, however, had his sights set higher than that, coming up with the knife-edge idea of dressing up as a schoolgirl, replete with blonde, pigtailed wig, rouged cheeks, blue eye-shadow and short school dress, blouse sleeves rolled up to reveal his tatts. Whether intended as some kind of psychedelic refraction of Angus's hyperrealist schoolboy, or merely a piss-take of Malcolm's much-loathed Skyhooks' own now regular is-it-a-boy-or-is-it-an-alien appearances on the show – or possibly both, with a dash of bourbon breath and weed-exhalation thrown in for good measure – it took everybody by surprise, including Malcolm and Angus, who snickered throughout the taping. Not least when Bon lit a cigarette halfway through the song – something that could not be imagined on a TV pop show today – then fell backwards during the vocal-to-guitar call-and-response routine to reveal bulging white 'knickers'. Angus recalled how 'Bon thought, well, if we come along and be who we are, he [Meldrum] will just walk away [thinking], "Oh yeah, ho hum." But when Bon showed up like that, [Molly] just went nuts!'

It left such an impression on both the show's producers and the Oz public at large, the band was invited back on to do it all again three weeks later – and again shortly after that. AC/DC would become part of the furniture on *Countdown*, making 38 appearances on the show over the next two years, regardless of whether they had a new single out or not. 'That show was hugely influential on record sales in Australia and they were on *Countdown* all the time,' remembers Browning. '*Countdown* really loved them – that was during the screaming-girl era.' Whenever they appeared on the show they tried to make an event of it. On one occasion Angus revived his Super Ang routine, leaping from a telephone box. On another they rigged up the set to make it appear as though he was piloting a propeller plane. Browning's carpenter at the Hard Rock became adept at knocking up whatever sets the band dreamed up. Hence also the giant spider's web used as backdrop for Bon to appear in a spider suit with eight arms, and the gorilla suit Angus wore the time Bon dragged him out playing wildly from a cage. On yet another, Bon came on wearing a red and white straw boater and striped blazer undone to the waist, his hairy chest exposed in laughing counterpoint, clutching an old man's walking stick with a crooked handle. If Angus was definitely not the stereotypical self-absorbed Seventies axe hero, Bon was most definitely not your average conceited heavy rock vocalist, either. More of a cabaret-style showman, in fact. Or a character actor, inventing the character of Bon Scott, gap-toothed, tattooed hard man of animated-movie rockers AC/DC. 'When he joined us he took us by the scruff of the neck,' said Malcolm. 'On stage it'd be: "Don't just stand there, you cunt" ... whatever AC/DC went on to achieve, Bon was also very responsible for.'

Arriving at the same moment in Australia as colour television, these *Countdown* appearances became a huge factor in the band's early success. Or as Bon later put it, 'If you don't show your arse to Molly Meldrum [on *Countdown*] you're fucked.' It was an unkind if deadeningly accurate put-down. Bon and Molly – a genuine Melbourne mover and shaker who delighted in describing himself as 'The oldest teenager in Australia' – would enjoy a fitful personal relationship. Yet it was Meldrum who became AC/DC's most influential supporter in these, their earliest, empire-building days. Jerry Ewing, an Australian-born rock critic who would go on to found *Classic Rock* magazine in London in the Nineties, was nine years old and living in Sydney the first time he saw AC/DC on *Countdown* in 1975. 'The next day at school it was all we talked about. And of course everyone my age picked up on the fact that Angus was in a school uniform. That was the link that got us in. Otherwise it could have just been another band. Literally, the next day we were all running around with our satchels on our backs pretending to play the guitar! Next thing, every kid had the album, *High Voltage*, with the red cover. Until then everyone's favourite band at school had been Skyhooks, which everyone kept on liking, and Sherbet. But they were more middle-of-the-road. Then AC/DC came along and they had more to do with the anti-establishment kind of approach. They actually scared parents.'

In April, hard on the heels of AC/DC's first *Countdown* appearances and with both album and single climbing the Australian charts, *RAM* published their first major feature on the new band. Writer Anthony O'Grady revealed how the first time he met Angus, 'all five foot five of him', the guitarist had approached him 'with homicide in his eyes' – due to O'Grady's review of the disastrous Sunbury festival, in which he mistakenly reported that the promoters had cancelled the band's appearance, because, he explained, 'the group had left the Festival grounds and were uncontactable'. Fortunately, Bon the Likeable was also present, steering the conversation around to *High Voltage*. 'It's real tough music so it's good to play on stage,' he said. 'Melbourne and Adelaide radio are playing stuff from it.' Though Malcolm warned, 'One of the problems with the album is the words. There's a lot of "dirty" words in the songs which they can't play on straight radio ... like on one line there's the word climax ... as in sex. And you can't have a climax on radio ... Wouldn't want to corrupt the kids, you know.' He also admitted that both he and Angus were not always so basic in their musical tastes. 'We were into jazz chords and progressive music ... the real complex time-change things. But that only lasted a year, cos really we grew up on rock'n'roll and we've been progressing through rock'n'roll ever since. It's the way it's played that we're really into. If we don't come off stage really sweating and abso-lutely stuffed we don't reckon it's been worthwhile out there.' Or as Angus put it, 'It's a lot harder to play something simple in a way that hasn't been played before, than it is to play something complex.'

Back on the road AC/DC were now on a roll. Evans may not have been the greatest bass player in the world but he fitted the bill. 'When you've got Malcolm on rhythm guitar and Phil on drums, you really are flying first class. If you can't play bass with these guys, find another fucking job, you know what I mean?' The youngest member of the band, and free from any musical decisions, Mark liked to have fun. Not least with what he calls his 'research assistants': taking his pick from the endless stream of young groupies the band attracted in even greater numbers since 'we'd been on the telly'. Where, though, just a year before that had spelled the death-knell for Colin Burgess and Dave Evans, Malcolm was a lot more secure working with the much younger, inexperienced Evans. 'Malcolm was a tough cookie. By the same token when we were relaxed and away from the band situ-ation, a night off having a few beers, playing darts and playing pool, we'd have a fucking ball, man. We'd be laughing ourselves fucking stupid [and] it would generally be me, Malcolm and Phil out drinking.

Angus wouldn't go out drinking then Bon would be off doing his own thing. We had great times but once it was business that personal side of it may as well have not existed.'

The worst times were always after a bad gig or one that Malcolm had deemed not good enough. 'Malcolm used to have this saying: "We could have been the fucking Beatles tonight and [the audience] still would have been the same." He was always very unexcited about anything. If it was a bad gig absolutely nothing would be said, but nothing would need to be said, because it would be like a refrigerator in the room. Like a fucking big iceberg in there – as quiet as you could possibly imagine. And you'd be going, "Fuck, okay." It would be oppressive, completely oppressive. But then those guys can get something across without saying anything, particularly Malcolm.'

The star of the show for Evans was always Bon. As a frontman, 'He was the gold medallist, man.' Angus may have been the centre of much of the attention, but from Evans's vantage point on the stage, 'Angus was riding shotgun. Angus was [Bon's] little mate onstage – his little partner-in-crime. I think that says a lot about Bon's stage presence and charisma that he was still very much the frontman.' It was the same offstage, he says. '[Bon] was a very warm-hearted guy. Sure, he could get out of control and stuff, but the guy had impeccable manners.' Once the band began to make it though, 'he did feel a very strong responsibility and a *duty* to the image of Bon Scott, which would probably cause him to push the envelope a bit too far on occasion, you know?' Some of that was front – 'When you looked at him, there was this hard-assed rock'n'roller, but inside there was a hippy, let me tell you' – but not all of it. 'He could be a hard-ass when you wound him up! He was a tough guy, I'll tell you. He was a softie at heart, but man, if you rattled his cage, he could fight. He could protect himself and a lot of people around him, oh yeah. Hard guy. Really hard guy when he got going.'

Just before Evans had arrived at Lansdowne Road, George Young had taken the band back into Alberts' Sydney studio to record a new single. It was important to keep up the momentum. As if to cover all angles, it was decided to write a new song – called 'High Voltage', a promotional no-brainer dreamed up by the ever resourceful Chris Gilbey. To add the finishing touch, George decided, it would be built around the chords A, C, D and C. It sounded formulaic and it was. Yet with George on bass and Phil Rudd now providing the metronomic drums, all Angus and Malcolm had to do was vamp it up, Bon layering the cake with typical rock'n'roll rebel icing, railing against anybody unhip enough to ask him about the clothes he wears or why he grows his hair. Short, anthemic, and, in retrospect, more authentically AC/DC-sounding than anything from the album it steals its name from, 'High Voltage' was the first classic single from the band – and their first real hit when it was released in June. The first AC/DC single to get added to all the major radio station playlists, as well as teeing up several more *Countdown* appearances, eventually peaking at No. 6 in the national chart, it also helped drag the album it was named after back up the charts. By the end of that Australian winter, *High Voltage* had topped 150,000 sales. 'For the population,' says manager Michael Browning, 'the album sales were just phenomenal.'

An indication of how far AC/DC had come was their headline appearance at Melbourne's Festival Hall – with Stevie Wright (and another future Vanda and Young protégé, John Paul Young) in support: a complete reversal of their show opening for Wright at the Sydney Opera House exactly 12 months before. This though was another part of Gilbey's marketing strategy. There was no way the band could have filled the venue on their own but with Wright on the bill too it became the biggest concert event in Melbourne that week. Certainly the subsequent film of the show – commissioned by Gilbey initially against the wishes of Ted Albert, who Gilbey says he 'pushed into it' – looks grand and exciting, helped again by some inspired 'editing' by Gilbey, who overdubbed applause lifted from George Harrison's *Concert For Bangladesh* album. 'We also had some guys waving big AC/DC banners that I think Chris paid to be there,' remembers Browning. 'It looked fantastic on video though.' Something that would have unforeseen reverberations when it began to get shown privately in London some weeks later ...

Conscious of the fact that while things in Melbourne had built in a pleasing crescendo for AC/DC, Sydney, conversely, both Alberts' and the Youngs' home, remained tantalisingly out of their reach commercially, George pressed for the band to return to King Street and begin work immediately on another album. The brothers were elated. It meant they could return home to the comforts of family life in Burwood. The rest of the band, led by Bon, who knew all about the pleasures Sydney had to offer, were also keen. With the three of them sharing one large open-plan room at the Squire Inn at Bondi Junction, most nights when they weren't working in the studio would be spent across the road at a club called The Lifesaver. Nicknamed the Wife Swapper, and populated by groupies with attention-grabbing handles like Mandrax Margaret, Amphetamine Annie and Ruby Tuesday (the latter soon to be made famous in an AC/DC song called 'Go Down'), life was an even bigger party than it had been at Lansdowne Road.

A bar-restaurant open each night until 2 a.m., the Wife Swapper became Bon's 'office' throughout July and August. Making himself at home, he quickly hooked up with another teenage girlfriend-cum-fan: 16-year-old Helen Carter, a Bondi beach babe who'd been a regular pub-goer since her early teens, and would later form the post-punk outfit Do-Re-Mi (who hit the Oz charts in 1985 with the single 'Man Overboard'). Sharing Bon's bed at the Squire, though, meant sharing the room with Phil and Mark too. 'Bon had the double bed because he was the oldest,' she would tell Clinton Walker. 'It was almost as if there was an invisible wall.' The Bon Helen recalled was 'meticulous' in his dress sense: basic jeans and T-shirt uniform but always 'perfectly laundered'; the sort of guy who washed his hair every day and styled it with a hairdryer. 'He was very proud of his hair. He wasn't just the archetypal grub rock'n'roller.' Once across the road at the Wife Swapper though, it was a different story. In public, Bon had an image to live up to, though he would always warn Helen in advance not to take his 'antics' there too seriously. 'You'd just be standing there trying to hold a normal conversation, and Bon would turn his back and say, "Don't look." The girl would just lift her dress and they'd start doing it. You'd think it couldn't have been any fun for anybody.'

Some extra tracks had already been begun during the sessions for the 'High Voltage' single: a straight-ahead recording of their live staple, Chuck Berry's 'School Days', and a re-recording of 'Can I Sit Next To You Girl', which lost a comma but gained immeasurably from the extra comic zest Bon's lascivious vocal was able to bring to it. More significantly, they also recorded another new original; a typically bumptious Bon lyric set to a suitably hobnailed blues riff called 'The Jack' – Oz slang for venereal disease; a rowdy call-and-response version of which had already infiltrated their live set.

'The Jack' was destined to become one of the key moments of the AC/DC live set, where it remains to this day; a showpiece routine which their audiences never seem to tire of – despite its plodding musical backdrop and tediously repetitive chorus. And of course it was inspired, as almost always, by true-life events – in this case, when Malcolm received a letter from a now forgotten one-night stand informing him she had VD and so, in all probability, therefore, did he. Giving the note to Bon to gloat over, 'I started playing a blues and we started [singing] together "She's got the jack". We sort of threw it away and didn't worry about it, but then a couple of days later we just had a jam with it with the guys, a slow blues, and Bon started singing it again. [It] just evolved out of that, really.' In fact, having 'the jack' was such a regular occurrence – the product of their habit of 'sharing' their groupies, as much as the 'quality' of the groupies in question, some of whom belonged to a brothel near to Lansdowne Road – Angus would later boast they 'got group rates from the doctor'. Bon said he became so well-known to the doctors and nurses at the 'clap clinic' that while everyone else was called by number, when it came to him 'it was just "Bon"'. The late *Melody Maker* writer, Carol Clerk, who got to know the band when they first came to London, recalled bumping into Angus in a bar once as he announced: 'It's Bon's twenty-first!' Knowing Bon was already closer to thirty, Clerk enquired further. 'It turned out to be [Bon's] twenty-first bout of gonorrhoea.'

Beneath the unbearably blokey exterior of 'The Jack', however, lay growing evidence of Bon Scott's gift as a lyricist. Concerned with what the conservative, family-oriented Ted Albert – who'd already looked the other way once with 'She's Got Balls' – would make of such graphic lines from 'The Jack' as *'She was number nine ninety-nine on the clinical list / And I had to fall in love with that dirty little bitch …'*, when George had a quiet word, asking him to change them, he was amazed and delighted when the singer merely grinned and came back with *'She was holdin' a pair but I had to try / Her deuce was wild but my ace was high …'* By turning the metaphor of 'The Jack' from VD to card game Bon had done something 'so clever', said George – also known for his ability to come up with lines on the spot if an idea wasn't working – he felt he was dealing at last with a singer he could really do business with. So clever, in fact, that while it was the latter idea that made it onto the band's next album, it was the original, 'dirty' lyric that Bon would always sing live.

As a lyric writer Bon had an amazing eye for detail yet wasted no time getting straight to the moral point of the story. He didn't care that it made him look bad sometimes, or even absurd. Life would do that to you too and his songs were all scooped whole straight from real life – often in such high style they rivalled the work of old world European minstrel-storytellers like Jacques Brel. As riff-makers, the Young brothers shared the same minutely telling addiction to detail, but again they didn't want to fuck around, they always got right into it: the smell, the action. The irony is that this intensely populist approach made them outsiders not just to the critics but to the entire rock'n'roll community of the Seventies. Yet because their songs always had humour, had attitude, in their desire to please no one but themselves they ended up appealing to everyman, becoming over time virtually critic-proof. 'He had years of lyrics that his previous bands wouldn't let him use,' Malcolm reflected. 'He could knock up a set of lyrics for a song overnight, with the help of a bottle of Jack Daniels. You'd read 'em and go: "That's fucking eloquent, Bon."' In fact, Bon would often struggle with his lyrics, and become uncomfortable when praised for them. Angus: 'If you asked him about his lyrics, he'd always just say it was toilet poetry. But he was gifted, believe me.'

Recording through the night at Alberts in July, the only other hiccup in the studio – and again it revolved around Bon – concerned what became the opening track, and something of a mission statement for AC/DC, 'It's A Long Way To The Top (If You Wanna Rock'n'Roll)'. The idea came from a line in Bon's notebook that George had picked up on. 'It was just sitting there. He hadn't written any lyric for it, just the title.' Again, the lyrics were diary entries – the no-holds-barred tale of what it actually takes to make it in a band. But set to such a joyously unstoppable come-on-in-the-water's-fine riff that actually getting there sounds like it's worth every rip-off, every disappointment, every broke day and lonely night. When George in a flash of inspiration suggested adding bagpipes to the maelstrom of guitars and drums – egged on by Bon having told him he used to play in a Scottish pipe band, not realising he meant he'd played drums, not the actual bagpipes – the singer, bending over backwards to please, simply grabbed the pipes and began blowing like his life depended on it as Malcolm and Angus looked on in comic disbelief. When, finally, he managed to get a passable drone out of them, George simply recorded the sound and, using the most rudimentary razor-blade-to-tape technique, spliced it all together. 'The whole song was made that way actually,' recalls Mark Evans. 'The riff came from these jams we were doing which Bon put words to and George sort of made something out of.' Released as their next single, the result was their biggest Australian hit yet.

Having to play the pipes live, though, became such torture for Bon it became his least favourite moment in the set. 'He grew to hate them,' says Michael Browning. 'In fact, I'd say having to play them put more pressure on him than anything else at that stage. It became one of those things the crowd always loved, but they were always going out of tune and Bon would be so out of breath from the show they could sound bloody terrible some nights.'

Other things were also starting to get Bon down, sending him into the blackest of moods. 'Having to finish off the lyrics, or write the lyrics, or kind of just having it all together so that it coincided with the conclusion of the recording process. That was a particularly stressful period, I remember, for Bon.' The three Young brothers would work together, the music written and recorded at lightning speed during the first week in the studio. But Bon would be left to come up with the lyrics on his own, expected just to have them all ready by the second week. Says Browning: 'He was a fabulous lyricist but you can't just pour it on and off, can you? He had a notebook thing that he used to put down ideas in it. I think he had concepts and ideas, then if Malcolm would come up with the riff, Bon would go, "Oh, yeah, I've got a song about 'TNT' ..."'

The track 'TNT' – and title of the new album – was built around a chanted chorus inspired, says Mark Evans, by Angus's stock answer to being asked how he was doing. 'Angus had the saying – "I'm TNT, I'm dynamite" – he used to recite that all the time, like a Muhammad Ali float-like-a-butterfly sort of thing. We had a guitar to go with that but once we got in the studio how it ended up was completely different, because George changed it around.' The thuggish riff Angus eventually concocted to go with it, with its baiting 'Oi! Oi! Oi!' opening gambit, anticipating the football-terrace backing vocals of punk by at least a year, conspired to make 'TNT' another that quickly became a live anthem. On the one hand, entirely throwaway – the first line of the second verse was lifted from a TV ad for fly spray – on the other, the product of more astute footwork on the studio floor from George. 'When we were doing the lyrics,' Angus recalled, 'Bon came in and said, "I'm getting stuck with this chorus." I was in the back there, chanting along, and George said, "What are you doing? Why don't you hop out and do what you're doing there? Try it." So it started from that.'

The remaining three tracks that would comprise *TNT* were all written and recorded during these late-night sessions and were all prime-time AC/DC belters. Beginning with 'Rock'n'Roll Singer', which dated back to Dave Evans's time again but now hit new levels of swagger and sweat with Bon's own lyrics and piratical vocals, and a riff so catchy it would later be 'borrowed' by reinvented Brit rockers The Cult for their 1987 hit, 'Wild Flower'. Of the remaining two tracks, the first, 'Live Wire', was a *tour de force* that would open almost every AC/DC show for the next five years; starting with an ominously rumbling bass figure like a distant train approaching at high speed, before erupting into full Bon-as-bad-motherfucker mode. The second track was a fast and furious piece of old-school rock called simply 'Rocker'. Full of semi-ironical references to Cadillacs, teenage dreams, blue suede shoes and tattoos, it's the sound of Fifties-style Jerry Lee Lewis channelled through the cheap stereo speakers of a teenage hoodlum from the Seventies. Less than three minutes long on record, live it would blossom to become a 10-minute Angus show-case, the one where he ran riot through the audience, taking the basic high-speed riff and spinning it like spaghetti into crazy new shapes as the band thundered away behind him.

With the album recorded, mixed and mastered in just two weeks, AC/DC continued on their mission to win over the rest of Australia, beginning with Sydney. A free show at Victoria Park was announced for early September and Chris Gilbey set to work devising a new radio campaign that would really ram home the group's image as credible rockers, as well as *Countdown* regulars. Taking his inspiration from a saying well-known at the time in the UK but less so in Australia – 'Your mother wouldn't like it' (the title of a nightly rock show on London's premier commercial radio channel, Capital, hosted by Nicky Horne) – Gilbey concocted a radio campaign based on vox-pop interviews done with young fans on Bondi beach. When most of them turned out not to have actually heard of AC/DC, he simply asked them to talk about whichever bands they did know and like, then edited down the tapes to make it sound like they were talking about AC/DC. Hence the radio voice asking: 'What do you like about Angus?' The answer: 'I like his legs!' coming from a quote about Sherbet singer Daryl Braithwaite. A further element was added when Gilbey picked up on the deep and sexy voice of a friend's girlfriend, who he told to 'do a stoned rave' as she pretended to be the outraged mother of a kid who wants to go and see AC/DC. 'She did this whole thing about how disgusting and awful AC/DC are – it was perfect!'

Gilbey added one final touch to the ads: the voice of well-known Australian radio announcer Mike Drayson, intoning the line Chris had written for him: 'AC/DC – they're not a nice band.' It worked: the

Victoria Park show was a triumph and the *High Voltage* album headed back up the chart again. Suddenly AC/DC were as big and well-known in Sydney as in Melbourne and, increasingly, everywhere else in Australia. Back in Melbourne, where the band had returned to sign a new five-year management contract with Michael Browning, the band's first major venue headlining tour of Australia was announced for December, in time for the much-hyped pre-Christmas release of the *TNT* album. Longer-term plans were also now afoot to get them over to London for a quick promotional trip. No AC/DC records had yet been issued outside Australia and New Zealand, and the chances of some UK-based record company executive wandering into a show in Sydney or Melbourne were so remote Browning felt sure the best way to make it happen was to put the band where all the top A&R men could see them – under their noses in London.

Meanwhile, with one foot of the band still very much in the pop world of *Countdown*, Browning had booked them into a week-long series of free school holiday lunchtime concerts in the girls' clothing section of the Myer department store in Melbourne. The idea was to ramp up the PR for the band while at the same time reinforcing their teenage fan-base – a no-brainer on paper that backfired spectacularly when thousands of fans tried to get into the first show. With the band literally swept off the tiny in-store stage, they had to stop playing half-way through the second song and make a dash for the safety of the changing rooms. Bon had his jeans partly ripped off and lost both his shoes, while Malcolm was knocked flying and came back with a large cut above his eye. The store, meanwhile, was wrecked, with the cost of the damage – and the many items simply stolen – reckoned to be in the tens of thousands. Pat Pickett, an old larrikin pal of Bon's who had recently talked himself into a job with the band as Bon's 'Percy' – personal roadie – recalls how 'they expected seven or nine hundred kids [but] seven to ten thousand turned up, something ridiculous. It was sort of terrifying.' Even when Pat managed to get Bon out through a back door and onto a passing tram, dozens of girls managed to follow them onto it. 'They [were] tearing us to bits. It was freaky …'

It wasn't just the girls that liked them either. With the band also astutely booked into half a dozen school halls and holiday camps, Angus recalled doing 'a gig for a school of deaf children. They sat at the front of the stage, put their ears to the ground and soaked up the vibration. And they fucking loved it, even the youngest ones.' As Jerry Ewing says, 'I guess it was similar to the way teenyboppers in England were into the Bay City Rollers. Plus it was Australian – no one had any idea that most of them came from Scotland – it was ours.' He was one of many 11-year-olds at his Sydney school now obsessed with AC/DC: 'We all had long hair. We all loved AC/DC. There were kids that didn't, but they were like the outsiders, the nerds. It was like every kid in Australia was into AC/DC.'

To add to the impression, in October the band was invited to perform live at the annual *TV Week* magazine King Of Pop awards, which were televised nationally. Unlike *Countdown*, watched faithfully each week by a loyal audience, the King Of Pop awards show was billed as family viewing, so drawing a much larger, broader-based audience – the first time AC/DC had been seen in this regard. Determined to steal the show, Bon again rose to the occasion, vamping it up in skin-tight white trousers, white drawstring waistcoat opened to the navel, no shirt, and a plum-coloured Teddy Boy drape jacket – all set off nicely by a bright red, outsized bowtie strapped across his bare throat. With Angus in what looked like a freshly laundered blue school uniform and Malcolm still squeezing his little legs into knee-length high-heeled boots, Phil and Mark having trouble keeping the grins off their faces, it became the most talked-about highlight of the show. Keen to leave the right impression on the show's producers, at the after-show dinner that night Bon pulled a large and noisy vibrator from out of his jacket pocket, waving it around in the face of a lady *TV Week* executive. Happy drunk Bon turned into angry drunk Bon, though, later, when he ripped apart dozens of issues of the magazine that had been left in piles for guests to take home with them. He then grabbed a cooked turkey from one of the catering tables and filled its empty carcass to the brim with champagne, and used it as a kind of surreal goblet, taking gulps of champagne between mouthfuls of the bird's meat. All of which he just about got away with; until he swapped the champagne for his own urine then handed it to Daryl Braithwaite, who happened to be passing, inviting him to have a swig – which the Sherbet vocalist duly did. Then spat out onto the floor as Bon looked on and roared with laughter, and the rest of the room pretended not to notice.

Bon was too drunk to realise he'd stopped being funny, but the fact is there was a genuinely antisocial side to AC/DC. As Anthony O'Grady later observed, 'You'd say hi to them and they'd look at you sideways like, "Whaddya saying hi to me for?"' It was also a sign of how out of control Bon's drinking had become again since finding success with AC/DC. Alcohol, it seemed, was something Bon simply could not do without – except on those occasions when he would 'white knuckle it' and go days, sometimes weeks without a drink, before descending into yet more bingeing. Even when he was off the booze he would still start each day by gargling Coonawarra red wine mixed with honey – the secret ingredient to his singing voice, he claimed. But then before a show each night he would also 'gargle' with port, which he said gave his voice its raspy edge. The fact that he didn't always spit out the gargled wine afterwards was neither here nor there. He said.

AC/DC's first nationwide headline tour of major venues kicked off on Tuesday, 4 November, with a sold-out show at the 5,400-capacity Festival Hall in Melbourne. Still playing pubs and clubs, hotels and school halls, practically up to the day the tour started, right from the word go everyone, including Michael Browning and George Young, who'd seen it all before, felt they were now operating on a different level. Nevertheless, as Angus would point out, the size of the crowds may have got bigger but the way they viewed the band hadn't. If anything, he laughed, things had got even more rowdy. 'Dodge a bottle here, dodge a fist there. The only time they'd stop trying to pick a fight with us was when it was hard and fast. Songs could start off slow but they might have to speed up in the middle!' Then there was the perennial problem of returning to places where previously they had laid waste to the town groupies – many of whom now had disgruntled husbands and boyfriends. 'Upsetting the diggers', as Bon put it. Malcolm recalled how at one show in Victoria, 'all the youth of the town were ready to beat the shit out of us!' They got used to running straight off the stage each night and onto the tour bus. 'They'd like a bit of a car chase, and Phil is a maniac behind the wheel so if any shit like that went on, Phil was doing his driving and all sorts of tricks. We used to get out in the bush roads and pull around corners, quickly pull over, all lights out, hide! And we'd watch the guys go screaming past, crank up and go back into town, then get their women ...'

Other times the band came up with more ingenious ways of getting out of trouble. When they played a special New Year's Eve show in Adelaide and there was a power cut halfway through the set, a near riot ensued, with hundreds of angry, drunken punters storming the stage and trying to smash the equipment. Overpowered, the band exited the stage, wondering what to do next. Fortunately, Molly Meldrum was there and it was he who suggested Bon take his bagpipes out into the crowd and try and provide some sort of distraction, until things calmed down again and/or the power was turned back on. The rest of the band, harking to the sound of smashing glass and breaking metal beyond the dressing room door, thought this a very bad idea. But Bon the Likeable decided to give it a go – after all, it was as though Molly had dared him and he wasn't going to back down in front of that cobber. Going out a back door and around to the front of the venue, moments later Bon seemed to appear out of nowhere in the middle of the crowd, perched atop Pat Pickett's muscular shoulders and blowing for all his might on those bloody bagpipes that he hated so much. Remarkably, it worked. The crowd began to listen then laugh at the sight of the shirtless and sweating singer wobbling around making a fearful noise. By the time the chimes of midnight were being called in the power was back on and the band was blasting away like nothing had happened. It was, says Mark Evans, 'a bloody good way to see in the New Year – and very typical of Bon'.

The same month 'It's A Long Way To The Top (If You Wanna Rock'n'Roll)' was released as a single. The band had already performed it twice on *Countdown* before it hit the shops, and by the end of January 1976 it had become the first AC/DC single to reach the Australian Top 5. The real celebrations, though, were kept for the chart performance of the *TNT* album, released in time for the Christmas shopping spree. Just as Chris Gilbey and Michael Browning had anticipated, initial sales were through the roof, the album selling more than 11,000 copies in its first week of release, taking it straight into the charts at No. 2, kept off the top spot only by Bob Dylan's newly released *Desire* album. Within weeks, *TNT* had gone to No. 1 – on its way to becoming the biggest-selling album by a domestic Australian act in 1976. As Harry Vanda later observed, '*TNT* was the one that really pulled the identity; like, this is AC/DC [and] that's who it's going to be and that's how it's going to stay.' The rave review in *Juke* magazine described it as 'an instruction manual for a rock and roll band' and that's exactly what it was. But then the promotional campaign Chris Gilbey had devised for the album was also extremely persuasive, white-label copies of the record being sent out to all the most influential journalists and radio people wrapped in a pair of red ladies' panties with a black-and-white insignia over the crotch that read simply: 'Dynamite'.

The second AC/DC album also helped send their first album back into the charts. Within 12 months, according to Browning, *TNT* had sold 'around 300,000 in Australia'. Added to the approximately 150,000 sales of *High Voltage* and the accumulated sales of their three Top 10 singles, and there were over half a million AC/DC records sold in Australia in the two years since Bon Scott had joined. Yet nobody was getting rich just yet. 'There was a stream of income from record sales,' says Browning, 'but I mean, the groups in those days were on a very small percentage of retail, so it wasn't huge. It wasn't like it is these days.' Indeed, on the band's meagre 3.4 per cent royalty rate, approximately 450,000 total sales at a time when albums retailed for around A$3.50, would have given AC/DC an income of around A$53,550, or very roughly speaking around £34,000. Split five ways, less Michael's 20 per cent management commission and tax, spread over two years, it was clear that Australian success alone was never going to be enough to do more than keep the band going long enough to make another album that was hopefully as successful. Fortunately for them, even as they set out on what they dubbed the Lock Up Your Daughters Summer Vacation Tour of '75–'76, Michael Browning was on the brink of something momentous that would make the achievement of conquering Australia seem simple and meagre by comparison. Something that would mean they could leave Australia behind. The gang had had their fun, taken what they wanted. Time now for them to move on to the next place of rich pickings ...

Phil Carson was a musician whose biggest claim to fame was working on the road in the late Sixties as the bass player for Dusty Springfield. By 1970, however, he'd swapped his guitar for a desk and was fronting the London office of Polar Music, the Swedish record label that was first home to Benny Andersson and Bjorn Ulvaeus – a working relationship that eventually resulted in Abba signing to Atlantic Records for America and Canada. By 1973 Carson had also moved on to become Senior Vice President at Atlantic – appointed when they opened their first London offices in Berners Street, just around the corner from Oxford Circus – and was a major contributor in the early Seventies in the development of its trio of groundbreaking English bands: Led Zeppelin, Yes, and Emerson, Lake & Palmer. Carson had also been responsible for bringing Richard Branson's fledgling Virgin Records label to Atlantic, via a lucrative distribution deal for the US, the first fruits of which was Mike Oldfield's multimillion-selling *Tubular Bells*, one of the classic albums of the period and which also became the soundtrack for one of the most memorable hit Hollywood movies of the era, *The Exorcist*.

In 1976, another British band that Carson was hoping to lead into the big time was Back Street Crawler, the outfit formed around the talented but doomed former Free guitarist Paul Kossoff, who'd been signed personally to Atlantic by its co-founder, Ahmet Ertegun. Naturally keen to try and fulfil his boss's ambitions for the intermittently interesting blues-rock itinerant, Carson had nursed along their debut album, *The Band Plays On*, only to see keyboardist and Kossoff's chief co-songwriter Mike Montgomery throw in the towel after it became clear the guitarist's chronic drug dependency was not going to change any time soon. Thinking on his feet, Carson came up with what on paper appeared to be the ideal solution: the recruitment on keyboards of another prolific songwriter – and former band mate of Kossoff's – named John 'Rabbit' Bundrick. Born in Houston, Texas, the 27-year-old Rabbit had arrived in Britain three years before as a member of American reggae star Johnny Nash's backing band. Offered the chance to play on Bob Marley & The Wailers' debut Island Records album, *Catch A Fire*, Rabbit became such a sought-after presence on the London session scene he found himself recording – and writing six of the ten tracks on – the post-Free album *Kossoff, Kirke, Tetsu And Rabbit* – before being invited to join the re-formed Free with both Kossoff and vocalist Paul Rodgers for what turned out to be their final album together, *Heartbreaker*, in 1973. Since then he had become the go-to keyboardist for artists such as Sandy Denny, John Martyn, Jim Capaldi and Kevin Ayers. At the time Phil Carson decided to seek him out as a possible replacement for Montgomery in Back Street Crawler, Rabbit had just finished playing on the soundtrack album for *The Rocky Horror Picture Show* movie. He was also being managed by the same company that handled Bob Marley, Peter Tosh and Gil Scott-Heron. Also working at the company was a beautiful young Australian go-getter named Coral Browning – Michael's younger sister.

'In those days the British music business was being run by a handful of companies all basically within walking distance of each other in London,' Carson remembers now. 'I remember calling Coral on the phone about Rabbit and her saying she'd swing by my office later that day to talk it over and go through the paperwork. Next thing I know there's the vision of a 23-year-old-ish willowy brunette. We laugh about this now because I still see her from time to time, but I'll never forget it. She's wearing this almost see-through Laura Ashley print dress. I managed to position her between the sunlight and my desk and there I am having a fucking good time, you know. She was pretty good-looking but completely professional ...' A deal was agreed for Rabbit to play on the next Back Street Crawler album, as well as join them for some American dates. 'The whole thing was done in fifteen minutes, but I was in no hurry for her to leave, you know? I'm quite happy to carry on chatting so when she says something about, "I hope you don't mind, but my brother has this group he's managing ..." I don't mind at all! I mean, in the Seventies, who the fuck cared about Australia? But I cared because Coral Brown looked really hot and she was Australian. At that point she could have sold me anything ...'

Phil sat there as this determined young woman gave him her pitch. 'She told me that the band had already sold over 100,000 records back home, which was huge back then for Australia.' His attention finally shifted to what it was she was actually talking about, when Coral pulled out 'this briefcase type thing, inside of which was like a mini-movie projector. I'd never seen anything like it before and suddenly my curiosity was really sparked. She turned it on and there was this film clip of this band playing a gig somewhere and the whole crowd going apeshit, holding up banners and things with the name of the band on it: AC/DC.' The clip came from the promotional film Chris Gilbey had commissioned of the band's Melbourne's Festival Hall show back in June. The briefcase came from Michael Browning's time in London with Billy Thorpe & The Aztecs. 'I'd seen it in a shop window in Melbourne, this little briefcase with a video thing that folded up in a briefcase. I thought to myself, wow, what a great thing to take over to London to show a clip of Billy and The Aztecs. Videos were made in film in those days so we transferred it onto a format that worked in this briefcase and I went over there and it worked really well. Everyone would be amazed that someone would come into their office and pull out this briefcase and show them a music clip.' When Michael left London he gave the case and cine projector to Coral, who had come over with him but now decided to stay on. Later, Browning had sent her the AC/DC tape purely on the off-chance that it might enable his sister 'to rustle up a few gigs in London whenever we finally got there'. Which is what Coral had been trying to do when she received the phone call from Phil Carson enquiring about Rabbit.

'She told me she was putting together an itinerary for them based on whatever pub and club gigs she could cobble together – hoping to get the band a record deal on the basis of dragging some A&R men down to them.' Carson, however, had other ideas. 'I think I watched less than two minutes of [the film clip] then told her to turn it off. Coral looked at me, like, "But you've hardly seen anything yet. Don't you like it?" I said, "I've seen enough. Let's make a deal. Get your brother on the phone ..."' It was nearly three o'clock in the morning in Melbourne but Michael Browning was used to getting phone calls in the middle of the night. According to Carson, he and Browning agreed a deal for AC/DC then and there for 15 albums at $25,000 per album in advance. 'One album firm, with options for two more albums a year and then more yearly options, adding up to fifteen albums, and a $25,000 advance with everything recoupable. Plus the record label – Alberts – at their expense had to send them to England. I told them to forget about bringing them in for a few club shows on their own, that I would put them on the next Back Street Crawler tour – much higher profile. Michael got it. He realised that for this unknown band from this country that nobody cares about to be signed to Atlantic Records and be guaranteed what ought to be a pretty decent tour of England, as against just coming over and hoping you're gonna get signed, really was a big opportunity.'

Michael Browning, however, has a somewhat different recollection. 'I knew it was our big chance to get the band out of Australia but didn't really do the deal until I flew over to London the following week. And I think fifteen albums is a bit exaggerated. I think it was probably for five albums. And I seem to recall the advances were $35,000, rising gradually for delivery of each of those albums.' Carson says he recalls the deal coming with a royalty of 12 per cent. This Browning does not dispute. 'The twelve per cent would have been what we used to call in Australia a third-party deal. The deal was between Atlantic and Alberts, it wasn't between the group and Atlantic. All of the royalties and advances went directly back to Alberts and there would have been a split between the group and Alberts – from memory, a fifty-fifty split on international income.' In short, the band would end up with approximately 6 per cent of Atlantic-generated revenue.

Out of that, says Browning, the band's 50 per cent share of the 12 per cent from international income would be set against un-recouped advances before they were paid out. 'They would have to recoup the advances that were paid to sustain the living expenses of the group when we first went over there [to London] and subsequent tour supports. I virtually didn't get anything out of it. To be honest, I just went and did the deal because I wanted to. And I think they paid my airfare to go over and tour. I think that was about all I got out of it.'

Atlantic coming in when it did was a big lifeline though, he says, 'because even though the record sales were good in Australia, no one was really that excited. It was always the challenge of doing it outside of Australia. It was just a given that you were gonna sell a lot of records here, given that whole teenybopper thing. I mean, it was good and everyone was happy. But it wasn't really what it was all about [for AC/DC]. The Atlantic thing, although financially it wasn't a huge deal, in terms of advances and that type of thing – it *was* a huge thing that we had the opportunity and the vehicle to do what we wanted to do, which was to make it internationally.'

Money-wise, AC/DC were able to take the Carson deal because they had that cushion of money already from their Australian success. They weren't rich but they weren't begging. 'The advances overseas weren't as crucial as they would have been for someone starting from scratch in England or America. Basically, what I did was go to Ted Albert and say, "Whatever the advance I end up negotiating, I want you to put that back into providing a source of revenue for the group to go over there, live there for a while and gig, do whatever." Which he agreed to, and allowed us to go over there and do what we initially did.'

For Phil Carson, the motivation was simple. 'I thought, nobody can say I've done a bad deal whatever happens, because I actually think they can sell a few records, by the way.' There was just one hitch. Jerry Greenburg in New York was the President of Atlantic. And while Phil ran Atlantic everywhere outside America, it was Greenberg to whom he had to report. Phil had never done a deal without first running it by Jerry. But Jerry was on vacation and Coral was very persuasive in her thin floral-print dress, so Phil just went ahead. He would deal with Jerry in his own time. He also had what he felt was one other important card up his sleeve. As he says, by 1976 'my position at Atlantic Records was totally fireproof. I was the go-to guy for Led Zeppelin. I was one of the only people [fearsome Zep manager] Peter Grant would talk to.' He had also engineered the deal that brought Mike Oldfield's *Tubular Bells* to Atlantic in America. Yet Carson's bravado would have both short- and long-term consequences for AC/DC's prospects outside Australia that neither he nor they could have anticipated. 'I told Coral to send me over both their albums and that I would take them home that night and listen to them,' he smiles. 'As far as I was concerned, the deal was done.'

Done perhaps but not quite dusted. And nor would it be – certainly not in America – for some years to come. Not that anyone, not even Phil Carson, was thinking that far ahead yet. No one, that is, except the brothers.

CHAPTER EIGHT

All in the Name of Liberty

The start of 1976 found AC/DC both on the road and in the studio. With the Lock Up Your Daughters summer tour in full swing and both the *TNT* album and 'Long Way To The Top' single still hogging the charts, but with the newly added promise of their first overseas trip now being lined up for April, it was important they get enough new material in the can to keep their profile at home high during the weeks and – they hoped – months they would be away. The problem was they didn't have any new material. They had gone into Alberts at the end of December to record a new single, 'Jailbreak' – during which a paralytic Bon passed out halfway through recording his vocal. A vamp cooked up between Malcolm and Angus at a soundcheck one day based on Them's 'Gloria' – an old Bon favourite from Valentines days – it would now be added to a new collection of songs they hurriedly threw together with George and Harry at King Street, between tour shows.

No wonder then that the results were patchy. With the studio clock running faster than ever, quality control came a poor second to simply laying down some stuff and quick. Nevertheless there were some gems lurking in the debris. Top of the heap was the song that became the title track of the album, 'Dirty Deeds Done Dirt Cheap' – a reconditioned 'TNT', replete with football terrace chanting, that name-checks both their previous albums among the dirty deeds the protagonist promises to do dirt cheap, but ramped up several notches as the band that had been playing together for nearly a year now turns an average rock'n'roll ditty into a powerhouse.

There was also 'Problem Child', with lyrics harking back to Bon's prison days and another signature Young brothers riff straight from the back of the bone yard. And this album's 'The Jack', another self-consciously crowd-pleasing nudge-and-a-wink anthem called 'Big Balls', delivered in a faux English toff's accent, the band prancing along behind like a circus pony. Plus a handful of the kind of lowbrow rockers AC/DC could now churn out in their sleep: not least, 'There's Gonna Be Some Rockin'', which sounds good enough to have been a highlight of their live shows but on record barely stands repeat listens; 'Squealer', its chief feature being how easily the band could turn what the desultory lyrics seem to imply is a love song into something fiendishly juvenile – fun as long as you didn't pay too much attention; worst of all though the dreadfully titled 'RIP (Rock In Peace)', so hackneyed it made 'Can I Sit Next To You Girl' sound inspired.

Balanced against these, however, were further highlights like 'Ain't No Fun Waiting Round To Be A Millionaire' – the title taken from a postcard home Bon had written while on tour. When Bon begins by intoning, 'The following is a true story' in which only the names have been changed 'to protect the guilty', he means it. The band, of course, make the whole thing sound like excellent fun, starting off at half-speed before switching gears to bring the number to a rowdy finish. The finished 'Jailbreak' track, which, though entirely derivative – Bon screaming camply for his liberty – was simply too catchy to shake off, was another highlight of the original Australian album. Best of all, though, was the surprisingly tender blues, 'Ride On', with its plaintive lines about empty bottles and empty beds completing the picture of the singer as his own empty vessel. This was Bon Scott baring his soul for once without any spin or knowing asides. That rare to the point of otherwise non-existent thing, a beautiful AC/DC ballad, 'Ride On' alone was enough to elevate *Dirty Deeds Done Dirt Cheap* to a level above its predecessors. Had they not been in such a hurry to finish it they might have bolstered it further by the inclusion of another track recorded during these sessions: 'Backseat Confidential', an unfinished track that would eventually resurface in superior form three years later as 'Beating Around The Bush'. Instead, when they released 'Jailbreak' as a single in Australia in June that year the B-side was the frankly tedious instrumental version of the traditional Scottish air 'Bonnie Banks Of Loch Lomond': two minutes of grinding guitars and boorish background noises they titled 'Fling Thing'.

Once again, George Young played a prominent role in the production and arrangements, signing off on all the melodies and lyrics. 'Whenever we're stuck [George] will give us a hand,' Bon told *RAM*. 'But we write our songs, play our own material. It's not a case of George pushing the band to where they couldn't get by themselves.' But, of course, that's exactly what it was. Except this time, with one eye now on London and cementing the new Atlantic deal, the pushing had been so hard the album was nearly derailed. According to Malcolm, 'The way we've always worked, especially on the early albums, was to write songs to fill the live set – not the album. If we knew we needed four or five fast songs to please the punters, we wrote them for the stage, not to put onto the next record.' Maybe so, but there's a thin line between capturing the exuberance of a live show on record and merely filling up tape so you can get back on the bus to the next show; one that *Dirty Deeds* weaved across like a drunk trying to navigate a busy road.

Back in Melbourne in February, they filmed a special performance of 'It's A Long Way To The Top' for *Countdown*, which featured the band miming on the back of a flatbed truck slowly cruising up and down Swanston Street in the heart of the city's business district. Malcolm would claim that he'd had the idea years before, but it was no coincidence that the Rolling Stones had launched their US tour the previous summer by playing 'Brown Sugar' on the back of a flatbed truck along New York's Fifth Avenue. Filmed early one Monday morning, as people made their way to work, the appearance of AC/DC, along with three extras dressed as Scottish pipers, hardly caused the kind of stir the Stones' traffic-stopping live performance had nine months before, but when the clip was shown on *Countdown* the following Sunday it once again stole the show. The following day

Alberts released the new AC/DC single, the album title track, 'TNT', backed with 'Rocker', another Top 5 hit that prompted what would be the band's last live in-studio *Countdown* performance for some time. Though they would be back by year's end for one final live *Countdown* performance with Bon, AC/DC was about to bid farewell to Australia, if not quite for ever, then for as long as they could. As former Guns N' Roses manager Alan Niven – a New Zealand-born former musician and writer well-versed in the Australian music scene – says: 'The greatest achievement of any Australian rock group has always been this: to get the fuck out!' That now became the overriding priority of AC/DC. As Angus would brag in *Record Mirror & Disc* in his first interview with the English music press, 'Success [in Australia] means nothing. We left on a peak rather than overstaying our welcome, and set out to plunder and pillage.'

'It was certainly our main goal and had been really from day one, I suppose,' says Michael Browning. 'Once we had the Atlantic deal it was just a case of tying up loose ends and getting on the plane.' Those 'loose ends' included a trip back to Sydney where they all checked into the five-star Sebel Townhouse hotel in Elizabeth Bay. It was here that Bon received his first royalty cheque for $500. The brothers also received cheques but theirs were for greater amounts, having written more songs, though they made a point of not discussing exactly how much more in front of Bon. Not that he appeared to care. Armed with his dollars and his all-expenses-paid hotel room, he spent the next couple of weeks chilling out between ad hoc late-night recording sessions for the new album, grooving along to a cassette of Donna Summer's 'Love To Love You Baby', a massive summertime hit in Australia that year and Bon's current favourite song.

The final *Dirty Deeds* sessions were completed the first week of March, at which point the party transferred back to Melbourne – literally in this case, as Michael Browning threw a champagne reception which served as a farewell party before the trip to London, and an appropriate setting to formally present AC/DC with their first gold records: three each for *High Voltage* and *TNT*. Bon was in his element, loudly cracking jokes, telling filthy stories, promising to give his gold records to his mum back in Fremantle. As he wrote to Irene: 'I told her to make a space on her mantelpiece. She told me to write some clean songs for the next one.' The brothers, though, were having a less fun time of it. They had been told that the writer Al Webb from *Juke* magazine was also expected at the party – currently number one on their shitlist for various disparaging comments he had made about the group in print; Malcolm and George spent half the night asking likely-looking suspects, 'Are you from *Juke*? Are you Al Webb?' But Webb wasn't there. Instead, *Juke* was represented that night by another writer, Frank Peters, who the increasingly worse-for-wear Young brothers convinced themselves was really Webb. Suitably fired up, Malcolm eventually marched over and grabbed Peters by the shirt and told him how 'fucking lucky' he was that he wasn't Webb. A shaken Peters left soon after. A week later *Juke* responded with a cover headline: 'AC/DC ATTACKS JUKE!', followed by a two-page spread inside, by Peters, detailing the incident.

Bon, meanwhile, was on the end of his own media scrimmage the same month when the Australian edition of *Rolling Stone* ran its first major AC/DC feature. The story opened with the image of the singer vomiting backstage after a show, due, he insisted, to a 'bad bottle of Scotch'. Anthony O'Grady, who was at the same February show in Sydney, recorded the scene in *RAM*, writing how Bon 'sometimes gets the same look that battle-scarred alley fighters have – a look of indifferent bloodlust. Kick 'em in the teeth and they'll just spit blood and get up again.' Off the record, O'Grady recalled how later that same night, back at the Young family home in Burwood, he and Bon were asked to wait outside in the car so that Malcolm, Angus and George could 'talk business'. Bon, clearly used to this sort of thing, meekly complied, before passing out in the back seat next to the bemused *RAM* writer.

Throughout these final few weeks, Browning kept the band working, gigging in Melbourne and Sydney and all points between. He also got them to film another promotional clip for *Countdown* for the forthcoming 'Jailbreak' single, not for release until June, by which time the band would be in London – 'like going to the moon in those days', as Mark Evans puts it. Shot at a remote quarry near Sunshine in western Melbourne, it was a rudimentary video typical of the times in its attempt to capture the narrative of the song – bad boy escapes the clanger only to be shot in the back by no-good cops, with Bon in the pivotal role, replete with pouches of fake blood timed to explode tied to his undershirt and little firecrackers positioned strategically among the rocks to simulate the effect of ricocheting bullets; Malcolm in comedy police helmet and toy gun. Browning also organised a photo shoot at Melbourne Gaol, where notorious Australian bushranger Ned Kelly was hanged in 1880. 'We had to put our necks through the noose on the gallows,' Malcolm later recalled. 'We thought, "Fucking hell, what if the fucking door drops?"'

There was one final 'farewell' Saturday night show at the old Bondi Wife Swapper, on 27 March, where Billy Thorpe got up to jam with them on the encore number, 'Baby, Please Don't Go', and during which Angus did something for the first time that was to become another trademark move of his at all future AC/DC shows: he dropped his shorts and mooned the crowd. He also used the long bar as his personal catwalk, running the length of it while still playing before coming to a stop with a knee-slide that sent glasses flying left and right. The following Wednesday – the night before they were due to fly out from Sydney Airport – there was one last party, this time at the Young family home in Burwood. It was Angus's 21st birthday and while everybody toasted him with beer, wine and whisky, Angus contented himself with an extra large helping of spaghetti bolognese – his favourite, straight from the can – and several tall chocolate milkshakes.

The following morning, after a very late breakfast, the band and their two most reliable roadies, Ralph and Herc, set off together for the airport. Just as Mark Evans had been promised exactly a year before, AC/DC would be in England. Most excited though was Bon Scott. The last time he'd made this journey it had been in the opposite direction, fleeing London and Fraternity and returning to an uncertain future as a broke and all but forgotten has-been. He had never stopped dreaming he might make a comeback some day but deep down inside he'd never really considered it possible. Now, fronting this band of young tearaways that he never really thought had much of a chance, his life had been turned around. Barely more than a year before he'd been a broken-down figure with a limp, happy to scrape the underside of boats and drive proper musicians around in someone else's borrowed car. Now here he was heading straight for the top of the mountain.

To mark the occasion, Bon got a new tattoo, his first for five years: a lion and a thistle, echoing the Scottish royal coat of arms, which he hoped would act as an amulet against ill-fortune. Unlike the Young brothers, who'd always had this next move down in their own minds as part of the bigger plan – more even than Phil or Mark, who as non-contributors to the writing side of things had always held out hope that sooner or later they would tether their wagons to a group of winners – Bon Scott really could not believe his luck.

He was right not to.

AC/DC flew out of Sydney on April Fool's Day, 1976. Nearly 37 hours later, after stopovers in Singapore, Hong Kong, Bombay and Bahrain, they landed at London's Heathrow Airport, where rush-hour traffic was starting to build on the long drive home for the weekend. It was a typically grey English spring afternoon, clouds like blanket covers. Despite the ravages of the long journey – 'I had time for two hangovers on the way,' wrote Mark Evans in his memoir – they were thrilled to be met at the airport by Michael and Coral Browning, and a long black limousine hired for the occasion by Atlantic Records. A house had been rented for them all to share at 49 Inverness Terrace, in Bayswater – a large terraced house that had been sequestered into different small apartments, where the five band members plus two roadies would live for the next eight months. It was crowded but 'like the Taj Mahal', says Evans, compared to Lansdowne Road. As usual, the brothers roomed together, as did Phil and Mark, while Bon was allowed his own small rooms at the very top of the house. First though they ordered the limo to give them a tour of the London sights, driving past Buckingham Palace, Trafalgar Square, Piccadilly Circus ... Malcolm remained typically underwhelmed, almost sneering, while Angus merely stared out the window and blew smoke against the glass. The others though gawped in genuine awe. 'Like looking at a Monopoly board' is how Evans remembers it.

The first AC/DC single on Atlantic – 'It's A Long Way To The Top' (backed with 'Can I Sit Next To You Girl) – was released the same day. Radio Luxembourg, then still an influential station despite its famously unreliable medium-wave signal, made it their 'hit pick of the week' and the band spent their first few days in their new lodgings trying to tune the station in on their newly bought transistor radios. 'It was good but not that good,' recalls Michael Browning, 'because you'd hear the record come on then halfway through you'd lose signal and it would vanish.' Used to hearing their music on Australian radio, the novelty quickly wore off. 'It was actually frustrating.'

More frustrating though was the sudden cancellation of a string of club dates they had been expecting to go out on in support of The Kids – formerly the Heavy Metal Kids. With their raucous street urchin charm and anthemic fist-in-the-air numbers like 'Rock'n'Roll Man' and 'The Cops Are Coming', The Kids would have made ideal touring partners for AC/DC at that stage. But the group, who'd recently been dropped by Atlantic, had subsequently fallen out with their talented but by then drug-addled singer, Gary Holton, leaving them in complete disarray. It was a setback but one the brothers could shake off, safe in the knowledge that they had the start of the Back Street Crawler tour – a much bigger deal – to look forward to at the end of the month. Again, though, their plans were thwarted when the band delayed the tour a fortnight, with just nine of its original thirty dates surviving the revised schedule. Their guitarist and founder, Paul Kossoff, in whom Atlantic's charismatic co-owner, Ahmet Ertegun, had shown such faith, had also become a victim of his out-of-control drug habits, suffering a fatal heart attack on a flight from Los Angeles to London two weeks before AC/DC arrived in London. Back Street

Crawler were a far more earnest proposition musically than The Kids, but in Terry Slesser they again had a frontman whose gravelly vocals and hard-man onstage image would have made a fine complement to Bon's own tough-guy persona, their signature song, 'It's A Long Way Down To The Top', providing a more considered side of Bon's similarly titled tale. But the band, though intent on continuing with a new guitarist, Geoff Whitehorn, had not had time to bed in yet. Kossoff was just 25 when he died. Rather than share the shock and sadness of his death though, both Bon and the brothers were mightily pissed off. 'That cunt Paul Kossoff fucked up our first tour,' the singer complained glibly in *RAM*.

Bon, however, had more to worry about than some cancelled shows. Visiting an old haunt from his Fraternity days, he walked into the same Finchley pub he'd worked in – and straight into trouble. Before he'd even reached the bar, he later recalled, he was smashed in the face by a pint glass – the old-fashioned panelled mugs with heavy handles – and knocked unconscious. When he came to he was in hospital – again. This time he'd dislocated his jaw and broken his cheekbone. The injury was so serious doctors were forced to make an incision at his hairline and insert a surgical tool to enable them to piece his shattered cheek back together. His face was covered in stitches and big yellow-blue bruises, both his eyes blackened. When pressed by police for his version of events Bon claimed to have no recollection of what had happened, just that a brawl was in full swing when he walked in. As he later wrote to Pat Pickett, 'It wasn't even my fight. I didn't see what hit me.' Behind the shrugging, nonchalant exterior though, Bon was badly shaken, convinced it was his 'bad karma' catching up with him – equally sure there would be more hell to pay later. He spent the next few days laid up in his bed at Inverness Terrace, while Coral fussed over him, feeding him soup and comics – he was currently into *Conan The Barbarian* – which he read propped up on one elbow, chain-smoking spliffs. On his next public appearance with the band – for a photo shoot, ironically outside a pub – he wore sunglasses to hide his face.

Atlantic, meanwhile, had rented AC/DC a rehearsal space to keep them busy – feel like they weren't completely wasting their time. But the band never rehearsed. The first time they went they ran through a few Elvis and Chuck Berry songs then slouched home again. They never went back. Instead, Angus shut himself away in his room, sitting on his bed playing the guitar, the TV blinking silently at him. The only time he got up was to fetch more tea and cigarettes. Not being a drinker or dope smoker left him pretty much confined to his own company. Malcolm, who was a drinker and smoker, at least went out for some fresh air occasionally, playing a round of pitch-and-putt golf in Hyde Park with Michael Browning. Lunchtimes, Mark and Phil could often be found in the Ducks And Drakes pub, where they discovered the quintessentially English delights of shepherd's pie and warm summer ale. The only one who had no fixed routine was Bon, who Browning later described as 'decadent, sex-crazed' but also 'more intellectual, more poetic, more sophisticated in his tastes' than the others. Bon, Michael added, 'was the kind of bloke who would have known a good wine'.

With everyone antsy about not playing, and the bills mounting up – Browning had budgeted the weekly upkeep of the band at £600; based on £50 per week wages for each member; £50 per week rent; and roughly £300 a month for food, transport and all other expenses – Michael pulled a rabbit out of the hat by persuading Richard Griffiths, then head of a small but powerfully motivated London booking agency called Headline Artists, to get involved. Griffiths, who looked after John Martyn (another untameable kindred spirit from Glasgow) and Eddie and the Hot Rods (who would become unwitting rivals to AC/DC in Britain that year), impressed the brothers immediately by organising their first official British show – a free, two-set gig on 23 April, at the Red Cow in Hammersmith. A pub with a rectangular live room at the back, the Red Cow was a small but significant presence on the lively London club scene, and despite Griffiths's best efforts would only offer the band a Monday evening slot – the slowest night of the week. They took it.

For the band this was a throwback to their earliest days at Chequers, when no one knew or cared who they were. At least Chequers always drew its own crowd, though. When the band strolled onto the tiny Red Cow stage for their first of two 45-minute sets, the 'crowd' was barely large enough to make the bar opposite the stage look busy. Playing essentially the same set as they had been doing for months now in Australia – except shorn of covers bar the proven-winner encore, 'Baby, Please Don't Go', which was considered obscure enough to be cool even in critic-conscious London – road-hardened by the 238 shows they had already played in the preceding 365 days, bristling with the added confidence of having two chart albums in that same period, and so bored by their limited London experience thus far, they ignored the deficit of audience members and simply went for it with even more abandon than had become their stock-in-trade; Bon eye-balling the crowd and addressing his songs to each one personally; Angus leaping off the stage into the unexpectedly ample space and running with his guitar like a soldier strafing the enemy; the rest of the band simply closing their eyes and pounding away with barely a break between numbers.

Malcolm Dome, now one of Britain's best-known rock writers and broadcasters, but then simply a diehard rock fan who'd picked up on the fact that a new band from Australia, said to be quite good, were playing a free show that Monday night not far from where he then lived, was one of the few faces in the Red Cow that night. He remembers being 'astonished at how good they were. Because it was their first gig here and at the Red Cow, I think we expected to see a new band. Instead we saw this absolute powerhouse, but so close-up in this virtually empty room it was amazing.' During the break between sets, he says, 'they were just hanging around and so I got chatting to them. Bon was being the *bon-viveur* and just spoke to everybody. He was talking about being over from Australia, and how the thing he was trying to get across to the others was that they had to start again. He said, "We're no one here but that's the great challenge. If we can make it here that's what's really going to establish the band."' By the time they started the second set, says Dome, 'the place was packed! It was unreal. There had been about twelve people there for the first. Whether they all went out and rang their friends, I don't know, but somehow word must have got out because it was absolutely rammed for the second.'

For Malcolm Dome, 'It was the start of me bumping into Bon Scott quite a lot at places like the Marquee and the Music Machine, partly to promote the band and partly because he always loved hanging out. He was a great character who liked to enjoy himself; someone with a great deal of charisma and personality and … life. There was always so much life about Bon.' He adds: 'I got to know Malcolm and Angus a little better later on from seeing them around at gigs but they were never what you call friendly people. They were always really wary, as if they were thinking, "If we get to know someone too well they're gonna stitch us up in the end", which was always a bit of a weird thing but that's the way they were.'

Dome goes on. 'Mark Evans you would see around occasionally. Phil Rudd was a boozer, enjoyed a good drink. Not much of a chatter, though. A drummer, if you want. Not surly, but someone who always made it very difficult for you to get to know him – he liked to choose who he'd hang out with. And that's the other thing about AC/DC. They weren't a gang, in the same way, for example, that Guns N' Roses were when they first came to London. They were five men against the world and united by that. AC/DC never really were. They were Angus and Malcolm, then Bon, and then the rhythm section. They weren't really united, even though they shared the same house. They weren't like "we are best mates". They didn't have that.' Mark Evans agrees. 'Nobody was in AC/DC because they were friends. You were just in it for the good of the band.'

Also at the Red Cow that night was a familiar face from Sydney: Buzz Bidstrup, who'd left Oz to 'go travelling' a year before and now found himself in London, where he'd been amazed to learn his old mate from Fraternity was now fronting AC/DC. 'I'd seen the band with Dave Evans and of course I knew Bon as this hippy guy, and I couldn't quite put the two together in my mind. But that night at the Red Cow there weren't many there but it was electric. I was living in West Kensington as a lot of Aussies did, so we turned up and after the show, Bon asked the inevitable question: 'Do you know where I can get some pot? I've got a bottle of whisky. Where are you living?' And so he turned up at our place and we smoked a lot of hash and drank some whisky and razzed around a bit. He was saying AC/DC were doing great stuff and it was all kind of go. Everything was happening.'

Three nights later they performed at the Nashville Rooms in West Kensington, where they were billed as an 'Antipodean Punk Extravaganza' – a tongue-in-cheek description of John Peel's. Ahead of the curve as always, Peel had been playing tracks from both the original Australian *High Voltage* and *TNT* albums on his Radio One show for several weeks already, coupling the name AC/DC with those of other, as he saw it, emerging new-style rock acts from abroad like the Ramones and The Dictators, and closer to home Eddie and the Hot Rods and Doctor Feelgood. You could see his point. Alongside Dave Evans, Angus-as-schoolboy had seemed incongruous, perverse; a freak. Scurrying around Bon onstage, however, with his short hair, tattoos and gap-toothed grin, Angus looked like part of a new dynamic: one that subverted the singer-guitarist paradigm as defined by Jagger–Richards. So while the music sounded trad to sophisticated London ears, what came across via rough, tough-guy Bon's anti-pseud lyrics and the spectacle of the idiot-savant lead guitarist cavorting purposely was a whole new take on rock, not dissimilar to the effect the punks would go out of their way to contrive: and one very much in keeping with the much more knowing post-Altamont atmosphere of the times. None of which meant diddly, as yet, to Bon or Angus, much less to Malcolm; if anything, being mistakenly called 'punk' was seen as an insult by AC/DC, who could not foresee the transformation the new scene would have on the musical and cultural landscapes of Britain and then the world. For now, the Sex Pistols – who had played second on the bill to future Clash frontman Joe Strummer's pub rock outfit, The 101ers, at the Nashville three nights before AC/DC headlined it for the first time – weren't even on their radar.

On Monday, 30 April, Atlantic finally released their first AC/DC album in Britain. Titled *High Voltage*, it was in fact an amalgam of the best from their two Australian albums, track selection personally supervised by Phil Carson. 'After I agreed the deal with Michael, Coral gave me their first two albums and I took them home that night and sat there with a bottle of wine and listened to them. It was obvious that most of the best stuff was on *TNT*.' In fact, only two of its nine tracks came from the original *High Voltage*: 'Little Lover' and 'She's Got Balls'. Carson chose those, he says, 'because they made a nice contrast to the other tracks. The best of the rest were all on *TNT*.' Indeed, the only tracks not taken from *TNT* were 'Rocker' – which would find a home later in the year on the international version of *Dirty Deeds Done Dirt Cheap* – and Berry's 'School Days'. 'They didn't need a cover on their first album here,' judges Carson. 'We needed to show they were more than just a great live band, that they could write their own material and that it was of a sufficiently high standard.'

Reviews were mixed, with the *New Musical Express*, then the biggest-selling weekly music paper in Britain, not even deigning to review the album, deeming it an irrelevance in the context of what else was going on musically that summer, from the Ramones arriving for their first UK shows in July to the return of the Stones for a string of high-profile dates in London in May. (The latter attended by AC/DC. 'They were terrible,' concluded Angus. 'We would have blown them off the fucking stage.') The *NME*'s main rival, the *Melody Maker*, did review *High Voltage*, but their writer Mike Oldfield concluded it amounted to little more than 'the same old boogie', even if the lyrics had 'a brash-ness and lack of sophistication that's always useful in the heavy brand of rock'. The old-fashioned fan mag *Record Mirror* suggested chirp-ily: 'These Aussie youngsters boogie ... with bagpipes!' But no one in the rock intelligentsia read the poptastic *Mirror* anyway. The only one of the serious music papers to get behind AC/DC from the start was *Sounds*, with its regular John Peel column and more populist approach. Their writer, Geoff Barton, trumpeted it as 'a tonic in the midst of the all-too serious, poker-faced groups of today'.

As Malcolm Dome says now: 'What did we really know about Australia, musically, in those days: Rolf Harris and Frank Ifield? There was nothing rock that had come out of there to make anybody go, wow, that's really good. So AC/DC were really something quite new. And you could tell Malcolm and Angus were still wet behind the ears in this new environment whereas Bon was instantly at home. Onstage the brothers betrayed none of this nervousness but offstage they were very nervous about being outside their comfort zone, and having to start all over again. But you have to give them credit for taking the risk. They could have stayed in Australia and made a good living but they decided, no, we're better than this and we want more. So they took the risk and came to London.'

By the end of May they were now able to charge for their shows: £1 to see them headline the Nashville on 31 May, supported by Johnny Thunder's Heartbreakers. Three days later they recorded their first session for John Peel's Radio 1 evening show – an exhilaratingly speedy run through 'Live Wire', 'High Voltage', 'Can I Sit Next To You Girl' and 'Little Lover', which was broadcast on 21 June – and the following day they headlined their first show at the Marquee: entrance, 70p. Ian Jeffery, who'd recently begun working for the band as their sound engineer and tour manager, recalls standing outside small venues like the Greyhound in Fulham Palace Road, 'saying to passers-by, "Come here. There's a great band on. Come on, you'll have a great time", virtually dragging people in off the street.' They had also finally begun doing their tour with Back Street Crawler – 'Back Scratcher', as the band insisted on calling them – pulling the rug from beneath the unsteady feet of the headliners almost every night. 'We could ambush bands,' says Mark Evans. 'People would come to the gigs and say, "Jeez, mate, this is a brand-new band but they sound like they've done five hundred gigs." They didn't know we had!'

Playing Birmingham's Barbarella's club on 29 May, Crawler vocalist Terry Slesser remembers giving Angus their £50 fee upfront 'so they could get a curry. I always said if I ever headlined I would give the support act every consideration: full PA, full lights, etc. My manager said, "Sless, while that is very admirable, I've *seen* AC/DC. They really rock and may blow you off the stage." I said, "No matter", and of course, AC/DC really did rock.' Blown off every single night, true to his promise Slesser remained matey with the newcomers. He could not have imagined though under what strange circumstances he would become briefly reacquainted with them again just a few years later.

Things really kicked into high gear in Britain for AC/DC with the advent of the Lock Up Your Daughters summer tour – title borrowed wholesale from their Australian summer tour of six months before: 19 dates at various Top Ranks and Civic Halls that began in Glasgow on Friday, 11 June, and culminated at the Lyceum Ballroom in London on Wednesday, 7 July. Sponsored by *Sounds*, this was a pivotal moment in the band's attempt to break through in Britain. The day after the tour began *Sounds* ran its first AC/DC cover story, replete with a picture of Angus looking his most demented on the front, and the headline: 'Would you give a job to this school leaver?' The story, by Phil Sutcliffe, served as a glorified advert for the tour, which *Sounds* readers were able to buy specially priced tickets for at 50p, on presentation of a cut-out coupon from the mag. The brainchild of Phil Carson – determined to make up for any lost face in the wake of the Back Street Crawler false start, and at the same time tighten the bond between the band and the only music weekly in the country that had seriously come out in AC/DC's favour – this would be more than just a regular AC/DC concert. For their 50p, ticket-holders would enjoy a whole evening's worth of entertainment, including films of live performances from other Atlantic-affiliated artists, including Black Oak Arkansas and the Rolling Stones. Each night the first 50 fans through the doors would also be given a free copy of the new AC/DC single – the non-*High Voltage* track, 'Jailbreak', already another Top 5 hit for them in Australia but not due for release in Britain until the end of July. Fans were also encouraged to come along dressed as schoolboys and schoolgirls. And instead of a support act, there was also a local DJ spinning records each night.

'Between the movies and AC/DC coming on we'd also have competitions for the best-dressed schoolboy and girl,' recalls Ian Jeffery. 'The audiences would be the judge. You can imagine in all those places, the guys would come on and it'd be: "Fuck off! Get off!" Then when the girls dressed in school uniforms came on and it was all, "Get 'em off!"' The winners at each event were invited down to London, all expenses paid, for the 'final', when John Peel would be the DJ and judge. 'It was fucking hilarious!' laughs Jeffery. The boys and girls were split into two categories: 'best-dressed school-boy' and 'schoolgirl we'd most like to'. Prizes consisted of various Atlantic albums, including signed copies of *High Voltage*, plus pairs of jeans and, for the overall winner, an acoustic Epiphone Caballero folk guitar; an incongruous gift in the setting of an AC/DC competi-tion but the best they had been able to rustle up for free from one of the guitar shops in nearby Denmark Street. Asked about the Lyceum show a few days later, Bon had already forgotten anything about the winning schoolboy. The successful schoolgirl, though from Harrow, Middlesex – still burned bright in his memory. Not least as she had also taken home an unexpected bonus prize in Mark Evans. 'Beautiful long legs,' Bon lamented to Anthony O'Grady, 'long blonde hair. She looked bloody sexy, really sexy, garters, suspenders, stockings, mini-dress ...'

Two nights later the band held a birthday party for Bon. He was 30; 'the Big Three-Oh,' as he called it, mock cheerfully. Michael Browning went to the trouble of booking a private room at the Russell Hotel in King's Cross. By 10 p.m., however, with the band and guests sitting sullenly around their tables, drinking without anyone to toast, it was clear Bon wouldn't be showing up. They were used to his sudden absences, but this felt bad; not even showing up for your own party, as arranged and paid for by the rest of the band. Pissed off, Malcolm simply got drunk; Angus was merely bored and eventually left alone, half expecting to see Bon tumble home in the early hours of the morning. But Bon didn't come back to Inverness Terrace that night or for the next three nights. Bon later laughed it off, claiming he'd 'fucked' his birthday in, starting just before midnight and continuing right through to midday the following day.

The truth, however, was somewhat more complicated. In fact, he had spent those days – his first away from the road since April, holed up in a tiny, one-room bedsit in Gloucester Road with his 'new girl-friend', an old flame from Adelaide days named Margaret 'Silver'

Smith. The same age as Bon, and with the same tastes for the exotic things in life, Silver had left Adelaide and begun 'travelling', not long after Bon had returned from the disarray of Fraternity's ill-starred London sojourn. 'I just set off around the world on my own and met a lot of very interesting people,' she recalled in a rare interview with 891 ABC Radio in Adelaide in February 2010. 'When Bon arrived in London with AC/DC I'd been here for quite some time.' She claimed Ronnie Wood from the Rolling Stones 'became a friend' and that they shared a house where she worked for him in some unspecified role. 'So I went to a lot of really interesting gigs.'

What Silver failed to mention was that she was a regular heroin user at the time she and Bon became reacquainted in the summer of 1976. By the time I met her, in 1979, she was a full-time heroin dealer, her modest third-floor abode in Gloucester Road red-flagged among the junkie cognoscenti of the West London music business as a good place to score 'gear' most any time of the day or night. With her croaky junkie voice, bleary smile and tough-cookie demeanour that allowed her to weigh up people as easily as she did grams of smack, Silver was no pushover. She may have been a rock chick, but she was hard in a way so-called hard men like Bon Scott could never be. And although the pair would enjoy what could best be described as an on-off relationship over the next three and a half years, it was one that took Bon into more direct conflict with the band than any other issue brought about by his recalcitrant ways. It also brought him into much closer contact with hard drugs; dicey territory for someone with his history of overdoing it. Indeed, there is a story dating back from this time, subsequently glossed over, that Bon suffered another heroin overdose during his earliest days with Silver – similar to the one that had landed him in hospital in Melbourne two years before, though no needles had been involved this time. It was just Bon mixing his prodigious alcohol intake with a few hefty lines of the one thing guaranteed not to mix with it: heroin. A mistake, to be sure; but a prophetic one, and not to be his last ...

Silver, who had no special fondness for AC/DC's music, and a positive dislike of the brothers in whose hands so much of Bon's fate now lay, saw herself and her London flat as offering a kind of sanctuary for Bon. 'Bon would sort of go off to this other world,' says Michael Browning, 'no one else would be involved in it at all. So there'd be the house where Malcolm and Angus and Mark and Phil lived, and then there would be wherever Bon went off to. But he was older and it was kind of accepted in that sense, that he had his own world. I don't think they liked it but that was just the way it was.' He says that Silver would rarely be seen at an AC/DC show. 'She was part of Bon's world, but she certainly wasn't part of the band's world. There was just the odd occasion where we would all be at the same dinner or something along those lines but that was about it. She was looked upon as being a negative influence.'

A more positive influence on the wayward singer was that of the band's new tour manager, Ian Jeffery. Jeffery already knew Phil Carson through working on tour with Yes. He had also met Michael Browning before, when touring with Rick Wakeman, who had head-lined the Sidney Meyer Music Bowl, in Melbourne, in early February 1975. Jeffery had first seen AC/DC by accident, on a night off, during a visit to the Hard Rock Cafe with the rest of the Wakeman road crew. 'It was this little room with this wall of sound coming from the stage,' he recalls. 'I turned round and said, "It'd be fucking great if they had a singer." Two and a half songs in, on comes Bon with this big jokey apology. "Sorry I'm fucking late I couldn't get off work ..." then just proceeded to slam us like you've never heard. Afterwards we were all like, wow! What the fuck was that?'

When, in May 1976, Carson phoned Jeffery to ask if he'd be able to work on the imminent *Sounds* tour, mucking in humping gear and mixing the live sound, 'I leapt at it. I mean, the band was com-pletely unknown, but I remembered them from Melbourne and knew they'd probably be fun. And they were.' Michael and Coral Browning were then sharing Coral's mews flat in Ossington Street, around the corner from Inverness Terrace. Michael had also rented a garage in Kensington and turned it into a makeshift office, often sleeping over on the couch after making late-night calls to Australia. Coral had also developed a soft spot for her older brother's latest protégés, especially

Bon, who she soon became a kind of personal shield for, like so many of his women friends did. 'Coral was one of the few people Bon really trusted,' says Michael. 'He'd put the big show on for the outside world, but with her he could be himself, and she became very protective of him.'

Ian Jeffery also quickly became part of 'the family'. When the tour ended he simply carried on working for them. 'Back then it was fun, we had relationships. When we were in London we would all go out together; our pub was the Warrington in Maida Vale. There would be places you'd all go together on a day off or a Sunday or whatever. Malcolm always used to come round. He would even bring Angus to the Warrington sometimes. Angus would have lemonade or orange but Malcolm would always start on pints and end up with a couple of stiff whiskies. That's when you knew it was time to go home,' he laughs. More seriously, 'Bon was the elder statesman. But it was always Malcolm who was in charge. Malcolm was the decision maker. Angus would always leave that to Malcolm. Every turn in direction they took, it was always Malcolm who led the way.'

When the band returned to the road on 16 July, it was for five club shows in Sweden. Brought up on the idea that Swedish girls were especially promiscuous – a Seventies view widely held at a time when Swedish porn was considered the best in the world – Bon was disappointed when the myth proved mightier than the reality. 'That shit about them being promiscuous is a load of shit,' he wrote home to a friend, complaining. 'I had to pull myself twice!' Three days before they flew out to Stockholm, they played their most prestigious London date yet: a performance of 'Live Wire' and 'Can I Sit Next To You Girl' filmed live at Wimbledon Theatre for a Marc Bolan TV Special, *Rollin' Bolan*. As an old T. Rex fan, Malcolm had to hide his excitement at the chance of meeting his former idol. He didn't want to blow his cool, shrugging it off to the band as 'nothing special'. But he stayed to watch Bolan perform his new single, 'Laser Love'. Dressed down in his new de-glammed outfit of baggy suit and tie, his corkscrew hair tamed into a short, side-parting, this was hardly the same rock idol Malcolm had put pictures of on his bedroom wall in Burwood.

He left disappointed, though happy in the knowledge that once again his band had 'blown off' the headliner.

Like passing ships, just as the overweight and drug-damaged T. Rex star seemed on an inexorable decline, so AC/DC's comet appeared to be burning ever brighter. By the time they'd returned from Sweden, Coral Browning had pulled off an impressive press coup, getting the *Sun*, Britain's biggest-selling tabloid newspaper, to run a page-length feature headlined: 'Power Crazy!' The timing of the article, which coincided with the airing of the Bolan special, teed up what was to became another major turning point in the AC/DC story: nine shows at the Marquee, beginning Monday, 26 July, spread over six weeks, ending with two shows on 7 and 8 September; a residency that became the go-to show that skin-peeling hot summer of '76. 'After the third show you couldn't get in, the place was so packed,' remembers Phil Carson. 'It didn't matter if you had a ticket or not it was just rammed. These were the days when [Marquee owner] Jack Berry would pack about a thousand people into what was a seven-hundred-capacity venue. It did make it all very exciting though.'

Michael Browning recalls the shows as 'the hottest I've ever been to – and I'm from Australia! The sweat was literally washing down the walls. You could see steam rising from the crowd.' Fans would start queuing outside the club mid-afternoon. By the time the doors officially opened at 7 p.m. the lines would be stretched all the way down Wardour Street and up into Oxford Street. Police were called more than once to try and control an increasingly out-of-control situation, while inside the club the crowd was such a crush that the only way paramedics were able to treat the dozens that routinely fainted or collapsed from heat exhaustion each night was by encouraging the crowd to pass the bodies out over their heads. By the last shows in September, the Marquee house record had been broken three times, Angus was ending the show down to just his stringy grey Y-fronts, and Jack Barry was proclaiming AC/DC 'the most exciting band I've seen play at the Marquee since Led Zeppelin'.

Between the Marquee dates the band ventured out to similarly sweaty shows in Birmingham, Burton on Trent, St Albans, Plymouth,

Penzance, Bath and several other hot spots. They also flitted back and forth to the continent, doing hit-and-runs in Holland, France and West Germany, where sales of *High Voltage* had replicated those in Britain, especially in West Germany, where the band were spoon-fed to the media as authentic British punk rock.

On 29 August, they appeared fifth on the bill at the final, Sunday, night of that year's Reading Festival, then the UK's largest annual rock festival. But that was seen as a disaster, and not just because it rained throughout the band's late-afternoon set. AC/DC may have been melting them inside the Marquee, but trying to get 50,000 wet, miserable people motivated halfway through the afternoon of the last day of the festival was another thing altogether. But if the mood was depressed when they left the stage to desultory noises from the uninterested crowd, the impression they left backstage threatened to undo all the goodwill the band had built up over the preceding months. Michael Browning would later claim that they had been unduly influenced by Atlantic Records. 'It was like, "This is the big time. You go there and get your own troupe backstage, sort of role-play being a superstar", and it kind of backfired.' John Peel, once again there in his capacity as DJ and arbiter of good taste, was no longer happy to be on the same side as these apparent upstarts, later claiming to be 'probably the first person ever' to sleep through one of their sets. While the *Melody Maker* put the boot in with: 'If you think the Sex Pistols are a gang of untalented jerks ...'

'[We were] just posturing,' said Michael Browning. 'Like, "No one's allowed on the stage, no one's allowed backstage when they walk through" ...' 'You could always tell when it had been a bad gig,' sighs Mark Evans. 'The dressing room afterwards would be like ice. No one daring to speak, everyone sort of avoiding Malcolm's eyes ...' On the bus home there was 'a heavy meeting' during which George Young – who'd flown in with Harry Vanda in time for the Reading show – tore into his brothers, yelling, 'Who the fuck do you think you are?' George was so angry he kept calling Mark Evans 'Dave' – after the earlier Evans in the band. When Mark corrected him all three brothers ripped into him too.

In fact, AC/DC was about to find itself on the wrong side – as far as the media was concerned – of everything. The same month a clip of them performing their new single, 'Jailbreak' – filmed at the Marquee – was aired on the Opportunity Rocks spot of Granada TV's *So It Goes*. Two weeks later, the Sex Pistols appeared on the same programme performing 'Anarchy In The UK' and upsetting guest presenter Clive James, who later recalled singer Johnny Rotten as 'a foul-mouthed ball of acne calling himself something like Kenny Frightful'. Lines were being drawn that would have a lasting influence on how AC/DC would be perceived. For now, though, Angus Young's school uniform and Bon Scott's short(ish) hair and characterful geezer vocals – as far removed from the chest-beating histrionics of a Robert Plant or Rod Stewart as the earliest releases by punk progenitors like the Pistols and The Clash would be – allowed them to escape through the net punk had begun to throw over self-indulgent 'old farts' like Zeppelin and the Stones. It was only a matter of time, though, before they were found out and brandished as not one of us by the punk archetypes in the British music press.

Meanwhile, in the wake of their woeful Reading experience, George Young and Harry Vanda decided to take the band out of the still sweltering heat of London and down to the fractionally cooler Somerset countryside for a long weekend at Vineyard Studios in Bridgewater. The idea was to record some new material for a proposed EP; something to plug the gap in Australia that had been left by their absence for most of the year. The plan now was to start playing dates in America, where the international edition of *High Voltage* would be released later that month. Then return to London and begin their first major tour behind the release of the *Dirty Deeds* album. In the end only three tracks were completed, none of which were deemed worthy for inclusion on a stand-alone EP. Of these, the best, potentially, was 'Dirty Eyes', whose galloping riff would later be recycled into one of the greatest AC/DC anthems of all, 'Whole Lotta Rosie', but for now was let down by lyrics that sat well below the usual level of wit Bon was known for. 'Love At First Feel', also recorded at Vineyard, appeared to have a little more going for it, but again was more filler than killer (and would, in fact, become a filler track on the British edition of *Dirty Deeds*). Most telling of where the band were, musically, at that precise moment though is 'Carry Me Home', where it becomes clear how the growing influence of punk on both the club circuit and in the music papers – and more overwhelmingly on the John Peel show, the only Radio One programme till then prepared to play AC/DC – was being duly noted by the band. Bon, in particular, had never sounded so brutish. The lyric concerned a night of heavy drinking with a girl the protagonist ends up depending on to carry him home. Seen, in retrospect, as weirdly prophetic of Bon's own fate, in reality it was far more reflective – as all Bon's lyrics, however trite, were – of the life he was already then leading. He'd been passing out from drink and/or drugs for years. Lately, though, it had invariably been whatever woman he was with at the time who had been moved to save him. 'We actually never really fought,' said Silver, recalling those days in that 2010 radio interview. 'But I found it was a difficult lifestyle and it was really frustrating when he was drinking. Sometimes he would not drink for long periods, and then just binge unexpectedly ... he could be difficult to manage.'

In the end, the EP idea was scrapped, as was another suggestion that a live album – the quick and easy (and cheap) option – be fashioned from some of the outstanding Marquee tapes. American reaction to *High Voltage* had not been encouraging; there were also hold-ups over getting their working visas for the US organised (not least because of Bon's criminal record). Instead, Michael Browning and Phil Carson had persuaded John Jackson at the powerful Cowbell agency to sign AC/DC, and put together their first headlining tour of major British and European venues. Cowbell was then the premier booking agency in the UK; signing with them meant another step-up in prestige for AC/DC inside the business and a higher profile among larger numbers of concert-goers than before. Cowbell moved quickly, putting together a significant European tour, combining club shows in their own right, and 23 shows – which they 'bought in' for them, industry parlance meaning: paid for the privilege of appearing on – opening at theatres and arenas for Rainbow in West Germany.

In Hamburg, following their show at the Fabrik cultural centre on 15 September, the band hired a local studio to record a song the eldest Young brother, Alex, now living in Hamburg, had written for them called 'I'm A Rebel'. With George once again in attendance they laid down the basic riff and Bon sank his teeth into the vocal, but the end result was hardly inspired, with its pat lines about being '*a danger to the public*' and '*the product of a screwed-up world*', but none of the reassuring Bon twinkle to add a nicely ironic polish. Again, the song remained unused, eventually resurfacing four years later when it became the title track of the second album by Solingen-based metal band – and AC/DC wannabes – Accept, whose more literal musical approach the song suited better. Leaving the studio unhappy that evening the band cheered itself up with a visit to the Reeperbahn, the famous red-light area of Hamburg's St Pauli district, where Angus spent a pleasant half-hour with a six-foot hooker who told him, 'Für you, little boy, nine Deutsche Marks!' As he later recalled, 'It was an offer too good to refuse.' Even though, 'she was twice me size.'

Nine days after their final show on the Rainbow tour, at the Congresgebouw, in Den Haag, Holland, AC/DC arrived at Southampton University to begin their most ambitious British tour yet: 16 shows at various universities and town halls that also included their first headline appearance at London's 3,400-capacity Hammersmith Odeon. Browning wasn't sure they would fill it but the weeks of sold-out Marquee dates ensured the venue was near capacity come the show. To coincide with the tour, 'High Voltage' became their next UK single, and though it bothered the charts not at all, it gave the music press something to talk about and tickets for the tour a further boost in sales. There were also a slew of incidents to keep the name AC/DC in the news and gossip pages. The show at the Oxford Polytechnic had to be cancelled when the college committee took a stand against what it described as 'the blatantly vulgar and cheap references to both sexes' in AC/DC songs. (A new date was put in at the end of the tour at Oxford's New Theatre.) After their show at the Birmingham Town Hall on Friday, 29 October, Angus – who now routinely dropped his shorts to moon the audience, much to their evident delight – was accused of masturbating on stage. Ludicrously, the vice squad was alerted and in Liverpool and Glasgow the band was officially warned they would be arrested if Angus tried to 'remove his underwear in public'. The real trouble-makers at Glasgow's City Hall weren't the band, though, but the crazed members of the front row that destroyed Bon's bagpipes. 'He put them down at the side of the stage,' said Angus, 'and, of course, all these kids grabbed 'em and tore 'em to bits! Then they set fire to the curtains! That was pretty much the end of that.' The *NME*, belatedly picking up on the AC/DC story, sent the veteran Phil McNeil to interview them. Barely stifling a yawn he allowed that 'With a sense of what sells rather than what's cool they could well clean up.' Again it was left to *Sounds* to make the case for the defence. 'The rhythms hit your heart like a trip-hammer,' wrote Phil Sutcliffe, waxing lyrical about the 'fluent solos from Angus' and 'the fascinating stage presence of Bon, leathery debauchee, a strange companion for the school kid'.

The highlight of the tour was their first headliner at the Hammersmith Odeon, on 10 November. A cold, rainy night in London, the Odeon was barely half full of paying customers but crawling with critics, radio people and various industry figures keen to see what all the fuss was about and the exhausted band's nerves were ragged. Backstage were various members of The Damned, Eddie and the Hot Rods and the Sex Pistols but nobody paid them much attention. The brothers, in particular, hyped up and ready to pop, were at their least talkative. Nothing must go wrong. The only one, as usual, who seemed utterly unfazed by the whole deal was Bon. Having travelled down overnight on the tour bus from their previous show in Norwich, Bon asked to be dropped off at Silver's bedsit in Gloucester Road, where he remained, in bed, until early the next evening. 'It's our first Hammersmith Odeon show, this really important gig, and he's half an hour late,' Mark Evans chuckles. They'd offered to send a car for him but Bon had insisted he take the tube instead – then got on the train going in the opposite direction. 'It got to show time and people were frantic,' says Evans. 'Then finally he arrived, all smiles.

Just told us the story and you couldn't help but piss yourself laughing. Just a funny guy.'

Not everybody thought so. In fact, things were about to turn very serious indeed for Bon Scott and AC/DC, as attitudes towards them hardened, at home and abroad; almost to the point of breaking.

CHAPTER NINE

A Giant Dose

The Hammersmith Odeon show was considered a triumph. Reviewed across the board, mostly favourably, even the *NME* was forced to think again, coughing up: 'The day, Gawd 'elp us all, AC/DC conquered London'. The only loud sniffing still to be heard came from Clive Bennett in *The Times*, who complained: 'Music of any sort must surely require more from performers than just the capacity mindlessly to bash their instruments into oblivion. It is in this primal state that AC/DC exist.' Interviewed about the tour in *RAM*, Bon claimed the best night was actually in Glasgow, 'our favourite place in the whole of Britain', where the kids 'are really mad' as most of them were 'Angus and Malcolm's relatives anyway'.

Two days after the Hammersmith show, *Dirty Deeds Done Cheap* was released in Britain. Already out in Australia, where it had tipped straight into the Top 5, again the track listing for the international version differed from the original home-grown product. When Geoff Barton, reviewing *Dirty Deeds* in *Sounds* – under the heading 'Same Old Song And Dance (But So What?)' – compared it to *High Voltage*, observing, 'So alike are they that tracks could be interchanged quite easily', he didn't realise how right he was. 'Rock In Peace' had been replaced with 'Rocker', from *TNT*, which had been left off the international *High Voltage*; while 'Jailbreak' was dropped completely in favour of 'Love At First Feel' from the aborted Vineyard sessions in September. As before, there was also a completely different album sleeve. In Australia, the cover had depicted cartoon versions of Angus and Bon in a pool hall, the former, eyes hidden by his school cap, giving a two-fingered salute, the latter, his right arm monstrously enlarged, the legend of the album title tattooed on his forearm. In Britain, however, Phil Carson had hired Hipgnosis – the design company then famous for their incongruous yet curiously affecting Led Zeppelin and Pink Floyd sleeves – to provide a cover for the album: a typically obscurantist Hipgnosis image of a group of individuals representing a broad demographic – young and old, straight and gay (presumably another misreading of the AC/DC insignia). But then, as Carson points out, 'We got it on the cheap', as it was 'a reject of somebody else's cover'. (A habit Hipgnosis maintained for many years, keeping all rejected work then selling it off at reduced rates to lesser artists.)

None of which appeared to affect the album's chances of success outside Australia, either way. So while it became another chart hit at home, *Dirty Deeds* singularly failed to make any impression on the British charts at all. For now, AC/DC's impact in Britain was restricted to their avid but still relatively small live following. They had high hopes, though, for what the New Year would bring – and what else might be in stall for them in America, where *High Voltage* was now picking up its first reviews and plays on FM radio, and where their first US single, 'It's A Long Way To The Top', was released in November. There, though, they would come up against the first serious problems of AC/DC's short but so far spectacular career. As Phil Carson says now, 'Nobody in America liked them. It was as simple as that. Not even my own record company.'

The review of *High Voltage* in *Rolling Stone*, published in early December, summed up the prevailing view. Billy Altman got straight to the point, calling AC/DC 'gross-out champions', insisting that with their arrival 'the [hard rock] genre has unquestionably hit its all-time low'. He concluded that 'AC/DC has nothing to say musically (two guitars, bass and drums all goose-stepping together in mindless three-chord formations)', adding, 'Stupidity bothers me. Calculated stupidity offends me.' Such was the fall-out from similarly negative reactions to the album, two promotional showcase gigs in Los Angeles at the Starwood club were pushed back indefinitely. There were some isolated incidents of radio support – most promisingly from the legendary DJ Wolfman Jack, on his nationally syndicated show from Los Angeles – but any suggestion that America would be just the next step on the ladder for AC/DC after Europe and Australia was about to be quashed in spectacular, near-fatal style.

With plans for an American visit now shelved until the New Year, AC/DC's quick-thinking young manager decided the most sensible option was to return to Oz in time for Christmas, for a hastily arranged summer tour. Conceived as a triumphant homecoming – they had originally planned to call it The Little Cunts Have Done It tour, before deciding to tone it down to the only somewhat less obnoxious A Giant Dose Of Rock'n'Roll tour – things got off to a reassuringly high-profile start when the band was met at Melbourne's Tullamarine Airport, on 26 November, by a large gathering of screaming female fans. There was also a press conference during which a drunken Bon and the bleary-eyed brothers did their best to sound triumphant while striking suitably humble noises about how good it was to be 'back home'. In fact, they were not happy at all about being back in Australia. 'It was a tough tour,' admits Michael Browning. 'The group didn't want to be doing it. I copped a lot of shit for making them do it. But it was a financial necessity. We had to fill the coffers up to keep doing what we were doing in England and Europe. But try explaining that to a young rock'n'roll band [that] didn't want to be there.'

To make matters worse, AC/DC's first major tour of Australia for nearly a year ran into problems almost immediately. Their first show back, at Melbourne's 5,000-capacity Myer Music Hall, had been a sell-out, with Molly Meldrum raving afterwards in *TV Week* about the band being 'the cause of yet another hysterical riot' as a couple of thousand ticketless fans stood locked outside. After that, though, things grew increasingly complicated. Despite the scenes at the airport, in no small part contrived by Chris Gilbey at Alberts to drum up some much-needed publicity for the tour, AC/DC had now shed the majority of teeny fans who had followed them so avidly during their *Countdown* days. A year is for ever for pop fans and most of them were now chasing other closer-to-home Australian stars like

Sherbet and John Paul Young – the latter the latest signing to the growing stable of artists George Young and Harry Vanda had brought to Alberts. The band's standing was then dealt a double blow by the arrival of punk, which even in Australia now decried long-haired hard-rock bands as out of touch and no longer relevant. Even the beer-guzzling diggers that had lined the bars during their pub and club gigging days had developed a certain grudging attitude towards AC/DC now they had 'buggered off overseas', as Browning puts it. Proof of which came in no uncertain terms when the band headlined the 5,000-capacity Hordern Pavilion, in Sydney, on 12 December, only to discover the place barely half full. 'They weren't really cool any more,' says Browning. 'In the end they really couldn't wait to get back to England.'

Mark Evans recalls other problems too. 'We got banned from a lot of the gigs. Angus was dropping his shorts and we had a problem with the tour programme where there was a quote on top of my photograph which said, "I want to make enough money so I'll be able to fuck Britt Ekland."' As soon as kids brought that home for their parents to see the office started getting calls saying the programme should be withdrawn and the tour cancelled unless it was. That nearly derailed the whole thing.' There was a further media contretemps when it emerged that the phone number Bon sang of in the title track to *Dirty Deeds* – the one he suggests to *'call anytime ... 36-24-36'* – actually belonged to a wealthy widow who threatened legal action after thousands of kids began calling her number day and night, forcing a contrite public apology from Chris Gilbey. Angus's bare arse also made headlines as a new threat to society. 'You see his backside in the papers more than you see his face,' complained Bon, only half joking. And there was sudden 'public concern' over reports that many of the band's most ardent fans were getting tattoos in emulation of Bon, leading to 'growing fears' that AC/DC fans could be putting their health at risk from homemade schoolyard tattooists.

It wasn't all gloom. *Dirty Deeds* had been another significant Australian hit, albeit not yet one as sales-heavy as *TNT*. Something Malcolm Young found cause for complaint in. *TNT* had gone to

No. 1. Why hadn't *Dirty Deeds*? What the hell was wrong with everyone? Despite these setbacks, the band was playing better than ever.
Absented from the pressure cooker atmosphere of a London then
increasingly in the throes of the punk revolution – the same day
AC/DC arrived back in Melbourne the debut single from the Sex
Pistols, 'Anarchy In The UK', had been released in Britain into a media
shit-storm – AC/DC forgot about maintaining the sharper edge they
had begun to contrive towards the end of that first stay in London, and
relaxed back into simply being their own filthy little selves. One of the
new highlights of the Australian dates was a passage of the show, just
before 'The Jack', called simply 'Gonorrhea' – an impromptu upgrade
on the traditional call-and-response routine between Bon's strained
vocals and Angus's manic guitar, built around the singer mangling
the lyrics to 'Maria' from *West Side Story*, a strangely subversive take
that burst the bubble of pomposity attached to most Seventies rock
shows, and further unleashed the foul-mouthed inner troublemaker
of the band. On tour, the brothers would room together. Mark Evans
and Phil Rudd would room together. That left Ian Jeffery to room
with Bon. 'Now that really was an experience,' Jeffery chuckles ruefully. 'The amount of times I would be in bed sleeping and Bon would
come in and be sitting talking to the TV thinking he's talking to me
or whoever! I'd reach over and put the TV off and he'd go to bed ...'

Just two years younger than Bon, Jeffery became closer in many
ways to the singer than his own band. 'We would spend many hours
hanging out just talking bullshit. Bon had his own little social calendar as well. He was a sociable guy, whereas with Malcolm and Angus
there was no socialising with other musos. It was maybe a hello or
a grunt every now and again. Whereas Bon would want to have con-
versations, want to go and see gigs and hang out and go to different
things. Bon would have friends and acquaintances all over the place.
He would write hundreds and hundreds of postcards. He was always
off down the post office, posting cards to people he'd met once or
twice, along with people that were really good friends of his. He was
just a different makeup, totally, to the brothers.'

It was a fundamental difference that Jeffery feels the brothers recognised, too, and respected – in their own ways. 'I think that Malcolm and Angus, deep down, really did appreciate who Bon was. But there was a front with them, where they wanted to be in charge as well. Bon knew just when to flaunt that as well, and how far to take it, exactly what he could do, when to walk away and disappear for a couple of days or whatever. But I think it would have been good if there was just a little bit more [involvement in the band's business side] for Bon. It was just, steady on, mate, we're in charge here. Nobody's the fucking star in this band, only the guy wearing the shorts, you know?'

Just when it looked like they would survive the tour well enough to enjoy their Christmas break – a neat endnote to what had been a daring but ultimately satisfying year – Michael Browning received another late-night phone call from Phil Carson. This one of a very different tenor, though, to the call he'd taken from the Atlantic chief just nine months before. 'In the middle of the tour, I got Carson telling me Atlantic Records in America didn't like the *Dirty Deeds* album. That, in fact, they were going to drop the group from the label. And that's when things got really bad.' Browning immediately flew to the Rockefeller Plaza offices of Atlantic in New York to see what could be done, but was met only by blank faces. 'Carson and the European affiliates of Atlantic all got it. But the Americans just didn't get it at all. I recall sitting down with Jerry Greenberg and their A&R guy and they were just giving me lip-service.' To add insult to injury, 'All they wanted to talk about was Skyhooks! I'm sitting there thinking, you've got to be fucking kidding! You've got a group with more potential than you can poke a stick at and all you want to talk about is the prospect of signing up another Australian group that I didn't think had any future in America whatsoever.' Flying back to Melbourne, it seemed to Michael as though for AC/DC 'it was very close to being all over'.

Unable to see how this still raw young band was going to fit into the formats of American AM radio stations then being gorged on the soft rock sounds of Rod Stewart, Elton John, the Eagles and Fleetwood Mac, even when Carson pointed out how well the international version of *High Voltage* had done in Britain and Europe, Atlantic's New

York boss, Jerry Greenberg, was adamant. Carson: 'I said, "I think you're making a very, very big mistake." But the drop notice was out, they were history.'

Though Browning was obliged to share the news with George Young and Ted Albert, the news was kept from the band, who were merely told Atlantic in New York had 'a problem' with the album, not yet that it wasn't going to be released, or that the band had effectively been dropped. In London, meanwhile, Phil Carson, outraged that his judgement and authority were being undermined in this way, was determined not to give up on AC/DC without a fight. 'I went to Neshui [the elder of the two Ertegun brothers who co-owned Atlantic] and showed him the sales figures that we'd got for *High Voltage*. Which were not awe-inspiring but considering we'd only paid $25,000 for the album, this was not so bad. There were about 10,000 sold in Germany, approximately 12,000 in England ... Maybe it had sold 40,000 overall. It had certainly earned its money back. Neshui saw it and backed me up and I re-signed the band at that point. I managed to claw it back in. And thank god I did ...' For both sides, though, there would be a price to pay. For Carson it meant reducing AC/DC's commitment to deliver a set number of albums by one. For Browning it meant a significant drop in overseas advances. 'To save the situation, I had to agree to drop the advance [on future AC/DC albums] from $35,000 to $25,000 – nearly a third. If I hadn't done that they would have been dropped.'

It was only now the situation had been resolved that Browning felt able to break the news to Malcolm and the others. Taking their lead as always from Malcolm, their reaction was predictable. 'There was always a siege mentality about the band,' says Mark Evans. 'But once we found out that Atlantic had knocked us back the attitude was, "Fuck them! Who the fuck do they think they are?" We were seriously fucking pissed off about it. You listen to *Dirty Deeds* now it's just a great gritty rock'n'roll album. But then you hear they weren't happy with the vocals, or they weren't happy with this or that. It was just all this fragmented stuff coming back.' There was never any suggestion,

says Browning, that the band should step back and consider soften-
ing their sound to make it more palatable to the American record
company. 'Malcolm's attitude was the opposite. Total disregard for
what Americans think.' Or as Evans puts it: 'We were all little guys.
None of us would accept being dictated to by anyone. You can joke
about it and call it the little-man-syndrome or whatever. But that's
just the thing. We were an arrogant bunch of fuckers. To have something like that was just, "Mate, we'll show you."'

Nevertheless, to be on the safe side it was decided the band should
hasten back into the studio and record a new album – one that the
American side of Atlantic would have no choice but to release. Thus, in
January 1977, AC/DC re-entered Alberts' studios in Sydney and spent
two weeks recording what came to be known as *Let There Be Rock*.
The result was the first truly explosive AC/DC album. 'If anything,
George Young was even more determined to prove the Americans
wrong than Malcolm and Angus,' says Evans. 'And cos of that, I think
they got it right.' From the sound of a whisky-guzzling Bon counting in the intro to the swaggering opening track, 'Go Down' – a song
about a real-life groupie from Melbourne named Ruby (as in Ruby
Lips, though her actual name was Wendy), known for her fondness
for giving head to the frantic finale, 'Whole Lotta Rosie', about another
real-life friend of the singer's lickin' stick, this one though weighing
almost 20 stone, via the title track, a heartfelt ode to original no-shit
rock'n'roll as evinced by one of the fastest, most joyfully headbanging
pieces of high-octane noise ever committed to what was still then just
poor weak vinyl, *Let There Be Rock* was the first truly classic, no-duds-
allowed AC/DC album. Thirty-five years on it remains one of their
best.

It sounded exactly like what it was. Written and recorded fast, fast,
fast, before the vibe had time to fade, full of blood and spittle and put-
a-fuck-into-it fun, fuelled by cheap speed and cold beer, topped up
with expensive whisky and at least a million cigarettes, some of them
smelling distinctly 'funny'. If Atlantic in America had been expecting something more in tune with the lukewarm milk of AM radio in
the mid-Seventies they were going to be sorely disappointed; tracks

like 'Dog Eat Dog' seemingly speaking directly to the suits in New York, in its disgust against the deal-makers and others the band was expected to trust. 'All the albums I made with them were all done in a two-week period,' says Evans. 'The songs were basically written in the studio. We never did a demo recording. But for me it was a watershed album. There'd been some great stuff before that, of course. But *Let There Be Rock* was where the band really found its length and really started sounding like AC/DC. It also holds two of my favourite songs: "Hell Ain't A Bad Place To Be" and "Let There Be Rock". The vibe on "Hell Ain't ...", the swagger that's on there, it still moves me every time I hear it. To me it's like the band's "Brown Sugar". I mean, if you're a purist and like the guitars being completely in tune and things being completely studio sterile, that song's gonna kill you. Cos the guitars are whomping all over the place out of tune. But it's just got that nasty gritty feel about it that says AC/DC.'

The whole album sounds like it's on the verge of spilling over into total chaos. Recorded as-live, mistakes were tolerated if the vibe was strong enough, the energy audibly crackling over the speakers on tracks like the romping 'Overdose', with its faltering feedback-heavy intro to a lyric suggestive of the symbolic link Bon had established in his mind between love and drugs – and Silver. Or the latest in Bon's long line of self-mythologising anthems, 'Bad Boy Boogie': so much hip-rolling swagger its jeans are halfway to its knees. Back in Sydney, and playing drums in The Angels, who had now signed their own deal with Alberts, Buzz Bidstrup was in the studio watching from the sidelines. 'It was all to do with the feel. It wasn't about perfection. They would play the riff until George said, "I think you've got the groove there." That might be five minutes, it might be ten minutes. Remember, there's no drum machines, no click tracks, nothing. They'd just hammer at Phil Rudd. Or if Angus was recording a solo, he would be climbing all over the amps and rolling around the floor. That was part of what made George and Harry good producers, they could actually get the band fired up to be so excited about what they were doing.' Angus later recalled seeing smoke 'pouring out of the fucking amp' at the end of the 'Let There Be Rock' take. 'George is fucking screaming, "Don't stop!"' The amp held out till the end of the song, when 'It melted,' Angus cackled. It was simply one of those albums 'where it was all cooking'. The real hero of that track though, for Mark Evans, was Phil Rudd. 'We did two takes of it and at the end of the first one I remember thinking, "That's the end of Phil for a couple of hours." But Phil said, "Let's go again *now*." I thought the guy was gonna fucking explode! From my memory I'm pretty sure they used the second take.'

The band had to scrabble hard for new material. Some of the new tracks like 'Bad Boy Boogie' had previously existed in miniature form. 'It was a title that was around and a riff that we'd messed around with a little bit maybe at soundcheck,' recalls Evans. 'Others like "Whole Lotta Rosie" didn't look like they were gonna happen at first, either.' With its staccato, looking-for-trouble intro and roguish vocal, 'Whole Lotta Rosie' was to become AC/DC's signature song: typifying the band at its most animalistic yet transcendent, in the same way 'Whole Lotta Love', from which it cheekily pastiches its title, had done for Led Zeppelin. Yet it began life as just another reconfigured number, this time of the track 'Dirty Eyes' from the Vineyard sessions of four months before. Says Evans: 'It didn't really happen. But then within the period of that week [in Sydney] it jumped and became what it was.' The real-life Rosie was a Tasmanian mountain girl: 'A *massive* girl. Bigger than the lot of us put together! In fact I think she ate one of our roadies!' he chortles. According to Angus Young, 'Bon had this fetish about big women. He used to party around with these two girls who were called the Jumbo Jets.' The one-night stand with Rosie, though, was of a different order, says Evans. 'How I remember it, back at the hotel we used to stay in, in Melbourne, there was a brothel out the back and Rosie used to run it. Then one day Pat Picket came running into my room saying, "You've got to come and have a look at this! He's fucked her!"' According to Bon, Rosie had simply been, 'too big to say no to'. When Evans followed Picket into the room: 'You could see this massive whale of a woman on the bed and you could see a little arm sticking out underneath with tattoos on it. Pat said, "Look, he's in there somewhere!" She was a good sport, though, Rosie – a real good person to have around. I can't confirm or deny whether Rosie was her real name but we knew her as Rosie, cos she had red hair.'

There was another little Bon ditty included on the original Australian and British and European versions of the album but which the American record company put their foot down about: 'Crabsody in Blue', a swinging blues – half 'Ride On', half 'The Jack' – based on Bon's sexual history since finding fame. Thirty-five years later the humour may seem strained, anachronistic. Set in the context of the times the song was written in though – the height of progressive rock with its portentous lyrics and multiple time signatures – 'Crabsody in Blue' is positively anarchic. It certainly proved too much for the Americans – and eventually the Japanese record company too – who replaced the track with 'Problem Child', from *Dirty Deeds*, the album the Americans had also just rejected.

As usual, backing tracks were all completed in the first week. Bon, who was given cassettes of the mixed-down, vocal-less tracks that he then 'scribbled words to', did all his vocals in the second week, during which Angus also laid down his various guitar solos. 'Bon would be locked away with his books writing lyrics and fitting them to the backing tracks,' remembers Evans. 'Except, that is,' he adds with a smirk, 'on those days when you'd go in there and he'd done a bunk and didn't come back for two days ...' Those were the days when he took off with Silver, who had also returned to Australia, to spend Christmas with friends in Adelaide, before rejoining Bon in Sydney in January. With Silver soon establishing good connections in Sydney and Bon drinking more heavily than ever, they made an odd pair; both stoned on same-difference substances. 'We hired a little motorcycle so we could get around,' she recalled. 'There were a few nights where I'm trying to go down the [...] expressway and he's on the back swaying away.' To outsiders, Bon seemed more in love than ever – and more in need of some place he could escape to away from the pressures of being in AC/DC. 'The Young brothers loved Bon, no two ways about that,' says Browning. 'But Bon had that leftover hippy thing of smoking dope, dropping pills and all that sort of thing.' Even though Malcolm liked a puff, says Browning, 'the Young brothers hated being around people like that. Alcohol was a different story. But anyone stoned, anyone in that kind of mindset, the Youngs hated it and Bon would have felt uncomfortable being with them in that sort of environment. So that was his trip. He used to go off and do all that sort of thing. They accepted it, no problems. [Bon] just sort of lived and travelled in a different world than [Malcolm and Angus] did.'

Although Bon and Silver would part again – the band already planning their return to London as soon as the album was finished; Silver, to return to her own, more separate London life, both with and just as often without Bon by her side – it was a relationship that would endure for what remained of his days. Says Evans: 'On the road sometimes he'd feel isolated. It's the way Bon was. I think it's probably drawing a long bow to call it depression. We all had our moments where you thought, what the fuck am I doing here, you know? But Bon had probably been on the road maybe ten years by then. Even with the success we all felt was coming, I think it wore a bit thin for him.' Getting away from the band, being in a totally different environment, even for a little, with Silver, 'He kind of needed that more than the rest of us.'

Let There Be Rock, the fourth AC/DC album, and easily their best yet, was released in Australia in March 1977 – and barely made the Top 20. Reviews were equally dismal. The headline in *The Sun*, in Sydney, simply read: 'What a Bore!' According to Ian Jeffery, 'That hurt them far more than America not getting their music; the fact that their own country seemed to have let them down.' So much so it would be several years before AC/DC deigned to return to Australia to tour. Instead, they flew back to London, but even there the tide seemed to be turning against them. Punk rock – in the shape of debut albums from The Damned, The Stranglers, The Jam and The Clash, to name the most prominent – had arrived in force now and suddenly AC/DC looked like being swept under the rock media carpet along with other 'dinosaur' rockers like Led Zeppelin and the Rolling Stones.

The band was typically defiant. Disdainful of both their playing ability – 'At least the Rolling Stones were competent musically,' Angus sneered – and their so-called rebellious attitude – 'The real punks were the [original blues] guys who had to fight from the beginning to get accepted [by a white audience],' declared Malcolm, citing Bon as more of a wild man than Johnny Rotten could ever be – the band's disdain for what they saw as an entirely artificial scene was further exasperated by incidents like the one where Malcolm stormed off the set after an Australian TV interviewer tried baiting him into saying something 'outrageous'. When the show's producer then ran after him, begging him to come back and storm off again so they could film it better, Malcolm's dislike turned to disgust. 'We were tougher than any of those punks,' he told the writer Sylvie Simmons in 2004. 'We used to sit there laughing at these guys who were supposed to be able to bite your head off, thinking, we could just rip the safety pin out of his nose and knock the shit out of him.'

Back on the road in Britain in March, when the *NME* tried to take the band to task for playing to the crowd rather than 'challenging' them, Bon dusted them down. 'These kids might be working in a shitty factory all week, or they might be on the dole. Come the weekend, they just want to go out and have a good time, get drunk and go wild. We give them the opportunity to do that.' Legendary US critic and proto-punk apostle Lester Bangs – in the UK on assignment for *Rolling Stone* – declared AC/DC to be 'so true to the evolutionary antecedents' of rock their songs weren't just about 'hold-my-hand stuff but the most challengingly blatant flat-out proposition and prurient fantasy'. Or as Bon told *Melody Maker*'s Harry Doherty, who travelled with them to some of the dates: 'We're a real down an' dirty lot. The songs reflect just what we are – booze, women, sex, rock'n'roll. That's what life's all about.' The only truth for the band, Bon suggested, lay out on the road. Beginning their biggest UK tour yet with a sold-out show at Edinburgh University, Bon called a halt to proceedings halfway through 'Dog Eat Dog', in protest at the heavy-handed way security were dealing with their admittedly out-of-control fans. A single was issued to coincide with the dates – 'Dirty Deeds Done Dirt Cheap' backed with older tracks 'Big Balls' and 'The Jack' – which Atlantic cleverly promoted with the slogan: 'All radio stations are banned from playing this record'. It wasn't true but you couldn't tell the difference, only 'good old Peely' on Radio One choosing to ignore the 'ban'.

The return to London had coincided, says Browning, with 'generally a feeling of, let's try and get this up to the next level. Not in the sense where the group tailor-made a record to that end, more just on a business level. It finally reached a point where I managed to get [the Atlantic department] who were in charge of the marketing dollars to put a reasonably good [budget] forward for that album [*LTBR*]. We got a little bit more aggressive in those terms.' With Australia flagging behind them, the idea now, he says, was to 'Keep moving forward and progressing. Their sound was developing too. It was getting heavier with every record. They were slowly [turning] into the kind of band that America would relate to. Slightly grander, more Zeppelinish, I suppose.' This newfound belief, born of the near-fatal crash of the Atlantic deal in America, now translated itself everywhere the band played, says Malcolm Dome. 'There was always this feeling with them that they were going to make it big. They had that real focus and determination. But then they had already done it in Oz. This was not first time around for them and that came through, despite a lack of support from the by now punk-obsessed media.'

The 18-date UK tour ended at London's Rainbow theatre on Friday, 11 March. Backstage that night, at the invitation of promoter Freddy Bannister, was David Krebs, then one half of the most powerful rock management company in America: Contemporary Communications Corporation, known in the biz simply as Leber–Krebs, after Steve Leber and David Krebs, who formed the company in 1972. With CCC, Krebs had overseen the careers in America of hard-rock giants like Aerosmith and Ted Nugent. They had also positioned themselves shrewdly at the centre of the new wave by signing the New York Dolls (later The Heartbreakers) and The Tubes. Krebs was no fool and knew exactly what he was looking at onstage at the Rainbow: a band with all the makings of superstars – but as yet completely unknown in America. He introduced himself to Michael Browning the same night. 'We discussed AC/DC doing some of his shows in the US,' says Michael, 'including an Aerosmith tour and his Texas jam festival. Both of which happened.' When Krebs suggested getting involved in the band's US management, Browning was far from cold to the idea. However, there was one snag for Browning. As he recalls, 'I enjoyed a good relationship with David. We eventually had a meeting about a year later to discuss a co-management deal where [a CCC upcoming management star named] Peter Mensch was also present and behind my back he reported back to AC/DC the details of what was discussed, which proved to me that he couldn't be trusted. If David hadn't involved Mensch the deal most likely would have happened.' Mensch hasn't commented, but whatever the reasons why the deal didn't happen, this would not be the last time Browning would encounter Peter Mensch.

The same day as that Rainbow show, the *Let There Be Rock* album was released in Australia, along with their latest single down under, 'Dog Eat Dog'. Given the apathy with which they felt the Australian public and media now treated them, they grudgingly filmed a mimed performance of 'Dog Eat Dog' at the BBC studios in Hertfordshire for the special 100th edition of *Countdown*, hosted by Leo Sayer, then at No. 1 in Oz with 'When I Need You'. It was a desultory affair. Instead of his usual shirtless appearance, Bon looked as though he'd wrapped up warm against the London cold in a fur-trimmed jacket, while Angus ditched the school uniform in favour of a blue-and-white hooped T-shirt. It had been a long day filming during which the drinks had flowed freely and by the end of it everybody was simply in a hurry to leave.

In April they flew out for the start of a 12-date tour opening for Black Sabbath. It was supposed to be another step up the ladder – new equipment had been purchased, extra road crew hired to help them operate it – but instead it turned into yet another disaster. At the first show in Paris, 'all the gear was blowing up,' complained Angus. He was so frustrated, 'we played about twenty minutes then destroyed the stage'. From that point on relations between the two bands became strained, to say the least – though, typically, Bon was a frequent visitor to the Sabbath dressing room, where he had resumed his mate-ship with Ozzy Osbourne, who shared his tastes in brothel creepers – worn onstage – and booze – a large anything, please. The tour came to a premature end though when AC/DC were sacked after some 'argy-bargy' between Malcolm Young and Geezer Butler. For years the story, oft repeated, was that Geezer had foolishly pulled a knife on Malcolm in the bar of the hotel they were sharing in Sweden – and that Malcolm had reacted as one would expect by flooring the hapless Sabbath bassist. In truth, it had only been a toy flick-knife comb. The result, however, was the same: AC/DC were on a flight home the next day.

Kicking their heels back in London in May, Mark Evans was the next to feel the cold wind of change when Michael Browning called him to a band meeting at which he was told his services were no longer required. Evans says he believes it was 'a commitment issue', adding, 'nobody could have been as committed to that band as the Young brothers were. I had a very healthy social side and I think that was viewed as being ... I was paying more attention to the social side rather than being committed to the gig.' Behaviour that was hardly likely to endear him to the brothers. Angus had never 'reckoned' him as a bassist anyway. Malcolm had gone along with it because Evans shut up and did what he was told and George played all the hard bass parts on the albums anyway. But just like Dave Evans before him, and before that Colin Burgess, once Malcolm got it into his head that Mark was getting a free ride – all the perks of the job without con-tributing anything of note, his days were numbered. Evans agrees that 'the boozing and birding' didn't help his cause. He laughs. 'It wouldn't happen before the gig, but after the gig if I had something lined up I'd be out of the dressing room five or ten minutes after the gig. I'd tell them, "Guys, great gig! See you later!"' He feels the turning point came after the final show at the Rainbow. 'There were some sound problems onstage. We went over well but it wasn't like when people used to go mental at the Marquee. Back in the dressing room, there was a VIP bar next door and I had a couple of research assistants [groupies] in there warming up. So I got changed into my clothes and was like, "See you in the bar, guys!" No one said anything.

[But] afterwards, I thought, I really should be staying in there a bit longer than this. If you don't want to be a scapegoat for a shitty gig, don't be first out the room, you know? But I was twenty-one and not thinking that far ahead ...'

According to Ian Jeffery though, 'It could have been for any reason. Malcolm would be off the rails at any given time.' As well as excess boozing, 'he liked a little smoke too and when you combine the two ... I've seen the wrath within the band let alone to people outside. If he thinks they're not cutting it, or talking to somebody he didn't know about ... just anything at any level.' To make matters worse, 'Mark was homesick. He wanted out, cos it was still a struggle then. And Mark was a guy who couldn't hold his drink and who drank because everybody else did. A couple of times they got into squabbles. I wouldn't say fisticuffs but slapping each other around. And at the end of that when they decided they were staying [in London], it was the perfect time for them just to say okay, that's your lot.'

Auditions for a new bass player began almost before Evans's plane had touched down again in Melbourne. Early suggestions had included Glenn Matlock, recently sacked from the Sex Pistols for 'liking The Beatles', and an occasional drinking partner of Malcolm's and Ian's at the Warrington. But that was 'never gonna happen', according to Jeffery. Glenn was already famous – more famous in Britain, at that point, than either of the Young brothers. Matlock also saw himself as a songwriter. Part of his problem in the Pistols had been his frustration at not receiving more recognition for his part in creating their best songs. There was no way Malcolm and Angus would have tolerated that kind of input into their music. If Glenn had found Johnny Rotten difficult to deal with, he would have found Malcolm utterly unplayable. There was also a suggestion that the band 'steal' 18-year-old Paul Gray from Eddie and the Hot Rods. But, again, the Rods – as they were now known in a bid to increase their punk credibility and play down their pub rock roots – had achieved a measure of fame, in Britain, at least, comparable to AC/DC's. For the brothers there seemed little to gain in bringing in a guy whose musical abilities were not discernibly better than Evans's, yet conceivably had even more of an attitude. Meanwhile, the band worked away in a small shabby rehearsal room in Victoria, half-heartedly auditioning a string of no-hopers who either couldn't actually play but had mistakenly taken AC/DC to be the 'antipodean punk band' of John Peel's reckoning, or hopelessly over-clever bass technicians reared on the Stanley Clarke school of playing, using the bass as a lead instrument when all Malcolm wanted was 'somebody reliable who would do what they're told and could keep up with him and Phil', as Ian Jeffery puts it. At one stage Malcolm was keen on tracking down former Manfred Mann's Earth Band bassist Colin Pattenden. When they had played at Randwick Racecourse in Sydney a few years before, the brothers had been impressed when they saw Pattenden break a bass string but simply carry on without missing a beat as a panicking roadie worked around him onstage, fitting a new string, mid-song. Michael Browning was aghast. As far as he was concerned, the well-meaning Pattenden may have been 'a good player' but his image was so cheerfully avuncular it would have made AC/DC look even more off the pace image-wise in this most image-conscious of times.

The answer came in the form of a journeyman English bassist named Cliff Williams. Born in Romford, on the outskirts of London, on 14 December 1949, Williams had spent his formative musical years as a teenager in Liverpool, where the family had moved when he was 11. 'Which was tremendous … that whole Merseybeat scene. Everyone and their dog was trying to be in a band – for the chicks.' Williams had begun playing semi-professionally at 13, being sneaked into pubs, pretending he was older. Leaving school, he worked 'in a metal shop for about a year and hated it'. Invited to spend three weeks in London in the summer of 1967, playing in clubs with 'some crap band' – actually, Jason Eddie and his Rock And Roll Show – when the mini-tour finished he never went home. Instead, he lived rough for a while, sleeping in a cardboard box under London Bridge. Eventually he got a job stacking shelves in a supermarket and snagged a part-time gig playing bass with the Delroy Williams Soul Show. Occasionally he would find himself playing on a session for some notable, like Alexis Korner, a jobbing blues and jazz musician whose fondness for giving try-outs to previously unknown young musos – was well-known. Mostly, though, Williams simply hung out, waiting for something to happen, taking short-lived factory jobs. Eventually he hooked up, via an ad in *Melody Maker*, with an 18-year-old guitarist named Laurie Wisefield – later of Wishbone Ash – forming the short-lived group Sugar. When that didn't work out, the pair got together with fellow journeymen, singer Mick Stubbs and drummer Mick Cook, and formed Home. As Williams later recalled, 'We had a few albums out in England, did a little bit of stuff. Never got too [far].' In fact, their debut album, the clottishly titled *Pause For A Hoarse Horse*, released in August 1971, led to support slots opening for big-name acts like Led Zeppelin and the Faces. A second album, simply titled *Home*, was described in the *Melody Maker* in its end-of-year round-up as one of the albums of 1972, but sales stubbornly refused to follow. A third album – the self-consciously conceptual *The Alchemist* (based on the Louis Pavel novel *The Dawn Of Magic*) – followed in 1973 and was trumpeted by *Disc* as 'a work of genius' but again failed to get anywhere near the UK charts. At which point Stubbs threw the towel in and Home fell apart. Cliff and Laurie's biggest claim to fame, in fact, was touring America later that year as part of Al Stewart's backing group. 'Just to get to America and see it!' Everything, though, 'sort of fell apart after that [and] Laurie went off to join Wishbone Ash'. Williams had soldiered on in a new outfit called Bandit but they 'didn't do too much of anything' and disbanded after just one eponymously titled album, released in January 1977.

At the time he got the phone call – from a pal named Jamie Litherland, then playing in noted jazz-rock goliaths Colosseum – tipping him off about the AC/DC auditions, Cliff Williams 'was kind of like thinking, maybe I was all done with it'. He was a decent player, but he'd had his chance and things had not panned out. Now he was 27 – considered old to be starting all over again, not least with a bunch of no-names from the colonies, as AC/DC were still thought of by most people on the London scene. Encouraged though by Litherland, and with nothing much else to do, Williams turned up for an audition halfway through May 1977. So concerned was Browning that the band choose the fresh-looking Williams over the talented but doughy-looking Colin Pattenden he spent the days leading up to Cliff's audition personally coaching him. Williams had never heard any AC/DC music, had never seen them play – aside from a vaguely remembered TV slot (probably the Marc Bolan show from the previous summer). When Cliff left the Victoria rehearsal room that first day, Browning was relieved to be told, 'Oh, man, he did exactly what we've been looking for!' Nevertheless, he was called back for a further audition, jamming on blues standards and occasional AC/DC numbers like 'Live Wire'. Again, Malcolm and Angus reported their findings back to Browning and again Cliff seemed to be 'what we've been looking for'. Nevertheless there were two further full-blown 'jams' – working more on AC/DC material, but also on his stage-craft, as directed by Malcolm. Ian Jeffery sighs. 'When Cliff joined, Malcolm told him: "You stand there and I stand here. When you've got to sing you walk forward, you walk backwards, you don't turn around. That's all you fucking do." You know, they'd both stride up to the mike together for the backing vocals, then they'd both stride back together and sometimes Malcolm will turn around and walk back. But Cliff was never allowed to do that. Malcolm was like, "You never turn your back on the audience, got it?"' Cliff got it, and Michael Browning was finally instructed to make a formal offer to the bass-ist, phoning him late on the evening of Friday, 27 May. After which, AC/DC finally had a bass player that could do exactly what they wanted: play good, sing well and do what he was fucking told. Malcolm cel-ebrated by grunting his approval. Angus lit another cigarette. It's not known what Bon's reaction was, if any. He had no say in the matter. Besides, he was probably already tucked up at Gloucester Road with Silver ...

The first thing Cliff Williams had to do on joining AC/DC was get a work visa to allow him to travel with them to Australia, where they hightailed it in June 1977, in readiness – finally – of the start of their first US tour in July. When the Australian Embassy in London refused to give him one, AC/DC simply took him with them anyway.

*

For a while in 1977, the whole AC/DC edifice, such as it was, had looked like crumbling. Though far from a spectacular commercial success, the international release of *Let There Be Rock* would start to turn things around for them, however. A relative flop in Australia, where it sold less than 25,000 copies, barely scraping into the Top 20, making it their least successful album at home, on the plus side it would become the first AC/DC album to shove its snout into the British album charts, albeit at a relatively lowly No. 17. It was released in Britain in a revamped sleeve, once again: where the original Australian and American cover had been a simple black-and-white image of a left hand – double-exposed – holding the neck of a guitar (the hand actually belonged not to Angus or Malcolm but to a guitarist named Chris Turner, then of the Australian band Buffalo), the UK version was an only marginally more interesting colour live shot of the whole band, in profile, from the side of the stage. (Though it hardly seemed worth it, the live colour shot later replaced the original fret shot on all editions of the album.)

Phil Carson knew they were still skating on thin ice in America, but that luck was with him, though, this time, in the shape of a new recruit to the New York office: one John David Kalodner. An up-and-coming A&R man whose infallible ear for hit rock acts had already seen him bring notable success to Atlantic in the shape of the British-American rock act Foreigner – whose debut album, released in March that year, had already sold a million copies – Kalodner was on his way to becoming the biggest driving force behind developing rock talent in America in the Eighties. Best of all, he was an old-fashioned record man in the purest sense, in that he let the music inform him. As he told me in 1984, 'I believe if the band is good enough, and prepared to put the hard work in, that eventually things will happen for them. Back in the Seventies, a lot of groups had the talent but not the work ethic. Or they were prepared to work but would let it slide in the studio because of drugs. AC/DC was one of those bands that seemed to have it all: talent, hard work and no major hang-ups. Even Bon, though he drank, always showed up on time ready to work. And they were *great* live. I liked them as soon as I saw them.'

Such was Kalodner's growing status, says Phil Carson now, 'The only reason *Let There Be Rock* came out in America, really, was because by then John Kalodner had joined Atlantic. John wasn't a musician but he had a unique capacity for understanding the connection between what a band is playing, what you can get on the radio, and what kids will buy. John knew [AC/DC] wasn't going to get on US radio much. But he said, "Yeah, I think this group's great. We should go with it." That's how the second American album became *Let There Be Rock*. And it made a bit of a noise and from then on it carried on. It still was not big, particularly in America. But it was gradually building and building.'

Though *Let There Be Rock* would not be made available in Britain until the autumn, it was released in America on 15 June – to collective sighs of relief from everyone bar Malcolm, who refused, in public at least, to 'give two shits what the fucking Americans think'. With the band planning on being away from home again for some considerable time, George Young ordered them back into the studio to get more material in the can. The idea was to bash out another album in quick-time, then put the band on the road in America, then Britain and Europe, than back to America, for the best part of a year. With Cliff still not legally entitled to work in Australia though, George again picked up the slack on bass. But they only got as far as the outline to two more ton-up AC/DC rockers in 'Up To My Neck In You' – a typical Bon double-entendre propelled by a typical Young brothers pedal-to-the-metal rocker – and the 'Let There Be Rock' sound-alike 'Kicked In The Teeth' – plus the bones of a truly superior tune that would not surface for another two years but would become another highlight called 'Touch Too Much'. The subsequent album – to be titled *Powerage* – would not be completed until early the following year. In the meantime, the band had their first US tour to think about. Not that anyone was showing it. 'Bon was off, as usual, doing his own thing, while the brothers acted like it was nothing,' Michael Browning recalls. 'It was only me that was panicking …'

There were two unofficial warm-up shows back at the Lifesaver, which gave Cliff Williams a chance to play properly with the band for the first time before an audience – billed as The Seedies, as a precaution against attracting the attention of Australian immigration, who still hadn't granted Williams a work permit, and also as a face-saver against the fact that AC/DC was no longer big enough in Sydney to headline the Hordern Pavilion. Nevertheless, with their gear piled up on the bar and leads snaking out the door to a van containing a mobile recording unit, the first Lifesaver show was 'like a bomb going off', according to Ian Jeffery. The second show, the following night, was even louder. Word had got around and hundreds of fans that couldn't get in simply hung on outside, listening to the music escape through the doors and windows. Halfway through, one crazed female fan jumped on the stage, grabbed the mike from Bon and shoved it up her skirt. 'I was laughing,' Fess Parker, from support act Big Swifty, told Murray Engleheart. 'She's stuck it right up inside her!' Meanwhile, a roadie was 'giving a good serve' to another girl on one of the back tables, as people were 'standing up on tables clapping'.

Browning also squeezed a video shoot into their schedule, for the planned release later in the year of 'Let There Be Rock' as a single. Filmed in a church in Sydney's Surry Hills, with Bon as the priest pontificating from the pulpit – albeit in reverse-colour white smock with black dog collar – and Angus, in green choirboy smock, replacing his schoolboy cap with a toy halo, the symbolism was comical yet entirely apt. This was AC/DC as fundamentalist preachers, sent by the Lord to gather converts and induct them into the eye-swivelling ecstasies of hardcore ass-shaking rock'n'roll. 'Let there be light!' Bon screamed, flapping his hands in mock Al Jolson style, before leaping from the altar like a swooping bat. What the video didn't show was his actual fall onto the front pews, where he landed so badly he ripped apart all the ligaments in his right ankle.

Three weeks later, on 27 July, with Bon still 'taking the medicine' for his badly injured ankle, AC/DC played their first show in America, at the World Armadillo Headquarters, a large spare warehouse in Austin, Texas, where they played second fiddle on the bill to Canadian heavyweights Moxy. 'They'd take place all over Texas,' explains Ian Jeffery of the Armadillo shows. 'The beer garden, the live band, the fucking pot den … We would go somewhere new in Texas every day.' The five band members and Ian would travel together in a station wagon, 'With as much kit and tackle as you could get in the back and a guitar each. Keith and Evo, the two crew guys, would be in a twelve-foot rider [a large haulage van]. I'd be on the phone talking to the American agent, Doug Thaler, going, "Where we off to today, Doug?"'

Doug Thaler was a fast-talking, forward-thinking 29-year-old maverick from upstate New York who'd started out as a gifted musician in his own right eight years before, playing keyboards in The Electric Elves (later The Elves, and later still just Elf) with future Rainbow and Black Sabbath vocalist Ronnie James Dio. Typical of the times, their debut 1967 single, 'Hey, Look Me Over', written by Thaler, was somewhere between a surf record, with furious drums and echoing harmony vocals, and the kind of post-beat, faintly psychedelic pop then being purveyed in America by the Lovin' Spoonful – and in Australia by The Easybeats, who had their only Top 20 US hit that summer with 'Friday On My Mind'. Late that summer both bands found themselves on a seven-band bill headlined by Gene Pitney – which is where Thaler 'first got to know George and Harry real well. There were some good guitar players on that tour but I remember George saying to me, "I've got an eleven-year-old brother at home that's better than anybody that's on this tour." That of course would have been Angus.'

Eight years later, Thaler had become a booking agent, working at Thames Talent in Connecticut, whose main clients, Deep Purple, Thaler had been working on when they were booked to play the Sunbury festival in Melbourne in 1975, where they got into it with local roisterers AC/DC. 'So I'd heard the name come up but I'd never put it together in my mind with George and Harry. Then when their first album came out in America in '76, although it didn't take off, it hit a couple of hot spots and I was getting calls from promoters out in places like Columbus, Ohio, and Jacksonville, Florida, asking if I knew anything about booking this act. I was the guy who did British acts like Be Bop Deluxe and the Strawbs and I guess they figured I might know something. I don't think anyone knew they were from Australia.'

When Thaler was headhunted early in 1977 by ATI – American Talent International – he planned to take both the Strawbs and Be Bop with him, so flew to London in March to firm up those arrangements, and also do a little talent spotting while he was there, signing up the Pat Travers Band and Judas Priest. When one night he saw that AC/DC were playing at the Rainbow he remembered the name and arranged to go. 'It was sold out and they were great. It was essentially just an earlier version of the same show you see today.' Impressed, he picked up copies of *High Voltage* and *Dirty Deeds*. When he discovered that his old pals George and Harry had produced both albums and that the guitarists were in fact George's younger brothers, he stayed up late that night and put a phone call through to Alberts in Sydney. 'I said, "I want to look after these guys." And [the Youngs] are very family kind of guys. So they knew me and they liked me, and I said I'm in a good place and I'd really like to work on this. Next thing you know, we've got a deal.'

What Thaler didn't yet know was how much trouble AC/DC were in with Atlantic in New York over their whole future in the US. Without major record company backing to help underwrite the tours, there was almost no point signing an act to his new agency. George knew that having their own American agent ready to go to work for them would be a huge advantage in persuading the Rockefeller Plaza office to get behind them at last, and allowed Thaler to believe, as he still does, that 'Jerry Greenberg was right behind them.' What Thaler hadn't anticipated, either, was how little enthusiasm there would be for his new overseas signings from his new boss, Bill Elsen, at ATI. Elsen had made his bones working at Premier Talent, owned by the legendary Frank Barsalona, who had booked everybody from The Beatles to Led Zeppelin. Eventually ATI would also become a big player in the American market, handling tours for Rod Stewart, Neil Young, Kiss and Dire Straits, to name a few. In 1977, however, they were still running a long way behind Premier. 'Bill was like, "What are we gonna do with all these baby bands you've signed?" I tried to tell him, look, we can't compete with Premier. If we wait for bands to blow up we'll never get them. We needed to sign bands before they blew up.' With Elsen still not convinced about AC/DC, Thaler delivered an ultimatum. 'I said, "Look, I can either book them via the agency or I can book them from home but either way I'm gonna work these guys."' Thaler ended up booking the first five AC/DC tours of America – with Elsen and ATI.

Ian Jeffery: 'We'd be trying to pick up $150; driving along with a Holiday Inn road book in the front of the car for directions. No travel agent. And Doug would tell us to go back to where we'd just come from cos they wanted another night from us.' They would pool their 'shitters' – small bills and loose change – 'to see if we had enough cash to scrape together a Dairy Queen': a meal at the cheap-and-cheerful fast-food chain then dotted all across America's freeways. Determination was the key; determination and sheer bloody-mindedness. Qualities the Young brothers had in abundance. 'It was all Malcolm,' says Jeffery. 'If there were arguments or discussions going on whatever, Angus would always leave that to Malcolm in the end. Bon was like the elder statesman, who everybody liked, but Malcolm was the decision maker, over everything. Even if Angus had strong points, Malcolm would be, "Fuck off, mate, we're not doing that."'

Bon Scott almost missed their first show when he 'wandered off', as Jeffery puts it, 'with all these Mexicans he'd befriended at some bar somewhere. The afternoon of the show, we're all down there getting ready and Bon is nowhere to be seen, and the brothers are getting more and more pissed off. They sent me back to the hotel to look for him but I knew he wasn't there. Anyway, ten minutes before they're due to go on, with the doors to the place long open and all the people there, I'm standing outside hoping and praying Bon's going to show up. Next thing there's this truck comes hurtling over the horizon, with AC/DC music blaring out of it! It's Bon with ten of his new best friends, all holding bottles of whisky and joints in their hands. It pulls up, Bon jumps out and says to me, "Ian, this is Pedro and this is Poncho, etc, can you get them all on the guest list?" Meanwhile, the brothers are going nuclear. But the gig went off without a hitch.'

A lot of his wayward behaviour on that first American tour, thinks Jeffery, was simply Bon's way of dealing with the task of starting all over again – again. 'This wasn't like it had been in Britain, where it was a case of getting in the music papers, and getting your face out there on the road. This was America, where they've got whole states bigger than Britain. You could do well one night in Jacksonville or wherever, then the next be playing to one man and a dog in Bumfuck, Arizona – waiting for Bon to turn up. We were sweating some nights in places we didn't know you could sweat.' Angus Young would recall just such an occasion when they took a last-minute booking opening for Johnny Winter: on paper, what should have been a complemen-tary pairing; the brash young rockers opening for the high-energy blues-guitar wailer. Instead, the audience, who 'were all out there for him', only became interested in AC/DC when Angus got a bad elec-tric shock from some faulty gear. 'They liked that,' he remembered. '"Hey, the little guy's lighting up."' When audiences did open up long enough to hear what the band could do, 'reaction was brilliant,' says Browning. 'I don't recall one gig that I could say didn't work. It was an instant rapport with the audience. Angus would do his thing at the end of each show. And even where the audience didn't know the songs, by the end there was always a big reaction.' Even if they didn't always get it, said Angus, 'they'd never go forgetting the little kid in the shorts and satchel, the one who behaved like a lunatic.' 'Some of 'em thought Angus was queer,' Malcolm added with a smirk. 'Then when he bared his ass ...'

Supporting REO Speedwagon in Jacksonville, Florida, Bon became acquainted with the good ole boys from Lynyrd Skynyrd, whose tough-guy frontman, Ronnie Van Zant, he had more than a little in common with. Taking a shine to their new friends from Down Under, the Skynyrd crew took Bon, Malcolm, Angus and Cliff back to their own band complex – a wooden shack in the hills – where they spent the next two days drinking and smoking and jamming on everything from 'Sweet Home Alabama' to 'Whole Lotta Rosie'. When Skynyrd then offered the band the chance to fly with them on their private plane to their next show, Bon was all for it. But Angus, whose teetotalism left him entirely out of the hell-raising Scott–Van Zant loop, passed on the idea. When Malcolm was also forced to decline when his girlfriend (later his wife), Linda, put her foot down, complaining she hadn't flown all the way to America from Australia to be left kicking her heels while Malcolm went off with 'the boys', Bon also very reluctantly turned down the offer. When, just two months later, Van Zant and five others, including Skynyrd guitarist Steve Gaines and his sister and Skynyrd backing vocalist Cassie were killed when that same plane crashed after running out of fuel en route from South Carolina to Louisiana, Bon and Malcolm felt better about their decisions. But only just. They were making new friends everywhere they went now. At their second of three showcase gigs at the Whisky a Go Go in Los Angeles at the end of August, Bon was approached backstage after the set by Kiss leader Gene Simmons. 'He said, "Look, we're touring in December and we'd like you to tour with us." And they toured to [thousands] of people a night.' It was an offer Simmons would make good on during AC/DC's second US tour later that year. By then, though, it was as if every major band in America wanted the newcomers to open their shows for them. Word about AC/DC was finally spreading.

'You could feel it building,' says Browning. 'Jerry Greenberg had hired two new executives from Arista Records. One was Michael Kleffner and the other Perry Cooper. And one of their first assignments for Atlantic was to do something with this group they didn't know what to do with. And that was really the saviour for America, the fact that we now had two champions at the record label, working on us every day. They came to the first couple of gigs, around the Florida area, Jacksonville, and Columbus in Ohio, where we'd had a fair bit of FM radio airplay and the crowds were good. And they totally got it, and really championed the cause. I can't speak highly enough particularly of Michael Kleffner, who's now deceased. But he was very, very important in American Atlantic's eventual support of the group. The rest of them, Ahmet Ertegun and Jerry, I don't think they ever really got it, to be honest, until the royalties started flowing through the system. I know Ahmet really thought them to be derivative and not that sort of innovative. I just think he thought they were a meat-and-potatoes rock'n'roll band and that was about it. If they make money, cool. But there was no great appreciation of them.'

Browning says it was also Kleffner who got the hugely influential American promoter Bill Graham behind AC/DC. 'Michael used to work for Bill as a security man, a bouncer, I suppose, at the Fillmore, in New York. And so he had a pretty good relationship with him, and it was through that that he got us on the initial Day On The Green festival [in San Francisco, the following summer]. So Michael was highly supportive. He knew some key people that were good for the band in America.' It was all about building relationships, being kind to Joe from Idaho. How did the brothers with their stand-off attitudes deal with that, I ask? 'There were people that they took to that they liked, in the business. And there were some they didn't really care for or resonate with. But for all that they were pretty aware of having to PR themselves with people. I think the band particularly liked Perry Cooper and Kleffner. And there were other people along the way, like Doug Thaler from the agency. He was important in the process.'

Ian Jeffery recalls how Cooper 'used to turn up and the first thing you'd see after he checked into the hotel was room service pushing two of these great big wheelies with beers and sandwiches and things. And we'd just follow it cos we knew we were going to Perry's and we'd get something to eat and a drink for nothing. That sort of thing goes a long way when you're stuck out in the middle of nowhere and you're travelling in a station wagon and a twelve-foot rider. Perry would stay at the same hotel as the band. He'd be in a bigger room but you'd go in there and help yourself. And he'd ask if there was anything else you needed. And that that was a comfort back then, to have someone from the record company you could relate to. Very cool guy.'

Another crucial contact in New York was Barry Bergman, from EB Marks, the band's American publishers, who Alberts had a long-term involvement in. Bergman was an ambitious, music-loving 32-year-old who'd been on the scene, 'enjoying several minor successes' before landing his first big full-time gig at EB Marks, where he became Vice President, helping launch the careers the same year of Meat Loaf and another hit Australian Vanda and Young signing, John Paul Young. 'Barry became a very strong ally of the group and mine,' says Browning. 'He ended up giving me office space in the building and everything. Because of Barry Bergman, Michael Kleffner and Perry Cooper, we suddenly had a really solid base of support in America that was just crucial. Without that it never would have happened.' Says Bergman now: 'I was convinced AC/DC had a future in America because I thought the live show was magnificent and if they were willing to put the blood, sweat and tears into doing what they had to do – go out there and pound the pavements – then I felt that something was definitely going to happen. I wasn't initially sold on all the songs. I felt they needed their signature song that hadn't arrived yet. But I felt they would find their audience out there on the road. I was never even thinking about radio at the time, because this was not a radio kind of band. This was a live band. This was a band that was all about the fans, all about working.'

Bergman remembers taking a phone call from Angus early on. 'He said, "Barry, nobody likes our music. Radio doesn't want to play it and I don't know what's gonna be." This was a couple albums in, and I said, "Angus, just keep doing what you do and the pendulum will swing. Greatness is greatness and the cream will rise to the top."' Nevertheless, Bergman knew it would be an uphill struggle. The fact that they were big in Australia and doing well in Britain and Europe, he says, 'didn't mean much over here. Nobody in America was looking at other markets.' Even after *Let There Be Rock* was finally green-lighted for US release, 'very few people believed in it'. Jerry Greenberg, he says, 'never really understood it. You gotta remember something else. It wasn't their signing, you know? We're in a business where people only care about what they've done, not what might be great. I would go up there [Atlantic] and say, "Hey, they're playing downtown here, we gotta bring some people" and they'd say, "Oh, who wants to see this?" It was the old story. Everybody likes to be associated with a winner but very few are willing to stick their ass out to create one – and stick with it when the whole world is telling you you're crazy.'

It was also through Barry that AC/DC pulled off a remarkable PR coup on that first US tour, when the band was presented with the Key to the City of North Miami, Florida, by the local mayor, Michael Colodny, the day before an appearance at the big local venue, the Spartatorium, on the bill with the Charley Daniels Band, at a charity event for muscular dystrophy, titled Day For The Kids. 'That was a very key thing that I pulled off for them,' says Bergman with some pride, 'another story that's never been told. They hadn't made it yet, this was before the breakthroughs. But the mayor was my first cousin! So I called him up and said, "We gotta do something here" and he said fine. We never told the world what was really going on. [Colodney] said, "I'll give them the key to the city at City Hall. Then throw them a luncheon and make this into a big deal." So that's exactly what we did.'

CHAPTER TEN

A Wolf in Wolf's Clothing

Although *Let There Be Rock* barely scratched the US Top 200 (peaking at No. 154), it was the start of a journey that would result, over the next three years, in AC/DC becoming one of the biggest rock bands in America. These, though, were hard miles they would have to travel. Arriving in New York, the last week of August, for two shows – third on the bill to NY punk elders The Dictators at a sold-out show at the 3,400-capacity Palladium, followed by a much smaller but more media-friendly spot, it was thought, at the punk-credible CBGB's, opening for local power pop new-wavers Marbles – just as they had in Britain a year before, AC/DC often got thrown in with the wellspring of punk and new-wave acts now flourishing in the United States as well. 'I booked them into the Palladium,' admits Doug Thaler. 'Not because I thought AC/DC was punk. To me it wasn't the Ramones. It was something else with a much harder edge than that. I just wanted to get them in front of as many people as possible at their first New York show and we did the whole three-dollar ticket thing with The Dictators and the Michael Stanley Band, who were also on the bill, getting the various different labels to underwrite it. Michael Kleffner was the one who booked them into CBGB's.' Looking to add a little credibility-by-association, Kleffner thought he was doing the band a favour. But if AC/DC left the Marbles crowd frankly baffled, it did lead to Bon being interviewed the next day for New York fanzine *Punk*, who asked him for the meaning of life. Bon shrugged: 'As good a time and as short as possible.'

Says Phil Carson: 'AC/DC were not a punk group. But somehow in

America they kind of thought they were because of the way Bon and Angus dressed ... Jerry Greenberg thought they were a hit almost by mistake. Because the American fans thought we better like punk cos it's hip but we don't like punk cos it sucks. But we like this, let's buy it. And that's how I think AC/DC really got its start in America, because of the look of them. And of course as soon as you got kids through the door to see them play they were hooked and the word started to spread ...'

The important thing was to keep the band working, keep the machine rolling, no matter what. On that score, at least, Atlantic could have no complaints. 'They came here determined to crack this country,' says Barry Bergman, who took it upon himself to push the boys at Rockefeller Plaza as hard as he could. 'They were the hardest-working musicians I had ever known. They would play for five people, twenty people, they never gave a damn. They played every joint and dive that existed and never complained about it either. There was no way they couldn't make it – *no way*.' Off the road, 'Malcolm ran it. Actually George Young ran it, but through Malcolm ... The band didn't make business decisions, George made them.'

Touring, in actuality, was the only way AC/DC knew how to make things happen; carpet-bombing every territory they set down in, with gigs and more gigs. Three days after the final show of their first US tour – at an Atlantic Records convention in Fort Lauderdale, Florida, on 7 September – AC/DC were in Belgium, at Poperinghe, for the start of a 22-date European tour across seven countries. Forty-eight hours after that ended they began a 17-date UK tour at the Polytechnic in Sheffield. *Let There Be Rock* had just been released in Britain and while the reviews tended to stay within already established parameters – more of the same = good enough, from *Sounds*; more of the same = we-told-you-so bad, from *NME*, neither friend nor foe magazine picking up on what a leap forward the album actually was – tickets for all the shows had flown out the door as soon as they went on sale. The band were relieved to hear it. While they had been away, Bon told Molly Meldrum in an interview filmed in London for *Countdown*, 'We honestly thought the punk and the new-wave thing might spoil it a bit for us, but it really hasn't. It was a big fad for a while and there are those still hanging on to it but the main thing about it is, it gave rock music a real kick in the guts, you know? We played here before the Sex Pistols were even sort of thought of and now people are beginning to realise they want something more than just some fella singing [he affected an angry punk voice] anarchy and rape ...'

As before, the highlight of the tour, in terms of prestige, was a headline show at London's Hammersmith Odeon on 25 October. As usual, there was a party afterwards that Coral Browning managed to get a few select rock writers into. 'They always had a downer on the British media,' recalls Malcolm Dome, who was there. 'Certain journalists, like Dave Lewis on *Sounds*, once they got to know him they didn't want to talk to anybody else.' There was also a significant contingent of other musicians at the show and party, demonstrating AC/DC's appeal across the new cultural divide engendered by punk. But for all their popularity with members of The Damned and Eddie and the Hot Rods, it was the heavy rock giants of the day that the individual band members felt most at home with: Pete Way from UFO, Brian Robertson of Thin Lizzy, fellow Australian Bob Daisley of Rainbow. 'Malcolm and Angus didn't trust anyone new coming into their world,' says Dome, 'let alone the punks who they really had no respect for. Whereas Bon had the attitude: "Until you prove otherwise, why shouldn't I treat you as a mate?"'

Bernie Marsden, once of UFO and Babe Ruth, then of Whitesnake, the band recently formed by vocalist David Coverdale after the messy demise of Deep Purple the year before, was another who'd recently become close to the band. 'I knew them all but it was Bon that I got to know quite well,' says Marsden now. 'We were drinking partners. Well, I used the term loosely cos I couldn't stay with him for *minutes*, let alone an hour or two. It was funny, because we were all a lot younger then of course. But I do remember thinking, "Hmmm, I don't know if I can cope with this." Also, it was expensive, especially in places like the Marquee, where we used to go a lot. But they always seemed to have a few bob in their pockets. Or they had a bloody good tab going wherever we were, so I enjoyed the company but I couldn't get involved in the extracurricular [activity]. I'd always been scared of drugs.' Bernie was just 25, still finding his way on the music scene. Bon was already past 30 and had been everywhere. Or so it seemed. 'He was a very, very powerful frontman. He kind of scared you a bit. Put it this way, I never heard anybody heckle him. I mean, you hear about this guy being a hard man and that guy, but I think Bon really was tough. I've seen him a couple of times in bars when people have started on him then very quickly backed off. He'd give them the look. Put it this way, when I was out with Bon I always felt pretty safe.'

AC/DC had been due to drive to Great Yarmouth the following day but the show got rearranged when the BBC called at the last minute asking if they would appear on their high-profile in-concert programme, *Sight and Sound*, simulcast on Radio One and BBC2 TV. The Sensational Alex Harvey Band – the home-grown Scottish act Bon so admired – had been booked to appear but had cancelled with just 48 hours to go when singer Alex Harvey walked out of rehearsals, announcing his 'retirement from rock'n'roll' along the way. It had been a strange week all round. Just days before, they had received news of the Lynyrd Skynyrd plane crash. There was simply no time to reflect though. The day after the final show of the UK tour, at the Cambridge Corn Exchange on 12 November, Bon flew with Silver to Paris – ostensibly to meet her old friend Ronnie Wood, who was then recording the Rolling Stones' *Some Girls* album at Pathé Marconi studios. With Wood and his chief crony, Keith Richards, then in the full throes of their own heavy-duty affairs with cocaine and heroin, the obvious supposition is that Silver was actually delivering 'a package' to the guitarists. Whatever the reason, Bon tagged along and spent the next 48 hours 'hanging out' with Wood and his circle. That is, until he happened upon another band working in a smaller secondary studio at Pathé Marconi: a new French outfit called Trust, who by strange coincidence were then recording their first single – a more punk-conscious version of 'Love At First Feel', with lyrics rewritten in French by vocalist Bernard Bonvoisin and retitled 'Paris By Night'. The French singer was amazed to have the AC/DC vocalist actually in the studio with them as they recorded it, and Bon and Bernie immediately became friends, laying waste to several Parisian cafes along the Left Bank as they caroused the late-night haunts of the 7th Arrondissement. By the time Bon left again on 15 November, he and Bernie were 'blood brothers', he said.

Bon slept for most of the eight-hour flight he then took to New York, and arrived wasted for the beginning of AC/DC's next step on the ladder to American success: opening at the Civic Center in Poughkeepsie at the first of four dates at medium-sized venues supporting Canadian stars Rush. From there it was straight on to the UFO tour for a swing through the South, including four auditorium-sized shows with UFO, and five of their own at small theatres and clubs. Whether alone or opening they now had a set packed with one knockout blow after another: 'Let There Be Rock' was the new opener, followed by 'Problem Child', 'Hell Ain't A Bad Place To Be', 'Whole Lotta Rosie', 'High Voltage' … as an opening act they were rarely granted the time to play encores, so they just turned the end of each set into one almighty encore: usually 'Rocker', expanded to a blood-spitting 12 minutes or more, depending on how the crowd was feeling it, which usually meant longer.

UFO bassist Pete Way recalls thinking AC/DC – the brothers in particular – were 'going out of there to absolutely kill us every night. You know, support bands don't usually admit they're trying to blow the headliners off the stage, but Malcolm, especially, didn't bother to hide it. He wouldn't even look at you before they went on. Even Bon, who'd be hanging out in our dressing room most nights, he'd give that little nod and a wink but you knew as soon as he went out there he didn't give a fuck about you. They were gonna steal the rug from under you first chance they got.'

Away from the stage, Pete and Bon – likeminded souls who only wanted, as Way says now, 'to get completely fucking out of it as often as possible' – would become 'good mates'. On that first tour together, though, says Way, 'It was Angus I got really matey with. After the show, the rest of his band would be off getting drunk or whatever, pulling birds. But Angus didn't really do any of that so he used to just sit around in the dressing room with me. Then back at the hotel, we used to hang out in each other's rooms. It was usually mine, actually, as we had better rooms than them. But it didn't matter. We just liked to have a laugh together. The funny thing was, I was going through the whole white line fever thing, but Angus didn't seem to mind. I'd be snorting coke. He'd be drinking Coke. And we'd literally stay up all night talking and mucking around, cos he had so much natural energy it was like being with someone on coke. Then in the morning he'd say to me, "I dunno why you need all that shit. Why don't you have a nice big breakfast instead?"'

Three weeks into their second US tour, Perry Cooper came up with the novel idea of taking the band into Atlantic's New York studios at 1841 Broadway, on the corner of 60th Street, and recording a live album – not for general release but serviceable to US radio stations, in the hope the one-off nature of the project would appeal to them enough to play tracks from it. Atlantic's NY studios were famous in their own right, having housed the birth of several rock classics, including in recent times two Cream albums (*Disraeli Gears* and *Wheels Of Fire*), the *Allman Brothers Band* album, *Loaded* by The Velvet Underground and a plethora of other rock-historic notables. The subtext of placing a not-for-general-release, radio-only AC/DC album alongside such names: this was something special. Sure enough, FM radio jumped on it and for the first time AC/DC songs such as 'Live Wire', 'Hell Ain't A Bad Place To Be' and 'Whole Lotta Rosie' became staples of American FM rock radio. 'It worked so well they ended up doing it with a couple of other artists too,' remembers Barry Bergman. 'They would press a thousand copies and send them out to radio to keep the band's name alive out there in between albums. They only did three or four acts in the series but AC/DC was the first.' Recorded before an invited audience of Atlantic and other AC/DC-affiliated dignitaries, Bergman was especially chuffed when Bon made his way through the throng to stick the mike under his nose and force him to sing along on the chorus of 'The Jack'.

Forty-eight hours later AC/DC began a four-show stint opening for Kiss at truly huge arenas, beginning in Memphis, before 12,000 people at the Mid-South Coliseum. The same weekend, in

Indianapolis, they played to 18,500 at the Market Square Arena. Two days after the final Kiss show in Fort Wayne, they joined the latest Aerosmith arena tour, opening before 9,000 at the Coliseum in Charleston. The night after that they opened for Cheap Trick at the Coliseum in Greensboro. More than 5,000 were there, the stage in the middle of the hall, half seated, half standing. With Aerosmith then in a drastic downward spiral, the result of being so loaded on drugs they had to be helped on and off the stage most nights, they were easy meat for AC/DC, whose high-energy performances, not least from the eternally straight Angus, who made it his duty to cover seemingly every inch of the venue, including through the audience, usually perched on Bon's shoulders, made the headliners seem even more wasted. Recalled Aerosmith guitarist Joe Perry, 'If you closed your eyes, you'd think [Angus] was standing there, tapping his foot. But he would be all over the stage, all over the amps – he never missed a note.' He said the Aerosmith road crew even had a name for Angus's nightly contortions, lying on his back whirling in a circle on the stage: 'bacon frying'.

Keeping up with their growing reputation as a live attraction were the never-ending stories of offstage shenanigans. Sometimes it was self-inflicted madness, almost always involving Bon – like the time he took off with a bunch of Hell's Angels he'd just met, to a cabin in the woods where they distilled their own bootleg whiskey. Malcolm, who he'd dragged along with him, recalled how they didn't get away until the following afternoon, 'playing pool, telling jokes, drinking the same rotgut these guys there are drinking'. As Joe Perry told *Rolling Stone* in 2008, 'Bon had so many miles on him. You could tell when he sang ... he was there, man.' Or as Bon himself told the American writer David Frieke in 1978: 'We just want to make the walls cave in and the ceiling collapse ... Music is meant to be played as loudly as possible, really raw and punchy, and I'll punch out anyone who doesn't like it the way I do.' Sometimes it was just being in AC/DC, the eternal outsiders, that brought the road fever on. More than once, because they simply didn't come across like rock stars – no extravagant silks and scarves and bodyguards for the Young brothers the way there were for Aerosmith, no outlandish hangers-on and freaks falling out of limos like with UFO – the venues' own security staff would question their presence, unable to believe these strangely accented, vaguely aggressive strangers could actually be part of the concert. 'We used to pull up at a show in a car,' remembered Malcolm in 1980. 'We'd tell 'em, "We're playing here tonight." But you couldn't get through to half these people. In the end, we'd just crash through. We pulled many a Starsky-and-Hutch through the gates.'

Barry Bergman, who often travelled with them in their tour bus, recalls the toughness of mind the brothers, in particular, always displayed. 'I must have seen over two hundred of their shows during those years,' he says, 'and I got to tell you something, these guys don't talk to each other when they're not working. These guys are not close when they're not working but when they're together, they're together. They used to argue and fight a lot but it was always about the show and how good it was and the quality of it. They were all about the fans. They were never about the industry or the business. I always felt that they were the people's band. They had no love for the industry and most of the people in it. They thought that most people in the business were full of shit. And they were right.'

At their show in Allentown, Pennsylvania, on 17 September – a headline gig at the local Community College, supported by The Dictators, the band they had opened for in New York a year before – the promoter, Tom Makoul, told Doug Thaler the next day that Malcolm and Angus had got into a fight standing in the wings at the end of the show, arguing over what to play as an encore. 'One brother knocked out the teeth of the other brother!' Thaler later recalled being told. The only one the brothers never got into a physical fight with was Bon: Angus because he loved Bon too much; Malcolm because, he said, 'Bon would have punched me back and I would remember that.'

January 1978. King Street, Sydney. There would be no AC/DC summer tour of Australia this year, even though it had now been over a year since they'd last played there – despite the fact that certain dates had been pencilled in, and in some cases actually advertised, for March. The dates were then cancelled because – the official story went – Cliff Williams was still being denied a work permit. But that wasn't true. Cliff was in the studio working with the band on what they hoped would be the best, most forward-thinking AC/DC album yet. The fact was, 'The [previous Australian] tour was such a painful experience for them,' says Michael Browning, 'the subject of them coming back just didn't arise again. It was just generally understood that we were on a mission to make it internationally, and America was really the important focus at that point.'

It was all about America and making an album, finally, that would 'do a job there'. For all his grumblings behind the scenes about stupid Yanks, for Malcolm Young the recent months spent touring America had been an eye-opening experience. Not just the people and the places – the sheer scale of the whole story of what it was like to be there, trying to make it in America – but the respect AC/DC was starting to get. Not just from newfound fans, but from other bands and musicians, other people in the insanely go-getting American music business: agents, promoters, publishers and producers – record company suits and radio station beards that just a year before either hadn't heard of them or, if they had, hadn't given them a chance, hadn't even considered their records worth releasing in America. For a band that had always, intrinsically, rejected the idea of taking itself too seriously, Malcolm now relished the glow he felt when the people of America, the biggest, most serious record-buying nation on Earth, began to treat AC/DC as proper, as real, as serious. Cracking it at home in Australia had never been more than a step, in Malcolm's mind, towards bigger and better things. Even Britain had been a pushover by comparison – the punks they arrived with easy to outfight and outplay. In America, though, they were competing with Aerosmith and Kiss, with Alice Cooper and Ted Nugent. Big names, no fucking around allowed. And for the first time Malcolm Young knew AC/DC would have to up their game if they were to be seen in the same take-no-prisoners light. For a man who had spent most of his life professing how little he gave a shit what anyone else thought, now, in January 1978, as AC/DC went back into the studio with big brother George and his cohort Harry to finish their fifth album, Malcolm cared very fucking much, thank you, what people were going to think of the finished thing.

Somewhere along the road between those early sessions of six months before and the end of their second US tour, opening for Blue Oyster Cult, in Pittsburgh, four days before Christmas 1977, Malcolm had decided *Powerage* would not be like AC/DC's other albums. Travelling hundreds of miles each day in the back of a cramped van with nothing to think about except what was coming at them from the FM dial on the radio, for the first time since they were kids the Young brothers got to hear a whole spectrum of rock music they would never have knowingly sat down to listen to without being forced into it. That meant hours and hours of Boston and 'More Than A Feeling', Steve Miller's 'Fly Like An Eagle' and Foreigner's 'Feels Like The First Time', day after day of heavy-rotation Rod Stewart, ELO, Alice Cooper, Kiss, Bob Seeger, Peter Frampton, Heart, Aerosmith and Queen, all of whom had huge Top 40 hits in the US that year. Above all, it meant listening to *Hotel California* by the Eagles and *Rumours* by Fleetwood Mac, not just the two biggest-selling albums of the year but of any year that decade.

By the time they were ready to go back into the studio in Sydney, in January 1978, Malcolm and Angus knew better than at any time before exactly what was needed if they wanted AC/DC to make it big in America; that this time they would have to do more than go into the studio empty-handed, throwing it all together as best they could in a fusillade of alcohol and fags and making-it-up-as-you-went-along, George-driven Aussie spunk. *Powerage* would have to be their heaviest proposition yet – but also their most musical. *Powerage* would need to show what AC/DC could do, demonstrating the one thing critics had got into the habit of expecting them not to achieve – *growth*. This time around the little dogs were determined not to get pissed on by the big dogs.

'With Cliff in the band and America finally sorted out, they now had the confidence to do that,' says Michael Browning. 'I mean, they were never shy but *Powerage* was where Malcolm, in particular, really wanted to show they were good musicians too.' As a result, *Powerage* would take longer to record than previous AC/DC albums, with ad hoc sessions spread across several weeks at the start of the year. Experiencing fully for the first time the midnight oil-burning intensity of AC/DC in the studio, Cliff Williams, for one, was convinced *Powerage* was special. It remains his personal favourite AC/DC album. There was clearly 'a lot of chemistry there', he said, 'just a real fiery energetic work environment'. Even though the sessions were spread out, when they started work in the studio, 'We got there and got down, and did the long-hour days … It was really a tremendous experience – and the album really turned out pretty good too.' A view Jerry Ewing shares. 'For me, *Powerage* is the definitive Bon Scott statement. It sounds like they just went into the studio and cut loose. And you can hear it. It's got a frantic energy to it.'

Energy and musical aplomb. Conceived as a showcase that would place AC/DC right up there with the American superstars they were now sharing stages with, *Powerage* was split down the middle between yet more ton-up AC/DC classics like the powerful opener, 'Down Payment Blues', and the more elliptical 'What's Next To The Moon'. In the former, the difference in mood is pinpointed by the change in perspective of Bon's lyrics, still writing about the long way to the top but no longer self-mythologising, talking instead of *'Feeling like a paper cup / Floating down a storm drain'*; the latter, with its circular guitar figure replacing the juddering block chords of yore, was simply the most transcendent moment on any AC/DC album yet, the lyrics staring past love and pain, focusing instead on that thing just out of reach. Whether intentional or not, it was the same yo-yoing dynamic throughout its nine tracks: one moment, a perfect-ten rock monster like 'Riff Raff', its crazed, spiralling riff belying its solitary verse about being lost in Mexico and pay-off line about almost literally laughing yourself in two. The next moment, another seductively mid-paced stroller built around a tight, almost pop guitar figure: 'Gone Shootin''. This time, though, the subject matter is truly murky. Not rock noir so much as the dark that falls when you least expect it, when you can least cope. A song about a girl who is always so loaded she says goodbye, given Bon's predilection for writing lyrics straight from his own life, it's impossible not to see at least part of this song being about his on-off relationship with Silver, the stoned travelling woman who is permanently somewhere else in her head. Certainly there is nothing celebratory about the timbre of the song, despite some lovely understated interplay between the two guitarists, not so much duel-ling or backing each other up in a fight but more ... dancing together, like real partners, with little to prove but plenty to show. Indeed, it's a track that would not have been out of place – in both its resigned, bittersweet lyrics and its understated yet emotionally rending playing – on either *Hotel California* or *Rumours*.

Of the remaining tracks, the lines between old-school, go-get-'em AC/DC and new, more measured see-what-we-can-do AC/DC are pleasingly blurred. 'Sin City' begins like classic AC/DC – towering intro, all-guns-blazing riff – but again the story is much deeper than on earlier city-at-night epics like 'Bad Boy Boogie'. On the surface, about a gambler going all the way in Las Vegas, it's also a metaphor for the assault AC/DC were now intent on making on the American charts. With its low-slung guitars and chugging drums, 'Gimme A Bullet' sounds more like the Lynyrd Skynyrd number it almost steals its title from than anything AC/DC had put down on vinyl before. The song – about a girl who tells her guy, *'Now you go your way and I'll go mine'* – again seems to refer back to Silver, with Bon crying for a *'bullet to bite on'* to help him with his pain.

The two tracks which close the album, 'Up To My Neck In You' and 'Kicked In The Teeth', also exemplify this new dynamic. Although both date back to the earlier *Powerage* sessions of six months before, only the latter sounds like it comes from an earlier era, albeit one where the band are at the absolute peak of jolly-roger bad-boy bigness, Bon literally screaming over the intro. 'Up To My Neck' sounds much more modern; Bon once more up to his neck in whisky-women and good-bad times, but the guitars and drums move with a staggered grace that has more to do with the Rolling Stones at their drug-binged mid-Seventies peak than the wall of block chords AC/DC had previ-ously relied on.

There was one other track, too, 'Cold Hearted Man', but that only made it to the very earliest vinyl editions of the album released in Britain – and these days is not included on any of the CD or downloadable editions. In truth it is no loss. A second-hand AC/DC number with music and lyrics from the bottom of the collective barrel, though that was not the reason it was eventually cut from the album. *Powerage* was destined to become an even more polarising album for AC/DC than *Dirty Deeds*. For all three Young brothers, it represented their best work to date; a breakthrough to another level musically that they all justifiably felt proud of. For Bon it was a milestone, too, in that he no longer felt obliged to simply come up with lyrics to order, the one-size-fits-all looking-for-trouble imagery of his earlier work, despite coming almost always from real life, replaced by lyrics with less immediate box office appeal, perhaps, yet much closer to the dark heart he was now sure had been broken beyond repair. As such, *Powerage* was the first AC/DC album that showed real signs that they had become more than just a beer-and-guts rock band. More inspired than Zeppelin, at this point, more playful even than Aerosmith, and more wise certainly than any of the next-generation metal bands they would find themselves lumped in with in the Eighties, they could not have imagined the reaction it would receive from the once again baffled heads at Atlantic in New York. This time, though, the repercussions would last not just for the lifespan of the album, but for the lifetime of the group.

Invited to Sydney to hear for himself what the band was up to, Doug Thaler arrived in February to discover everyone in high spirits. 'It seemed a very exciting time for them. The Young brothers were good guys [and] I got to see George and Harry again and see the band working and rehearsing.' Before AC/DC, Thaler had represented both the Sensational Alex Harvey Band and Thin Lizzy, and Bon, in particular, loved to pump him for stories about both Harvey and Lizzy's flamboyant poet-singer, Phil Lynott. Having been an increasingly frequent visitor to the Thalers' 10th Street New York apartment, Bon now reciprocated by making it his duty to show Doug around the most rock'n'roll joints Sydney had to offer. Thaler recalls, 'Bon was living in a motel in Bondi with his girlfriend [Silver]. And one night he and I went to the Bondi Lifesaver. Rose Tattoo was playing. There were five guys and four of them had different-coloured hair and one of them, the singer Angry Anderson, had no hair at all. Angry is singing a song then he goes and throws up on one side of the stage. Then he sings another song and goes and throws up on the other side of the stage. I walked into there with Bon and there's a big glass window by the front entrance and it was clear that a human had been thrown through it not long before ...'

Thaler detected a difference in Scott's demeanour, though, the next time he saw him, just a few months later at the start of their next US tour, when Bon seemed to be 'going for it' even more than usual. As Thaler puts it, none of AC/DC 'were big druggers. Angus I never saw do anything except smoke cigarettes and drink tea. Malcolm liked to [drink and] dabble with a little pot and so would Bon. But Bon ... after his girlfriend left him in '78, that's when he started to go downhill.'

Bon's latest troubles with Silver had begun in the aftermath of completing the *Powerage* sessions. Instead of relaxing on the beach with her and thinking about how bright the future looked with a great new album in the can and more European and American dates being lined up, Silver seemed more interested in hanging out with a new 'friend' she'd made named Joe Furey. Furey was working as a roadie with Rose Tattoo. Unlike Bon or the Tatts, though, Joe wasn't a 'grog merchant', preferring to indulge in what was also Silver's favourite pastime: getting stoned on heroin. Silver has always maintained that she and Joe were never lovers, yet neither has denied how intimate they quickly became. I knew them both, for a period, in the late Seventies, when they lived in London, and they certainly came across as very much a couple. Even though they lived together, though, it was never clear if they were having sex. They seemed more like brother and sister; enablers, perhaps.

According to those who were there, Bon professed to like Joe himself, his only concern being that Silver liked Joe more than she did him. Knowing his drinking was probably a big part of why she chose to spend more time with Joe than him, Bon took to seeing a hypno-tist, to try and stop drinking. Sitting on the beach each day, white-knuckling it, Bon soon fell off the wagon and took to going down to the Lifesaver, knowing he wouldn't be drinking alone for long. His brother Graeme, who came to visit him around this time, later told Clinton Walker that by February 1978 Bon would be at the Lifesaver 'drunk most nights, and he'd still go home on his bike'. When Silver suddenly announced she was taking off for Bangkok with Joe, Bon was devastated. Yet with AC/DC due back in Britain for their next tour in April, there wasn't much he could do to stop her. Silver told Walker: 'I made the decision to break up when we left Australia. Bon couldn't accept it, he was still very emotionally dependent on me, so we said, okay, twelve months, have a twelve-month break.' In fact, they would never be together as a couple again.

According to Doug Thaler, the break between the two was far from clean. 'What I was given to understand, and it was so long ago I can't recall what Bon told me and what the other guys told me, but apparently they were living together in a motel in Bondi and what money they had was his, and it wasn't much but they had it in a joint account and she just, I guess, she took off – cleaned out the account and didn't say anything to him. It started to go downhill for him after that.'

As if to make matters worse, Michael Browning now received yet another crushing phone call from Atlantic in New York: they didn't like the new album. 'The delivery of that album wasn't met with very much enthusiasm at all,' he admits. 'It wasn't just America this time, either. I'm talking all over.' The problem, as Michael saw it, was that *Powerage* was 'more of a statement about themselves, and credibility and, you know, having something that they were really proud of as musicians, as opposed to something that was really needed to take it to the next level'. Having invested heavily in the band by now, how-ever, Atlantic didn't simply block its release in the US or threaten to drop the band from the label. They did something almost as bad, at least in the eyes of the three Young brothers. They insisted they 'fix it'. Browning sighs. 'A lot of it was unsaid. It wasn't like anyone came out and said this is not good enough or commercial enough or whatever. There was nothing ever really directly stated. It was just an overall vibe that you got.' He knew they were in trouble, he says, when even Michael Kleffner, their former champion, 'suggested' they record another track: something specifically commercial that the label could give to radio – and that radio would actually want to play.

'It was one of only two times I ever recall them caving in to Atlantic and saying, all right, we'll do what you want,' Ian Jeffery says. Re-entering the King Street studios in March, they recorded exactly the kind of two-dimensional self-consciously good-time track they had worked so studiously to avoid doing on the album: a two-bit piece of head-bobbing guff called – apparently with full pun intended – 'Rock'n'Roll Damnation'. 'It had a chance of being a great song,' says Jeffery, 'but when you add in tambourines, maracas and a shuffle, you know … it's not quite what it's supposed to be.' Nevertheless, 'Rock'n'Roll Damnation' did what it was supposed to do, at least in Britain, where it gave AC/DC its first legitimate, albeit still relatively minor hit, peaking at No. 24 in June 1978, along the way occasioning a true symbol of British success: the band's first performance of *Top of the Pops* – then the nation's biggest weekly TV pop show. 'It was like going back to the *Countdown* days,' says Jeffery, 'all teeth and arse and miming to the hit. They absolutely fucking hated it! But then it was a mediocre record and afterwards they turned round to Atlantic and said, "See, you don't know what you're fucking talking about, do ya?"'

Michael Browning, however, was more sanguine about this latest development. As he says, 'I know a lot of fans out there think [*Powerage*] is the best record they ever made. But in terms of what was needed on the business end of things, it didn't happen.' As for the single, 'It was pretty much a deal-breaker. They had to do it. [But] that was the first time they were on *Top of the Pops* and that was kind of the break I think Atlantic were looking for to get out of the commercial doldrums. That's where we needed to be at that point in time and there was nothing else on *Powerage* that was gonna put us there, so …'

On paper, it all seemed eminently sensible. With 'Rock'n'Roll Damnation' added at the last minute to the new album as the opening track, expectations were high for its release among the Atlantic sales force – or higher, certainly, than they had been until then. In reality, though, the initial performance of *Powerage* – despite selling steadily enough in the UK to give the band its first gold record (for over 100,000 sales) by the end of the year – appeared low-key compared even to *Let There Be Rock*. It barely made the UK Top 30, where *LTBR* had reached No. 17, and the reviews in the music press, though generally positive, again harped on about the similarity of the material to their previous albums – something that had now become the defining theme, it seemed, of any discussion in print on the merits or otherwise of the music of AC/DC. The brothers, who had put so much into the album, were utterly aghast, their frustration only increased when word kept creeping back about how little their own record company thought of it too.

Increasingly, the only place left where life made sense was out on the road. On 28 April, they began their longest UK tour yet: 27 dates that would underscore their transition from upstarts to mainstream headliners. The third show of the tour, at the Apollo theatre in Glasgow, was recorded, as other shows had been sporadically in the past. In America, Atlantic had noted the breakthrough success of Kiss via two live albums: *Alive*, released in September 1975, which gave Kiss their first US Top 10 chart hit; and the follow-up, *Alive II*, released in October 1977, which had done even better, giving Kiss their first multi-platinum album in the US, as well as dragging previous studio albums back up the charts in its trail. Like AC/DC, Kiss were not a band renowned for their originality. Instead, their reputation lay in the unmatchable ferocity of their live shows. With the *Alive* series (there would be two more *Alive* releases over the years), Kiss had transformed the idea of releasing a live album – seen till then as, at best, a contractual stop-gap – into a commercial driver. With *Alive II* still hogging the US charts as *Powerage* struggled to a peak of No. 133 (the 'Rock'n'Roll Damnation' single didn't register at all in America), the idea of 'doing a Kiss' and releasing an AC/DC live album began to be openly discussed in the upper-floor offices at Rockefeller Plaza.

Not everybody was convinced, though. In Australia, where *Powerage* was now officially the worst-selling AC/DC album so far, reaching only No. 22 before quickly falling away, Ted Albert was looking to squeeze a little more juice out of the existing catalogue by issuing a greatest hits collection. Ostensibly titled *12 Of The Best*, and conceived specifically with the Australian market in mind – though Alberts intended to sell it to Atlantic as good for them too – it would contain two tracks from the original *High Voltage* – 'Baby, Please Don't Go' and 'She's Got Balls'; four from *TNT* (still their best-selling Australian album) – 'It's A Long Way To The Top', 'The Jack', 'TNT' and 'High Voltage'; three from *Dirty Deeds Done Dirt Cheap* – the title track, 'Problem Child' and 'Jailbreak'; and three from *Let There Be Rock* – the title track, 'Dog Eat Dog' and 'Whole Lotta Rosie'. There would be none from *Powerage*. Atlantic wavered over releasing it internationally, attracted by the fact it would cost next to nothing to produce, but concerned by the fact there had only been three AC/DC albums released thus far in America, four in the UK, none of which had been a significant chart hit. The idea of a 'best of' from a band most fans still hadn't actually bought an album by seemed premature, even injurious. They nixed the idea, in favour of a live album. But Alberts felt it would do no harm to release *12 Of The Best* in Australia, at least. Indeed, it might provide a necessary financial fillip at a time when Alberts were pouring more money than ever into AC/DC, with ever more slight returns. There were no longer any easy-money gigs to be had in Oz. Meanwhile, the costs of keeping the band on the road in America, where even their few headline gigs barely paid the rent, and their big support slots cost a fortune in 'buy-ins', were only partly being underwritten by Atlantic. Everything else – from the wages for their road crew to that bottle of whisky Bon insisted be waiting for him after every show – was coming out of Alberts' bank account in Sydney. The only area where AC/DC's revenues had begun to sharply increase in 1978 was through the new, expanded lines of merchandise they were now selling at their shows; from simple T-shirts and tour programmes emblazoned with the lightning bolt AC/DC logo, to a new line in patches that could be sewn onto denim jackets and jeans, to various logoed wristbands, posters and other memorabilia. In the decade since The Beatles pioneered the idea of selling secondary, non-musical merchandise off the back of the group's name – but sold the idea so cheaply to any franchise that came along they made only a fraction of the profits – merchandising in the music business had grown into an ever more sophisticated operation. By 1978, the idea of placing a band's logo – in effect, its signature – on various, clearly band-derived products, had begun to take hold. AC/DC became one of the first mid-level rock bands to use it as a significant revenue stream to keep their operation afloat. Others quickly followed suit and by the early-Eighties bands like Iron Maiden, Rush and Motörhead were making more money from their merchandise than they were from record or ticket sales. AC/DC were one of the first, though, to recognise how much value the collector-mad, mostly male rock audiences put on owning these products. From that perspective, it's easy to see why Alberts had been so keen to release an AC/DC greatest hits. They got as far as designing a sleeve for the album and sending out a press release announcing its imminent release when – under pressure from the band, in the shape of George, and backed by Atlantic, who feared it would interfere with their own plans for a live album that autumn – Alberts reluctantly pulled it from its schedules.

With George and Harry back in the studio sifting through live tapes from the recent Glasgow Apollo show, plus various live recordings from the last American tour and, going further back, to Australia on the Giant Dose tour, in preparation for the live album it had now been decided Atlantic would release in that year, by July AC/DC were back touring America. Still squeezing in their own headline shows at clubs and small theatres wherever it was feasible, mostly the tour concentrated on getting them in front of the biggest audiences possible, tour-hopping from opening slots with Rainbow and Alice Cooper, to Journey and Aerosmith, Doug Thaler using every contact he had to push the band along. 'The fact that they were so good at blowing the main band off each night made it easier and harder,' recalls Thaler. 'It meant you always felt pretty confident no matter where you booked 'em they would kill.' But word was now getting out. 'One thing the big headliners don't like at all: the young support act getting all the attention.' It was Michael Kleffner, though, whose longstanding relationship with promoter Bill Graham landed the band a spot on the biggest outdoor event in the rock'n'roll calendar that year: the Day On The Green festival, then into its third year. Staged at the massive Oakland Stadium, outside San Francisco, on 22 July, the headliners were Aerosmith, Foreigner, Pat Travers and Van Halen. But according to the review the next day in the *Pasadena Star-News*: 'It was little-known Australian group AC/DC that brought 70,000 fans to their feet ... The quintet's 10.30 a.m. show aroused the crowd with a moving set of power rock'n'roll.' Even *Rolling Stone*, still holding the group at arm's length, was forced to concede, when reviewing their set opening for Rainbow at the Palladium in New York in August: 'There's nothing new going on musically, but AC/DC attacks the old clichés with overwhelming exuberance.'

Two weeks into the tour, they were joined on their own headline dates by a San Franciscan outfit called Yesterday And Today – better known in the Eighties as Y&T. Their singer, Dave Meniketti, says the most memorable thing about their three-night jaunt together was that Bon spent the entire time travelling on his band's bus. 'We didn't think too much of it other than, oh, there's this cool band that we're playing with and the lead singer is so pissed off that the guys in his band don't wanna party in the bus that he figured, 'Hell, I'm hanging with these young guys! They'll party!' And we did. I remember us pulling into gas stations and him and [wild man Y&T drummer] Leonard [Haze] going into the gas station's little store and buying like Jack Daniels and stuff like that, and coming back onto the bus. I mean, it wasn't a bus it was like a large Dodge van with a padded bottom that we all were like sitting around in. But it was crazy. It was a great time. I also remember that they couldn't find Cliff [Williams] one time after a show. He'd gone off with some chick and didn't leave any number where he was going or anything. The bus was ready to leave and it was hours late and they were like, "Oh my god! What are we gonna do? We don't know where he is!"'

Going off and hanging out with the support band was becoming a habit for Bon now. 'It became the usual thing,' says Jeffery, 'half an hour to go to show-time and everyone wondering where the fuck is Bon. Next thing he'd turn up with a bunch of strangers, all waving whiskey bottles and smoking joints.' Jeffery remembers a particularly memorable occasion when the band headlined over Cheap Trick and Molly Hatchet in Jacksonville – the same moonshine territory that had been among the first to pick up on AC/DC. 'We were doing a three-dollar-a-ticket radio-sponsored tour with Cheap Trick. And it was flip-flop, one night they'd close and one night we'd close. Standard PA and lights, you shared it whether you were headlining or not. No compression in the PA, you can only have purple lights, that sort of thing. In Jacksonville, Cheap Trick was supposed to close it. It was sold out, you know, eleven thousand people. Jam-packed, right, where normally we'd be playing to a couple of thousand. Cheap Trick said, there's no fucking way we're closing. You're fucking finishing the show. And it was fantastic! They played "Whole Lotta Rosie" and it was the first time we heard the crowd chant "Angus!" over the intro. There'd been little bits of it before but that was the first time we'd heard it in this gobsmacked hall full of fucking people, drunk, just having a party enjoying themselves!

'We get back to the hotel and there's a wedding reception and we're down there drinking and having a great time.' As usual Bon stayed with it till the hotel bar closed, and, as usual, Ian stayed with him to keep an eye. 'The rest of the guys had already gone to bed by then but there's me and Bon and as usual Bon would have all his best friends with him that he'd met that night. But eventually we went upstairs and it turns out we're on the floor where the honeymoon suite is. The guy's got his bride there and he's pissed out of his head and she's sozzled too. I opened our door but the guy's there and he can't get his key in his door. Bon says, "Here, mate, let me help you with that." So I put my bag in the room, came out and there's Bon with the bride swept up in his fucking arms disappearing into our room! He slams the door and I'm standing there, can't get in, locked out of my room, thinking: "Bon's knobbing the bride. I better get downstairs and get a spare key and get back upstairs and rescue the woman and save Bon from arrest!" It was a classic ...'

Not everyone found Bon's increasingly drunken behaviour so endearing. Says Barry Bergman: 'I told Bon he was gonna die young if he didn't stop drinking. But Bon told me, he said: "I live for the day." He was an absolutely sensational human being. He was a very kind and caring and loving human being. But I'll tell you, he couldn't help himself. He was an alcoholic.' Bergman now found himself getting closer to Angus. 'After a lot of the shows, the band would go back to the dressing room, meeting fans or picking up groupies, or whatever the hell they were doing. [But] Angus didn't drink. He was into hot tea and Coca-Cola. I didn't drink either. I never drank or did drugs. So he and I used to go out for something to eat and talk. Angus is a beautiful human being. He's a very intelligent guy. Banging chicks and all that, that was never really his big thing. He was about doing the work ... It was Bon who was the party animal.'

Opening for Thin Lizzy at the Royal Oak Theater, in Michigan, on 13 September, the AC/DC gang mentality exerted itself again as, halfway through their set, they came under attack from a posse of uniformed in-house security men, who rushed the stage in an attempt to stop the show. When the first officer to arrive made the mistake of grabbing Bon's arm, he received a head-butt in the face for his trouble, sending him crashing to the floor. At which point the rest of the band threw down their instruments and along with their roadies all joined in a free-for-all fight on the stage. As usual, Bon had become 'close friends' with Thin Lizzy and their crew ('He used to come into our dressing room and pretend to like us so he could drink our beer,' Lizzy guitarist Gary Moore later told me) and order was only restored finally through the intervention of Lizzy's own management and record company team, who were there. The trouble had begun when Ian Jeffery, who was still doubling as their sound engineer, was punched and dragged from the mixing desk after 'refusing' to turn the sound down. According to the security team, the show had

exceeded a local ordinance proclaiming that any sound over 100 decibels was simply 'noise' and would have to be shut down. The 'Decibel
Deputy', as he was called, had apparently clocked the sound level from
AC/DC's mixing desk to be over 125 decibels and demanded Ian do
something about it. Misunderstanding the word 'loud' being yelled
in his ear by a stranger, Ian had replied, 'Yeah, and we're just starting
to cook!' To which the DD had responded with a sharp punch to his
back, which he in turn was rewarded for with a Jeffery-sized boot to
the chest, sending him flying off the podium. Cue: pandemonium. 'I
was being physically carried out the door! I broke free, ran down the
side of the building and got back in to see Malcolm looking at me like,
"What the fuck are you doing? Why aren't you at the desk?" I yelled,
"They threw me off, too loud!" At which point, Malcolm throws down
his guitar and starts chucking all the monitors into the pit! All the
Tasco guys who were in charge of the monitors went nuclear and a
big fight then broke out between them and our crew.'

Ian managed to grab Malcolm and the others from the resulting
melee and get them back to the dressing room. But Malcolm still
wasn't having it. Demanding of Ian, 'Show me the cunt!', he marched
over to the promoter – 'Who really didn't have anything to with it,'
says Jeffery – and punched him in the face. That's when the police
were called. In the end, the promoter agreed to withdraw the threat
of an assault charge in exchange for the band paying $20,000 to
cover the cost of equipment damage. The details sorted, though, the
band resumed their set to huge, if somewhat baffled, cheers from the
1,700-strong crowd.

'For little guys, the Youngs were tough,' says Jeffery, 'absolutely
tough as nails; Malcolm much more so than Angus. But I tell you
what, Angus is a wiry character. I would not get on the wrong side of
him, that's for sure. Their frameworks belie everything. If there was
something that got them to that level, size didn't come into account.
You go do what you've got to fucking do. You don't think of what the
repercussions might be. And that's what they were like.' The only
one who ever really stood up to Malcolm, he says, was Bon. 'But in a
much different way. Bon was that character where he had authority.

Bon was a loveable character. Other times, you spoke to Bon, you knew: this needs to be done and it needs to be done now. He would have his scenes with Malcolm and Angus but if Malcolm wanted to get pushy, Bon would let him push, then say: "What's that for? That's not necessary." He would come from that point of view all the time. And he would never lift his hands to one of his other band members. If one of them wanted to punch him he would like give them that look and say, "You don't need to fucking do that, you know?"' As a result, though they came close, Bon and Malcolm never actually came to blows. 'I saw a couple of times where it got really threatening, you know, but it stopped short of that.'

When they weren't having a go at each other, AC/DC would be putting the fear into the bands they were opening for. The late Ronnie James Dio, then the frontman of Rainbow, recalled being caught off guard by Malcolm Young when the two bands toured together. 'The first time I ever met Malcolm he came into our dressing room looking for beer, as they'd gotten through their rider in about five minutes. He never said hello, just, "Where's the beer?" I recall [Rainbow bassist and well-known Scottish hell-raiser] Jimmy Bain muttering something under his breath. The next thing you know, Jimmy had gone to sit down and Mal had pulled the chair from under him. But that's what they were like. Young and brash. They'd had to fight for everything ...' Or as Gary Moore would tell me, 'They were fucking unreal. People used to talk about Thin Lizzy being a gang, but we had nothin' on them! These guys weren't fucking kidding. The brothers especially could be very scary. Angus wouldn't look at you before a gig. They were all out to get us, to blow us away. And they succeeded, actually. The only one I didn't have a lot of time for was Bon. He seemed a decent enough bloke, but he was so drunk. One time he was so drunk he could hardly speak, then he'd go on and his singing would be brilliant. Very strange ...'

It was also around this time that Phil Rudd began showing serious signs of road fever. Like Bon and Malcolm, Phil not only liked a drink but was also inordinately fond of good strong sticky weed. Add in the copious amounts of cocaine that was now the *lingua franca* of any high-profile American tour in the 1970s – as indeed it mostly remains to this day – and Rudd, who'd always been a ball of nervous energy, was starting to crack. By September, as AC/DC burned their way across the American Midwest, 50 gigs into a 66-date tour – at one point playing ten nights straight without a break, a ludicrously heavy schedule no artist of a similar stature would dream of undertaking these days – Phil's mental and physical well-being was in such a parlous state he had to be checked into hospital between shows, where he would be heavily sedated in order to get some 'rest'. Silver would later tell Clinton Walker how Bon, in particular, 'was pretty freaked out by the way they just propped Phil up and made him perform ... There was no actual concern for Phil's long-term well-being. And basically, that was pretty much their attitude to Bon too, with his drinking. Nobody really seemed to give a shit that he was killing himself, as long as he got out there and did it.'

Others would not agree with that view, but one person who did care very much about the state of his old friend was Vince Lovegrove, who joined the tour in Atlanta in August, as Bon's guest, and would later write an article about it for *RAM*. Watching the band play at the Atlanta Symphony Hall, sharing the bill as co-headliners with Cheap Trick, 'Very impressed, I was,' Vince wrote. 'Personal driver, ritzy hotel, the best looking groupies I'd ever set eyes on. I mean, it was the real thing. I thought, if anyone deserves it, Bon does ... He said he'd make it and he was making it: in style.' Lovegrove said he saw Bon through new eyes after the show as he changed out of his battered old denims and into an expensive, three-quarter-length leopard-skin coat, then nabbed the bottle of Scotch that was always now waiting for him backstage in the dressing room. This, Bon explained only half-jokingly, was him in 'wolf in wolf's clothing' mode. Playing the part of the rock star to the hilt in the only way he knew how: by 'going for it'; by 'getting out if it'; by saying 'fuck it'. Sharing a taxi back to his 'ritzy' hotel, the Plum Tree Inn, Vince recalled sitting with Bon in his 'luxurious' hotel room: 'Bon and me, an Australian photographer, a few groupies, and the odd Seedie wandering in and out in an attempt to find the action.' The only action that night, though, wrote Lovegrove, occurred after the groupies had grown bored and the photographer nodded off, and the two old band-mates 'became self-indulgent about the good old days'.

It was at this point that Vince extracted an unexpected confession, as Bon began to tell him how 'tired of it all' he was. 'I love it,' Bon went on. 'But I want to have a base. It's just the constant pressures of touring that's fucking it. I've been on the road for thirteen years. Planes, hotels, groupies, booze, people, towns. They all scrape something from you. We're doing it and we'll get there, but I wish we didn't have these crushing day after day grinds to keep up with.' For Bon, the rock'n'roll life was 'all there is', he told Lovegrove. But he could no longer 'hack the rest of the shit that goes with it'. Recalling that night more than 25 years later, Vince recalled Bon telling him how he'd 'got the best deal because I'd settled down and wasn't on the road any more'. How Bon was 'getting sick of this' and talking about moving back out to the countryside somewhere. 'He said, "I'd like to settle down, live an ordinary life like anyone else and just play guitar."'

The drunken, small-hours ramblings of a road-worn old showman they might have been. But there was a degree of yearning there too, thought Vince, which also fuelled the heavy drinking. Bon had given his all to these kids – AC/DC – but he was no longer a kid himself, and more painfully aware of the fact with every mile they drove down the never-ending road on the 'highway to hell', as Angus had taken to calling the American tour of '78. Something, surely, would have to give ...

CHAPTER ELEVEN

Blood on the Rocks

Bon Scott and Phil Rudd may have started to crack, but that had to be their business, as far as the AC/DC schedule was concerned. With the live album – non-ironically but nevertheless all too aptly titled *If You Want Blood ... You've Got It* – set for release on 15 October, AC/DC had just four days off between the final date of their marathon US tour, opening for Aerosmith before nearly 9,000 people at the Coliseum in Fort Wayne, Indiana, on 3 October, and the start of their next European and British tour: 32 shows in just 37 days, across eight countries, culminating in two sold-out nights at London's Hammersmith Odeon, on 15 and 16 November.

With the ten-track live album serving as both documentary proof of AC/DC's growing status as one of the premier-league live rock acts in the world and as a *de facto* best-of, George Young and Harry Vanda had done a decent enough job of sprucing it up for mainstream consumption, mixing out obvious mistakes, choosing the best takes of the tracks, cleaning up the lead and backing vocals and bringing the whole package up to studio standard, as was common for officially released live albums, then as now. One of the simplest tricks they used in the studio, which added to the atmosphere of the record considerably, was the addition of crowd noise, overlaying pre-recorded waves of applause between the tracks, so that the songs conveyed more of a sense of a live occasion than the actual gigs, where there would often be lulls between numbers as Bon casually chatted to the crowd, announcing the title of the next song in an offhand way that drew little reaction from the audience.

These were just the trimmings though to a dish that needed little adornment. AC/DC live was a genuinely thrilling proposition. Released on Friday 13th, *If You Want Blood* ... would include all the obvious crowd-pleasers like 'The Jack' (its strictly live, 'dirty' lyrics included on record for the first time); 'Whole Lotta Rosie' (with new crowd chant of 'Angus! Angus!' over the juddering intro recorded for the first time, thereby embedding it for ever into the consciousness of all future generations of AC/DC concert-goers); and lengthy barn-storming encores of 'Let There Be Rock' (distinguished by the very real roar of approval from the Glasgow crowd at seeing the band return to the stage wearing Scottish football shirts) and 'Rocker', cleverly edited down from its usual 12 minutes-plus to a more radio-accommodating three minutes dead. As a result, *If You Want Blood* ... finally opened the doors for AC/DC to the UK Top 20, climbing as high eventually as No. 13. To mark the occasion, Phil Carson threw a party backstage after the first Hammersmith show where Bon got so drunk, according to *Melody Maker* writer Steve Gett, he 'needed the stomach pump before getting to his feet again'. Gett was joking – but only just. Bon was in such bad shape that, backstage before the second night at the Odeon, he told Phil Lynott, who was there, to expect 'more of a club show tonight, I'm fucked'. Speaking on the phone that afternoon to the *Herald* in Melbourne, Bon had admitted that the only noticeable effect chart success in Britain was having was on 'my intake of alcohol. I can now afford to drink twice as much.'

The plan after that had been to return home to Sydney for Christmas, ready to record a new album in the New Year before taking off for their first tour of Japan in March. Behind the scenes, though, a new storm was brewing.

In America, despite the months of touring over the preceding two years, putting themselves in front of the biggest audiences available around the country – in spite of the word-of-mouth which was growing, as evidenced by the upswing in theatre venues available for them to headline their own shows in, and the increase in merch sales, the strongest indicator of a band's increasing or decreasing popularity at ground level – the live AC/DC album did not repeat the success

Kiss had had with their two *Alive* albums, reaching a paltry No. 113. Very small potatoes indeed for an act which Atlantic in New York was expected to keep backing to the hilt with tour support and marketing dollars.

It was now that what Michael Browning calls 'the discussions' began in earnest over at Rockefeller Plaza. Everyone agreed AC/DC had something. Good live band, hard workers; good songs, albums made relatively cheaply. What they didn't have yet though were any hits. Not in America, baby. And that's where everyone's – including the brothers' – focus now lay. Maybe it was the singer, enquired Jerry Greenberg, not for the first time. Maybe he didn't have the right voice for American radio? Maybe they would do better with someone else? Browning began to hear that kind of talk a lot now from New York. Indeed, the late Seventies and early Eighties were a time bedevilled by American record companies complaining about singers – particularly non-American singers – with the 'wrong voice' for US radio. At a time when the rock music getting played on US radio tended towards the high-end slick of acts like the Eagles, Fleetwood Mac, the Steve Miller Band and Boston, acts whose singers tended towards a much higher, more mellifluous register than Bon Scott ever sought out, it's easy to see why Atlantic struggled to see past this 'problem'. But then the music business, then as now, has a short memory, and it had only been a few short years since Rod Stewart, Robert Plant and Paul Rodgers had been considered the 'right' voices for US rock radio. What this overlooked was how unique and characterful Bon Scott's voice was. The irony being that in less than two years AC/DC would enjoy greater sales success in America than any rock band previously with a singer who made Bon sound like Doris Day.

Bon's predecessor in AC/DC, Dave Evans, speculates: 'I don't know if it's true or not because I wasn't there but I heard from several people that for a while there before they cracked it in the USA, certain people over there weren't very happy with Bon's vocals, and there was contemplation of replacing him. Now Bon would always have been mindful of the fact that when he joined the band AC/DC was successful. We'd had a hit record. We'd played all the major venues in Australia – and still they were quite happy to sack me. He knew it didn't matter how big the band was, he had to keep looking over his shoulder.'

Says Browning: 'Yeah, look, there was that kind of discussion going on. Not in a blunt either-do-it-or-we-drop-you type way. But Bon's voice was just not accessible and they were never going to really get huge radio airplay in America with his voice. There was that kind of conversation going on.' For now, however, Browning kept such ideas from all three brothers, judging he could best handle them alone. 'I pretty much kept them immune from that type of conversation. I knew how much they loved Bon and getting rid of Bon would never have been an option. So there was no point in repeating or relating. It was just something at Atlantic, we'd have the conversation maybe but that was as far as it ever went.'

When Michael refused to relent about Bon, the discussions took a new turn. Maybe the band needed a new producer. 'That was part of it. It was Bon and a new producer that would give them a sound that made sense in America, on American FM radio. Or someone who could possibly make Bon sound a little bit more accessible, that was the idea. There was a *lot* of pressure coming at me from that point on. The general feeling was that they needed new producers who had more of an understanding of what was happening sonically, in America in particular.'

Driving the conversation was Michael Kleffner, backed by Jerry Greenberg. Recalls Barry Bergman: 'I wasn't in those meetings but I would speak with Michael Kleffner a lot and I know that he believed they needed a new producer.' In January 1979, Kleffner flew to Sydney to break the news personally. 'He took a trip to Australia to sit down with George and Harry and tell them, "Hey, if you really care about your brothers, you've got to step down."' This was never going to be news that George, in particular, was going to take well. Nevertheless, Kleffner was adamant: for AC/DC's career to take off in America, and for Atlantic in New York to continue investing in their future, George would have to step aside and let someone else take over in the studio. What's more, Kleffner had just the guy in mind. A week later there was a new face in the studios at King Street: that of 36-year-old Edwin H. Kramer – Eddie to his friends, of which he was about to discover he had none in Sydney.

Born in Cape Town, South Africa, in 1942, Kramer had made his name in London in the Sixties, working as the in-house engineer at various record company-owned studios. His break came in 1966, when he took a job at Olympic Sound, in Barnes, where he engineered albums for an impressive array of chart acts, including The Beatles and the Rolling Stones. When an unknown young American guitarist named Jimi Hendrix arrived at Olympic just before Christmas 1966, it was Kramer that helped him and his producer-manager, former Animals bassist Chas Chandler, record his debut album, *Are You Experienced*. Kramer would remain Hendrix's sound engineer for every album he made before his death in 1970. Kramer then co-produced a succession of posthumously released official Hendrix albums, notably both *The Cry Of Love* and *Rainbow Bridge*, which contained all the material the guitarist had been intending to include on what would have been his next double-album. On the strength of his impeccable credentials, Kramer had gone on to record with many other high-profile artists, including Joe Cocker, Derek & The Dominoes and, most famously, Led Zeppelin, working alongside guitarist and producer Jimmy Page on five Zep albums between 1969 and 1975. Now living in Miami, by the time Michael Kleffner approached him to work with AC/DC, Eddie Kramer had also become the producer of Kiss's best-selling albums, including both *Alive* albums and, in 1977, their biggest chart hit, *Love Gun*.

Still a guy who can drop names like Brian Jones and Jimi Hendrix into his conversation, Kramer admits that back in January 1979, when he first met AC/DC, 'I was a little impressed with myself, shall we say.' This was not an approach likely to endear him to street toughs like Malcolm and Angus. In fact, with all three Young brothers still fuming over Kramer's unilateral appointment by the suits in New York, they were ready to go to war. George was especially galled as he felt he – and to a lesser, more supportive sense, Harry – had been the key to whatever successes AC/DC had already achieved. He and

Harry were also then going through their own most prolific period of success. Having turned Alberts into *the* rock label in Australia, following AC/DC with similarly domestically successful rock acts like Rose Tattoo and The Angels, they had more recently diversified to provide giant international pop hits for John Paul Young, another expat Glaswegian that had grown up in Sydney, whose Vanda and Young-penned single 'Love Is In The Air' had been a Top 10 hit all over the world in 1978 – including America, where Atlantic were now claiming George and Harry lacked any understanding of the workings of modern-day radio formats.

'George had been fabulous for them,' concedes Browning, 'but he lived 12,000 miles away and hadn't been to America for years. American FM radio had a sound that you had to experience to really understand what it took to break a band in America, through that medium.' Ultimately, adds Browning, 'even though now everyone says the best records [AC/DC] ever made were with George and Harry, the concept of finding a record producer that was gonna crack the American nut was the right thing to do. Atlantic just happened to choose the wrong guy. In typical American record company thinking, they went, "This guy's been involved with Jimi Hendrix and Led Zeppelin, therefore he's gonna be the guy that AC/DC need." At that point, I don't think Atlantic had any idea how influential George and Harry were – George in particular. And, of course, it didn't go down all that well with Malcolm and Angus either. They really felt pretty bad about it. It was a very difficult period. You knew they weren't happy. But they kind of went, if that's what's got to happen, if that's the only way we're going to continue making progress internationally, then that's what we've got to do.'

Working up ideas with Kramer in the same studio they had created their first five albums in with George and Harry was a predictably uphill task for the new producer, who recalls: 'Kleffner was a friend of mine and he'd seen the success of Kiss.' When he showed Kramer a video of AC/DC playing live, 'I said, "This band is incredible!" And I guess that started the whole conversation.' Kiss were a tremendous live band that Eddie had managed to capture the essence of on record.

If he could do the same for AC/DC . . . But, as Kramer points out now, 'The record company thought I was the perfect choice, not realising that in order for something like this to work the band had to agree. But the band in Australia was very much in charge of their own destiny and really had very strong opinions about what they wanted and how they wanted it to sound. By the time I arrived there the writing was already on the wall that this was not going to work.'

A situation not helped by the upturn in Bon's drinking: always heavy it had recently become excessive even by his standards. 'I went there,' says Kramer, 'hung out with them, tried to do some demos with them, and realised that there was an obvious difficulty with the singer too. He had the most incredible voice but trying to keep him in check from his drinking was a very tough call. And I didn't quite realise that at the time. But I think more than anything the band resented me being foisted onto them. [It] was like sticking a pin into them. In addition to which, I don't think I was the right guy for the job. My attitude was wrong. I don't think I was earthy enough or tough enough . . . They needed somebody like their older brother and I wasn't that. I was the antithesis of that.'

After just two days, they called it quits and Kramer told Kleffner to bring the band over to Miami, to start work proper on the album. 'We started rehearsing in Florida and that's when the proverbial shit hit the fan.' Malcolm recalls: 'I remember he looked at Bon and said to us, "Can your guy sing?" He might have sat behind the knobs for Hendrix, but he's certainly not Hendrix, I can tell you that much.' In a letter home, Bon complained that Miami was boring: 'an Elephant's Graveyard for geriatric Jews'. Of Eddie Kramer, he simply said: 'It turns out the guy was full of bullshit and couldn't produce a healthy fart.' For Michael Browning, it was simple: 'Kramer had no idea about song material, what was cool, what was not cool. His whole focus was really just on how to make it sound better. It was a hopeless situation.' Made worse, Kramer counters, because 'Bon was drinking like crazy and didn't have any lyrics.' Until then, they had always had George to lean on in the studio; to help the brothers write and arrange the material. Kramer: 'He was the older brother and they were used to him and he was used to their ways. I was not. I could tell Kiss what to do. I understood them very well. I didn't understand AC/DC. [It needed] quite a bit of reconnaissance, and gentle sort of figuring out who they are and the personalities involved. I wasn't there from the beginning. I wasn't *one of them.*' You weren't part of the clan? 'Oh, my god! You've just hit on the right word – clan. Because they were so tight together, that was part of the magic of the band. They were so instinctive. They each knew what the other was going to do. To bring me into that, it was like [throwing] a monkey wrench into the mix.'

The sessions with Kramer staggered on for three weeks, at the end of which the band had filled several cassettes with 'bits and pieces', including the halting riff to a work-in-progress they'd dubbed 'Highway To Hell' – after Angus's description of their last American tour – and the bones of another song that would eventually make it onto the next album as filler, a weak attempt at a US radio hit called 'Love Hungry Man'. Mostly, though, according to Malcolm, 'We came out of it with nothing.' The nadir, says Browning, was reached when Kramer tried to get them to record 'Gimme Some Lovin'', a 1966 hit for the Spencer Davis Group.

There would be a price to pay for the disaster of the experiment with Kramer – and this time it would be Michael Browning who coughed up. With the brothers, he says, there was always 'a degree to which the messenger really cops it. It was definitely part of my demise from the group.' But then, as he admits, 'it wasn't a great period, when I'm the manager and suddenly the group were in Miami with a producer they didn't want to work with. I was in New York and the group were down there getting frustrated as hell, so obviously I would have been part of the array of people that they weren't very happy with at the time.'

As part of his own effort to break the band in America, Browning had recently begun sharing a rented apartment on 48th Street, New York, with two expat South Africans he'd recently hooked up with named Cedric Kushner and Clive Calder. Kushner was the 30-year-old son of a grocer who'd arrived in America at 21 to try his hand as a boxer. Weighing 400lb, at his peak, if Cedric caught you with a hook you went down, but his size made him slow and easy to hit, and by 1974 he'd worked as a Ferris wheel operator on the Jersey Shore and as a pool cleaner at a Miami hotel. At which point he returned to New York and got into rock concert promotion, starting with past-their-best names like Steppenwolf before striking gold when a little-known band named Fleetwood Mac that he had been supportive of in the clubs suddenly hit pay-dirt in 1977 with the zillion-selling *Rumours* album. From that point on Kushner was a player, promoting rock shows artists like Bob Segar and the Doobie Brothers, at prestige NY-area venues like Madison Square Garden, Boston Garden and the Nassau Coliseum. Kushner was a single, good-time guy who liked rock'n'roll and loved AC/DC. Michael Browning not unreasonably considered him a strong potential ally. Clive Calder, meanwhile, was a former musician turned music biz entrepreneur whose company Zomba – after the first capital of Malawi – had started in London in the early Seventies as a management company but since expanded into recording, distribution, production and publishing, opening an office in New York in 1978. Calder's star client was a young South African named Robert John Lange – 'Mutt' to his friends – who had worked with Calder and his business partner, Ralph Simon, for years, producing domestic hits in South Africa, before the three men, all roughly the same age, pooled their resources and relocated to London in 1974, where Lange's career began to take off. 'We were politically very much opposed to the old apartheid regime,' Simon was quoted as saying. They were also attracted to the idea of applying skills learned in the tiny South African music business – where a mere 10,000 copies would land you a No. 1 record – to the vastly more lucrative British and, eventually, American music businesses. Again, for an outsider to the US music business looking for like-minded friends, Clive Calder looked like another potentially powerful ally to Michael Browning.

When Michael received an angry phone call from Malcolm late one night in January 1979, telling him he refused to work one more day with Eddie Kramer, Michael happened to be sitting around the apartment with both Clive and Mutt Lange.

'I got off the phone and just looked at Mutt and said, "You have *got* to make this record." He was sitting right next to me after I got off the phone call from Malcolm, and I just hammered the shit out of him to make the record. Clive was going, "No, no. He's doing the Boomtown Rats, he's doing City Boy. AC/DC haven't got a big enough base. Mutt's not going to anyone that sells under 500,000 units ... etc." But I just didn't stop. I just hammered them and by the end of the night I'd convinced Clive and Mutt to do it. I called Malcolm back and said, it's cool, I've got Mutt Lange. And he said, "Who? Who's he?" I gave him some names Mutt had worked with but he hadn't heard of any of them. I just remember Malcolm saying, "We couldn't give a fuck. We've got to get anyone – anyone! – but Eddie Kramer!" They didn't care, as long as it wasn't going to be Eddie Kramer. So that's how that whole thing with Mutt started.'

Though neither Browning nor Lange – nor any of the Young brothers – could have known it yet, it was to be a game-changing decision for all involved. 'It wasn't as if I had a choice,' says Browning now. 'I knew Mutt had done some good stuff for City Boy and the Boomtown Rats. But that wasn't really what I based his ability as a producer on. Mutt and Clive had played me stuff he'd been working on with his ex-wife Stevie, who was in a group called Night and it just really blew me away. It was really more that, that gave me the confidence to tell Malcolm he was gonna be fabulous.'

Born in Mufulira, northern Rhodesia – now Zambia – in November 1948, Lange came from a privileged background: his German mother was from a prosperous family and his South African father was a mining engineer. Nicknamed 'Mutt' at school – a name he may have liked because it belied his upper-middle-class origins – Lange grew up listening to his father's country records, favouring voodoo yodellers like Slim Whitman and Hank Williams. As fellow South African – and fellow producer – Kevin Shirley explains, 'The nature of the South African government in that time was so Conservative-Christian that rock music was really frowned on. Woodstock was

frowned upon, LSD and anything to do with drugs was all suppos-
edly part of this evil genre. Certainly in our house we didn't have any
rock'n'roll. The only thing we had was Simon and Garfunkel, no Elvis
Presley or Beatles, no nothing.'

It wasn't until Lange was sent to Belfast High School in the eastern
Transvaal that he really connected with pop music. Starting his own
band playing rhythm guitar and singing harmonies, Mutt became a
big name on South Africa's miniaturised music scene. Trevor Rabin,
part of home-grown South African pop sensations Rabbit in the
mid-Seventies, and the singer-guitarist who relaunched Yes virtually
single-handedly in the Eighties, with the innovative production of his
hit song 'Owner Of A Lonely Heart', recalls seeing Lange perform in
the late Sixties. 'He would do Joe Cocker's version of "With A Little
Help From My Friends" and he would sound and look just like Joe.
It was extraordinary. Mutt was an amazing singer. He could do anything with his voice.'

Rabin was an equally adept singer and musician. Before Rabbitt
he had briefly been part of Clive Calder band Freedom's Children –
a heavy-handed mix of prog and psych rock before such terms had
been invented – and when Calder moved into production Rabin went
with him, as an all-purpose session hand. It was through Clive that
Rabin then met Lange, also now reaching out into production. 'I used
to do all Mutt's sessions in South Africa, as a guitar player. I did *so*
much stuff with him.' It was now Rabin learned what every musician that would subsequently work with the earnest producer would
discover. In the words of Bob Geldof, Mutt Lange was 'a martinet – a
perfectionist who drove others as hard as he drove himself'. Trevor
Rabin chuckles at the description. 'I remember Mutt and I had one
kind of awkward moment in the studio. I was doubling a guitar part
and he stopped and said, "It's just a tiny bit out." And I'd done it and
done it and finally gone, "Oh, god, Mutt. Are we splitting hairs here?"
He said, "Well, they're *my* hairs."' He laughs. 'Outside of that he was,
I think, the best producer to come out of South Africa.'

Part of Lange's abilities, Rabin feels, came from the heavy restrictions put on him as a musician in South Africa in the apartheid era.

'Western rock music was banned, we had no big-name artists coming to play, the live scene, such as it was, was very small and closed off.' Working on a succession of what became known as *Springbok Hits* – compilation albums of Western pop hits re-recorded and sung note-perfect by Lange and his regular studio crew, led by Rabin. As Kevin Shirley, who cut his teeth as a musician and producer in the same studios as Lange and Rabin, and would go on to work with Led Zeppelin and Iron Maiden, to name just two, explains, 'Because we had these boycotts because of apartheid, we just didn't get any new music whatever. Mutt would get the seven best singles, whatever they were, flown in every week, and he would copy them in the studio. And they would make these things called Springbok Hits that would have six No. 1 hits on one side and six No. 1 hits on the other. He would copy the productions, he would copy all the singing and playing – and they were fantastically well done. We had no way of hearing the originals but I've since heard them and he did an incredible job. So not only was Mutt this incredible musician and producer, he could work virtually in any style, no problem.'

Says Rabin: 'Here was a guy who could write music, play music, had his own thing. And now he's got the best singer to sing his songs in Stevie, who has just this marvellous voice. But Mutt just really got to the point where no one [in South Africa] could understand what he was about and I think that's why he left. Before he did, there was one album I played guitar on for Mutt, which was really a significant record for him in South Africa' – a self-titled album by Cape Town funk singer Richard Jon Smith. 'It was one of the first times [Mutt worked with] a guy who had a lot of credibility as a musician as well as an artist who was doing well. Mutt took him to a completely other level. But Mutt never tried to promote himself. He was the same as he is now, just very quiet and very into himself. Very unassuming, no arrogance involved, it was pretty extraordinary ...'

By the early Seventies, Mutt had married Stevie van Kerken – known professionally as Stevie Vann, and already a teenage star in South Africa – and started a band called Hocus. But with virtually nowhere to play – 'not more than once anyway', as Rabin says – such a huge talent quickly outgrew its confines, and the newlyweds headed off to London, under the aegis of Clive Calder and Ralph Simon, and formed a new group, called Stephen, who were signed almost immediately by Dave Dee – another expat South African, and former Sixties pop star, now working in A&R for Warners. But when their debut single, the jaunty, highly polished 'Right On Running Man' – like proto-Stevie-Nicks-era Fleetwood Mac, five years ahead of the curve – failed to make the charts, both Langes began to sense their luck running out. The stress proved too great for the marriage to survive and by 1976 Mutt had found a new love in Belfast-born Oonagh O'Reilly, and was back in the market for producing other artists.

His first notable success came with a Birmingham sextet called City Boy, whose busy guitars, strident keyboards and complex vocal arrangements helped to overcome an image partway between bookworm and disco dad, but whose musical needs suited Lange's hyperefficient talents perfectly. He was able to sing or play better than any of them, so the band were happy for their still unknown young producer to school them through five albums, finally making the UK Top 10, in 1978, with the hit single, '5.7.0.5', which also reached the US Top 30. By then, Lange's name had become known in the London-based music business as a producer who could bring the best out of often unpromising material; artists like Graham Parker who did the business live but could never quite capture that energy on record. Lange produced Parker's breakthrough second album, *Heat Treatment*, in 1976 – though the short, balding singer in the sunglasses never thanked him for it, complaining the production was 'too stiff' for his liking. Others, like Clover, featuring a young Huey Lewis, understood better and wouldn't move in the studio without Mutt there to guide them. Albie Donnelly, whose soul-driven band Supercharge were another newly signed act that benefited from the Lange school of rock, recalls Lange staying in the band's communal house in Liverpool during the recording of their first major label album, *Local Lads Make Good*, sleeping on the couch and having a cold bath every morning because there was no heating. 'Mutt didn't drink, didn't smoke and was vegetarian. He was very hard working and very determined, so it was on the cards really that he would become successful.' Donnelly would become Mutt's saxophonist of choice, guesting on hits by the Boomtown Rats and Graham Parker. While still others, like Canadian blues-rock guitarist Pat Travers, then recently signed to Phonogram, remembers spending 23 hours locked in a London studio with Lange, before 'coming out with absolutely nothing'. Lange, he says, 'spent four hours on a bass drum' alone.

The closest Lange had previously been to a band with a sound like AC/DC's had been in 1977 when he produced the debut album for The Motors, notably the opening track and first single – and minor chart hit – 'Dancing The Night Away', with its long stately intro eventually bursting forth into blistering, multi-layered guitars and big, sing-along chorus. But The Motors had no recognisable frontman, no easily identifiable lead guitarist and, with the exception of the truly exceptional 'Dancing The Night Away', no fully formed songs to speak of. Mutt had taken them as far as he could and back in the space of that one album. AC/DC, with the comparatively vast back catalogue, already sizeable audience and inbuilt born-to-be-belligerent attitude finely honed to a razor-sharp, blood-pointed tip by the recent upheavals with brother George and clueless Eddie, would be something very different for the producer with the fair curly hair and even fairer, infinitely curlier musical mind.

At the time AC/DC went to meet Mutt Lange, at pre-production rehearsal at E.Zee Hire studios, in March 1979, neither side knew or, frankly, cared much about the other. If Lange had been apprised of the situation *vis-à-vis* George Young, he certainly showed no sign. While Malcolm later joked that if he'd known their new producer was then enjoying his first major UK chart success with the Boomtown Rats, 'we'd never have let him through the door'. Yet it was the artistry that the precisely attuned producer had brought to the raggedy-arsed Irish punks that encouraged Phil Carson at Atlantic, for one, to think he might just be the man to bring the polished sheen to AC/DC so beloved of radio, not least on the ads-driven airwaves of North America. 'Rat Trap', the Rats' first No. 1, just four months before, had been produced by Mutt almost to sound like The Easybeats meets AC/DC: clever insider pop with big anthemic rock choruses. Such easy-on-the-ear catchiness was not easily attained, though. Geldof recalled how the Rats had made their demo for their first album in a small Dublin studio in a matter of hours. 'With Mutt the recording lasted eight weeks. We did seventy-eight takes alone for "Lookin' After Number One".' As Geldof found out, and the Youngs were about to discover, 'the sound had to be broken down into its component parts in order to give [Lange] greater control in the final stages of mixing the instruments together'. Living in an apartment next door to the studio, they would begin their working day at 10 a.m. and often not finish until 2 a.m. 'We felt inadequate, the more so because Mutt himself was a brilliant musician and was impatient with our fumbling.'

All the Young brothers knew of Mutt Lange, the first time they met, was what Michael Browning had told them about him: that he was 'a genius', the sort of introduction that had both Malcolm and Angus curling their lips. Ian Jeffery laughs as he recalls that first meeting. 'Mutt Lange turns up with a mop of curly hair and green wellies on, and they're all going to me, "Who the fuck's *that*?"' Trevor Rabin imagines the scene all too clearly, he says. 'He would have walked in with just this quiet, friendly but very quiet confidence. He would very quickly gain your respect and deliver. And when you deliver and you're not arrogant and you just keep delivering, people have respect for that and they go along with it, and they trust it.'

According to the log diary kept by in-house engineer Mark Dearnley, basic tracking was begun on the new AC/DC album, at Roundhouse Studios, in London's Chalk Farm, on Saturday, 24 March, with all recording completed exactly three weeks later on Saturday, 14 April. The first track they worked on was the title track, 'Highway To Hell'. The instantly arresting guitar–drum intro had been conjured up in Miami, on the day they snuck off from Eddie Kramer, to work alone, with Angus grinding away on guitar while Malcolm bashed at the drums. All was nearly lost though when the engineer recording them took the only cassette of it home, where his young son playfully unravelled it. Fortunately, Bon, who was always rewinding his own worn-out cassettes, carefully put it back together the following day and the tune that was about to transform all their lives was restored.

The fact that the intro sounded like Free's 'All Right Now' – itself a close cousin of the Stones' 'Honky Tonk Woman', via John Lee Hooker's 'Boogie Chillun' – was not lost on their new producer, who promptly hired Tony Platt to help him mix the final edits. Lange, Platt says now, was looking for 'someone that would give it that kind of dry, punchy rock thing, and he knew I'd worked at Island Records in the old days with those sorts of bands, including Free'. It was, as Platt puts it, 'that feeling of space and time' that characterised the whole album. Tracks like the obvious single, 'Touch Too Much' – retrieved from its flailing, earlier incarnation and remade into a smooth-as-nylons, top-notch toe-tapper – and the pulsing 'Get It Hot' were, on the surface, cornerstone heavy rockers, yet, as Platt points out, 'they are both quite slow- to medium-paced. One of Mutt's things that he brought to AC/DC was how to really work a groove. They may have been an out-and-out rock band but you could now dance to all their tunes. Or most of them anyway ...'

Even scorching-hot new numbers like 'If You Want Blood (You've Got It)' – a particular favourite of Mutt's simply because he liked the then novel idea of making a track with the title of a previous album – with its bugling 'Brown Sugar'-style intro and barrelling chorus, was impossible to listen to without moving yourself out of your seat. Whereas George Young had always encouraged them to simply give it their best shot and damn the niceties (like tuning and time-keeping), Mutt insisted on everything being in perfect balance, melodically, rhythmically, harmonically, so that when each song explodes into action it does so against a backdrop that contrasts rather than competes for attention.

In this way, he even coaxed from them tracks that took their foot off the pedal long enough to almost be called ballads. In the case of 'Love Hungry Man', the beat was essentially no different to 'Highway To Hell's, but the idea was much less in your face. Although the band

– Malcolm and Angus in particular – came to see that track as the bridge too far that Mutt forced them to cross on the album, refusing even to play it live, it still sounds good on American radio to this day. On the final track, 'Night Stalker', Lange even took them back to the kind of blue electric rainfall they had only ventured to once before – on 'Ride On'. But if 'Night Prowler' musically exceeded its elegiac descendant, Bon's lyrics were something else: the tale of the kind of beast that literally waits for you to '*turn out the light*' before it '*makes a mess of you*'. Perhaps if the music hadn't been so convincing the song would have fallen into a more Alice Cooper-type horror. But Lange's production seems to rule out any thoughts of contrivance or theatre. It just sounds mean – and dirty.

Lyrically, other tracks like the bouncing 'Girl's Got Rhythm' and 'Beating Around The Bush' – the latter, successfully remodelled from the discarded *Dirty Deeds* track 'Backseat Confidential', with a new, flintier riff barely one remove from that of Fleetwood Mac's 'Oh Well' – came straight out of the same bottom drawer as the rest of Bon's dirty-mind fantasies. Musically, though, this was a whole other universe. Still blues, all rock, but taken to such an exalted level it simply bounced like forked lightning across a pearl white moon. The craft that went into 'Walk All Over You' was like a George Young production in reverse. Where something like 'Let There Be Rock' or 'Sin City' covered similar terrain, Lange was able to introduce a more sophisticated set of dynamics that turned an otherwise average blues romp into something touched by greatness. Similarly, 'Shot Down In Flames', with its faux spontaneous intro and lemon-squeezing, back-slap rhythm, was pop-rock taken to its zenith.

'Mutt took them through so many changes,' says Ian Jeffery, who was there at many of the sessions. 'I remember one day Bon coming in with his lyrics – I forget which song it was now, but it might have even been "Highway To Hell" – but he starts doing it and we're all sitting round in the control room, and Bon's struggling, you know? There's more fucking breath than voice coming out. Mutt says to him, "Listen, you've got to coordinate your breathing." Bon was like, "You're so fucking good, cunt, you do it!" Mutt sat in his seat and did it without standing up! That was when they all went, "What the fucking hell we dealing with here?"'

According to Malcolm Dome, 'Bon said to me when they worked with Mutt Lange on *Highway to Hell*: "Thank God we got rid of those other two" – meaning Vanda and Young. He felt they were holding the band back and that they had a real tunnel vision of what the band should sound like. And he felt that Mutt Lange coming in opened it up. And if you listen, you can see he was right. "Let There Be Rock" is still absolutely brilliant. Yet I knew what Bon meant, because Vanda and Young seemed to have this "Young vision", as it were, like it's the Angus guitar and the Malcolm rhythm that really matters and everything else fits in around that. I think Bon felt frustrated and that he wasn't being able to get through what he could. Then Mutt Lange coming in suddenly gave him the opportunity to open it up a little bit. As a result, *Highway To Hell* was a real leap up.'

Mutt also taught Angus some useful lessons, instructing him to play his solos while sitting next to the producer, 'So I can tell you what to play,' Jeffery recalls Mutt telling the gobsmacked guitarist. 'Angus was used to playing in the studio with his four Marshall cabinets, but Mutt wanted him to work on a tiny little amp in the corner of the control room. He said, "Sit here and I'll tell you what I want you to play." Angus was like, "You fucking will, will ya?" But he sat next to Mutt and Mutt didn't force it on him, was just kind of pointing at the fretboard and "Here, this" and "Hold that" and "Now go into that" and etc. It was the solo from "Highway To Hell", you know when he goes straight into that unforgettable first solo' – a wonderfully sustained burst of playing that begins at 2 minutes 12 seconds and continues right through to the juddering climax 26 seconds later. 'That ringing note that held and then he just climbs into it, you know? It was fantastic! And that really stood them all to attention on Mutt and they knew they had a real thing going. Because he never forced himself, he just had suggestions for whatever it was [and] they were ninety-nine per cent right. He wasn't asking them to do anything he couldn't do himself, or getting on their case saying it's been wrong in the past, nothing like that. He really massaged them into what became that album.'

Behind the inspiration lay plenty of sweat, too. Often when the band turned up at the studio each morning, Mutt would have been there for hours already. Always first in and last out, sometimes he would just sleep on the studio couch, working after everyone else had gone home, going through the day's performances, weighing, judging, discarding. Yet, as Lange would be the first to acknowledge, the interaction between artists and producer that created the first genuine AC/DC masterpiece was not just a one-way street. On his second day working with them at the Roundhouse, Mutt told Malcolm: 'You're the best band I've ever worked with.' Famously reclusive, Lange has almost never given an interview. Once, though, in the late Nineties, and typically obliquely, he agreed to a short question-and-answer session online. Little can be gleaned from his all-too brief answers. But when he says, at one point, 'sometimes when you're lucky in life you can make the trends happen', it seems clear he's referring back to his work with AC/DC. When he adds, 'It's always by accident and chance, but it happens', this is more than false modesty. Despite his plenitude of gifts, Mutt knew that he alone could not make AC/DC, or any other act, successful, no more than that notorious old gangster-manager Don Arden could, as he famously put it, 'polish a turd' and turn clients of his like the Small Faces and ELO into chart gold. First and foremost the act had to have talent; then came the polishing. Nobody, though, ever polished a rock band quite as shiny or as dedicatedly as Mutt Lange now polished AC/DC. Like a master finding his muse, AC/DC had provided the producer with his greatest canvas. Unlike the punk-conscious acts he'd toiled with previously in London, who couldn't play above the minimum standard and were full of convoluted ideas about what was or wasn't acceptable to the pseudo-intellectual rock press, AC/DC not only could play – their chops honed by a thousand gigs in every type of venue, big and small, these past five years – they didn't give a fuck what anyone else might have to say about it after the fact. They were about broad strokes, inclusiveness, rock you didn't have to think about but could dance to all night long. Unrestrained for the first time by self-consciousness, bolted-on artifice, Lange was able to apply the full panoply of his immense talents to the AC/DC album. What's more, he could surely relate. Weren't the songs like those of the country music artists he would have adored growing up? Blood and sawdust songs full of bold, fidgety emotion and devil-may-care humour, brimming with sin and redemption, the band's insatiable desire to put out and please, to dazzle and demolish you, like a breath of fresh air after the clogged-up feelings and spastic dances of Deaf School, Graham Parker, the Boomtown Rats and all the other young ideas-driven college acts Lange had been working with in London.

Lange had added in that solitary online questionnaire that 'When you're searching for the fortune and fame, you need to avoid notoriety. There's no upside in being well-known. You need to always be under the radar like a hidden shadow. I learned this early in my career. I've always been a private person. I don't value being in the media spotlight. I'm fortunate to be able to avoid it.' Be that as it may, those three weeks in London with AC/DC, in the spring of 1979, were about to change the lives of all involved, for ever.

The first time Michael Browning heard *Highway To Hell* was at home in his apartment in New York, where Malcolm had come to play it for him. 'It was obvious from the word go it was something special. The difference between *Highway* and *Powerage* was chalk and cheese. I thought the title track was the absolute breakthrough track that they needed for America and then we sort of got into the process of working out the cover and all that sort of stuff.' More to the point, the powers that be in New York agreed. 'We all liked what Mutt Lange did,' says Barry Bergman. In America, 'We went from 50,000 and then up to 75,000 albums [with *High Voltage* and *Let There Be Rock*] to 125,000 and then up to 175,000 [with *Powerage*] to 250,000 with the live album. But we needed to break it out, and this was the record would do it. *Highway To Hell* made both AC/DC *and* Mutt Lange in America.'

But if everything was beginning to look rosy again on the surface, as ever with AC/DC, there were rumblings beneath ground that few saw coming. Atlantic decided they didn't like the title, and tried to get the band to change it. 'They freaked,' remembered Malcolm. 'They didn't want that title.' The fear was that the band would be mistaken for devil-worshippers. A quarter-century later Phil Rudd is still confounded. 'If you'd have been on the road with us for those years up to that point, you'd have known exactly what we were talking about.' The brothers were insistent: the title stayed. Or else. There were also questions about the album cover: a nondescript band line-up shot, its only stand-out feature that Angus was wearing a pair of plastic toy devil horns on his head. An earlier photo from the same session had Angus on his own on the cover, not just with horns but also a curly little forked devil's tail, but that had been rejected by the band, says Jeffery, 'because it was fucking shite'. They were not to be budged though on the simpler one that was finally used. 'Who the fuck do they think they are?' Malcolm told Ian.

Meanwhile, in New York, there was further fall-out from the appointment of Lange when Michael Kleffner, who had championed AC/DC in America for so long but whose recommendation it had been to hire Eddie Kramer, found himself out in the cold after a bitter altercation with Clive Calder. 'Michael Kleffner got very pissed off with me for sacking Eddie and getting Mutt onboard,' explains Browning. 'He ran into Clive Calder a couple of nights later in a club in New York and started putting shit on Mutt Lange. And Clive called Jerry Greenberg the next morning and within a couple of hours Michael Kleffner was fired from Atlantic Records. It was just a drama that unfolded. It was just all this shit that was unfolding because of the change of producer.'

Unfortunately for Browning, the ripples didn't end there. Excited on the one hand that things were finally starting to move for the band in America, Browning not unwisely decided his own position could do with shoring up, in anticipation of the big push he felt sure was coming stateside, and entered into a partnership agreement with his other New York flatmate, Cedric Kushner. 'I needed a big injection of capital and Cedric had it,' says Browning. 'That was a fairly major fact. They didn't really think he was the right person though and in hindsight they were right.' According to Ian Jeffery, and we

only have his account of the meeting, Browning's unilateral appointment of Kushner was doomed from his very first introduction to the
band. 'We had just got back to London and Michael turns up with
Cedric Kushner, this 300-pound overweight American. This is in
the fucking car park. This guy comes up, like "Hello Malcolm, hello
Angus." Malcolm's going to me, "Who's this?" I've got no idea. So I
got Browning to one side and said, "Michael, who's this guy?" "Oh,
yeah, yeah, yeah, he's my new partner." That was it. The guy was history before he'd had a chance. Not only was he fucking going up to
them and introducing himself before letting them decide whether
they want to acknowledge him, he's introducing himself as Michael's
partner! They hadn't been told. It hadn't been discussed. So that was
it. Not a chance in hell of surviving with the brothers after that.'

There were other issues too. A four-date Japanese tour had been
booked for early March, at a time when it was expected the band
would have finished working on their new album with Eddie Kramer.
When those plans got shelved and new time was booked in London
with Mutt Lange, what was to be the band's first tour of Japan was
kept in the diary. According to Browning though, 'There were some
immigration issues' and the dates were cancelled at the last minute,
causing huge consternation in the band camp. 'The equipment had
already gone over there by the time we cancelled,' Browning explains,
'and it meant we had to pay for everything even though we wouldn't
actually be going.'

With the band also forfeiting an appearance fourth on the bill below
Aerosmith, Van Halen and UFO, before a stadium crowd of nearly
110,000, at the Los Angeles Memorial Coliseum on 8 April – and
along with it a much-needed pay day – because they were now going
to be in the studio with Mutt, Malcolm Young was on the warpath by
the time AC/DC finally returned to the road on 8 May, in Madison,
Wisconsin, the first of 11 co-headline shows with UFO. It was at the
next show – a sole headliner at the 2,000-capacity Tennessee Theater
in Nashville – that the shit finally hit the fan.

'I flew down there for the night,' Browning recalls, 'and it was in
the band room, after they came offstage, an unbelievable argument

happened between me and the group. Just out of nowhere, me and Malcolm and Angus, basically. There was just an almighty flare-up and that was it. I was fired.' Afterwards, riding the tour bus back to the hotel, 'It was the most solemn bus ride you could ever imagine. [After which] I spoke to Malcolm I think twice on the phone, because there had to be a bit of a transitional thing. They had a tour coming up of England that I had to convey, and a few things like that. And that was it. The rest was just lawyers.'

Browning now insists his demise was as much to do with the fact that 'Mensch was out undermining my relationship with them like you wouldn't believe, because he was desperate to get involved with them. Mensch had been circling for a while.'

According to Ian Jeffery, however, the decision had nothing to do with wanting to bring Peter Mensch into the picture and everything to do with the brothers' ire over what they saw as the mismanagement of their affairs – beginning with the removal of brother George from the production hot seat up to and including the appointment without their prior approval of Cedric Kushner.

'Everybody was on a hiding to nothing. They hated the fucking world and everything in it. When we got to Nashville, Kushner was getting these fucking gigs lined up, which were horrible. The band said, that's it, you're fucking finished, we're going home. "Browning, we're sacking this guy. We're gonna go camp out in New York at John Clarke's" – which was the lawyer with Marks Music, which was their publisher then. They said, "We're gonna go back there and we're gonna get them to line up managers and we're gonna find somebody so we can continue here." This is midnight in the dressing room. They said to me: "Ian, fucking sort it out. No more gigs."'

While Browning spent a miserable night in his hotel room unable to sleep, Jeffery was on the phone, first to Doug Thaler at ATI, letting him know there would be 'a pause', as he chuckles darkly now. Then to John Clarke, George Young, Perry Cooper and anyone else he felt needed to know immediately. 'I said, "We're going to New York. They want to meet managers."' Once there, 'a whole slew of managers were lined up for them to meet. All the managers came to them but they just didn't stand a chance when they walked in. The only one who wouldn't come was Leber–Krebs, who was the biggest management company of that time, who said you've got to come to us.'

Speaking today from his office in New York, David Krebs laughs off such a claim. 'That's ridiculous. I was a fan of theirs from 1977. I desperately wanted to manage them because I knew they'd fit in with the kind of groups we were building.' Most successful music companies in the Seventies were run by yin-yang teams: two-man teams where each man represented either the 'music' or 'business' side of the operation. In this case, Steve Leber, bespectacled, serious, balding, was the fine-print man; his partner, David Krebs, the one who saw his office as a den, smoked pot, wore jeans, drank at lunch and talked about the bigger picture. At the time their main clients were Ted Nugent and Aerosmith, both in their late-Seventies arena-headlining primes, if not quite at their musical peaks any more. AC/DC had supported both acts due to the good relationship Doug Thaler enjoyed with the duo, but also because back in 1977 David Krebs had offered Browning a deal to take care of the band's management affairs in America. Although Browning had declined, 'David had always stayed in touch and been a gentleman to me in his dealings,' says Browning.

'There was a standoff going on at first,' remembers Jeffery, 'because the brothers didn't like being told they had to go to them. In the end they said, okay, those cunts think they're so fucking big, we'll go see them. We walk in there and Leber and Krebs have got this long office corridor with birds sat at every desk – rock'n'roll floozies dressed up to the nines with tits hanging out and you can see their knickers. And this guy steps out of an office with a suit and a tie and a shiny forehead – he's Leber. It's like oh my god, what have we walked into here! David Krebs' office was locked but he had the total rock'n'roll office – dim lights at nine in the morning, fish tanks, purple lights. You could smell the pot. Angus walks in there and it's like, "Do you want a drink of anything?" And he's like, "Yeah, cup of tea ..."' He laughs. 'Confused them totally ...'

Jeffery says Krebs asked them: 'How much are you earning at the moment, five hundred, fifteen hundred?' Malcolm replied: 'Depends, you know. Ian would know more about that.' Ian kept a straight face and said, 'Yeah, in that ballpark.' In fact, with the *Highway To Hell* album not due for release for another two months they were barely covering their costs at that point. Jeffery: 'Krebs said: "Well, I have Aerosmith, Ted Nugent, and we're doing this series of the World Music Festival in Texas, Day On The Green on the west coast. Big shows in Cleveland, 80,000 people a night. They're all my bands, they're all my festivals. What if I say I'll put you on these shows and I can get you a million dollars by the end of the year?" We all looked at each other like, what's this cunt on? Then Malcolm said, "Okay, smart-arse, we'll take you up on that. We're not gonna sign with you though. You put us on all these shows and if our bank balance gets close to that then maybe we'll tell you we'll join you."'

Speaking now, David Krebs chuckles and denies having any knowledge of this conversation. Nevertheless, the following day AC/DC had resumed their modest co-headline theatre tour with UFO, including a near sold-out show at the Palladium, just down from the Leber–Krebs office in New York. Good as their word, once they had come under the LK wing, the band was now studding their own shows with jewels like their third-on-the-bill appearance to headliners Boston, at the 55,000-capacity Tangerine Bowl, and their fourth on the bill slot at the Mississippi River Jam II festival, to headliners Heart, in June. By now Krebs had taken them out of the theatres with UFO and started putting them into arenas opening for whoever the headliner of the day happened to be, starting with Journey; as incompatible a bill as could be imagined at which AC/DC managed to steal the show – again. And again. Of course, there were still the usual Bon-sized bumps in the road. Opening for Canadian stars Triumph, at the Kiel Auditorium in St Louis, on 1 July, Bon confronted Triumph singer Rik Emmet over a 'misunderstanding' to do with Bon's 'lady friend', who, it turned out, had previously been a good friend of Emmet's. In one version of events, when ungentlemanly comments were attributed to Emmett, Bon stepped in. Literally, in this case, resulting in Bon taking the stage that night with a large bandage wrapped around a big toe, having taken mercy on the rapidly retreating Emmet by aiming his boot at a backstage lamp instead.

The brothers barely noticed. They were more focused on the special 4th of July show Leber and Krebs had booked them into at the 50,000-capacity Winnebago County Fairgrounds in Illinois, where they were second on the bill to Cheap Trick. The first of several arena show dates opening for their old friends, they were also the first AC/DC shows when they added 'Highway To Hell' to the set. By the end of July they were opening at arenas for another LK act, Mahogany Rush, and on 21 July they played third on the bill to nearly 60,000 at the Oakland Stadium, in San Francisco, behind Krebs's top earners, Ted Nugent and Aerosmith. A week later they were fifth on the bill to the same headliners at the 82,000-capacity Lakefront Stadium in Cleveland.

'Every day when we were out playing all these shows,' recalls Ian Jeffery, 'Aerosmith's tour accountant, Peter Mensch, would come in the dressing room and say, "If you guys don't play 'Dog Eat Dog', Ian's not getting paid tonight!" And they'd be like, "Okay, we'll play it just for you, shall we, Peter?" It was done as a gag but in fact you could tell Mensch just really liked that song. That he just really liked the band.' The brothers took note.

By the time the tour ended on 4 August, with their first ever appearance onstage to nearly 20,000 at Madison Square Garden, once more opening for Ted Nugent, they didn't yet have the million bucks in their bank that Jeffery says Krebs had promised them, but with *Highway To Hell* now in the stores and another 47 of their own arena-headlining dates lined up for September and October, the brothers felt they were well on their way at last. AC/DC signed their new management contract with Leber–Krebs on Monday, 6 August, before flying back to London for a few days off before their next run of shows began a week later. There was only one condition.

Ian Jeffery: 'At the end when Leber and Krebs and that were patting each other on the back the brothers said, "No, no, no. We're telling you something, we want Mensch. We don't want to be handled through twenty people, when we make a phone call we want someone who's *ours* and we want Peter Mensch." Krebs came to me and said, "But he's one of our tour accountants." I said, "That's who they want. Get him or you won't be their manager." And that's what happened. So it was fantastic for Peter as well. Except then they said, "And by the way, he needs to move to Europe. We live in fucking London.""

Again, Krebs denies any recollection of this conversation. On the contrary, he says, 'Having someone go out as a tour accountant was an amazing learning experience. Like the equivalent of a rock'n'roll MBA of sorts. We did that with Louis Levin, who ended up working with Michael Bolton.' Having the band elect Mensch as their day-to-day point of contact was actually a relief. 'I really had my hands full. I was a hands-on manager with Aerosmith and I was certainly a one-hand manager of Ted Nugent. So how much can you have on your plate?'

In the summer of 1979, Peter Mensch was a 26-year-old Jewish New Yorker. Self-doubt, second-guessing, keeping his mouth shut, none of these things troubled him. They would do so even less as the next few years flew by and he became one of the most powerful rock managers in the world; when his own management company, Q Prime, would become in the Eighties what Leber–Krebs had been in the Seventies: the biggest and the best. For now, though, living in London for the first time, running the day-to-day management of the fastest-rising international stars in the rock business, AC/DC, he was simply running to catch up, to prove himself worthy. Fortunately, he had a font of wisdom to call upon when he needed to, named Cliff Burnstein, a fellow New Yorker and former Mercury Records executive also schooled in the Leber–Krebs way of doing things. 'Peter took Cliff with him into AC/DC,' says Jeffery, 'because Cliff was part of the whole thing, you know, smart, smart, smart guy. Peter was the mouth and Cliff was the brains.'

While Burnstein remained in New York, however, Mensch could rely on Ian Jeffery to 'tip him the wink', as Ian puts it, about surviving the music business in London, and the two, so different outwardly – the pent-up New Yorker with the yadder and the tood next to the laidback Londoner who wore his knowhow and pocket full of secrets lightly – became close. 'When Peter first came over we had to slap him around and tell him how to behave,' says Jeffery affectionately. 'Record companies, every person in the world fucking hated him. Who was this arrogant guy coming in here telling us how it's done?'

Burnstein was the opposite, turning up for meetings with his papers in a plastic Safeway bag. 'He'd just turn up with his shopping bag, with his groceries and his *New York Times*. People would look at him like he'd just wandered in off the street.' Years later, when he was offered the presidency of Columbia Records, on the proviso he cut his long shaggy hair and shave off his bird's nest beard, Burnstein refused. As a joke, Ian once had AC/DC's merchandising company, Brockum, make Cliff a leather shopping bag. 'We copied Safeway's completely, but we made the bag black instead of white. Cliff loved it and said thank you. Then filed it away and carried on with his fucking Safeway's bag!'

Yet it was this combination of the apparently insouciant and the undeniably brash that appealed to AC/DC, not least the brothers who recognised fellow individuals when they saw them; fighters just like them that took an almost perverse pleasure in undermining the conventions of the games they found themselves playing, no matter how high the stakes or great the potential rewards.

'Put it this way,' says Ian, 'they never ever got close to either of those other guys, Steve Leber or David Krebs. The biggest mistake [Steve] made was thinking Angus was the route into this band. I remember him sending two limos to take us all to a party at his house out on Long Island. Took two fucking hours to get there and when we did it was all this swingers thing going on. It was nuts, all these people dressed up, then all dressed down again. All we wanted to do was have hamburger with chips and a pint. We saw what was going on and it was like, "What are we fucking doing here?", you know? And the other thing was, Steve Leber thought the way to the band was through Angus. That's how much he hadn't listened or done his homework, you know? He didn't have a clue that it was Malcolm that ran the show. And whenever there were arguments Angus would always end up siding with Malcolm. They never got close to Leber and Krebs at all. Peter and Cliff, though, they were just ... different.'

With *Highway To Hell* released in Britain on Friday, 27 July – a week earlier than in the States – AC/DC was back doing British and European dates throughout August. The usual carpet-bombing tour would come later in the year. For now this was major appearances at a select series of high-profile events as part of the general promotion for the new album. Two weeks earlier they had flown over from America for a one-off show in Arnhem, Holland, highlights of which were to be televised on the Dutch version of *Countdown*. They started the show with 'Highway To Hell', which would be the first single, to ensure it got the highest prominence on the show, and ended with 'If You Want Blood ...' (the B-side of the new single), again to ensure everybody got the message about the forthcoming album.

It was a fateful occasion, too, for Angus, who met his future wife, Ellen, part of the Dutch television production team. Ian Jeffrey recalls they met back at the hotel after the show. He says, 'she was hanging round the lobby, you know, waiting to meet Bon. Of course Bon was already having too good a time, went to bed etc. So Phil came down, had a go, of course she wasn't interested. Then Angus comes down, by then it's three or four in the morning and we're sitting round having cups of tea. Next thing you know she's on a plane to London with us, and is still part of the furniture now.'

It had been a similar situation with Cliff's wife, Georgiana, says Jeffery, who the bassist met when the band was once staying at the Kensington Hilton, in London. They had been checking in at the same time as a group of TWA air hostesses. 'Cliff came down later and said, "You remember that bird I was chatting to at reception? She rung me up when I got to me room." The next thing we know we're all going to the wedding.'

On 17 August they played at the Jazz Bilzen festival in Belgium, where 'Walk All Over You' and 'Shot Down In Flames' also got an airing. The following Saturday afternoon they were third on the bill at London's Wembley Stadium, behind The Stranglers and The Who. Phil Carson had tried to get AC/DC onto the bill at the two shows at Knebworth that Led Zeppelin headlined that same month.

According to *Sounds* magazine editor Alan Lewis, who had done so much to help promote AC/DC in Britain at a time when no other major music magazine would support them, 'It would have been a great pairing, kind of a meeting between the old guard of rock and the new. By then Zeppelin's standing in Britain wasn't what it was and we were getting far more readers' letters about AC/DC. You can't help wondering if they felt threatened in any way by these upstarts?' According to Carson, however, the reason for Zeppelin rejecting the suggestion of having AC/DC on the Knebworth bill with them was far more prosaic. 'Robert Plant didn't like them, simple as that. He thought they were derivative – which, let's face it, was hard to argue with.'

No such problems though for Pete Townshend of The Who, who had in the recent past singled out *Let There Be Rock* for praise, while at the same time seeing AC/DC as posing no threat whatsoever to his own fragile ego. Playing to nearly 90,000 people at Wembley Stadium should have been another tangible leap up in the public imagination for AC/DC, with an added bump in credibility being on the same bill as golden age rock overlords The Who and next-generation punk underbosses The Stranglers. Instead, as with the Reading Festival three years before, expectations outstripped reality by some distance. Things got off to an inauspicious start when Angus had to hold Bon back from 'sorting out' The Stranglers. Although they were all older than the brothers in AC/DC – in the case of drummer Jet Black, older by eight years even than Bon – and essentially posing as a notional 'punk' band, but whose musical frame of reference went back at least as far as that of AC/DC, The Stranglers – known for their obnoxiousness – found it amusing to taunt Bon and the others for being 'dope-smoking hippies'. Angus later told *Mojo*'s Phil Alexander how he had counselled Bon to make his point onstage, channelling his anger into giving such a fiery performance the haughty Stranglers would struggle to follow it. 'So that's what happened,' said Angus. 'We got up, gave it everything and turned the place upside down. We walked back in the dressing room afterwards, the room's full of dope, and Bon goes: "Who's the fucking hippies now then, cunt?"'

So stirred up were the band that when the sound suddenly failed halfway through 'Whole Lotta Rosie' and didn't return till they had already started the next number, 'Rocker', none of them appeared to notice, simply playing through as the crowd looked on askance. 'Definitely somebody was fucking messing with the equipment,' says Ian Jeffery. 'AC/DC was roaring. Whether it was The Who or their road crew, I don't know, but something happened.'

Better times lay ahead. The following weeks AC/DC played their first shows in Ireland – two nights in Dublin headlining at the Olympic Ballroom, an old-fashioned seat-less dance hall famous for its raucous crowds, followed by two nights north of the border at Belfast's Ulster Hall, where its 1,000 seats had been taken out to allow almost 2,000 standing fans to enjoy the show. In an era when the Northern Ireland 'troubles' were at their height, the band's hotel was surrounded by barbed wire and they were warned not to think about going out exploring on their own. Bon later recalled the Irish shows, though, as among 'the best we've done outside Scotland. The crowds are just fucking mental over there. Partly because they don't get many bands playing there, I suppose, but mainly because they're Irish – and fucking mental!'

When they again shared an outdoor festival bill with The Who, before 75,000 at the Zeppelin Field in Nuremberg where Hitler held his infamous Nazi party rallies in the Thirties, fearing a repeat of the 'power cut' at Wembley, Ian Jeffery and his crew made sure to do a tour of the equipment before the band took to the stage. 'I remember climbing the fucking scaffolding at the top of the PA, checking out all the bins and the horns and things and half of them weren't working, they'd turned them down. I ended up climbing the fucking speakers too because I knew they'd turned half of them off.'

Later that night, back at the hotel where all the bands were staying, Townshend walked into the bar, Angus recalled, and told them: 'You've done it again, you fuckers! You stole the show!' Bon, though, wasn't in the mood to be friendly, whether Townshend had really known what his crew was up to at the show or not. He taunted him: 'Here, Pete, buy me a drink?' knowing that Townshend was then on the wagon, having struggled with an alcohol problem for years. Bon, said Angus, 'was just rubbing it in'.

The way people in denial about their own drinking or drug problems tend to do when confronted by someone in the same quandary actually trying to do something about it.

CHAPTER TWELVE

The Place Down Under

It was around this time, the late summer of 1979, that I first met Bon Scott. It was at Silver's flat in Gloucester Road where I had gone to score heroin. I was not a junkie. That is, I would certainly not have characterised myself as such at that time. I was simply a partner in a PR firm called Heavy Publicity specialising in rock bands, and we rarely, if ever, travelled anywhere without drugs. Among our clients were bands such as Black Sabbath, Pat Travers and UFO. It was through the latter that I had come to know Silver. Her 'best friend', Joe Furey (now known in London smack-buying circles as Joe Silver) had worked as a roadie occasionally, as I recall, for UFO and some of our other clients like Wild Horses – the band formed by Bon's pal Brian Robertson after the guitarist had been fired from Thin Lizzy for being too much of a handful even for Phil Lynott, both of whom were also involved with heroin on a fairly regular basis by then. Silver had been introduced to me as 'a good smack dealer'. And so she proved. The fall of the Shah of Iran at the start of the year had led to a wave of Iranian immigrants to the UK, along with a particular batch of heroin quite distinct from the cream-coloured Chinese variety that had until then been the norm. Unlike the China-white, as it was known, the new Iranian heroin was a rich brown colour and much more 'lumpy', making it more difficult to dissolve into a spoon ready for injecting, and more suitable for placing on silver foil and lighting from underneath, in order to smoke – to chase the dragon, in the parlance of the times. Silver, I was reliably informed, had plenty of 'the brown' – which also came with a reputation for being far stronger, and cheaper, than the Chinese.

As a young PR in the late Seventies, I did most of my networking with bands and journalists across a dusty mirror upon which would be placed several lines of cocaine and, soon enough, when it was time to 'cool out', heroin. Sometimes you would mix the two and make a 'speedball' – everyone's favourite: the bubbles and beluga of drug concoctions. Indeed, when it was felt we had spent a great deal on the above in order to seduce various music journalists to write favourable pieces about one of our artists – or when we had simply been entertaining our client rock stars with same – we would bill them back for the money, under the expenses heading 'Champagne and flowers for the band'. Useful code which most rock managers understood all too well.

Drugs, back then, were simply the *lingua franca* of the music business, especially where the artists were concerned. To arrive at a meeting with one without any 'Charlie' or 'Henry' on you was to come empty-handed, and perceived almost as a slight. Nobody discussed addiction. There was now a phalanx of private 'Doctor Feelgoods' in Harley Street ready to ride to the rescue should that eventuality occur. Nor was overdosing given much consideration, except in the sense of it being bad form to do so under somebody else's roof – or 'turning blue in someone else's bathroom', as Keith Richards, the doyen of drug etiquette, memorably put it. Coming across Bon Scott at Silver's tiny apartment was hardly a shock to the system then. Indeed, Silver often spoke of him on my previous visits, her charred junkie voice slowing to a crawl as she talked of taking care of him, cashing his cheques and sundry other 'helps'. I did not know they had once been lovers. I assumed merely that she was another hanger-on looking to justify her role in his life beyond simple drug pusher. Meeting him at last at her flat was hardly a big deal. As I recall he was bent over a mirror smothered in lines as I arrived. Silver had barely introduced us when he handed the mirror over for my inspection.

He was not as I expected him to be. Having worked with my fair share of 'wild man rockers' I had become used to them trying to live up to their reputations, especially on first meets. Bon was different, though. Quiet, almost introspective, very mannerly, offering me a line and a joint, the way a vicar might offer you tea and cake. I confess, I do not recall now, over 30 years later, whether it was heroin or cocaine we were snorting together, only that I had only ever seen or snorted heroin in Silver's presence before. Either way, it was simply no big deal. In 1979, big boys – rock boys – did both, at their leisure. There was nothing to explain, certainly nothing you might expect to repent later. I liked him; that was all. He seemed nice, even a little shy. When Silver began droning on about how well the band were doing in America now and that they were about to take off for their next long tour there, he began to fidget, saying nothing to interrupt but clearly uncomfortable with the unmistakable note of pride in her voice. Like his success was somehow also hers in some significant part. Not that she appeared to notice. She was too out of it. Had been, it always seemed to me, from way back when. I made my score and left them to it.

'They were chalk and cheese,' says Ian Jeffery now. 'They shouldn't have been compatible but somehow they were. They were perfect.'

By now *Highway To Hell* was on its way to becoming the biggest-selling AC/DC album yet. For once, reviews in the British music press were uniformly good, though still somewhat grudging, as if ashamed to be enjoying such anti-intellectual, unashamedly populist fare. The headline in the *NME* proclaimed in upper case: 'THE GREATEST ALBUM EVER MADE'. Then in much smaller type underneath: '(In Australia)', then describing AC/DC as 'a band who practise the science of overstatement to a ludicrous degree and succeed'. Even their staunch *Sounds* ally, Dave Lewis, while giving a general thumbs-up to the album, felt obliged to point out that '*Highway To Hell* marks no new adventurous groundbreaking for AC/DC.' Nobody picked up on the extravagantly lush, even intricate sound their new producer, Mutt Lange, had gifted them. Nobody grasped the sonic leap forward they had made. Certainly nobody predicted a big hit. Merely that more of the same seemed of itself a strong enough card to play at a time when the new wave was impatiently pushing, sometimes to its own detriment, at musical envelopes every week.

286

A truer sense of the new album's very different approach was felt more immediately by how much – and how quickly – it began to sell. By the end of August, *Highway To Hell* had reached No. 8 in the UK albums chart. It was also in the US Top 40 by then, cause for huge celebration over at Rockefeller Plaza if not at the 48th Street apartment Mutt Lange had recently returned to. He hadn't sweated blood to make a Top 40 album. As hungry as the band for a taste of raw, bloody-as-hell American success, it wasn't until September, with the band back touring there and the album perched at No. 17 in the US chart, that Mutt – and with him Phil Carson and Jerry Greenberg and Peter Mensch – finally felt able to breathe out again. By the end of the year, *Highway To Hell* would also take AC/DC back into the Australian charts, reaching a restrained but pleasing No. 24, their highest chart placing back home for three years.

Further encouragement arrived when the 'Highway To Hell' single was released in America the same month. It didn't hurt that the first wave of 'classic rock' stations that would become ubiquitous across the American radio landscape in the early Eighties had begun to broadcast, with the slick, perfectly attuned rock steady of the new AC/DC sound a shoo-in for inclusion on their new daytime playlists. Nor that momentum behind the band was now reaching fever pitch with the commencement of their first headline tour of arenas; nor indeed that the record was simply so catchy. But for the first time AC/DC – and their new single – became a regular, heavy-rotation feature on American radio. 'Highway To Hell' would peak at No. 47 on the mainstream pop charts, becoming the most played new rock single by a non-American act since Bad Company exploded there five years before.

'They'd done it, they'd cracked it,' says Ian Jeffery. 'Not that they'd seen any real money yet but they knew it was coming and it'd already started to make a difference.' Eschewing support slots in favour of their own headline dates, they upgraded their tour bus to a luxury 18-seater with bed and bunks for 12. There was colour TV and state-of-the-art video and stereo equipment for the brothers to flop out in front of. Phil Rudd began demanding – and getting – a full-size

Scalextric racetrack in his hotel room at every tour stop. It wasn't quite a victory lap yet. Still only featuring three or four numbers from the new hit album in their live set, early on in the tour, headlining the Long Beach Arena in Los Angeles, which they did for the first time on 10 September, they barely half-filled the place. In New York, in October, they couldn't even sell out the 3,000-capacity Shea's Buffalo Theater. Across America's heartland, though, where the shit gets righteously kicked and on a good day only the walls drip blood, they were monsters: selling out the 12,000-capacity James White Civic Coliseum in Knoxville; packing over 13,000 into the 12,000-capacity Charlotte Coliseum in North Carolina; running roughshod across Texas with Southern rednecks Molly Hatchet heehawing in support.

The only one of AC/DC for whom nothing much appeared to change was Bon Scott. He was drinking more heavily than ever, though, and his antics – missing a flight from Phoenix because he stayed in a bar trying to score with a woman; riding on Molly Hatchet's broken-down bus, getting wasted on whisky and rye rather than hold the fort on what was the band's most important tour – were beginning to seem less funny and more desperate by the day. He was also smoking dope non-stop and snorting cocaine on an almost daily basis. Others report seeing him 'gobbling down pills by the handful'. For the first time, Angus, who had always looked up to Bon and loved him, even when he was at his most unreliable, began to openly fret. Malcolm, unsure whether to pull the trigger or not, chose to look the other way – for now – having already decided on a reckoning when the tour was over and their future in America, which he had already sacrificed his older brother for, was more safely secured. Doug Thaler, about to go on to bigger things and handling his last tour as AC/DC's American agent, recalls: 'At the time we were out there on the *Highway To Hell* tour, Bon was in rough shape. He was drunk most of the time or sleeping it off so he could sober up and get drunk again. He was starting to have a real problem. The last time I saw him [was] the last date on that tour [in] Chicago. I saw him at the hotel in the afternoon. He was so drunk he could barely stand up. He didn't acknowledge me. He had a couple of chicks with him and he was going over to the elevator but he was in very rough shape for broad daylight. And I know the guys were starting to have problems with him by that time because of that reason.' Years later, when he was managing Mötley Crüe, one of the most notorious hell-raisers of their era, Thaler would check the entire band into rehab. Back in 1979, though, 'The idea of rock stars going into rehab hadn't occurred to anybody yet. If you were hurting you took a drink or a shot of something and you felt better. I don't think anybody realised the lasting dangers of drink or cocaine.'

It was the same story when, just four days after the end of their American tour, the band arrived back in Britain for the start of their next UK tour: 13 dates that included multiple nights at the country's biggest concert venues: two at the Apollo in Glasgow; two at the Apollo in Manchester; four at the Hammersmith Odeon in London; two at the Empire in Liverpool; one at the 10,000-capacity Bingley Hall in Stafford. By then, says Bernie Marsden, whose band Whitesnake was about to have its first hit album with *Love Hunter*, Bon's drinking had made him 'the talk of the town ... legendary. I think you always knew that Bon was on that ... not self-destructive path but that if he didn't pull it in at some point he would hurt himself, you know? A bit by default, really, because of how much he was drinking. Those chasers – those quadruple Scotches – they've got to catch up with you.' As for drugs, 'In those days, it was social. I mean, all I ever saw of Bon was the rock star and drinking. But there was always what else was involved.'

Opening for AC/DC was a young band from Sheffield called Def Leppard, wangled onto the tour by their prospective new manager – Peter Mensch. Leppard singer Joe Elliott remembers the tour as 'one massive fucking life lesson! We were on a real high at the time, loads of good press, new band recently signed to a big record deal, now this tour. We knew we were hot. Then after the first show we stayed behind to watch AC/DC and that's when we realised – fuck this, we're in trouble! They were so nice to us, especially Bon, who would give you money out of his own pocket for a drink or a curry. But also Malcolm and Angus, who didn't talk much, just sort of grunted if you'd done a good show. Then went on each night and proceeded to kill us stone dead! They were fucking unbelievable. I remember thinking: right, okay, we're in with the big boys here. We better get our act together.'

Backstage at the Bingley Hall show, another familiar face could be seen. That of Mutt Lange: there, though, not to see AC/DC but, at the invitation of Peter Mensch, AC/DC's trusted new lieutenant, the new boys, Def Leppard. The reviewers might not have got it, Malcolm and Angus may not have felt obliged to acknowledge it, Bon may have been too drunk to care any more, but Mensch was savvy enough to know exactly where and how the story of AC/DC had been so dramatically transformed. Now, with the signatures of the teenage wannabes from Sheffield fresh on a Leber–Krebs contract, again naming Mensch as the key man in the operation, he was determined to cut to the chase and get Mutt onboard there too post-haste. That is, as soon as Mutt had finished recording the next AC/DC album ...

After the UK tour, there had been 29 dates across Europe, focused on West Germany – where they did 16 theatre shows supported by up-and-coming British metallists Judas Priest – and 10 in France, where *Highway To Hell* had gone to No. 2. Plus one each in Belgium, Holland and Switzerland. By the time AC/DC did their final show of the year at Birmingham Odeon on 21 December – the end of a 'back-by-popular-demand' five-date add-on to the earlier UK tour – they had been on the road for almost nine months without more than a couple of days off here and there.

You get a flavour of just how worn out Bon Scott was in the film shot in Paris by French film makers Eric Dionysius and Eric Mistler, released a year later as the in-concert movie *AC/DC: Let There Be Rock*. Originally hired merely to make a promotional video, a misunderstanding between the pair and Mensch, who thought they wished to make a feature-length documentary, led to the two Erics eventually gathering footage, including backstage shots and brief snapshot interviews, over three days in Metz, Reims and Lille, before filming the whole show at the Pavillon de Paris on 9 December. In it, Bon looks every one of his 33 years, his gaunt face framed by more hair than he'd allowed himself since his Fraternity days, now seemingly a lifetime ago – as though he truly no longer gives a fuck what anyone else thinks, including, perhaps especially, Malcolm. And although he smiles for the camera and appears to put on a fair show for the French audience, the poses are not even ironic, merely rote, the inevitable plastic white cup full of whisky glued to his hand, his movements stiff, as though he was in pain.

One thing the cameras do not capture is how much time Bon spent away from the rest of the band offstage. Hooking up with his friend from Trust, vocalist Bernie Bonvoisin, the two travelled not on the tour bus but by train to each date. The two had a lot in common: both had started out as drummers, but had found greater fame fronting powerhouse rock bands, and both saw themselves as rebels by nature. 'We talked about doing something together,' Bonvoisin later recalled. 'I was thrilled.' Nevertheless, he admitted he was shocked to sit with Bon while he knocked back three double whiskies in quick succession one morning. By the time they had arrived in Paris, where the show was to be filmed, Bon had lost his voice. 'They had to call a doctor to him,' said Bonvoisin. When the doctor left, Bon poured himself a large whisky and Coke and made a toast to 'Doctor Whisky!'

When the tour finally ended two weeks later in Birmingham, Bon was so floored he slept for most of the 26-hour flight home, waking only to pick at the in-flight meal and guzzle as many free miniature bottles of Scotch and bourbon as he could stay awake for. Back in Sydney, exhausted and still drinking heavily, but separated at last from the rest of the group, who had scattered to their girlfriends and wives, Bon could look forward to three weeks off before returning to Europe for nine final shows in January. He intended to make the most of them, and while the brothers made plans to spend some of the money they'd made on buying their own properties, Bon splashed out on a new motorbike for himself: a red Kawasaki Z 900, with a top speed of 135 mph. He would ride it without a helmet, and fuelled by another night's heavy boozing, thundering around Bondi beach as though he hadn't a care in the world. Or certainly acting like somebody who didn't care any more. He also rented himself a flat, in O'Brien Street in Bondi, the first time he'd ever been able to afford the luxury of living alone. Not that he was ever alone much. The 'Highway To Hell' single had given AC/DC their first Top 30 hit in Australia for three years, while the album had reached No. 13 – hardly the dazzling heights of their early days in Oz but still their most significant hit since those times. AC/DC were news back home all over again and Bon revelled in the renewed attention, doing newspaper interviews and lapping up every drop of adulation at every pub and club he got blotto in. One of the big nights out he had was with his old mate from Adelaide days, Peter Head. 'We went out, bought some booze, got some dope and went to a party,' Head would later tell Murray Engleheart. The next morning, they awoke in adjoining rooms at Head's flat 'with women whose names we couldn't remember'. Bon didn't stick around long enough to discuss it, though. 'He suddenly got up, walked out and I never saw him again.' The previous night, however, Bon had begun to tell Peter how sick he was of leading the rock star lifestyle. He said, 'what he really wanted now was to settle down and have kids'.

His most significant visit, though, was the one Bon paid over the three-day Christmas weekend to his parents' home in Perth; the first time in three years he had been home with the family. Like the rest of his friends, Isa and Chick couldn't help noticing how much their son's drinking had escalated. But then it was the holiday season and New Year – Scottish Hogmanay – was always a time of hard drinking into the night and next morning. As Isa would later put it, 'You didn't tell Ron what to do. I never went too far. I just said I didn't like him drinking but you get to that stage they don't listen to you.' What they wouldn't have seen, either, was what went on behind the locked door of the toilet, Bon having a little toot now and then before carrying on drinking.

Flying back to London again in January, Bon didn't feel rested so much as spaced out, Sydney already seeming more like a dream. The bike and the new flat, though, had at least given him a glimpse of what might be. The first thing he did when he returned to a snow-bound England was arrange to have his own place in London too.

With Silver's help he found a small but 'posh' flat in a portered mansion block called Ashley Court, in Morpeth Terrace, a short walk from Buckingham Palace. Silver lent him a few sticks of furniture, knick-knacks and kitchen utensils, to help him move in without too much hassle. Forty-eight hours later he had left the flat to fly to Cannes, in the south of France, for MIDEM, the annual trade fair for the music business, where AC/DC were being presented with French gold records for both *If You Want Blood* . . . and *Highway To Hell*, and a British gold and silver for *Highway To Hell* – followed by seven more shows around the country. Bon was back in his new flat again by the end of the month, though, after a show at Newcastle's Mayfair – rescheduled from the UK tour of November.

There was one final show, on Sunday, 27 January, at the Gaumont theatre in Southampton, another leftover from the UK tour. This, though, was a significant occasion for Bon in another way: the night he began a short but vivid fling with an attractive young Japanese girl named Anna 'Baba', who Bon had been introduced to earlier that day, while having lunch over at Ian Jeffery's Maida Vale flat. Anna was an old friend of Ian's Japanese wife, Suzie. When he and Ian left to join up for the drive down to Southampton that afternoon, Suzie and Anna came with them. Returning to London in the early hours, Anna spent her first night with Bon at Ashley Court. The very next morning, he took her in a taxi to her flat in Finsbury Park, where he told her to grab her things and bring them back with her to his place. Years later, Anna told Clinton Walker that Bon was 'like the sweetest gentleman'. She certainly received a great deal of his attention over the next three weeks. When, on Wednesday, 6 February, AC/DC were filmed at Elstree Studios miming to their new single, 'Touch Too Much', for broadcast the following night on *Top of the Pops*, Anna went with Bon. The rest of the band was bemused but not out of sympathy with him. Angus was due to be married to his girlfriend, Ellen, in a few weeks' time and Malcolm had already settled down to fatherhood with his wife Linda, a former protégé of Fifa Riccobono's at Alberts in Sydney that Malcolm had been seeing off and on since the earliest days of the band. 'Angus got married cos Malcolm got married,' says Jeffery, only half joking. But if love wasn't necessarily in the air, the band were grateful at least for the steadying effect Anna seemed to have on their singer, who claimed to have given up whisky for sake, small hot flasks of which Anna would serve to him at home while he rolled joints and lolled about on cushions. It wasn't true – in fact, Bon was drinking and drugging more than ever, the sake merely added to his list of must-have consumables – but it's telling that Bon felt the need to project that idea to the others.

He and Anna also became regular visitors every Sunday to the Jeffery household in Maida Vale. 'Bon would come over with Anna every Sunday,' says Ian, 'and we'd go down the pub and [Suzie and Anna] would make Sunday lunch. We'd have a few pints then go back, watch the football on the telly, have Sunday lunch, then a quick kip. Then around six or seven o'clock we'd go back down the Warrington, and they'd come with us, you know?' Jeffery recalls how Bon would dote on his infant daughter, Emma. 'He would always bring her presents and play with her. She *loved* him to death. My wife loved him to death. *I* loved him to death.'

One event Bon didn't take Anna with him to, though, was to see UFO at the Hammersmith Odeon, a couple of days before the *Top of the Pops* taping. Instead, Bon turned up backstage with Joe Furey. According to UFO bassist Pete Way, Furey had been invited along in his role as Silver's partner in crime. 'Joe Silver [Furey] brought the smack down, you know. Bon was backstage [when] we'd had it delivered. Joe had the smack and [Bon] maybe snorted some, I'm not sure. We were just drinking as normal. But in those days it seemed perfectly all right. You could do some smack and wouldn't even notice the difference,' adds Way, who was five years younger than Bon. 'Physically, we were younger and your body could handle it.' Your body, perhaps, but not your face, and Bon's looked decidedly 'dusty' on *Top of the Pops*. Given their experience of TV performances going right back to *Countdown* days, it was a lack-lustre performance all round, Angus going through the motions while Malcolm and Cliff all but faded into the background. The single, which Mutt's engineer, Tony Platt, had thought would be

'I told him if he didn't quit drinking he was gonna die.'
Bon Scott, living up to his image, 1979   *(Getty Images)*

Bon Scott's grave in Fremantle, today *(Getty Images)*

A rare shot of Brian Johnson onstage without his trademark flat cap, 1980

(Getty Images)

Fly in the ointment. The post-Rudd line-up, circa 1988. Simon Wright far left
(Getty Images)

Blow up your audience. Even as record sales tanked in the 1980s, AC/DC's crowds just got bigger *(Getty Images)*

More on the road hell. Razors Edge tour, 1992 *(Getty Images)*

Angus and Malcolm onstage with Ronnie Wood of the Rolling Stones, Toronto, 2003 *(Getty Images)*

The brief, but unexpectedly successful, Razors Edge line-up, London, 1991. Chris Slade (bald), at the back   *(Getty Images)*

Last train home. Brian and Angus on stage during the start of the Black Ice tour, 2008
(Getty Images)

It's no longer about the music, but the *idea* of AC/DC. Left to right: Elaine Hendrix, Courtney Cruz and Sarah Cawood 'a huge hit', limped the following week to No. 29 then fell out of sight again.

AC/DC had never been about singles, though, and the following week would find Bon visiting Malcolm and Angus back at E.Zee Hire, where they were already pushing around ideas for the next album, scheduled to be recorded with Mutt and Tony in harness again in April. Not at the Roundhouse Studios this time though, but at the exquisitely appointed, Chris Blackwell-owned Compass Point Studios, in Nassau, capital city of the exotic Bahamian island of Providence. 'It was tax reasons,' says Ian Jeffery. With the rate of UK tax from income then running at 83 per cent, 'they'd been told by their accountants to make their next album anywhere *but* Britain, basically'.

Calling in at E.Zee to see the brothers on Friday, 15 February, Bon found them working away on the bones of two new tunes: 'Have A Drink On Me' and 'Let Me Put My Love Into You'. He'd already begun piecing his usual 'odds and sods' notes for possible lyrics in his various notebooks and scraps of paper, but he wasn't in the mood to sing. Instead, he jumped behind the drum kit and told them, 'Let me bash away.' The brothers were happy with that, it allowing them to forge away on their guitars while Bon – aping Phil Rudd's deceptively simple chugalug style – pounded out a beat to the intro to 'Let Me Put My Love Into You'. The mood was high. The previous day word had reached them from Peter Mensch that American sales of *Highway To Hell* had now reached one million, and that they would be receiving their first platinum album from Atlantic in due course. Alone that afternoon into early evening, Malcolm and Angus Young thrumming away on their guitars, chain-smoking Bensons and tossing around ideas and insults in equally good-natured measure, the old man stomping away on the drums as he had told them he could the first time he met them, over five years before, his dreams of being a singer backburner'd just as theirs of becoming rock stars were beginning to come true, it seemed, briefly, to Plug the roadie and whoever else happened to stick their head round the door that the mood inside Studio One was happy, even hopeful. When Bon returned home to Anna that night he was

elated, telling her how this next album 'is going to be it'. A message
he felt strongly enough about to phone Isa in Australia and repeat.

'We were down at the rehearsal room and he came down to see us
and said he was just about ready to go for it,' Malcolm Young would
recall 30 years later. 'He was starting to recharge his batteries. He was
looking really good ...'

Sunday, 17 February, was not a normal Sunday. Revved up by his visit
with the brothers at the rehearsal studio, the previous day Bon had
told Anna she'd have to leave – for a while, anyway, until he'd got his
work done writing lyrics for the new album. Having her around was
too much of 'a distraction', he said. Maybe she could stay with Suzie
and Ian for a while. But instead of going over for Sunday lunch that
weekend, Bon asked Anna to stay one more night and cook a typically
Japanese meal for his friends from Trust, who he had invited over,
along with Rose Tattoo guitarist Mick Cocks, also recently arrived in
London. Trust were in town recording their album *Repression*. The
previous Wednesday Bon had turned up at the studio, where he and
Bernie Bonvoisin had made an impromptu recording of them duet-
ting on 'Ride On', Bernie taking the earnest lead as a stoned and
drunken Bon howled and mugged along, the band grinding away
behind them. Bon had also boasted of having worked on English
translations of seven or eight Trust songs, as he had told Bernie he
would back in December. He didn't have them with him, he said, but
would show them to him at the dinner on Sunday.

Years later, Anna would describe the occasion to Clinton Walker as
like a 'last supper'. Early the next morning, before Bon came to, Anna
left the flat and caught a bus over to Suzie's. It was a chilly Monday
morning and she hoped Bon would phone her later, see how she was
doing, at least. That evening, though, when Ian and Plug came back
from E.Zee Hire, they said they hadn't seen Bon all day. Anna began
to fret. She had been seeing portents of doom hovering around Bon
like flies for days, she said. Certain 'sad looks' she'd noticed when he
didn't know she was looking. The firmness with which he gripped
her hand, as though trying to tell her something: 'not for our bright

future but something so hopeless, maybe in a tormented hell', as she put it in her broken English. And, like everyone else, she couldn't help but notice how much he drank, starting the day with a large tumbler of neat whisky while listening to records, mixing Eric Clapton's *Slowhand* with John Lennon's *Imagine*. When the phone in Maida Vale rang just after 11 p.m. she jumped in surprise. It was Bon. When Anna asked what he was doing Bon told her he was at home alone, 'Drinking and writing lyrics.' He was planning on going to the studio the next day so was going to bed soon, to get some rest, he said. Anna took that to be Bon's way of letting her know she wouldn't be invited back any time soon. Suzie gave her a blanket and she spent the night on the couch.

Only Bon wasn't planning on an early night. In fact, he'd already rung Silver, asking if she'd come out with him. He didn't care where; he just wanted to see her. Coming down these past weeks after nine months on the road, getting his own flat in London for the first time, seeing some real money in his pocket at last, he had begun to reflect deeply on the past, where he'd been, what he'd learned, what he'd left behind. What he felt sure he'd lost along the way. It was partly this feeling that had drawn him back home to Perth at Christmas. Now just in the last few days he'd begun to make phone calls to old friends and acquaintances, in some cases people he hadn't seen for years: Coral Browning, Doug Thaler, David Krebs, even Irene ...

But Silver wasn't up for it. Where was there to go on a dreary Monday night in London? Especially when you could be home, snug as a bug, just you and your big bag of brown? Bon said, 'Just come out for a drink.' But Silver wasn't drinking. Junkies drink about as often as they bathe. Booze just doesn't go with the gear. Or as Pete Way, one of Silver's best clients back then, puts it, 'It's not normal to have a bottle of champagne with you while you're trying to get [the heroin] in.' Instead, Silver suggested Bon might like to hook up with Alistair Kinnear – another junkie acquaintance of Silver's, who she had briefly shared a flat in Kensington with two years before. That was where Bon had first met him. An aspiring bass player, like many fringe players that existed on the outer limits of the London music business, Kinnear had scraped by without ever making a dent on anyone's consciousness. Other than drug dealers and their significant others, that is. But he was on the guest-list for a show at the Music Machine, in Camden Town, later that night, Silver said. And so Bon, desperate to get out and lose himself in the crowd – any crowd – said okay, tell him to come and pick me up, then put the phone down and poured himself another drink, thought about making some more calls, the last of which he made to Ian Jeffery, where Anna picked up the phone and he was forced to tell her one of his stories ... again.

Headlining the Music Machine that night was a new-wave outfit called Lonesome No More, featuring vocalist Koulla Kakoulli and future Cult guitarist Billy Duffy. Kakoulli was best known for her vocal contributions to recent recordings by The Only Ones and Johnny Thunders, both of whom were notorious for their predilection for songs about and direct experience of heroin. Indeed, it was Koulla's big sister, Zena Kakoulli, wife and manager of Only Ones singer Peter Perrett, who had organised the guest list at the Music Machine that night. Zena and Peter, who along with the rest of The Only Ones have commendably cleaned up their acts in recent years, but were well-known junkies in London back then. Though there has never been any suggestion that anybody else present at Music Machine that night knowingly gave Bon Scott heroin, merely that the milieu Kinnear and Bon were entering was condusive to rock'n'roll behaviour of various types. It is almost inconceivable to me that some at least were not carrying heroin – specifically Alistair Kinnear, the tall but physically frail-looking son of a doctor who, according to Silver, had driven to Silver's Gloucester Road bedsit earlier that evening, where he was still 'visiting', when Bon phoned. From Kinnear's then home in East Dulwich to Silver's place is a good 45-minute drive; quite a detour to make for a 'visit' on an evening when he was planning on going on somewhere – Camden Town – in the opposite direction. Unless, of course, Kinnear had a compelling reason for wanting to stop by Silver's place. As a fairly frequent 'visitor' to the same apartment in those days, the answer seems all too obvious to me, though the reader may wish to draw a different conclusion, as others have. Interesting, too, that Kinnear, breaking a 25-year silence on the subject in 2005, should insist he wasn't there at all; that he had merely phoned Silver, 'to see if she wanted to come along, but she'd made other arrangements for the evening'. And it is possible, of course, that if Kinnear did have drugs with him that night he had obtained them from other sources.

Whatever route he took, driving to Bon's at around 11 p.m., Kinnear would later recall that the singer was already 'pretty drunk' when he picked him up, and saying in an interview with the London *Evening Standard* just two days later how at the Music Machine '[Bon] was drinking four whiskies straight in a glass at a time.' Speaking 25 years later, however, he maintained that 'Bon and I both drank far too much', that night, 'both at the free bar backstage and at the upstairs bar as well'. Again, a strange claim to make for someone who Silver now insists 'wasn't much of a drinker' – presumably as well because, like her, he preferred junk to drunk. Kinnear had added, 'I did not see [Bon] take any drugs that evening.' What, old Road Test Ronnie? Why would he want to take drugs on a boring Monday night out at the Music Machine, surrounded by people likely off their heads? A bored, depressed, lovelorn, drunken Bon, suddenly fancying a snort, a blow, a bump? Give it here, mate …

As Ian Jeffery says now, 'Nobody ever thought anything different back then. You'd drink twenty pints because everything else that was going down there *enabled* you to drink twenty pints. It was rock'n'roll! It was the same with that little upstairs bar at the Hammersmith Odeon. You'd go down a flight of stairs to the ladies' bog cos no one ever used it, no one knew it was there, rack 'em out [lines of cocaine and/or heroin] and get back up to the bar. I mean, they would have been dabbling in everything, you're right. But mainly they would have been drinking, having a good time. The rest would have been, "Oh, okay …" It wouldn't have been the other way around. Just like give us a bag of crisps, or something like that. Like, yeah, I'll have one of those, and just chucking it down your neck, you know? Cos it was fun. You wouldn't want to be left out.'

'At the end of the [after-show] party I offered to drive him home,' Kinnear explained in the same 2005 interview. As they trundled down the Euston Road in Kinnear's Renault 5, 'I realised that Bon had drifted into unconsciousness. I left him in my car and rang his doorbell, but his current live-in girlfriend didn't answer. I took Bon's keys and let myself into the flat, but no-one was at home. I was unable to wake Bon, so I rang Silver for advice. She said that he passed out quite frequently, and that it was best just to leave him be to sleep it off.'

'I realised that Bon had drifted into unconsciousness ...' Again not quite how Silver now remembers it. According to Silver 'I got a phone call about one in the morning from a very distressed Alistair saying, "He passed out! He passed out! What do I do?"' In other words, a panic call to a heroin dealer. Yet if Kinnear was especially concerned, why didn't the son of a doctor simply drive him to a hospital? Because he, too, was drunk and feared police involvement, perhaps a breathalyser test and the loss of his driving licence? Drunk drivers have certainly done worse things when trying to squirm out of that one. Or might it have been simply because he was carrying some smack he'd bought earlier and was terrified out of his mind that the snort – or two – he might likely have offered Bon that night had caused the blackout? As a Harley Street doctor well-versed in dealing with music business figures from the Seventies, but who prefers not to be named here, says, 'Alcohol and even a small amount of heroin can be a lethal combination.'

Back to Alistair: 'I then drove to my flat on Overhill Road and tried to lift him out of the car, but he was too heavy for me to carry in my intoxicated state.' At which point, he phoned Silver again. In fairness to Silver, alarm bells may have taken longer to ring for her, simply because she had seen Bon blackout so many times before. Speaking in 2010, Silver issued a dry chuckle as she recalled the many previous occasions when Bon had blacked out on her. 'I once have to admit to abandoning him at Victoria Station,' she said, as though it were the most natural thing in the world. 'It was during the daytime but, yeah, I just left him there and went home, hoped for the best. He found his way home or someone saw him home.' So when a still panic-stricken Kinnear rang her again from his Dulwich flat, complaining, 'He's down in the car, I can't get him up here!' she told him, 'Well, take down some blankets.'

Kinnear: 'So I put the front passenger seat back so that he could lie flat, covered him with a blanket, left a note with my address and phone number on it, and staggered upstairs to bed. It must have been 4 or 5 a.m. by that time, and I slept until about eleven, when I was awakened by a friend, Leslie Loads. I was so hungover that I asked Leslie to do me the favour of checking on Bon. He did so, and returned to tell me that my car was empty, so I went back to sleep, assuming that Bon had awoken and taken a taxi home.'

Kinnear then slept soundly for another eight hours. When he awoke from his comatose state, it was dark outside, wintery and cold. It was a while before he got himself together to go out again. He was on his way to visit his girlfriend, who was in hospital, he later claimed. But when he got to his car, at around 7.45 p.m., Bon was still there, flat on his back where Kinnear had left him some 14 hours before. No sign of sick anywhere, as later assumed, but cold to the touch, deathly cold. This time Kinnear didn't waste time ringing Silver. Perhaps advice from a dealer only being useful when the OD case is still breathing and there's a chance the police don't have to be involved? Alistair knew he was past that. About 14 hours past it. Instead, he drove the car straight to the A&E department at King's College Hospital, where he finally got help to lift Bon out of the car at last. Out of it Bon and into it Alistair; their fates now for ever entwined.

When a by now utterly freaked out Kinnear was told Bon had been pronounced 'dead on arrival', he gave them Silver's name and phone number and fled the scene, not wanting any more to do with it. This time he didn't bother to ring Silver himself. When the hospital phoned her they didn't say Bon was dead, just that he'd been brought into the hospital and it was serious, and that she needed to come down. Fretfully, Silver agreed, taking Joe with her. Less than 24 hours since the panic calls from Alistair Kinnear telling her Bon had blacked out and couldn't be woken, it's hard to imagine the ex-girlfriend and heroin dealer wasn't already harbouring fears of what she might find when she got there. Fears that were not allayed when she and Joe were taken into a small room, brought a cup of tea, and told to wait for the doctor to speak to them. When the doctor finally arrived and broke the news, 'I just freaked right out,' Silver told Clinton Walker. 'I just shut down.' Needing to inform the next of kin, Silver explained she didn't have a number for Bon's family, so gave them Peter Mensch's office number. Then when she got back to her flat, she phoned Angus Young, who recalls her being 'hysterical'. She gave him the hospital's number and Angus phoned King's College but couldn't get anyone to confirm or deny anything about it as he wasn't family. So Angus did what he always did in times of trouble, he called Malcolm. Although it would be Malcolm who eventually took it upon himself to phone Chick and Isa with the terrible news, the first person he called was Ian Jeffery.

'I got a phone call like 2.30 in the morning from Malcolm,' says Jeffery. 'Just like, "He's dead." I said, "Who's dead? What are you talking about?" He said, "Bon's fucking dead." I said, "No, he's not." He yelled, "You think I'm fucking *joking*, do ya? You think I'd *fucking* joke about a thing like this!" He went off at me and I'm like, "No, of course not, Malcolm." He said, "Well, he is! *He's fucking dead!*"'

Anna Baba, still staying over on the couch at the Jeffery flat, was woken by screaming from the next room. When she went to investigate she found Suzie sobbing in Ian's arms. She fell to her knees and asked if it was Bon? 'She took my hand and nodded. Her face furrowed by tears. Has Bon died? I asked again.'

Jeffery rang Jake Berry, another member of AC/DC's road crew who lived nearby, and he came straight over. They sat and drank tea, 'In total shock and disbelief.' Then Mensch rang. 'He said, "We have to go and identify the body and I think you should be there."' Jeffery didn't want to go, he says, but he agreed. Jake drove him to Mensch's place, then Mensch and Ian drove together to the hospital in Victoria. 'We're in the hospital and it's fucking chaos at 6.30 in the morning, cuts, bruises, people getting back from being out all night. It's the casualty bit where people are getting cleaned up.' They were taken to a room. It still hadn't quite sunk in for Ian, though, who was still half expecting to find Bon had somehow survived – yet again.

'We turned this corner and it was suddenly like we were in a vacuum. No noise. I grabbed Peter's arm and I said, "He's in there, Peter." And we got to the door and I said to Peter, "I'm not going in. I don't wanna see him." Peter was like, "For fuck's sake, you're coming in." I said, "Peter, it's him, and really I don't wanna see him like this." So Mensch said, "Okay, I'll go in." Then he came back and he says, "Yep, it was him." And it was silence. It was *chaos* in there but when I turned the corner there was this whole vacuum, everything stopped. I saw the door and I knew.'

The *Evening Standard* broke the news later the same day. The following morning most major British papers carried an item about it. The story was reported much the same way in all of them: left in car to sleep off a night of heavy drinking by a musician friend, Bon Scott was found unconscious the following evening; pronounced DOA at hospital. Police said there were no suspicious circumstances. *Standard* reporter John Stevens interviewed Kinnear at his flat, quoting him as saying, 'I met up with Bon to go to the Music Machine, but he was pretty drunk when I picked him up.' He'd left him in his car, he said, because 'I just could not move him so I covered him with a blanket and left him a note to tell him how to get up to my flat in case he woke up. I went to sleep then and it was later in the evening when I went out to the car and I knew something was wrong immediately'. It was this story, along with Kinnear's potentially disingenuous quotes, that formed the backbone of every story subsequently printed around the world. And to which much of the official version of Bon Scott's death is still attributed, four decades later. This was no ordinary rock'n'roll OD. This poor devil died by accident, enjoying himself on a night out, having a few drinks with friends.

A story that appeared to be backed up by the official coroner's report, which followed the autopsy on Friday, 22 February: the verdict 'Death By Misadventure', the cause 'Acute Alcoholic Poisoning'. The Coroner, Sir Montague Levine, was quoted as saying that Scott had been 'the captain of his own destiny', adding, 'This young man of great talent was a consistent and heavy drinker who died from acute alcoholic poisoning after consuming a very large quantity of alcohol.'

And that appeared to be that. Only of course it wasn't. Within days the conspiracy theories were flying back and forth between London and Sydney; including the outlandish idea that the band's new management had arranged for the singer to be killed, both to claim the insurance and so as to replace him with a more stable and sober character, ready for the push to the commercial summit planned for that year. A strangely counter-intuitive argument for a band then poised on the threshold of true international success and therefore in greater need of their extraordinary frontman and lyricist than ever before. And if they had been going to get rid of him, they would have just sacked him. Just as they had everybody else they'd grown weary of; just as they would continue to do.

Less easily dismissed were the behind-closed-doors suggestions that it had been more than just alcohol that had caused Bon Scott to fall asleep and not wake up. When I ask Ian Jeffery now if he thinks it possible Bon had snorted some smack the night he died, he says simply, 'That could well have happened ... Who knows if that part took [place] afterwards, cos I never went on to the Music Machine that night.'

The nearest the brothers would touch on the suggestion there might have been heroin involved was a quote which appeared in *Sounds* in March 1980, just weeks after his death, when Angus told Dave Lewis about the time Bon 'was somewhere one night and the people he was with filled him full of dope and things and he was really drunk then too. But fortunately they took him to hospital and they kept him for the day and he was all right then.' However, in *Mojo*, in 2006, Malcolm Young alluded to darker secrets when he told Phil Alexander of his belief that police were following them for weeks after the death. 'All our phones were tapped around that time,' he said. 'You could tell. I'd try and make a call and things were getting tougher. Obviously the cops were listening in, but it's just like anything else. If there was a sinister side to [Bon's death], they would listen to the band guys and see what they were talking about.' He added, enigmatically: 'We weren't there but we knew exactly what went on there. We still haven't told what we know because it's more of a personal thing for Bon.' Before concluding, 'Bon was really low and Bon was a big drinker, so that night he went a little bit further. But he didn't drink himself to death that was for sure. He had too much to live for.'

Speaking on the 30th anniversary of Scott's death, Silver claimed: 'He died of major organ failure and at the autopsy [inquest], the doctor's report said that his organs were like those of a sixty-year-old man – his heart, liver etc.' No one else I have spoken to, though, that was there can recall any similar 'doctor's report'. However, Kinnear later recalled how the day after Scott's death became public, 'Silver came around to see me. She told me for the first time that Bon had been receiving treatment for liver damage, but had missed several doctor's appointments.' Ian Jeffery snorts with derision when I mention this to him now. 'If Bon had been seeing a doctor, I would have known about it, and I never saw any notes, any prescriptions, never took him to any appointments.' Indeed, according to some reports the autopsy showed Bon's liver and general health were actually in reasonable condition.

The fact that there are conflicting reports is not conclusive in itself. Silver was far from the only one who had recently noted the deterioration in Bon's general well-being. And what of the coroner's report? Surely if there had been any drugs involved, it would have mentioned this? Perhaps not, according to two doctors I spoke to for this book, both of whom declined to allow me to use their names because, as the more eminent of the two put it, 'It's not my case', but both of whom were most emphatic about the degree of 'discretion' all coroners exercise from time to time. 'Certainly in cases of suicide, a coroner will nearly always choose to come to some other conclusion, because of insurance claims and because of family distress,' explains the first, a senior figure at a general practice outside London. 'In this case, he may well have chosen to gloss over the heroin, it being such a taboo subject, particularly back then. Or they may not have done a specific test to look for anything else, simply noted the extremely high level of alcohol in the bloodstream and deduced it was that, and put it down as death by misadventure.'

This view is backed up by the second doctor I spoke to, an eminent Harley Street physician with decades of experience dealing with musicians, among other high-profile public figures. I ask: if the coroner didn't put it in his report, does that mean there could not have been heroin in the body? 'No, it doesn't mean that. Yes, there could still have been heroin there.' So the coroner wouldn't necessarily have looked for or found heroin? 'No, not necessarily, no.'

What is known is that Alistair Kinnear disappeared from his address at 67 Overhill Road shortly afterwards, and remained under the radar for the next 25 years. In 1983, he moved to the Costa del Sol, where he appears to have lived on a fishing boat, before going missing believed dead under mysterious circumstances in 2010. In his only interview in the intervening years, given in 2005 to the late Maggie Montalbano, Kinnear said, 'I truly regret Bon's death. Hindsight being 20/20, I would've driven him to the hospital when he first passed out, but in those days of excess, unconsciousness was commonplace and seemed no cause for real alarm.' Why then, though, the panicked phone calls in the middle of the night to Silver? Kinnear is right: passing out was commonplace in those pre-AIDS days when drugs were still considered consciousness-expanding and over-drinking considered manly, even heroic. Except, that is, for heroin, which even then was considered the big no-no.

It's interesting to note, too, how Kinnear still felt obliged to quote the coroner's report, as if to defend himself. 'The Lambeth coroner's report cited acute alcohol poisoning, and death by misadventure,' he repeated not for the first or last time, almost as if speaking to himself. Yet, as he said, 'It has since been speculated that Bon choked on his own vomit, but I can neither confirm nor deny this', adding, 'There was no vomit in the car, and contrary to other reports I've read, he was not wrapped around the gearstick when I found him.' Indeed, there is no official suggestion of asphyxiation, of hypothermia, of heart failure or seizure or any of the other ghastly side-effects attributed to alcohol poisoning. Heroin users – that is, long-term addicts, as opposed to the occasional 'joyrider' Bon Scott was – are remarkably up on the dos and don'ts of their drug. Whenever possible, you do use clean needles but you don't do it in public. You do go to doctors for help when you need to but you don't under any circumstances go to the police. You do like to get high, always. But you don't – ever – try mixing it with booze. It's a commonly held belief that more drug users have died that way than any other. Is that what happened to Bon Scott then? It is my belief that it is. No mystery to it for me, just a great deal of deliberate obfuscation – certainly by the man who was there and who should have known better.

On 5 February, 2010, almost 30 years exactly after his hand in Bon Scott's death, Alistair Kinnear was reported in Sydney's *Herald Sun* to be the subject of 'his own mystery after disappearing with a yacht on the way to Spain'. According to the wire, he and two other men had set sail on a 13-metre wooden-hulled sloop named *Danara*, leaving from Marseilles, France, in July 2006. They were heading to southern Spain when they apparently vanished. 'We tried to get the coast guard and everybody else to look, but nobody could find anything,' his son Daniel told the reporters. 'So he's missing, not legally declared dead. We have to wait seven years for that to happen.' The story concluded, however, by saying, 'Soon after Kinnear went missing, a person claiming to be *Danara*'s skipper contacted authorities to say Kinnear was safe but did not want any contact with his family. The message passed on was, "Please forget me." However, his son is certain he is dead, and wonders if foul play may have been involved.'

As for Silver, she also disappeared off the radar for a time. Her explanation: 'Of course, there was massive publicity and stuff and, to be honest, both of us really just hid from the press at the time, because it was just too difficult to … you know … have done some press would be intrusive at a time like that. But it did affect [Kinnear] very, very strongly.' Intrusive for whom, one has to ask. If it's true what Malcolm Young says now about all their phones being tapped by the police in the weeks that followed Scott's death, can it be just coincidence that Silver was finally busted for dealing heroin later that same year? She'd lost her passport so was unable to flee, and 'went down hard', as Clinton Walker puts it now. 'There seems no doubt [Bon] loved her,' says Walker, 'but they would never have settled down the way Bon dreamed of. She was just the wrong woman for him, at that time at least.' Silver's 'soul mate', Joe Furey, escaped the bust, having left London for good within weeks of Scott's death. Silver eventually reappeared in Adelaide, where she reportedly finally got off drugs in 1986. She declined to respond to requests to be interviewed for this book.

The first Isa and Chick Scott heard of their son's death was when Malcolm Young phoned them. It had been Isa's birthday just two days before. They had just returned from an evening out at a senior citizens' club when the phone rang. 'I hope I never have to do anything like that again,' said Malcolm. 'I just screamed,' remembered Isa. 'I nearly tore my hair out.' Isa then rang Irene, who told her she'd only just spoken to Bon on the phone a few days before. Still in shock, Irene phoned Mary, then Vince Lovegrove, the latter, though horribly shaken by the news, was not entirely surprised, either. 'Irene phoned me late one night and I was completely devastated,' he later recalled. 'Here was a guy who deserved success, who deserved to be happy in life [but] I don't think he died happy.' The next day, the *Sydney Telegraph* reported: 'When Bon Scott died in London yesterday, a little piece of Australian rock history ended.'

Other 'mysteries' that have continued to hover around Bon's death include the story of 'two big men' who Australian *Rolling Stone* alleged went around to his Ashley Court flat and 'rifled through everything'. The implication: cleared it of any incriminating evidence, including drugs and/or any finished lyrics Bon may have left behind that could still be used on the next AC/DC album. Anna Baba would later claim she had been misled by Ian Jeffery into believing he had packed all Bon's notebooks away in the suitcase with his other personal belongings that were sent home to his parents in Australia – only to find it wasn't so when she visited Chick and Isa a few months later. While Silver claimed that when she phoned Peter Mensch asking if she could go round and retrieve the bits and pieces she had lent Bon just weeks before, he brushed her off. Mensch had previously paid lip-service to her, knowing the important place she seemed to occupy still in Bon's private life. After his death though, she was simply 'no longer relevant'. She also claimed that Bon's wish to be buried in Kirriemuir was not respected.

All of which can be cleared up very simply. The two 'big men' that went around to Bon's flat to 'clear it up' were Ian Jeffery and Jake Berry. 'If it was my gaff I'd want someone to come and clear it up too', as Jeffery says now. As a tour manager he was also used to dealing with things that were 'well crazier than that. Basically, it was just to put his things in a plastic bag. But it was a "just in case", you know. A quick sweep, before anybody thought: "Rock star. It's not just any-body, it's a rock star, let's get round there quick", you know?'

There was another reason Ian and Jake went around too. 'We had to go through the mechanical process, the press stuff, etc.,' explains Jeffery. 'You know, Phil Carson [and] that whole side of things got involved. But before that, we decided we'd move [Bon] to like a funeral rest home in Paddington. And we would have an open coffin – not an open coffin, but part of it open so if people wanted to pay their last respects, they could. Then I said to Mensch, "You know what, Peter? We can't have people fucking going in there and seeing this shroud or whatever you want to call it." I said, "Let's go round to his apartment and get his T-shirt and some jeans." You know Bon always liked his white T-shirt with the sleeves rolled up, and his jeans with his belt on. So we went round and got that and took it to the coroner place and said please can you put these on him? And at that point, I went in and saw him there and ... there's no words can describe it. He was in his jeans and his T-shirt, there he was, ready to fucking go on and give it a Whole Lotta Rosie, you know?'

Ian also packed up Bon's stuff, ready to return to Australia. Though he doesn't say so, you can tell from the shrugs and sighs why he didn't allow Anna back in there, too. As AC/DC's tour manager, and Bon's roommate and personal friend, Ian had seen dozens of girls come and go from Bon's life. Only weeks before Anna there had been the cutie he ended up in bed with in Sydney; before that a 'semi-steady' that worked for ATI in Los Angeles. 'The only one he ever loved was probably Silver. And he hated her too.' Anna, for all her kindness and love, had only known Bon for three weeks. Virtually his last act had been to ask her to move out of his flat. In the end, Ian Jeffery was only doing what he'd always done: looked out for Bon's interests first, whatever the girl's name was. Or who she thought she was in the singer's life.

Nevertheless, as he now concedes, 'His girlfriend [Anna] sat outside [the funeral home] for three days and didn't move. My wife would go round with soup and tea for her. She wouldn't move from the spot. My missus wouldn't go in though because she was just distraught.'

He did also take it upon himself to clear out the flat of drugs. Who wouldn't have done that for a friend, in those freewheeling days? The guy was dead. The last thing anyone needed was further besmirching of his name with posthumous criminal investigations. Again, all part of the come-what-may job for any top-line tour manager, then as now.

As for Silver not being allowed near the place: Peter Mensch is no fool; neither are the brothers. They all had Silver's number, knew where she was at. As Michael Browning so quaintly put it, 'She was seen as a negative influence.' If it was true that Malcolm and the others 'knew exactly what went on there' and were already convinced that Bon 'didn't drink himself to death that was for sure', Silver would have been the last person they would let anywhere near their business now. Regardless of the fact that she can hardly be held directly responsible for his death whatever the circumstances. Silver sold smack; she didn't force people to get drunk and take fatal overdoses.

One person Ian did make a point of paying a visit to was Alistair Kinnear. 'I didn't know Alistair. I'd never met him,' he says, 'but I spoke to him. I got hold of him straight away and I've gotta believe that [his story] is true. I could see it that way. He would go back to Victoria, cos it's on the way back to his house. And if somebody's sleeping in the car and you can't move him [and] you're not gonna wake him, you're certainly not going to carry him up two flights of stairs, you know?'

No arguments there. The only question none of those who were there that night has ever answered for me, without hiding behind the coroner's report first: what exactly was it that caused Bon to black out that night?

Michael Browning asks another important question which has never been answered properly. When he heard Bon had died, he says, he thought of Silver and of smack, but mostly, he says, he thought of his sister Coral. 'You know, my sister was very, very good at looking after Bon when she worked for me. And I suppose what crossed my mind is, why was he in that position, where he can be that vulnerable, and die in a car, on his own, out in some street somewhere? It just struck me as being a situation where he wasn't really being supervised the way he probably should have been. Coral was kind of like his minder, in a way. I mean, she had that relationship with him where he could always confide in her or call her if he was in trouble. She'd know where he was. We thought, well, what's he doing in that situation? Who was looking after him? There was enough money around at the time to have a minder. We all knew he was capable of overindulging and putting himself in that situation, so why wasn't somebody with him, looking after him, keeping an eye on him?'

Writing about that night over 25 years later, Vince Lovegrove echoed Michael Browning's initial thoughts. 'Those of us in Australia who knew Bon well, those of us who had known him since the Sixties, could not quite comprehend how, on the edge of international success, he could die alone in a car, parked in a lonely London street, in the middle of winter, with not a friend in sight.' Speaking now, though, the guy Bon replaced in AC/DC, Dave Evans, says he's not surprised at all. 'I had a private conversation with Bon, which will remain private, by the way. But I wasn't surprised when he died all alone and friendless ... I don't blame anybody in particular. But I wasn't surprised that he went like that, at all.'

Pete Way, whose own heroin addiction would overshadow the rest of his life, losing him first his career then not one but two wives to drug overdoses over the coming years, says, 'More than the people who investigated his body, I know damn well what can happen. It's nearly happened to me a few times.' Then tells a story, built on the many years' perspective he now has on the subject of early graves through 'rock'n'roll misdemeanours', as he only half jokingly puts it. 'I was talking to a friend about Michael Jackson, when he died, saying isn't it amazing, you know? And he said, "Well, how did you *expect* him to die?" So in a way, without taking anything away from Bon's spontaneous desire to reach the heavens, actually it could have happened to any one of us. As the Stones song said, "It's just a shot away" …'

Pete says the last time he saw either of the Silvers – Joe (who to be clear wasn't with Bon that night) – was backstage at a UFO show, in LA, in April, just a few weeks after Bon's death. 'We were playing Long Beach arena and he was there. It was as if it hadn't happened – but then it wasn't his fault. He didn't go [to Bon] "Have this and that." If you'd asked him to give you another line, or buy a bit more and that, he's not gonna say no. He's with friends, and Bon *was* a friend. At the same time, he's not gonna say no because he doesn't want to fall out with you. So in a way we're all as guilty. But then again, I went home. Bon didn't. It's like anything. People die of real alcohol overdoses, or drugs. Our dressing room was, like, you walk into it at your own peril …'

He croaks with laughter that turns into a very old dry cough.

CHAPTER THIRTEEN

What Did You Do for the Money, Honey?

The cremation took place in Fremantle, on Friday, 29 February 1980, where the following day the ashes of Ronald Belford Scott were buried in the Memorial Gardens, in the shade of the flowering eucalyptus.

Isa and Chick had received a letter from Ted Albert which spoke of losing 'a really good friend. There are not many people in the entertainment world, unfortunately, who you could call a friend, though the public often are made to think differently, but Bon was one of the real exceptions – a genuine person with a generous nature and a real wish to make others happy.' That much was certainly true. When, though, Albert added that Bon 'was not one, as so many of us are, to always be dreaming of better days and hoping for better things. He was a realist, who lived for the present and was quite happy to live each day for itself and to be content with his lot', he was surely being kind. Bon Scott was a born dreamer, who had spent his entire life looking for something better than his 'lot'. A prison-scolded larrikin in his youth, a heavy drinker and indiscriminate drug-taker in adulthood, he was also an inveterate womaniser, a roamer, a poet and a singer. He read a lot – anything he could get his hands on, on the road, from books of history and biography to magazines like *Penthouse* and *Mayfair* – and wrote a lot. Not just lyrics but poetry, letters, postcards, or just thoughts scrawled as they came in the notebooks he always took everywhere with him. He was also funny in person, generous with his time and money, hard working, and, at the time of his death, as reckless as ever. When people ask how he

313

could have died alone, in someone else's car, outside a building he had never been to before, full of drink and almost certainly drugs, the answer is how could he not? Sir Montague surely got it right when he described Bon as the captain of his own destiny; something that few who attended his funeral would have disagreed with.

It was a small, no-frills service, just the band and their entourage, plus Fifa Riccobono from Alberts to join the forlorn gathering of friends and family. No photographers, no TV or radio crews. It wasn't even covered by the local media. 'There were a lot of kids outside,' shrugged Angus. '[But] it was better being quiet, because it could have been very bad if a lot of people had just converged there.' A few weeks later, Ted Albert paid for Chick and Isa to fly to Singapore for a holiday. They had also been told by their accountant that they could expect significant royalties, as next of kin, more than enough to see them through the next couple of years. In fact, the royalties never stopped, as *Highway To Hell* and all the other AC/DC albums Bon Scott helped make so tremendous would become multimillion sellers as the years went by and their son's status as rock icon and legend just grew.

Ian Jeffery remembers how when they were making preparations to fly the coffin back to Australia, Angus came to him, '*adamant*, totally adamant' that, as he put it, 'Our mate's not below us. We're not going on the same plane as Bon is. We're not having him sitting beneath us while we're up there.' Ian reassured him: 'Don't worry. I'll take care of that. So I'd got everything arranged. Atlantic flew us all back first class, the band, me, Mensch ... We were gonna pick up all the Alberts people – Fifa and George and Harry – and make our way to Perth, it was perfect. Took the flight, we took the thing down, picked up in Sydney, went on to Perth. And we're just getting ready to go and I look out the window and I see a coffin going down ...' There had been a mix-up when the original flight the coffin was booked onto had been cancelled, and ground crew had seen it as their duty to get the coffin home as soon as possible, rearranging for it to be loaded onto what turned out to be the same flight as the band. Ian nods his head sadly. 'There was so much stuff I went through which

I never fucking want to go through again. Anyway, I could see this coffin on the runway, so I sat Angus down and said, "I'll get your bag, mate, don't worry about it." Once I'd seen them take that thing off and take it away, I let Angus stand up. Thankfully, it was dark, so he didn't notice anything.'

They checked into a hotel in Perth. It was too late at night to go to Bon's parents' place. But first thing in the morning they all went over to pay their respects and give their condolences to Isa and Chick. Ian continues: 'By this time his poor parents had just been lambasted by the press – Rock Star Overdoses! So we went round there and his mum came out and she was totally what you'd think: so distraught. But she was so grateful for everybody coming, you know? She was so happy to see everyone. We went in there and typical thing, you know, sandwiches and cakes and a cup of tea. And what she'd done was, she'd set out five chairs for the band – and four had come in to sit down. She realised then that her son was dead and that we'd come here to tell her. Cos she'd just been hiding for two days. It was a simple thing of laying five chairs out and when she came to the fifth chair it just gushed out like it was a waterfall. I was fucking distraught. I was so, so sorry for that woman ...'

Mark Evans, who saw the guys when they got back to Sydney before going out for the funeral in Perth, says simply, 'It was as bad as you could possibly imagine.' But then, as Angus said, 'Nobody knew what to do. I'd just got married – it was hard to take in. We were so depressed.' The day after the funeral Phil flew home to Melbourne for a break; Cliff went with him. The brothers flew back to London with Ian Jeffery and Peter Mensch. It was now that Mensch tried passing a list of possible replacements to Malcolm, who waved him away. Not because he was thinking of quitting, though he and Angus had had a brief conversation about changing the name, which they rejected out of hand, but because he wasn't ready to deal yet with the practicalities. This wasn't like replacing Dave Evans, or any of the others the band had left behind on the road. After the funeral, according to Malcolm, it was Chick that said to him, 'You've got to find someone else, you know that. Whatever you do, don't stop.' But there was never any chance of that. The Youngs had come too far to stop now. Especially when they knew they were this close to making George's dreams come true at last. In a *Rolling Stone* interview, published later that year, Angus was quoted as saying, 'I was sad for Bon. I didn't even think about the band. We'd been with Bon all that time; we'd seen more of him than his family did.' In the very next sentence, Malcolm admitted that within 48 hours of returning to London 'I thought, "Well, fuck this, I'm not gonna sit around moping all fucking year." So I just rang up Angus and said, "Do you wanna come back and rehearse?"' Angus added, 'I'm sure, if it had been one of us [that died], Bon would have done the same.'

It was no longer a question of whether AC/DC should replace Bon Scott but who with. Finally, Malcolm and Angus looked at Mensch's list. Then set about compiling one of their own. Molly Meldrum appeared to have made up their minds for them when he began talking openly on *Countdown* about Stevie Wright replacing Bon. But it was an absurd idea. With Wright in the midst of a full-blown heroin addiction again, he wasn't even on the list of possibilities. Rumours began to spread about other Australian notables, like 24-year-old Cold Chisel singer Jimmy Barnes, who certainly had the voice and the looks – and, coincidentally, was an expat Scot, and yet another of Bon's night-on-the-town drinking buddies – but was already a fixture in the Australian pop charts and therefore unlikely to fit Malcolm's main criterion, which was to find someone that didn't come with too much baggage. Barnes himself now claims he wasn't even approached. 'The whole thing was a complete urban myth – I never even spoke to the guys about it.' He had, in fact, already replaced Bon once before – Fraternity in 1973. History, though, was not about to repeat itself.

Then there was the Australian singer Allan Fryer, who was on the list. 'He was my choice, actually,' recalls David Krebs. But Fryer was almost too perfect – so much so he later formed an AC/DC mini-me with Mark Evans called Heaven. But as Malcolm Dome says, 'You meet Alan it's just like meeting Bon. It's exactly the same character – the same *joie de vivre*, the same drive. Like, wow, no wonder they turned you down. They didn't *want* another Bon. You can't blame them for not wanting another Bon.' There were also the usual suspects: Angry Anderson, John Swann, 'all those guys that were down in Australia – they were never in the equation,' says Ian Jeffery. 'They were never going back there for a singer.' Other would-be Bons included former Moxy singer Buzz Shearman, but his vocals had already been so damaged from years of touring with the Canadian hard rockers the idea never got off the page.

When proper auditions finally began in March, at Vanilla Studios in Pimlico, a converted garage near Vauxhall Bridge (the same place The Clash had written most of the *London Calling* album six months before), AC/DC found themselves deluged with what Ian Jeffery now characterises as 'would-be David Coverdales more than would-be replacements for Bon Scott'. He laughs at the memory. 'They'd all get the mike stand and put it between their legs and they'd all wanna sing "Smoke On The Water" ... They'd not got a hope in hell.'

Tony Platt had been at work in the studio with Mutt Lange one afternoon when they got news of Bon Scott's death. 'Mutt went out to take a phone call and when he came back he was white as a sheet: "You're never gonna believe this. Bon died." We both just sat and looked at each other for fifteen or twenty minutes. What do you say, you know? Everybody thought he was invincible. He was a kind of Keith Richards character. You just thought, well, he's just one of those people; he's got the angels looking down on him.' Already booked to make the next AC/DC album, Platt admits there was also a sense of, oh fuck, there goes the album. 'Of course. I think you'd be a liar to say that wasn't going through your mind. I think the answer came back, we're gonna consider the options. It wasn't very long though before Malcolm and Angus said, "We're gonna carry on. Find a singer and get on with it." I'm not a psychologist but I imagine it's probably a very good way to get through something like that.'

Once auditions were underway in Pimlico, cassettes of the sessions considered most promising would be sent on for Mutt to listen to. 'We were listening in the car [to work] every day to rehearsal tapes from the auditions. Sometimes it was hilarious. They had a sort of shortlist but there were all sorts of people pitching up. And we'd thought of a few people that we thought we should put forward. We sat and compiled a bit of a list to throw at them ...'

One of the names on the list Mutt suggested was a little-known singer from Newcastle, in the band Geordie. Angus, who recalled Bon telling him about the Geordie singer years before, was intrigued. 'Bon had said he was a great rock'n'roll singer in the style of Little Richard. And that was Bon's big idol, Little Richard.' Malcolm, though, who also recalled Bon talking about Geordie, was disdainful. Ian Jeffery remembers him telling Lange, '"He's a fucking big fat cunt. How we gonna have a big fat cunt singing with us?" Mutt's like, "I think you're confusing him with the guitar player." "No, I'm not! I've fucking seen Geordie. He's a big fat cunt!" So we're going through all those things and all these different singers are coming in, down there in Victoria, in the studios, and everybody forgets about this guy Brian Johnson for a while.'

Instead, attention turned to Gary Holton, once of the Heavy Metal Kids, who the band had supported all those years before. Holton had the barrow boy front and scallywag charisma, but he lacked the vocal range. Mutt didn't see it. Gary Pickford-Hopkins, who'd toured with Rick Wakeman in Ian's days of working with him and had also been in Wild Turkey, had the right kind of bluesy, soulful voice but less of the charm. Tony Platt suggested Snips (real name: Steve Parsons), formerly of Baker Gurvitz Army and, before that, Andy Fraser's much-heralded though commercially unsuccessful post-Free outfit, Sharks. 'The guy had an extraordinary voice,' says Platt.

Bon had left behind a lot of boxes for any replacement to tick. So far, though, the only one who had come close was another fugitive from a band they had toured with in their earliest days in London – Back Street Crawler vocalist Terry Slesser. Malcolm and Angus still remembered Newcastle-born Slesser as 'the good bloke' from the Back Street Crawler dates four years before. 'They had just returned from Australia and Bon's funeral,' Slesser recalled in 2009. 'It was a pretty grim scenario. I broke the ice when I suggested doing "Rocky Mountain Way" as a "non-Bon song" to get things going. We all relaxed a bit after that. I had a couple glasses of Mateus [Rosé] and Angus had a cup of tea. We ran through "Whole Lotta Rosie", "Highway To Hell" and "The Jack". It was all pretty enjoyable. Malcolm thought he was recording the rehearsal onto a Revox [reel-to-reel recorder] but discovered that it hadn't taped. I didn't fancy doing it all again. It was all a bit exhausting and emotionally draining.' It was an attitude unlikely to endear him to the brothers. 'He came in and they kind of liked him,' says Jeffery. 'I would have thought he had a good chance of getting the gig, but he kind of let himself down, you know? He didn't really cut it. I thought that Gary Pickford-Hopkins, who was on the want-back list, might be the one. But Malcolm wanted to take another ad out first though, see who else showed up.'

They were starting to clutch at straws. 'At one time they were talking about Noddy Holder,' Jeffery reveals. 'But they didn't think they would get him. And Malcolm said, "People will just say that's the singer in Slade. We can't have him even though he would be fucking brilliant."' Finally, 'There was one day when we had no one coming round and we're all sitting there jerking off going, what are we gonna do?' Out of exasperation more than hope, Malcolm told Ian to try and locate the guy Mutt had been blethering about: the fat cunt Geordie singer. 'So I managed to track Brian down to Newcastle and ask him if he could come down. He said, "Fucking hell, man. I'm working for me brother's roofing company, I can't just come. Plus I haven't got the money for the fare." I said, "Get on a train or a plane, I'm paying for it." He says, "You fucking are? Who are ya?" I said, "I can't tell you anything but really I'm gonna pay for everything."' Johnson offered to get the train, Jeffery told him to fly 'cos it was quicker. Then bought him a ticket over the phone and rang him back and gave him the details. So he came down. We sent a car out to pick him up at the airport, and we waited. And waited ...'

Downstairs at the rehearsal room there was a 'green room' with a pool table. 'A couple of the crew, Barry and Evo, were in there playing pool. So I'm upstairs with the band waiting for this guy who's supposed to come in at two o'clock. It gets to 2.15, then 2.30 ... ' Going downstairs to make a phone call to the airport to see if the flight had been delayed perhaps, Ian found Barry 'standing there with a guy with a fucking hat on. So Barry goes, "How's it going up there?" I said, "We're still waiting for this guy Brian to come." This other bloke goes, "Brian? I'm fucking Brian." He'd come in thinking that Barry and Evo were in this band he was gonna be auditioning for. Barry and Evo never thought to say anything. They thought he was just one of the studio guys who'd come in for a game of pool.'

Counting to 10 before speaking, Ian took Brian upstairs to meet the band. 'He was smoking when he came in, which went down well with the brothers, who introduced themselves. And then he realised who they were. They sat around chatting and you could see that nervousness coming in where Angus just wanted to get on with it.' Asked if he'd like them to play one of their songs, or something he'd like to choose, Johnson told them: 'Nutbush City Limits'. Ian: 'They looked at each other like, what? Not even we thought of that one! But they started playing it and he grabbed the mike, took it off the stand, wrapped it around his hand … It was almost like déjà vu Bon, except it was on his same hand like Daltrey used to do, you know? Bon would take the lead and wrap it round the other hand. So off they went and fuck, it was raw and you could see Angus get up out of his seat and start tapping his foot. Malcolm was just sat down observing, but you could see the little sparkle lighting up in everybody's eyes. Then they played a blues thing. Then they tried a couple of theirs. From that moment, it was history.' After Johnson left, though, 'Malcolm says, "We've got some guys coming tomorrow and the next day. You never know. Let's see 'em." But anybody who came through that door, even if they were good, didn't have a fucking chance. They'd made their mind up.'

A couple of days later they flew Johnson back down again from Newcastle. As before, he was late. 'About three hours later, just as we're thinking of going for some tea, he bounds in. He hasn't told us that he's had a phone call to go and do a TV commercial. Remember the old Hoover ad? *It beats as it sweeps as it cleans …* He was doing that the same day! He'd used our ticket to get down, went over there and did that, picked his money up, then came over.' He laughs out loud.

'But as soon as he walked in they went straight into a little blues, jamming. It was a done deal. Then they had a whole set laid out for him to sing. No problem. He was the best guy for the job by a million miles.'

Tony Platt remembers him and Mutt listening to the Brian tape. 'It was obvious. It's as much about the spirit of what you do, and AC/DC ... I don't think it's [unfair] to say none of them is virtuosos ... but you bring them all together and that sum of the parts is just something else completely, and it works. That's why the decision to have Brian in there was an inspired one, because they obviously recognised how it works and therefore they were bringing in somebody that would cement that properly.'

Of Anglo-Italian blood, Brian Johnson was born on 5 October 1947, in Dunston, Gateshead, on the south bank of the River Tyne, so was only a year younger than Bon. Johnson's father, Alan, had been a sergeant major in the Durham Light Infantry and, later, a coal miner. His mother, Esther, had been born in Frascati, in Italy. Performing and singing – 'Showing off!' – had been in his blood as long he could remember. Joining the local school choir when he was nine, he had also taken part in various small stage shows with the Scouts, even had a modest role in a locally televised drama. His first band was the Gobi Desert Canoe Club, about which little is known besides its fourth-form name. After that he joined short-lived heavy rock outfit Fresh. His first money-gig, though, was in a cabaret act called The Jasper Hart Band, peppering their Top 30 covers with songs from the hippy musical *Hair!* It was from this unlikely conglomerate that Johnson and other members of the band eventually formed Geordie.

Signed to EMI's Regal Zonophone imprint (then home of Procol Harum, The Move and T. Rex, among others), Geordie made the Top 40 with their very first single, in December 1972, the frenzied 'Don't Do That'. Pitched somewhere between the blokey-glam lines of Sweet, who they supported, and Slade, who they looked to for inspiration, their follow-up, 'All Because Of You', in March 1973, actually made the Top 10. But with only one real setting to their musical dial – rock-dressed-as-pop, played by grizzly bears in knee-boots – commercial decline set in almost immediately. They delivered live and released one half-decent album with their 1973 debut, *Hope You Like It*, but their final hit was the minor Top 20 success of their third single, 'Can You Do It'. Their second album, *Don't Be Fooled By The Name*, released in 1974, saw them out of the absurd glam get-ups and into gangster outfits, replete with cigars and toy machine guns, but the image change couldn't save the album from being a flop and the game was all but over. Johnson walked out after their third album, *Save The World*, in 1976. But the promise of a solo career lasted for just one single, the frankly appalling ballad, 'I Can't Forget You Now', replete with syrupy strings and a melody so thin Johnson could have rolled his ever present tobacco in it. By the time Ian Jeffery rang him in March 1980, Brian Johnson had separated from his first wife, Carol, and was living in the spare room at his mother's house. Recently, he had begun performing in a new version of Geordie, in which he was the only original member, concentrating more on heavy rock crowd-pleasers like 'Rock And Roll' by Led Zeppelin and 'Nutbush City Limits' by Ike and Tina Turner. 'It was a good wage packet every week,' he recalled in 2011. 'Not massive, but good. We did "Whole Lotta Rosie" to finish the set off with, which we'd just learned a couple months before.' Between gigs, he was also picking up work wherever he could: roofing, voiceover work, working in a garage, anything that paid – Brian Johnson wasn't young enough to be fussy any more.

He recalled that first phone call from Jeffery but telling him: 'Nah, I've been bitten before. I had three Top 10 hits with a band called Geordie. And after three years we were as broke as when we started. Those were the days of the great rip-off. I just said I'm not gonna do this again. I was away from home all the time, missed me daughters growing up ...'

It was only after Jeffery offered him a plane ticket and a car to pick him up from the airport that he thought he'd give it a go – 'And, boing!' When he found out it was AC/DC he was auditioning for, it never crossed his mind that he might have got the job. He just wanted to get home to Newcastle to tell the boys in Geordie that he'd sung a couple of songs with AC/DC. 'I just thought, I'm sure they'll have a big star guy.' Asked why he thinks they chose him, he becomes thoughtful. 'Yeah, I don't know, they were looking for a certain kind of singer. The boys, they were just dead sure what they wanted and nobody else knew and I'm sure a lot of people were left shaking their heads.' When they asked him to come back down to London for his second audition, he recalls telling them: 'Well, I can't just be popping up and down to London, it's fucking expensive. I've got a gig here. Playing me little band on the weekend ...' Asked if he could take Monday off from work, just to have another blow, with all travel expenses taken care of as before, he finally acquiesced. 'I'll tell you what, I'll take Monday and Tuesday off and I'll come down.'

It was at this second meeting in the Pimlico rehearsal room that the brothers first introduced him to a new song idea they had begun working on. 'They said, "We got this one song, we got a riff and we're gonna call it 'Back In Black', but that's all we've got, just a title and it's for Bon. It's a tribute to Bon. But we haven't gotten any words and all we've got is ..."' He hums the now famous lumbering riff. 'That's all it was. I went, "That's it?" And they said, "Yeah, well could you sing [the words back in black]?"' Grabbing the mike he waited for them to count in and begin playing the riff again then just started screaming: 'Back in black!' The brothers looked at each other then told him: 'Do that again.' He did it again, only louder this time: *'Back in black!'* and, just to keep the vibe going and because it was the first rhyme that came into his head, added, *'I hit the sack!'* The brothers put down their guitars and, as Johnson recalls, Malcolm said, '"Right, listen, let's sit and talk here." And I said, "No, no, I cannot be here for long." Then they said, "Could you sing 'Highway To Hell' for us?"' But he didn't know the words, so Angus sat down and wrote them out for him. Then they ran through the song a couple of times because Johnson had never heard it before, 'And then I sang that for them and they went "Right." Then I said, "Okay, well, I'll get in touch with you again." I went home and the telephone rang and it was Mal. He said, "Listen, do you want to come to the Bahamas with us and record the new album?" I said, "Are you telling me I'm in the band?" Then he went, "Well, yeah."'

Gobsmacked, Johnson was unsure how to react. He needed a moment to process. He said, 'I'll tell you what, I'm putting the phone down and give me a ring back in ten minutes, just to make sure this isn't a hoax.' Ian Jeffery recalls Malcolm, at this point, wondering if it was the other way around, and it was Johnson who was 'taking the piss'. He advised Malcolm, 'Just ring him back. I knew he was genuine. But I knew it was all coming out of the blue for him. I don't think he could believe his luck.' Malcolm gave it five then called Johnson back, confirming the offer. No money was discussed as yet. For now it was enough just to know he'd landed the gig. '[Malcolm] rang us back and it was definite and I had a bottle of whisky because it was me father's birthday and I got a bottle of whisky for him [but] he wasn't there. There was nobody in the house. I was like, "Yay! Oh, fuck!" And me dad came back to a half a bottle of whisky and I was sitting [there, saying], "I'm gonna do it" ...'

The formal offer followed the next day: a trial period of six months with a wage of £170 per week, plus out-of-pocket expenses. 'The lads just said, "Listen, we'll put you on a wage for six months and if it doesn't work out, then nobody's hurt." I said [to myself] these guys are straight shooters, there's no bullshit.'

The official announcement that Brian Johnson, formerly of barely remembered glam rockers Geordie, was to be the new singer of AC/DC, following the death of Bon Scott, was made on 1 April 1980. Nobody jumped for joy. Least of all David Krebs, who told Mensch he didn't really get it. As he says now, 'I thought Bon Scott was amazing. I think Brian is great but Brian is not my kind of singer. It's like the guy from Slade. It wears off – on me, at least, after a while.' From the outside, it seemed like a strangely underwhelming choice. The guy from *Geordie*? Are you *kidding*? Nobody could even remember what he sounded like, let alone picture what he looked like. Maybe it would have been better to just fold the band after all ...

There were two weeks of rehearsals in London, where Mutt came along and sized up the situation too. Then they were on their way to Heathrow airport for the flight to the Bahamas. 'I'll always remember coming back down to London for those two weeks of rehearsals and all these people were popping in and out to take a look at us,' Johnson recalled. 'I was sitting there and I looked up and Ozzy Osbourne was standing there having a look, like. I can appreciate it, they all loved Bon. But I remember thinking to myself, "Oh Brian, what the fuck have you got yourself into?"'

It wouldn't be until his first album with AC/DC, *Back In Black*, released just months after Bon's death, that critics and fans discovered just how well Brian Johnson would be able to fill Bon's shoes. Against quite literally death-defying odds, somehow AC/DC had come up with an album every bit as good, if understandably much darker, as anything they had ever achieved before. As time went by and the magnitude of their achievement, and its commensurate success, sank in, many would consider *Back In Black* the greatest AC/DC album of all. Producer Kevin Shirley now rates it as 'my all-time favourite album, next to Miles Davis and maybe a Beethoven violin concerto. It's certainly the best rock record that's ever been made.'

He may have looked like a cross between Albert Steptoe and Andy Capp, with his gamekeeper tweed cap and endless smoky tabs, but Jonno, as he quickly became known, had a voice like the sound of a giant gargling with nails and a presence as warm and inviting as a welcoming pub fire. He also had a penchant for double-entendre lyrics that almost matched Bon's own. Mostly, though, he had the inestimable help, support and guidance of Mutt Lange. Which was just as well as Johnson arrived in the studio for the first time as the singer in AC/DC shaking with nerves and terrified that he wasn't going to be able to deliver. Even talking to the crew freaked him out, most of them having worked for a number of other big acts too. 'I was a fish out of water,' he recalled in 2011, 'never been anywhere like that before.' To add to the tension, the budget for the album was still relatively small and with tour dates already being slotted in for the end of June, time was incredibly tight. Yet here they were expected to not only come up with an album that was as good as the ones made with Bon Scott, but an album that was able to build on the commercial breakthrough of *Highway To Hell*. Johnson's journey from Newcastle to Nassau was going to be a test – for all of them.

As if echoing their darkest fears, they arrived in Nassau to find the island at the mercy of one of the worst storms it had seen for years. Arriving at night, even the customs officials proved hostile, confiscating all their guitars. The band protested that they were here to work, 'But they just didn't like the look of us,' said Johnson. Expecting blue seas and white beaches, 'When we got there it was pissing it down, there was flooding and all the electricity went out, nay TV. We just ended up sitting there for three days until the weather broke and the guitars were cleared ... I think it was a case of a bit of bribery and then magically we got the guitars back.'

The band, who had heard so much about the 'glamorous' studios, were disappointed to discover their rooms were no more than small grey cells, only big enough to contain a bed and a small bedside table. The first thing the resident housekeeper told them was that they should lock their doors each night, because of local outlaw Haitians that came down from the hills at night looking for rich tourists to rob. Johnson laughingly recalled how 'she bought us all these six-foot fishing spears to keep at the fucking door! It was a bit of a stretch from Newcastle, I can tell you.' They began to take the threat more seriously when they learned of the plight of singer Robert Palmer, who lived nearby. 'Two guys broke into his house and held his mother and father hostage and shot his dog. Killed his dog in the house with a gun! There were dangerous bandits and we had to walk about 150 yards in pitch black roads to get from the house to the studio. It was fucking awful.'

Sessions finally began with Tony Platt finding the 'sweet spot' in the studio where the snare drum sounded best. 'We set the drums up around that. Then I built big booths for the guitars. The bass went into a separation booth. But it wasn't a particularly separate separation booth so a bit of it would bleed through onto the other microphones. And I set it up like they were onstage – Angus stage right, Malcolm stage left; Phil behind and Cliff to one side behind Angus. I knew when we mixed it, it was going to be panned like that and so I thought let's make it as close to how you'd hear it live as possible.' The vocals were all done with Brian working on his own with Mutt, beginning with guide vocals which he did sitting next to the producer in the control room, singing along as the band played in the live room.

The first track they worked on was another incomplete title and riff the brothers had worked up called 'You Shook Me All Night Long'. Johnson: 'Being a car nut [I sang], *"She was a fast machine, she kept the motor clean ..."* I wrote that in a night. "Here lads, what do you reckon?"' They liked it enough to encourage him to start recording a rough vocal. 'The boys weren't in because Mutt never wanted the boys in when I was singing because he knew I would be nervous and then he heard it and he went, "Hmm, I don't think it's gonna work, Brian."' Lange thought there were 'too many words'. According to Johnson, 'actually it wasn't Mutt, it was his wife, his new wife that went, "I think it's too many words." Well, you know how guys are. She had big tits and everything.' More seriously, Lange also felt the rhythm wasn't working and decided to slow it down. 'He said, "Try it my way",,' and began to sing it in half-time. 'That was when I realised that Malcolm is pretty much the captain of the AC/DC ship.' When Mutt played the slowed-down version with fewer words to the band, 'Mal came in and heard it and went kinda ballistic. He was like, "What the fuck are you doing? You've taken out the rock'n'roll!"'

Working on the lyrics to 'You Shook Me ...' occasioned another turning point experience for the new singer. 'I remember sitting in my room writing that and I had this blank sheet of paper and this title and I was thinking, "Oh, what have I started?" And I'll tell you something and I'm not scared of being called a sissy and I don't believe in spirits and that, but something happened to me that night in that room. Something passed through us and I felt great about it. I don't give a fuck if people believe me or not, but something washed through me and went, it's alright, son, it's alright – this kind of calm. I'd like to think it was Bon but I can't because I'm too cynical and I don't want people getting carried away. But something happened and I just started writing the song.'

For Malcolm, once he'd made his feelings felt to Mutt about 'You Shook Me ...', he remembers it as one of the easiest tracks to record; the other being a straight-ahead rocker called 'Shoot To Thrill'. For Johnson it was 'Rock And Roll Ain't Noise Pollution'. 'I didn't know what to do at the start so you can hear me there having a fag at the beginning. Mal just said to go with it so I put my head-phones on, put a tab in my mouth and just took a breath. For some reason middlemen were in the news at the time, the top guys weren't getting the blame and the work force weren't getting it either, it was the middlemen who were this grey area. I must have picked up on it and it just went from there.'

The hardest song Brian had to write the words for, though, was 'Hells Bells', the brothers' overt tribute to Bon. '[It was] about six songs in, and me head was down and I was spent. Mutt came down and he said, "Are you alright, Brian?" And I went, "I think I'm just dried up on this song ... I've already done 'Back In Black', and that was, like, devilish." It was a pretty tough call and I just couldn't think. And just then there was the mother of all thunderstorms coming in – the wind before the storm. It looked nasty out cos we were right at the sea. "Jesus," I said. "The neighs of the thunder are coming in." And [Mutt] said, "There you go, there's a start, Brian. The roll-ing thunder ..."' Staring out the window, Brian mused aloud: 'I said, "It's fucking pouring rain, look at the wind it's coming on like a hur-ricane and look at that lightning flashing ..." Honestly, I was like a reporter.' Suddenly, the words came in a rush. '"*Across the sky ... You're only young but you're gonna die ...*" And I just looked at it like an animal. "*Won't take no prisoners, won't spare no lives, nobody putting up a fight, I got my bell ...*" Cos there was a bell ringing, an alarm bell ... "*Get my bell, gonna take you hell, gonna get ya, Satan gonna get ya ...*" It was ten minutes. I said, "*Mutt, thank you*" ...'

As the track that would open the album, 'Hells Bells' began with the ominous tolling of a bell. Mutt loathed the idea of using pre-recorded bell sounds, so when they returned to England he sent Tony Platt to find a real church bell, which he eventually found at a church in the Midlands. Indeed, the atmospheric bells and guitars which roll in over the long intro like a dank fog across a swamp, acted as a suitably respectful way of beginning the first AC/DC album since Bon Scott's death just weeks before. Once they had decided to go with it, along with the other great Bon tribute the album is named after, 'Back In Black', they had found their way to continue their story without causing offence to friends or family – or most of all those fans who might have felt aggrieved that they could even think of going on without their beloved, bad Bonnie boy.

There was also a strictly no-drinking rule in the studio. Gone were the days when Bon would do his vocals with a bottle of JD in one hand and a big fat spliff in the other. The only exception being the day Malcolm got a phone call telling him his wife Linda had given birth to their first child, a daughter they named Cara. 'Malcolm came down and said, "It's a girl" and that was the first time I saw Angus take a drink. He got a bottle of Jack Daniel's and he went, "Aw fucking great mate", and he drank.' Five minutes later 'he was put on somebody's shoulders and taken to bed. Never saw him again – poor sod. But he was just so ecstatic for his brother you know? It was a wonderful night and we just continued and we got rambunctious and fucking got plastered.'

As with Bon, Mutt spent an inordinate amount of time on his own with Brian, simply getting his vocals right. 'I'd come in and he'd work me until honestly, I thought me ears were gonna bleed. He would say "try this one" or "do it this way" and of course he hadn't seen the words, I was literally writing the words in me little room as the tunes came down.' It reached a farcical stage on the track 'Shake A Leg'. 'It was the highest fucking song I think I've ever fucking sung in me fucking life. And I don't think I could ever do it again, there's one note in there – it's so fucking high and even after I done it – "Holy fucking shit," he said, "I didn't think he could get that." Well why did you fucking ask us, you dick? "Well, I just wanted to see where he could go with it."'

Angus Young would later observe that the main difference between Johnson and his predecessor was that 'Bon leaned very hard on the rhythm when he sang. His other great gift was lyrics.'

Hitting the nail on the head, he added, 'Bon and Brian had a different sense of humour. Bon's was more subtle. You'd wonder what he was talking about and half an hour later you'd be rolling with laughter when you finally got it. Brian's just as clever but his humour is more direct. You catch it straight away.' Yet on *Back In Black* that difference had not yet become the yawning chasm it would assume with subsequent AC/DC albums. Why was that? Conspiracy theories have run riot for years. The wildest being that not only did Bon actually write a great many of the lyrics on *Back In Black* before he died, but that he had actually recorded several demos of songs that later surfaced there, including the title track, and most especially 'Have A Drink On Me' and 'Let Me Put My Love Into You', which the brothers admitted he had rehearsed early, instrumental versions of just days before his death. Talking in 2000 to *Classic Rock* writer Philip Wilding, for a special piece marking the 20th anniversary of the album's release, Malcolm dismissed the charges out of hand. 'That is complete bollocks. I wish we had rehearsed the album with Bon. Think about it, if we had an album with Bon on it then that would have gone out, obviously. It'd be a total fucking disaster to sit on that, know what I mean?' He added, 'I wish he had written some of the lyrics. You can't compete with Bon's lyrics, he was born with this real talent for that.'

However, Malcolm Dome claims that shortly before he died, Bon 'showed me his book of lyrics. He had sheets of lyrics that he kept in a file, carried them around. He'd been showing me some of the ideas he'd been working for *Back In Black*. Not the song "Back In Black" but songs that were for the next album. There were a couple of lines, like, *"She told me to come but I was already there"*, which ended up in "You Shook Me All Night Long" – that's a Bon lyric. And I saw it. I saw it written down. There were lyrics, lines used, on *Back In Black* that Bon wrote. [But] he wasn't credited and to this day no one's really sure what happened. I don't think he wrote whole songs at all, I don't think he even got close to finishing whole songs. But there are lines in there that I know.'

The suggestion has been that when Ian Jeffery went to Bon's flat the day after his death to clean it out, he picked up Bon's lyrics. In the same interview with Wilding, Malcolm did concede that Jeffery passed him 'a note with some scribblings of Bon's and that was within a few days of his death'. Adding: 'There were a couple of little lyrics on there but there was nothing with a title or that would give you any idea of where his head was at, at the time ... There wasn't even enough to build up into something that would stand up to Bon's reputation.'

According to Tony Platt, 'Everybody chipped in. Brian worked on the nucleus of it but there were always a few lyrics that were missing or something that didn't quite work with the rhythm or the metre, so things got changed. I can distinctly remember on "You Shook Me All Night Long" everybody sitting down just throwing ideas forward. *"Double time on the seduction line"* was one of mine, I'll always lay claim to that one,' he smiles. Certainly a track like 'Given The Dog A Bone', though a powerhouse musically, sounds like the sort of Bon-era title the brothers might suggest, while the crass lyrics definitely sound like they were written by committee. Some were 'too lewd and over the top', others were 'just too stupid'. Other tracks, like 'What Do You Do For Money Honey', dated back, Malcolm said, to the original *Powerage* sessions three years before. George Young had come up with the title, and 'we all chipped in on' lyrics.

Did Bon write any of the lyrics? 'It *may* have been that there were some lyrics lying around,' says Tony Platt now. He pauses while he thinks it over. 'I mean, it wouldn't have been unusual that he ... he ... The process of how they write is, um ... Malcolm and Angus would come up with the riffs so if [Bon] was around he might have come up with a couple of those things ...' Should Bon have got a credit then? 'The whole album was a credit to Bon,' Platt says somewhat irritably. 'The album was made in his memory. It's so fucking obvious I don't know why people don't jump straight away to it, you know? Whether people think [Bon] was swept under the carpet or anything like that, it just wasn't the case. You've heard Brian saying he felt that Bon was in the room when he was singing the vocals. He made reference to that several times when we working on the album. You felt the spirit of Bon was there, because he was sort of the band he was inevitably going to have an influence.'

Ian Jeffery is less defensive on the subject. 'You've gotta give Mutt Lange a lot of credit there for writing most of the lyrics,' he insists. 'He was responsible for most of the stuff at Compass Point. Malcolm and Angus obviously pitched in a lot of it but I heard from Evo and Barry that a lot of it was Mutt.' Is it true though that some of the lyrics came from some of the notebooks you'd kept? 'Yeah, well, I wouldn't say it was a notebook. It was just scraps of paper.' With some of the lyrics that Bon had written? 'Yeah, yeah. Of course it wasn't "Back In Black" or anything then. There was not even anything to put to riffs. It was just some things that Bon was noting down as he would go along, as he was being given tapes by Malcolm and Angus. Like, see what you can do with this, play with this. I don't think it had got too far down the line at all. Bon would always have pieces of paper everywhere. He'd hear something, something would be on the news or the radio and he'd jot things down.' And did some of that end up on BIB? 'Yeah, you know, a few of the lines are in there. But [not] titles or anything like that. It hadn't got that far.'

Released worldwide on 25 July 1980, exactly a year on from *Highway To Hell*, Bon's final album with them, the new album, with Brian Johnson, *Back In Black* both broke the mould for AC/DC and repaid the faith shown in them by their longstanding fans. With its cathedral-like Mutt Lange production, its high-quality songs that still contained enough of Bon's DNA to afford them true greatness, and, most reassuring of all, with a new singer who had clearly taken to his task with the kind of relish Bon himself would surely have applauded, *Back In Black* was a better album than even the impossible-to-please Young brothers could ever have imagined; so resoundingly defiant of the bleak circumstances of its blooded origins, it would quickly take on a life of its own, beyond the hopes and aspirations of the band or even their fans, and out there in the stratosphere where only the truly great rock giants lived. More than 30 years and over 40 million sales on, it has become the second biggest-selling album of all time, superseded only by Michael Jackson's *Thriller*. Meaning the vast majority of people who have bought it – and continue to buy it each year – would not consider themselves AC/DC fans, as much as simply aficionados of good music, whatever the genre it happens to represent. A staggering achievement, up there with the untitled fourth Led Zeppelin album or The Eagles' *Greatest Hits*, but even more unexpected because the band that produced the album were held in such little regard at the time of its release. And even more remarkable given the fact there were no hit singles from the album; no MTV videos to rally round; no nothing except the usual round of endless AC/DC shows and more shows – hitting the road in what even then was beginning to be thought of as strictly old school.

Back In Black was also a transformational album for fans of rock. Arriving the same year as debut albums from Iron Maiden and Def Leppard, and breakthrough chart albums by Judas Priest (*British Steel*) and Motörhead (*No Sleep 'til Hammersmith*), it instantly became absorbed into the next generation of heavy metal bands that were about to blow up over the next decade. AC/DC had never seen themselves as heavy metal any more than they did antipodean punk. At the end of the day, though, they didn't give a fuck what anyone wanted to call them as long as they bought their records. In the Eighties, more people would buy AC/DC records than at any time before or since. The greatness – the total heavy-osity – of *Back In Black* and the richness of the back catalogue saw to that. But there was another factor. Metal fans have always been easily seduced by symbols of sacrifice; martyrs to the cause. In this context, Bon Scott was not seen as the wandering minstrel he really was, with an anything-goes weakness for booze and drugs and a careless, some might say selfish, attitude towards his own safety that ultimately betrayed the love of his family and friends. He was seen as a heavy metal hero. The most formidable kind: a *fallen* hero, lost in battle, fighting the good fight for rock and metal, riding the 'Highway To Hell', whose memory, swaddled 'Back In Black', would always be celebrated by glory of the 'Hells Bells'.

Paradoxically, or perhaps all too understandably, Ian Jeffery was one of the last AC/DC fans to fall for the whole deal. 'I remember

Mutt called me up from Nassau after about six weeks and said, 'Get rehearsals ready, Ian, we're coming home.' I was like, six weeks? You've got a new guy down there, you've got 'em on an island, which they fucking hate, conch stew, they can't stand that, when can we get back to some proper food, you know? And you got the job done in like six weeks? No fucking way!' Nevertheless he booked rehearsal time at E.Zee Hire and confirmed with Mensch and Leber–Krebs that they would be ready to begin touring by the end of June. Yet he didn't actually ask to hear the new Bon-less album. Not yet. 'It wasn't until we were loading the bell into the first gig, when Malcolm came and gave me the cassette. We were mixing up in the balcony and Malcolm comes up with Angus and says, "Here's the record, Ian, what do you think?" We put it on and I'm going, "Yeah, pretty cute, yeah." It was one of those things where it was kind of a transitional, kind of different to what you expected. But once you'd played it a few times and you were walking round with little doubts or lingering things in the back of your mind, next thing you were fucking singing the songs. You didn't know the words but you were humming 'em. Oh mate, everyone in the crew was walking round humming those riffs. They were just spine-tingling, toe-tapping moments where you just couldn't stop. And then when you heard them play it – fucking hell! For me, it was absolutely classic, because for me, as a sound guy, there was space. Malcolm is just the ultimate player for me. The fucking metronome. He stands there and the right leg starts going and it's just – boosh! And you're off. The sheer immenseness of it is like a tidal wave effect, it still pushes you along as the song begins to build and build. There was nothing dropping out as the solo came in. That wall was still moving through all of the songs.'

There were also yet more grumblings from Atlantic, who again considered the title – yes – too dark. But not so dark as the all-black cover, which nearly caused them to throw the baby out with the bathwater. 'They didn't like it but the band was in a position to tell them to fuck off by then,' says Ian Jeffery. 'They had Leber–Krebs behind them and they had an album that everyone in New York knew was a hit, no matter what.'

Even Malcolm Young had a somewhat delayed reaction, not really understanding what the band had in their hands until he was with Mutt in the mixing room in New York. 'Fucking hell,' he announced, 'this is a monster.' Or as Mutt's fellow producer Kevin Shirley says now, 'There's just an incredible architecture to it. It's *the* benchmark record for sound. The production on that record is so melodic, it just sounds so good. And it's so well structured that it crosses the genres.'

It certainly did. In Britain, where sales had spiked since Bon's death, the build-up to the new album's release had led to no fewer than four AC/DC singles entering the UK Top 75: 'Whole Lotta Rosie' (No. 38), 'High Voltage' (No. 48), 'Dirty Deeds Done Dirt Cheap' (No. 54) and 'It's A Long Way To The Top' (No. 55). When the *Back In Black* album was released in Britain at the end of July, it went straight to No. 1 in the UK. It also returned AC/DC to the near-top of the Australian charts for the first time since *TNT* in 1975, only kept from No. 1 by the new Police album, *Zenyattà Mondatta*. It also went to No. 1 in Austria, Canada and France, and made the Top 10 in Norway, and by the end of 1980 had earned AC/DC no fewer than 27 platinum or gold album awards from eight different countries.

The only place where *Back In Black* didn't immediately hit was, ironically, the place, like all Mutt Lange albums, it had been built specifically to conquer: America. In fact, it nearly caused Atlantic to spill their soup when it entered the US chart first week of release at a lowly No. 189. By then they had also begun their first US tour with Brian Johnson at the helm, headlining at mid-level arenas and large theatres, where crowd reaction was as strong as ever but critics tended to cast a sceptical eye on their new recruit. Def Leppard singer Joe Elliott, whose band had once again been invited to support AC/DC by Peter Mensch, were coming to the end of their first successful US tour when they opened for the band at the Palladium in New York on 1 August. 'It was one of Brian Johnson's first gigs on the *Back In Black* US tour,' Joe recalls. 'It was also my 21st birthday so I remember it really well. The reviews were just brilliant for us: "This great new rock band". But for AC/DC, I wouldn't say the daggers were out for Jonno but the eyes were on him, like saying, "You're not Bon Scott."'

It was only a temporary blip, though; the calm before the storm. By the time the band had begun their first tour of Australia for four years, in February 1981, *Back In Black* had heavy-stepped it all the way in America to No. 4, beginning a stay in the Top 10 that would last for nearly six months.

Yet while they celebrated back 'home' in Oz, with a huge outdoor summer show before 30,000 people at the Showgrounds in Sydney, supported by their Alberts label-mates The Angels and Bon-connected mates in Swanee, not much had changed behind the closed doors of the AC/DC dressing room. BON LIVES! graffiti may have grown like a rash in Australia over the preceding 12 months, but the party held backstage afterwards was all about reinforcing just how amazingly well AC/DC were doing now without their old man. There to see the band presented with 40 gold, platinum and silver records from all over the world were faces past and present: the entire Young clan, headed by George, and Harry Vanda; Peter Mensch; Ian Jeffery; Ted Albert; various members of Rose Tattoo, The Angels, Swanee and the Ted Mulry Gang. Even Mark Evans showed up. 'It was the first time I'd seen the band play since I'd left them. And here's the intro, then Brian singing, it was just bizarre! But really poignant, seeing them without Bon. I was in the VIP area and there were two mates around me so they gave me a bit of room. But I was really unsettled by it a couple of times. But if it was difficult for me, those guys lived through it, playing those songs every night, and living through that. What they did and the way they dealt with that transition, man, I've got nothing but the utmost respect for those guys. It was so fucking gutsy.'

No doubt. The only person missing from the back-slapping was Angus, who'd slipped away before the throng had been allowed anywhere near the backstage area. As usual, he just wanted to get out, grab something to eat, guzzle down a Coke and smoke another fag. Now, though, he had wife Ellen to accompany him. The only other person missing from the picture was one of the people that had done more for AC/DC than anyone outside the Young clan: Michael Browning. He'd not been invited. Once you were on the outside with AC/DC, there was no way back. Browning never heard from any of them again. As he says, 'It's the way of the Youngs. They rewrite history to suit themselves. I don't even think they do it to be nasty. It's just the way they are, they way they're made.'

What Brian Johnson was feeling this far into the trip – four shows from the end of his first world tour as the singer in AC/DC – has never been properly recorded. Partly because Jonno is far too canny a lad to do his dirty washing in public. Partly, perhaps, because he simply wouldn't have known how to express what must have been at times deeply conflicted feelings. By then he was definitely 'one of the lads'. Three months into the tour, with *Back In Black* at No. 1, Mensch had to come to him, he recalled, and said, 'I think we'd better talk.' Offered a lucrative contract, 'I signed it and they were great.' Here he was enjoying the kind of fame and fortune he had spent his entire adult life dreaming of and striving for, only to feel his moment had passed when, against all odds, he finally found himself where he'd always fancied seeing himself: at the top of the mountain, looking down. Yet Malcolm had made it clear to him right from their very first gig together at the start of the tour, at the Palais Des Expositions, in Namur, Belgium, eight months before, exactly where Brian Johnson stood in the AC/DC scheme of things.

'It was his first gig and it was obviously a big deal,' says Ian Jeffery. 'There were banners in the crowd with Bon's face on them, and people obviously waiting to see what this new bloke is gonna be like. I thought as a welcome gesture, to make him feel at home, to play "Fog On The Tyne" over the PA just before they came on. The crowd were singing it. I thought it was a nice touch. But Malcolm laid into me afterwards. Like, "What the fuck do you think you're doing?" The whole bit.'

Maybe it was that which soured Malcolm's mood before he went on, but the already stressed guitarist was in grim mood as the band ploughed into their first number, which was 'Hells Bells'. 'I remember I'd had a word with Brian before the gig,' says Jeffery. 'I said, "Whatever you do, don't fucking talk too much." Cos Bon never said much, he just said what he had to say, "All right, lads!" Then he'd walk back and get his head down and let the band take over. But Brian got carried away. It was his first gig, thanking people for welcoming him and that, cos the crowd was great. It was like they were saying, "Thank you for continuing this thing. Bon would love this, that this thing didn't get curtailed."

'And I remember after the second song Malcolm walking up to him and going, "Shut your fucking trap!" Then started the next song.'

Afterwards, Malcolm read Johnson the riot act. Jeffery: 'He was told, "When you get out there you fucking say hello, you say good-night and shut your trap. Nothing in between." So he was given his sort of orders right there and then. It was very rough to go outside of that, you know? What a tough situation, though. Boy, did I feel for him then.'

Bon was his own man. Did Jeffery think the new guy, whoever it had been, the brothers would have laid down the law to, because they simply didn't have the same respect for someone just walking in as things were getting good? That they used Bon's absence, in fact, to get things more like they'd wanted them all along? He nods his head. 'They would have been certain about that whoever it was. That was just part of the tablet you picked up. Here it is, fucking read it once, there'll be a test, you know?'

Jeffery admits that it took him quite a while to finally warm to the new singer. 'Not because he was a bad bloke. And *Back In Black* was fantastic, but it took me a long, long, long time to get used to the voice. It's probably not the right thing to say, but it was almost like the magic was gone. It took me a long time to fucking just say, "Well, he's not here – Bon. This is Brian, let's just get on with it. Let's keep it going." Brian was a nice guy but it was very difficult for me to get really, really close to him. Plus as well he was being part of this big thing that was just starting to come as well. He was like feeling his way, but in a very nervous way. He was very scared to cut loose or do anything, in case ...'

After the album had taken off, Jeffery recalls, 'They said to him, "Go and find yourself a house." And Brian wanted to get this big house which was right in the middle of this roundabout in Newcastle. It had previously been owned by some Newcastle entrepreneur. It was this huge house and Brian was like [Geordie accent], "Are you sure, canny lads? I don't wanna overextend myself." They were like, "Listen, if we tell you to fucking buy it you go and fucking buy it." Then the first times we went to visit him there, typical Brian, he's closed down fifteen of the sixteen rooms. He's living in the kitchen with a little telly in the dining room next-door, cos he doesn't want to spend on electricity. He'd taken all the light bulbs out so no one could switch 'em on and leave 'em on. You go upstairs and his brand-new Halliburton case is open at the bottom of the bed. He hasn't even unpacked from getting back off the road. We had to persuade him to put the lights on so we could play snooker. You'd look in his fridge and there'd be a couple of bits of mouldy cheese, a bit of ham and maybe a little bit of butter, next to it a bucket full of drinks in cans.'

Everybody had taken so long to finally believe in the idea of having Brian Johnson, not Bon Scott, as the frontman in AC/DC, it had never occurred to them he might be having trouble believing it too.

CHAPTER FOURTEEN
Two-Fingered Salute

As the razzed-up Eighties arrived like a drunken gatecrasher at the now winding-down party that was once the Seventies, it was no longer the figure of the svelte golden god, standing astride the mike, long mane of hair framing a coquettish pout, that embodied the face of rock. Nor was it the yang to his yin, the lead guitarist, swaying like a cobra, hypnotised by his own wasted elegance. Instead, by the summer of 1981, the biggest noise in rock was being made by a 26-year-old man dressed as a schoolboy, replete with bad haircut, skewwhiff school cap, wildly swinging satchel and a guitar turned up to 11; sitting on the shoulders of a screw-faced singer in a flat-cap that made a sound like a concrete mixer grinding up babies.

Goodbye Led Zeppelin, their breakup now officially confirmed. Hello AC/DC, whose latest album, *Back In Black*, had gone to No. 1 in Britain and was now on its way to selling more than 20 million copies in America. An album whose appeal was so broad, despite its dearth of hit singles, it was now on its way to becoming one of the biggest-selling of all time. Against all odds, AC/DC had not only survived the hole beneath the waterline that Bon Scott's death represented, they had positively thrived. As Angus Young said, not only had *Back In Black* succeeded beyond their wildest dreams, 'We knew that this new line-up would work, and that we wouldn't have to worry about the past any more. We had found success with a new voice and that was a big relief.' The future of AC/DC was suddenly looking 'very relaxed, I'd say'.

That may be how it looks now with the benefit of 30 years'

hindsight. At the time, however, whether they consciously realised it or not, the future of AC/DC was about to become defined in ways nobody inside the band could have predicted. There's a thin line between feeling 'very relaxed' about your future and falling victim of hubris. If *Back In Black* was the story of a band making the biggest album in rock just months after their singer had died, the story of its follow-up would be one of opportunities missed, decisions made in the heat of the moment that would affect the band's entire career, and of the ultimate consolidation of an idea that went right to the heart of the AC/DC story: that this was more of a clan than a band; that they didn't need anybody outside that clan to tell them what to do or how to do it. Or so they had and would always believe. As Ian Jeffery says now, 'I look back on those years up to when Bon died as the absolute best of my life.' The hard graft done, from here on in, it should have been plain sailing. Shouldn't it? Ian sighs. 'We didn't know it yet but the really hard part had only just begun ...'

It didn't have to be that way. By the summer of 1981, as AC/DC arrived in Paris to start recording the follow-up to *Back In Black,* the building blocks for yet more mind-boggling success were solidly in place. Not only had AC/DC managed the seemingly impossible – replacing Bon – they had top management, a genius producer and the world's biggest record label behind them. They even had a cool title for the album that would represent their next, most important step: *For Those About To Rock ... We Salute You.* What could possibly go wrong? Speaking in London in the summer of 2011, Brian Johnson denied feeling any pressure as they began work on *For Those About To Rock.* 'Of course the label wanted it sell just like *Back In Black* did, but we knew damn well that's not going to happen cos you can't do that. You can't write songs with the intention to sell a million singles or albums – unless you are some pop act. And we didn't have a problem with that. I mean, we tried, and we did well – but we never felt any outside pressure, because we didn't let it in. I think we were very confident after the success of *Back In Black*. And we had every right to be.'

That's not how others involved with the band at that time remember it though. 'Everything was going great till Atlantic stepped in and fucked it up,' says Jeffery. In America, where Jerry Greenberg had recently been replaced at Atlantic by a new president, Doug Morris, those old feelings of insecurity over what a band like AC/DC could actually offer a label with a roster as blue-chip as Atlantic's had never really gone away, not even with the astounding success of *Back In Black*. With the arrival of Morris, the feeling returned that, at best, AC/DC might just be a flash-in-the-pan. A here today, gone later today deal that the label should make the most of while it lasts. Hence Morris's grab-it-while-you-can decision not to wait for the follow-up to *Back In Black* but to rush-release instead the five-year-old *Dirty Deeds Done Dirt Cheap*. For Malcolm and Angus, who'd never gotten over the ignominy of having the album pulled from the US release schedule in the first place, this was the last straw. According to Phil Carson, still running Atlantic everywhere outside America, 'Doug Morris called me and said, "I've just found this old AC/DC album in the catalogue which we never put out. If we stick it out now it will give us something for the fourth quarter and we'll all walk away with big bonuses." I was furious. I said, "How are you ever going to consider releasing a Bon Scott album after we've just broken our balls introducing the public to Brian Johnson? I think it is *crazy*." I told him, "Yes, you'll have a hit, but it won't be anything like *Back In Black*." He said, "If we put it out now we'll sell two million, easy." I said, "You're right, you'll sell two million and that will be it, you'll have created a sales plateau and they'll never recover from it." His attitude was, like, so what? I don't think he really believed they would be around for long anyway. I said, "I think you're crazy!"'

So crazy, Carson resigned over the decision – before being 'talked out of it' by Atlantic's legendary co-founder, Ahmet Ertegun. 'That's when the war I suppose started between Doug and I, which continued. Oh boy, it was a war. Because he knew I was fireproof and didn't like it at all.' Nevertheless, he never forgave Morris for his decision. 'There's absolutely no doubt in my mind. If they'd waited for the next album [with Johnson] it would have been an even *bigger* album. It was one of the most crass, stupid decisions any record company ever made. Doug Morris may be the biggest and most important record company executive in the world but to me he is a moron, for that decision. So there you have it.' He pauses then adds, still furious all these years later: '[Morris] destroyed AC/DC at that point, destroyed them. So I feel very strongly about that.' He laughs but his eyes are burning.

Released in America for the first time in April 1981, nearly five years since its original UK release and absolutely in defiance of the band's wishes, *Dirty Deeds* reached No. 3 in the US, one place higher than *Back In Black*'s peak, but, just as Carson had predicted, sold only two million copies there at a time when *BIB* was now topping five million. As a result, says Carson, the 'sales plateau' for all subsequent AC/DC album releases in America would be similarly downsized. Not for the first time in history, short-term record company greed had stymied long-term artist career growth. The band, who were apoplectic with rage but didn't have the power to stop the release, did their best to cover their record company's tracks, claiming the release of *Dirty Deeds* was essentially to counter US bootlegs of the album. 'There were thousands of pirate tapes, shit-poor quality and expensive,' Johnson told *Creem* magazine. 'So rather than they [the bootleggers] get the money we thought we'd put it out.' When the album 'went straight into the charts', he added, without a trace of apparent irony, 'I was more fucking chuffed about it than [the rest of the band] were.' More chuffed certainly than Malcolm and Angus Young – particularly Malcolm, who swore a blood oath not to allow anyone from Atlantic near the band ever again. Angus was more sanguine. There would be other albums, like the one they were working on now, the real follow-up to *BIB*, and the fans would understand that. But Malcolm was having none of it. Heads would roll. It was a question of when not if. It was with this bloody-minded attitude that he arrived in Paris in the summer of 1981. Woe betide anyone who stood in his road.

Paris, Monday, 6 July 1981. With the band having spent a week rehearsing and settling in at the Arabella apartments in Montmartre – 'which they hated', according to Jeffery – AC/DC turned up to begin work on their next all-important album at EMI's Pathé Marconi studios. With Malcolm still fuming over the recent turn of events, nobody was particularly happy. Having come off the road four months earlier richer than they had ever been before, the five band members had enjoyed the first extended break of their careers; Angus by settling down to married life in Holland; Malcolm and Phil, similarly, in London and Melbourne, respectively. Cliff, meanwhile, had bought himself a 'rock star hidey-hole' in Hawaii, where he had been joined, briefly, by Brian, en route to buying his own new pad in Florida. 'They were doing what used to be called their "two years out" for tax reasons,' recalls Tony Platt, who recommended the studio to Mutt Lange. 'I can't remember why they didn't just go back there [Nassau] again,' says Platt, 'it may have had something to do with Angus and Malcolm wanting to be nearer home.' It was partly that, and partly because they wanted to feel more in control. You couldn't just take off from Compass Point, or have the family over for the weekend. It was an island – literally and figuratively – and you were stranded until finally someone came to rescue you, once the job was done.

As always, the first order of business for Mutt was capturing the drum sound which he would use as the foundation stone upon which to build the rest of the album. Immediately, though, there was a problem – and not just with the drums. While AC/DC arguably owed everything to Lange's meticulous, almost OCD approach to record production there was no denying the tensions his unusual methods were now creating within the band. As Mutt would later concede, 'Some of them believe I was a merciless tyrant in the studio and obsessed with absolute perfection with each song.' A statement his friend and fellow producer Trevor Rabin qualifies by pointing out that 'The thing about Mutt is he's never been interested in being popular with the people he's worked with. Mutt would have the courage and the judgement to say to himself, "I don't *care* if I'm going way over budget or not cos if I don't I'm not gonna get there" and he will persevere until he gets there. Mutt has this *incredible* ear, to always land up with the perfect thing, and I don't think there's anybody like him. I *know* there's nobody like him.'

Lange's career had also 'gone nuclear' by then, both in tandem with the two multi-platinum albums he'd made with AC/DC and separately in recent months with Foreigner, the already huge Anglo-American band whose Lange-produced fourth album, simply titled *4*, was released worldwide four days before he arrived in Paris to begin work on his third AC/DC album. The first single from the new Foreigner album, 'Urgent', released two weeks before, was already headed for the US Top 10. Three months later, a follow-up single, 'Waiting For A Girl Like You', would become one of the biggest-selling hits of the year all over the world, giving Foreigner their first – and only – American No. 1 album along the way. For a producer of Mutt Lange's supreme self-confidence, this was less something to boast of and more merely affirmation of his innate greatness. There's no doubt that AC/DC made Mutt Lange as much as Mutt Lange ever made AC/DC. By the time they began working together again in Paris in 1981, though, both sides, for different reasons, were already looking past their latest collaboration towards what both sides felt were much bluer skies. Mutt knew AC/DC, no matter how complete their cornering of the hard rock marketplace in the early Eighties, would never be capable of coming up with a song as transcendent as 'Waiting For A Girl Like You', which for him at that time represented the apotheosis of his talents. AC/DC were starting to question whether they really needed all the added extras a Mutt Lange production entailed. AC/DC was a band built on the one thing Mutt did not excel at: spontaneity. A little molehill that was about to grow into a mountain. In that regard, the album got off to a bad start by the almost absurd lengths the producer now went to, to find a studio in Paris which could provide him the precise drum sound he would be willing to work with.

According to Lange's engineer at the Paris sessions, Mark Dearnley – brought in as a last-minute replacement for Tony Platt when a schedule backfire meant he couldn't make Paris – they spent 'the first three days just on the snare drum sound'. Dearnley, who'd first worked with AC/DC and Lange two years before on *Highway To Hell* – and between times with the producer on Def Leppard's breakthrough platinum album, *High N' Dry* – explains how 'I got to the point where at the end of day two, Mutt said, "What do you think of that?" I said, "I haven't got a clue!"' He laughs nervously.

It took nearly ten days for Lange to decide he was never going to find the sound he was looking for and call a halt to the sessions while another studio was hastily arranged. Over the next two weeks, says Dearnley, 'we tried out a number of studios'. Setting up 'for a day or two' in at least three different locations before Lange finally decided 'that it all sounded better in the initial rehearsal room' – a cold stone room at Quai de Bercy, where Lange now ordered in the Mobile One portable recording studio from London. 'In the end we even used the PA that they'd been using for rehearsals for the drums,' says Dearnley. 'So I had kick-drum and snare miked up through a PA, separately fed to four speakers in the room facing the drum kit. We had it tuned up so it was like borderline on the verge of feedback.' He pauses. 'That was the first time I'd ever done anything like that. All Mutt's invention ...'

The delays were starting to eat away at the band, though. Angus believes that, unlike *Back In Black*, this time 'probably most, if not all' the songs had been written long before they got to the studio. 'We are always well prepared. We go in the studio with complete songs and we know what we want. We don't fuck around much – unlike Mutt Lange. But that guy has always been slow. Real slow. He'd need for ever to get anything done. Otherwise it would have been in and out in a week, I'd say.' Johnson shrugged: 'I think that's just the way [Mutt] ticks. He's a thinker, you know. He takes his time, and he does it his way. As long as it works, that's fine. But fuck, I could have done with less waiting around.' Asked to describe a typical day at Bercy, Johnson chuckled ruefully. 'Angus, Malcolm and myself on a big sofa – waiting!' Angus: 'Yeah, I don't think it would have been anything scandalous really. Just some guys that were bored shitless ...' The other thing you'd have seen was Malcolm scowling a lot. 'It was taking too long,' he complained in *Mojo* in 2004. 'He was trying to outdo *Back In Black* for sound, and it was the sound he was looking for whereas we were thinking of the music – and the performances were starting to suffer.'

Pissed off at what he saw as Mutt's 'fannying around', according to Ian Jeffery, Malcolm was also now questioning every aspect of the band's operation. Added to his personal hit list where Atlantic and Lange now vied for top spot was the band's management, in the shape of Peter Mensch. 'They felt that they were being compromised,' says Jeffery. 'Stuck out in Paris they felt isolated. They were struggling with the record to start with. They were starting to get into contentious situations with Mutt. It wasn't flowing in the studio. They weren't writing like they were used to. That whole side of things wasn't happening.'

By now it was the first week of August – just two weeks before AC/DC's first big live show for six months: headlining the Castle Donington Monsters Of Rock festival in England. Though the date had been booked months before, this was not how the band saw themselves preparing for what would be their biggest ever show in the UK. According to Brian Johnson, 'we were shitting ourselves – fuck, we haven't played this! We haven't [rehearsed] anything!' Their fears were not unfounded. Remembered now as one of those drear rainy days that disfigure so many outdoor British festivals, Donington '81 also featured piss-poor live sound (the BBC, who were recording, were blamed for an electrical fault) and a decidedly under-par performance from the headliners. Relying on the same set they'd already toured around the UK the year before, though the roughly 65,000 fans there that day seemed appreciative enough, the band knew they had badly undersold themselves. 'It was just one of those days,' says Jeffery. 'The BBC did something that buggered up the sound, which we were getting blamed for. It rained and the band wasn't really ready for it, even though the date had been in the diary for a long time before. It just sort of added to all the other things that were going wrong in Paris.'

Adding insult to injury, Malcolm had been stopped going up the ramp to the stage by an unthinking security guard for not having the correct stage pass. 'I'm in the fucking band!' Malcolm snarled at him, before Jeffery intervened. Returning to Paris the next day Malcolm was in vengeful mood. Somebody would have to pay; in this case, Peter Mensch. It was to be one of the most significant decisions they ever made, and the first move in what would become over the next few years a complete dismantling of the support network that had taken the band from also-rans to arena-headliners. And it would nearly cost them their careers.

From his days as tour accountant for Aerosmith, when Mensch had been appointed AC/DC's 'key man' after impressing them on their first US tour with Leber–Krebs at the helm, Mensch had worked night and day to build AC/DC into a hugely successful international act. It was Mensch that oversaw the successful launch of *Highway To Hell* in America, procuring crucial tour supports in America to the biggest acts, then upped their game until they were the ones taking out support hopefuls; Mensch who had been there to pick up the pieces when Bon died, and Mensch who had steered the ship out of dangerous shallows, turning personal tragedy into professional triumph with the game-changing *Back In Black* campaign. Ian Jeffery recalls how Mensch dutifully moved to London in 1979 to be near the band, and how for the next two years 'Peter was their man every day – *every* day. Hands on, totally.'

Yet Mensch was not the kind of hands-on manager that saw himself as their personal friend or drinking buddy. He might have a beer with Malcolm on occasion, just to be sociable, but mostly he was into building empires. For two years AC/DC had been a crucial building block of that burgeoning empire. By 1981, however, Mensch was spreading his wings as a manager in his own right, signing rising British stars Def Leppard while scouting around for more. 'Peter can deal with five different bands at five different levels on every given day, easy,' says Jeffery. 'Once you understand his system, that's it. He's a physical, loud guy, that's the way he gets things done. And most of the things he's done he's thought through and they're good plans. They make sense. That's how Mensch operates.' Now, though, with frustration mounting for AC/DC in the studio, 'I think they felt Peter was becoming part of this big thing where the personalised things, the caring were no longer there. [But] Peter never stopped caring about AC/DC, believe you me.' That wasn't how the band

– how Malcolm and the clan – were seeing it, though. Five days after what the history books now record as the first of what would eventually become three epochal Donington headline appearances over the years, AC/DC fired Peter Mensch. Asked now why he thinks he was fired, Mensch declined to be interviewed for this book. He did send the following message by email, though: 'I was never told why I was fired. They called their lawyer, who called David Krebs, who called me. It was the Thursday after the first Castle Donington Monsters Of Rock show. And that, Mick, is the only question I will answer.'

Says Krebs: 'AC/DC fired Peter. I defended him. I told them they were way off base.' According to Jeffery, 'They just felt that Mensch was only turning up when it was time to give them more float [money], saying, "Why are you not done yet?" He wasn't being in sympathy with them and feeling what they were feeling. They felt a bit isolated and they felt they were being pushed and it was going wrong with Mutt, you know. It wasn't happening in the studio and hadn't been for a while. And Peter hadn't seen that ...' Nevertheless, for Jeffery, who would effectively take over as the band's day-to-day manager, 'It was a bombshell.' Ian told them, 'I don't think anything has changed with Mensch. Malcolm's like, "Well, it fucking has!" At that point, you may as well just let him have another drink and go through the reasons why, you know. It's done, it's finished.'

Back in Paris the same could not be said for the new album. Mutt, who'd been fretting over the sound from day one, now insisted he wanted to hear the album on an actual piece of vinyl before going any further. 'Something was troubling him,' remembers Jeffery. 'He said, "I wanna go over and get it mastered at Sterling Music in New York." So me and Malcolm took Concorde over. We didn't tell Krebs or the record company. Malcolm didn't want anybody to know we were coming. I said, "We'd better let somebody know we're going, shouldn't we?" He said, "Fucking hell, you're sounding like Mensch now!" And Mutt was like, "Whatever you do, Ian, don't play the record, because the acetate, if it gets played even once it changes everything."'

When they arrived in New York later the same day they drove straight to Greenwich Village, where Sterling Sound was then located, and set to work cutting an acetate, with the help of Bob Ludwig, who did all the mastering in those days. As a safety precaution, they cut two. Afterwards, Malcolm and Ian went round to visit John Clarke, the band's New York-based lawyer. 'Just a courtesy call,' explains Jeffery. 'He was an older guy, in his sixties, even back then, but he was part of the family, you know?' It was Clarke who insisted that as a further courtesy, before they flew back to Paris, they really should call Krebs, and at least say hello to Ahmet and Doug Morris, too. 'He said, "Just to let them know it's all going well and that you're fine and you don't need anything." John turns it into this, just say hello thing, everybody sees you, it's been a while. It will get everybody going again. Malcolm says, "I guess we could fucking do that, couldn't we?"'

None of this had been part of the plan. Once they got to Rockefeller Plaza though, says Jeffery, and everyone had been alerted to the fact that Malcolm Young actually had an acetate of the new album in his possession, 'the pressure's on, right? Have a drink. Let's go up to the boardroom, where they've got a big stereo. I'm whispering to him: "Malcolm, we can't play this fucking record to them. Mutt specifically said not, it will change everything." He says, "We've got another one." So in the end he plays it to Krebs – and then he plays the other one, once. Thinking one play of each, Mutt will never notice. Meanwhile, I'm thinking, this is fucked, so I said to Malcolm, "Shall we go [back to Sterling] and press another one?" He says, "[Mutt]'ll never fucking know! He doesn't know what he's talking about anyway. One play doesn't do any harm." We get the plane back that night. We played it to Mutt and the first thing he said was "This has been played, Ian." It had become such a big point. It was a $20,000 operation in those days. But Mutt didn't want to send it, and Malcolm didn't want it going out anywhere without him. He was like, "I'll go with it and I'm taking Ian with me."'

The band was now becoming so bored waiting for Mutt to put the finishing touches on take after take Dearnley recalls how 'they would jam for hours just for the fun of it. I've got outtakes of Angus singing "Feelings" and stuff like that.' He adds: 'It's part of Mutt's process to spend a lot of time with it and I can see how that can be aggravating. They must have felt there was a lot of hanging around. There probably was, especially with using the PA. It was one of those sounds that would move with any slight drum change ... there would be a lot of stop-starting because of that sort of thing.'

While Angus now concedes that Lange 'did a great job' on *For Those About To Rock*, and that 'the album sounded real good', Malcolm, still on a mission after dusting off Mensch, had already decided he'd seen and heard enough. Years later, he had suffused the subject sufficiently in his own mind to describe it more as a natural parting of the ways. 'It was actually time to call it a day really,' he told Philip Wilding. '*Highway* was always his favourite album.' By the time they got to Paris two years later, 'The recording process was changing and Mutt was right at the forefront of that. The whole thing was getting longer and longer and *For Those About To Rock* had been such a hassle, moving from studio to studio, we'd been all over the fucking shop.'

According to Ian Jeffery, however, the Young brothers' reasons for firing Mutt Lange were far more prosaic. There was all the 'hassle', for sure. But there was also the money. 'You know, when you're paying somebody three, four or five points of $500,000, that's one thing.' After *Back In Black*, though, if, as Jeffery says, 'you're paying them that on $10 million, it's another thing'. It was at this point, suggests Jeffery, that attitudes towards Lange really hardened. 'It was, "What the fuck are we paying this guy all this money for? We can fucking do it!" It soured when they started to look at the figures that Mutt was being paid. Not realising the different step that this whole new creation had gotten them to. It soured because of what they were paying him. They felt that they didn't need him. "We've got the fucking engineer, Tony Platt, and that's all we need. We write the songs and now we know what to do, we've done a couple of albums here with him, we know what the game is, game's up, you know, we don't need him any more."'

The famously reclusive Lange has never opened up about his own feelings as to being dropped by AC/DC. According to Trevor Rabin, 'Mutt's got a very thick skin so I don't think he would have cared one way or the other, personally. What Mutt brought to AC/DC, if I was Mutt I'd say, "Well, I have as much to do with those albums as anything – and I'm still paying you guys a lot of money." In other words, "Whatever I earned, so did you." [The three Mutt-produced albums] are still the best AC/DC albums ever. They should be kissing his feet.' Lange's only recorded comment, years later: 'Angus has a certain vision for his music, which works for him.' An interesting choice of words considering it was always Malcolm he'd really had to please. 'By the time we'd completed the album,' Malcolm later reflected, 'I don't think anyone, neither the band nor the producer, could tell whether it sounded right or wrong. Everyone was fed up with the whole album.'

Listening back now, it's not hard to see why. Tracks like the first single, 'Let's Get It Up', while benefiting from a typically lush, minutely detailed Lange production, are so pedestrian as to be formulaic; something that could never have been said of even their most mediocre Bon-era tracks. For the first time, AC/DC sound like they've got something to live up to; some 'sales plateau', in Phil Carson's memorable phrase, and to hell with the consequence. Double-entendres had become single; riffs no longer simply recycled as worn thin and disposed of. Even more discouraging, on tracks like the cringe-inducing 'Inject The Venom' and the self-consciously tremble-tremble 'Evil Walks' the band sounded either pathetically comic or, worse still, positively mean-spirited. The only track of its ten that reached the same level as the best tracks on Lange's two previous AC/DC albums was the titanic title track. Starting as usual with a chorus and riff concocted by Malcolm and Angus, Johnson's lyrical theme was supplied by a book Angus had come across about Roman gladiators titled *For Those About To Die We Salute You*, taken from the oath each gladiator would address the emperor with as they went into battle: 'Ave Caesar morituri te salutant' ('Hail, Caesar, we who are about to die salute you'). Said Angus: 'We thought, "For those about to rock" … I mean, it sounds a bit better than "for those about to die".'

A 'journey' song, in that it starts relatively slow before moving through the gears towards a tremendous all-guitars-and-drums-blazing finale, its other signature motif was the sound effect of cannons blasting off as a prelude to its scorching climax – inspired by the cannons fired at the wedding that summer between Lady Diana Spencer and HRH Prince Charles. The band had been at the rehearsal room in Bercy when Angus noticed 'the royal wedding thing' on the TV in the night manager's office. 'You could hear these cannons going off,' he recalled. At which point a light bulb went on in his head. 'I just wanted something strong,' he says now. 'Something masculine, and rock'n'roll. And what's more masculine than a cannon, you know? I mean, it gets loaded, it fires, and it destroys.'

With the recording sessions finally wrapped at the end of September, Atlantic hurried to get the new AC/DC album out in time for Christmas. Released in the UK on 23 November, 1981, *For Those About To Rock ... We Salute You* was largely greeted with joy by fans and critics still basking in the heat of its mega-hit predecessor. It did not, however, follow *Back In Black* to No. 1, peaking at No. 3 behind the Human League's *Dare* and Queen's first *Greatest Hits*. And while it did provide the band with their first No. 1 album in the US, as Phil Carson had predicted sales only reached the same comparatively modest levels of *Dirty Deeds*. Indeed, more than 30 years on, *FTATR* has sold four million copies in the US – roughly 20 million less than *BIB* and, astonishingly, two million less even than *Dirty Deeds* eventually managed.

Nevertheless, *For Those About To Rock ...* remains the last truly iconic AC/DC album. So powerfully embedded did the image of cannons become they even had a cannon as the cover illustration on the album. When the subsequent world tour began in the US on 14 November, along with the 2.5-ton Hells's Bell that had first appeared on the *BIB* tour, suspended above the drums by a crane, there were now two dozen 'cannons' added to the stage-show. 'There were twelve-a-side black boxes [in] two rows of six that looked nothing like cannons!' Jeffery laughingly remembers. 'Until they were lifted up from the ground behind the PA and barrels popped out – then they worked. Built by Light and Sound Design. Fire!'

The scene backstage had also changed significantly. While the band had never been short of groupies in Australia and Britain – particularly the insatiable Bon – now for the first time in America AC/DC were attracting the kind of high-heeled, spandex-and-boob-tube-clad groupies previously reserved for Zeppelin and the Stones. With most of the band now married, however, as Brian told one American reporter, 'You never fuck them. You shake hands and that's it. That's for the crew. They're the ones with the passes, not us!' It was a neat line that drew a suitable veil over what were fast becoming uncrossable lines. It wasn't just the groupies the band was now filtering out of their increasingly blinkered vision. More than on any previous tour, AC/DC now had things all their own way. With no Bon around for backstage visitors to enjoy a drink and a laugh with, the job fell to Brian and occasionally Cliff to keep the party fires burning. Which if you liked a pint and a roll-up they were good at. The days of running off with whatever group of hell-raisers happened to come around town were long gone, though. By the time this writer caught up with the band backstage at their second Castle Donington festival appearance two years later they didn't even mingle with the rest of the bands. 'I like a nice cup of tea,' Angus would patiently explain, 'and a bit of quiet before the show.' Malcolm, it seemed, just liked to be left the fuck alone.

Singer Dave Meniketti, whose band Y&T opened for AC/DC on the UK leg of the *FTATR* tour in September 1982, recalls how 'The very first show their stage manager told us, "Okay, this is your first gig with AC/DC over here, we just wanna tell you a few things. You're gonna get stuff thrown at you, you're gonna get probably coins thrown at you, you're probably gonna get booed off the stage. That's just the way it is with AC/DC's fans [in Britain]. They're really crazy and they don't like anybody opening up for them." We'd never actually had that happen to us before – it probably got us shaking in our boots a bit.' As it happened Y&T went down just fine with the AC/DC fans. Backstage, though, they were still treading on eggshells. 'Brian Johnson and Cliff Williams, in particular, were the guys that used to hang all the time – at hotels or backstage. I mean, those guys were always good to us. They would invite us into their backstage room after their show while the guys were eating. We felt a little bit uncomfortable at times because I remember, somebody told us, you know, Malcolm is a real hard-ass, so don't say anything that's gonna piss him off or you'll be off the tour in five minutes. And our drummer, Leonard, would get into arguments every once in a while with some people about things. Somebody told him, don't say anything about the United States to Malcolm, he hates them. And if you try and, like, defend the US or something he's gonna go off and you guys'll be off the tour. So we were like worried that Leonard was gonna get into some discussion with Malcolm and Leonard was gonna go, "What are you saying!" But it didn't happen luckily. Malcolm was all business for the most part. He certainly didn't give us any bad vibes or anything. But it was just this sort of attitude that was put down to us. Like, you know him, he's like the guy so you better not make him mad, you know? He wasn't exactly the kind of guy that would hang after a show or come up to you or anything like that. And Angus was always a sweet guy. But you know, obviously you get on the road and you're tired at the end of a show. Some people like to hang after that, some people don't.'

More irritating for Malcolm and AC/DC in America were the renewed protests from various right-wing Christian groups, whose tanks had been amassed on the AC/DC lawns since Angus had been depicted wearing toy devil-horns on the cover of *Highway To Hell*. On one level, the 'god-botherers', as Brian called them, could be dismissed as just plain silly. He recalled a leaflet handed out by some Jesus freaks circling the environs of the Cobo Hall in Detroit where the US tour began, which claimed: 'The Bible says the Word of the Devil is Evil and so is rock'n'roll'. 'I don't remember the Bible mentioning rock'n'roll,' he wheezed.

The Christian Right were far less easy to brush off than that, however, with TV evangelists pondering whether AC/DC stood for 'Anti Christ/Devil's Child'. Suddenly everything they had ever done was called into question: violent cover art (the *If You Want Blood* ... sleeve on which Angus was depicted being decapitated by his own guitar); demonic possession (a deliberate misreading of a quote describing

355

the way Angus became 'possessed' onstage); paedophilia (Angus's fault again for dressing onstage like a schoolboy); and endless misinterpretations of the band's real name – a big favourite, Assault Christians/Destroy Christians. Not only were AC/DC denounced publicly as 'sexual degenerates', they were now proven 'devil-worshippers'. It was a story that continued to follow the band throughout their US tour, with the self-avowed Christian Right citing new tracks like 'C.O.D.' (an acronym not just for Cash On Delivery but Care Of The Devil, they claimed) and 'Evil Walks' as more proof of the band's diabolic intentions. Even ostensibly more clued-in institutions like *Rolling Stone* jumped on the AC/DC-are-bad-for-you bandwagon, describing them in their Record Guide as 'an Australian hard rock band whose main purpose on earth apparently is to offend anyone within sight or earshot. They succeed on both counts.'

Asked in 2011 what they made of the Christian groups protesting outside their shows back then, Angus smiled. 'We thought that was funny.' Brian was more philosophical: 'That was the best promotion we could get. We took them over from Black Sabbath, you know. They were probably the same people calling Ozzy and Geezer [Butler] Satanists.' He paused for a puff on the inevitable roll-up then added: 'I don't know – maybe they were fanatics for hire.' Angus chimed in: 'That's right – they got paid by the hour.'

By the time the *For Those About To Rock* world tour reached Europe at the end of 1982, a year after it had begun, things were at last running smoothly. Bernie Marsden, then guitarist with Whitesnake, who opened for them, and had known them all since his days as one of Bon's party-hearty London friends, says, 'Things were different now. They had turned into a fully fledged stadium rock band, with all the effects and the presentation. It wasn't the band I'd seen before but internally it was still pretty much the same because they were playing some of the old stuff as well. Even though the show never changed that much every night, you never really knew what was gonna happen because of Angus and the way he presented himself onstage. He would never be less than interesting, put it that way. Some nights you couldn't take your eyes off him, he was so caught in the moment. I think Brian was always aware of that and not try and do the whole thing of interacting with him. I know he would lift him on his shoulders like Bon used to, that was all part of the show. But Brian would just get up there and sing with that voice, you know. He never tried to be Bon.'

Aside from Brian, 'who you'd see at the hotel maybe', the other members of the band made themselves scarce outside the shows themselves. Marsden's fondest memory revolves around what he calls 'the legendary AC/DC pub' that would be erected backstage each night – to save the band actually rubbing shoulders with real people in an actual bar. 'There's a jukebox in there and a dartboard and a pool table. It even had beer on tap, with pumps and a barrel.' After their first show together, in Germany, he recalls: 'We finished, went down to the dressing room and got cleaned up a bit, came back up – and they still hadn't gone on. They were playing darts! Angus said to me, "Come on, you be my partner. We're trying to get a double eight to finish." While there's fifteen thousand Germans yelling, "A-C-D-C! A-C-D-C!" Just going mad. And I suddenly realised – we could have played an hour and a half and it wouldn't have mattered one iota. They're baying for blood out there. They just *want* AC/DC so bad, the better we warm them up the better for everyone.'

Marsden, who made a point of staying to watch from the side every night, remembers 'never realising until I watched it from that angle, how much work Angus puts into the show. Angus is wringing wet before he goes on. He gets himself *really* fired up. And then you've got the complete other side of it with Malcolm just locking it down, standing there cool as a cucumber. Then Phil Rudd, every third or fourth song, instead of smacking his snare drum he'd smack his thigh. After one show, he said to me, 'Look at that'. He'd got this permanent sort of never-been-able-to heal-properly cut on his thigh, he'd hit it so hard with the stick each night – for years.'

By the time the tour finally ended, at the giant Hallenstadion, in Zurich, on 12 December 1982, AC/DC had confirmed their status as one of the biggest touring attractions in the world, big enough to have turned down a million dollars to open a stadium show in America for the Rolling Stones. 'Malcolm had decided they weren't ever going to open for anybody any more, simple as that,' Jeffery says. 'Any other band would have given their front teeth to open for the Stones at that point. Not Malcolm. His attitude was "Fuck that. We're better than them anyway."'

Album-wise, however, *For Those About To Rock* would prove to be a watershed for the band. Without the old team of Mensch and Mutt to guide them, AC/DC's recording career was about to take an unforeseen turn – and not for the good. For established figures like Mutt Lange and Peter Mensch to be effective the band needed to cede elements of control they were simply no longer prepared to give. It had always been Malcolm's band. Even when George Young was calling the shots in the studio, or Angus was out front, spinning like a top, it was always Malcolm who had the final say. Now, in 1982, as AC/DC found themselves perched at the very top of the rock world, Malcolm felt there was no need to congratulate anybody, other than himself. From here on in, the world of AC/DC – the band that, during their formative years fronted by Bon Scott, had been an open invitation to all-comers to join in the fun, now, with Brian Johnson and everyone else doing as they were told by Malcolm and to a lesser extent Angus – became a closed shop. No longer mindful of anyone outside their own inner circle, as Ian Jeffery reflects, it had always been a case of 'You're either totally in or totally out with them.' Now, though, the clan was drawing in even tighter. The bigger the apple got the more Malcolm squeezed the pips, looking for loose ends, hangers-on, impatient to oust any that dragged him or his precious band down.

Says David Krebs, 'For the first six months after Peter was gone, I personally took on AC/DC – and it was a mistake. Peter had done a great job [and] I think he was very hurt that happened. But I never really had a relationship with Malcolm. Before he died, the person I spoke to most was Bon Scott.' Now, though, Krebs would be thrown into close contact with the Young brothers – and did not enjoy the experience. 'You know the old adage, familiarity breeds contempt?'

He describes their working relationship from this point on as 'stilted. The game was totally being run by Malcolm by then.'

Despite their personal transgressions, their bad manners and worse moods, their plotting and ploughing, their endless denial of everything outside their own forward charge, musically and meta-phorically, the gods of rock had been kind to AC/DC up till then. Allowing them to ride the waves, up and down, back and forth, turn-ing misfortune into an advantage whenever somebody or something seemed poised to snatch it all away from them. Now, though, with more money, more success and more things being handled their own way than ever before, their luck was about to change. Like all power-ful clans, the Youngs sought to control every inch of their destiny, almost to the exclusion of all else. How could they have known that just at the moment they had finally been able to assume complete control, their touch would desert them, or that things would have to get a great deal worse still before they might ever have the chance to get better again – if they were lucky?

CHAPTER FIFTEEN

The Master Switch

Having effectively become AC/DC's day-to-day manager through-out the *For Those About To Rock* world tour, Ian Jeffery was offi-cially given the job the day after the final show in Zurich, in December 1982. An end-of-tour meeting had been called, presided over by David Krebs, John Clark and the band's new accountant, Alvin Handwerker, all of whom had flown in especially from New York, and which Jeffery had also been invited to attend.

'They were all talking about what are we gonna do next and what are the repercussions and etc. At one point, they said to me, "Can you give us a few minutes here?" So there were obviously things they didn't want me to hear. No problem, cos I was still the tour manager then.' Ian went for 'half a lager' with the road crew. He hadn't fin-ished his drink before he was called back again. 'I walked in and John Clark said, "Well, they've taken the decision, Ian, and you are now the manager." I said, "I'm what? I don't know how to manage a band! But if it's something you think I can do ..."'

His position was clearly laid out for him. As their manager, 'I would never take decisions. I would always say I'll go back and speak to Malcolm and Angus. Never Angus and Malcolm; Malcolm and Angus. I was more like their guardian than their manager. I never made any big decisions on their behalf, I always reported back to Malcolm and Angus and let them decide what they wanted to do. The only point I made was that I'd do it as long as it didn't change my day-to-day routine from what I was doing already. I didn't want to suddenly be on the other side of the fence to the band. I didn't want to be like their Mr Ten Percent, you know? But there wasn't none of that or any percentages talked about. It was just, that's it.'

The only improvement in his position financially came later when Krebs invited Ian into his hotel room for a chat. 'Malcolm always told me, "Don't take any shit from him. If he says anything, tell him to fuck off." But obviously that was a lot easier for him to say. Anyway, Krebs went into some waffle, then: "We were thinking of the big picture. You really are the closest to the band, Ian. We're glad to have you in place and we're thinking we'd like to give you a little bit of extra money. We were thinking about maybe giving you two grand." But I was in the middle of something and so I told him I'd get back to him later. As soon as I got out though Malcolm took me for a drink and said, "What did that fucking cunt want?" I told him the story and that he'd offered me two grand. Malcolm goes, "He fucking what? You tell him you want fifty grand! And if he wants to say something about it you tell him I told you to say that!"

'So that's what I did when I went back later. When [Krebs] picked himself off the floor he said, "Now come on, Ian ..." I said, okay, I'll tell Malcolm that you refused then. From there it was a done deal. And back in those days, that was a chunk of change! Malcolm was brilliant about it. "What does that cunt want?" I said, well, he is your manager, Malcolm. "He's a fucking prat!" Krebs was still the manager but I had now become *everything* to them. They would run things by me before they asked questions of everyone else.'

As with previous incumbents in the job, however, being the manager of AC/DC was a double-edged sword. Essentially, Jeffery was there to do what he was told. Overall strategy was no longer something Malcolm or Angus Young were interested in handing over the responsibility for. They no longer sought anybody's advice, they simply dispensed orders. Your job was to carry them out – fast. Or else.

There had been a short break in the New Year but preparations for the next AC/DC album – their first without either Mutt Lange or George Young to guide them – were already underway by March. Still officially British tax exiles, they had planned for a month's rehearsals at the same studio location on the Channel Island of Jersey used by Iron Maiden. But when Maiden decided at the last minute that they wanted it, Jeffery, in his new capacity as day-to-day manager, found himself scouring the neighbouring Isle of Man for alternative venues.

Ian eventually located 'an old bed and breakfast, which had about eleven bedrooms'. The owner was from Bolton, a retired embalmer. Ian booked it for two months: 12 bedrooms, a cook, and total privacy. Ian did a deal for him to soundproof the bar, egg boxes, foam all over the room. Ian also bought TVs, plus aerials, and gave them to the owner, for each room. Ian was relieved to find the band liked it. It was in the middle of the Isle of Man: two-minute walk to everything, the town, the sea.

Jeffery would phone Malcolm and Angus every day, making sure they were all right. He'd bring PDs (day-to-day expenses money) over once a week from the mainland, talk to the crew, make sure everyone was happy. 'They were all fine. They never went out because there was a bar at the hotel! Just help yourself and the guy would charge us at the end of every week. They were like pigs in shit.' Until one Friday 'it all went fucking wrong, when Malcolm hit the roof and we were gonna fire the cook'. He'd asked for shepherd's pie but he'd called it cottage pie. The cook made it but when they all sat down to dinner, Malcolm took one look and said, 'What the fucking hell's this shit?' Shepherd's pie was supposed to have a thick crust. This crust 'was all thin and flat and mushy'. The cook told Malcolm: 'It's what you asked for: cottage pie.' Malcolm says: 'I want shepherd's pie, you cunt!' The cook wouldn't let it lie: 'Well, you said you wanted cottage pie and this is how it's made.' Ian: 'So Malcolm just took it up and threw it at him! The guy started crying … Malcolm was like, "Get rid of this fucking cunt, sack him!" I said, "Well, okay, that's up to George the owner of the hotel." But I was gonna go back to the road chefs and bring someone in. But that was the fragility of it all.'

Malcolm was always a hair-trigger away from blowing his top. The only difference was he was making up the rules as he went along now. But instead of alleviating the pressure of making a new album and going out on the next world tour, it seemed to add to his stress levels. Jeffery: 'They were under a schedule of their own making. They thought they had a great record and they went down to Nassau and I stayed behind to make sure the hotel was all stripped out and they could get it back to normal. Then go into meetings with Carson in London about the ongoing schedule; paying the bills. All the stuff I now had to do.'

In April, they returned to Compass Point Studios in Nassau, with Malcolm stepping into the role of principal producer, and Tony Platt drafted in as the Mutt-we-like – engineering and mixing the record. They recorded 13 tracks, ten of which would comprise the lo-fi disaster known as *Flick Of The Switch*. Platt did what he could to manage expectations. But as he recalls, 'By that time they were more at the mercy of the machine even though they felt they were taking control of everything. Management and record company said, "We need to move it into a slightly different space. Can you make it somewhere between *Back In Black* and *For Those About To Rock*?" In my estimation that was probably not the best of things to do. But I didn't have enough authority to push back on that. I didn't have the authority that Mutt had.' Officially, Platt was there simply to engineer, with the brothers taking the role of joint producers. In reality, however, he was the one with his hands on the controls. Doing what he was told. The way Malcolm liked it. 'I also don't have the musical ability, the musical comprehension or arranging capacity that Mutt has. So there were a couple of very important components that were gonna be missing when I was there. And in that respect they had perhaps unpicked too much of [Lange's painstakingly layered sound]. At the same time as that there were all these internal frictions going on. They were knackered – really, really tired.'

Musically, says Platt, 'The reference point for the new album was actually BB King's recording with Johnny Winter of "Mannish Boy", the one with everybody in the room whooping. That was the reference point that Malcolm gave to me. He wanted it to feel like that.' In other words, about as far away from the signature Mutt Lange-produced AC/DC sound as they could get.

And did Platt feel he was able to achieve that?

'No.'

Does he feel they even came close?

'No. No.'

He admits now that, by the end of the album, 'I felt slightly disappointed by it. I didn't feel like we'd achieved the goal. I think there were far too many other things going on.'

One of which was the volcanic eruption between Malcolm and Phil that led to the drummer – one of the absolute key components in the quintessential AC/DC sound – being next to be fired from the band.

As the years passed, Malcolm Young, realising his mistake, perhaps, would downplay what actually happened in Nassau. 'It wasn't a thrown-out-of-the-band bust-up,' he told *Mojo* in 2004, 'just an out-and-out go at each other.' The next thing Malcolm knew, he said, Phil had jumped on a plane 'and that was it, he'd gone home. It was later on that the word came that he didn't want to do it any more.' The truth, though, was much more frightening.

Ian Jeffery had arrived in Nassau just five days after the band. It was late on a Friday night when Evo (Keith Evans) picked him up at the airport. As soon as he arrived at the studio, Angus offered to play him the record. Jeffery, exhausted from his 10-hour overnight flight, responded by saying he'd love to hear a couple of songs. To which Angus replied, 'No, do you want to hear the record? We're done.' Says Jeffery: 'I was like, *what*? But I'm sitting with Angus in the control room and he's got his foot tapping, and he's hearing everything else that he thinks is going on. And I'm like … what are you gonna say to them? Yeah, sounds great. You're not gonna say, what a fucking pile of shit that is, let's get going here, you know? As far as they were concerned, they were finished. But I was sitting there thinking, well, it's not Mutt, you know? It was back to being an Alberts Production again – except without George and Harry. Even with Tony at the helm it had gone back to that sound. Still AC/DC but it didn't have that wall of sound, with all the separation, that you had with Mutt. They thought Tony knew everything, had everything the same as Mutt.'

As he lay in bed that night trying to sleep, Jeffery wondered if it still might be salvageable, if he could sit down and talk to them; get them to go back and look at a couple of tracks. Plans there were foiled before he'd even had a chance to try and implement them when the most almighty row broke out. 'It was a couple of nights later. I remember Malcolm kicking my door in roughly. "Get this fucking cunt on a plane tonight!" He was talking about Phil ...'

Not knowing what was going on, stalling for time, Jeffery explained that there were no planes out of Nassau at that time of night. Malcolm raged at him: 'Well, fucking get him out of here and find a hotel for him!' The reason behind Rudd's beating and subsequent expulsion from the band remains shrouded in some degree of mystery. Inevitably, the internet is awash with rumours. From the drummer's allegedly increasingly out of control appetites for drugs and alcohol, to various behind the scenes infidelities involving women of American and Dutch origins and even whispers of an illegitimate child. Reportedly, Rudd's alcohol abuse hit an all-time low at an Atlantic Records party for the band some months earlier, when he not only turned up late but became so drunk he was unable to finish the encores. That said, there is no evidence of any band intervention or of any attempt to talk some sense into him prior to their arrival in Nassau.

I ask Ian Jeffery, who was there, why Phil Rudd received such a hiding from Malcolm Young? His voice lowers to a whisper. 'I really don't want to go into details because it was a personal situation, nothing to do with the album. Something had happened and Malcolm just snapped. He just went up, kicked [Phil's] door in and dumped one on him. And that was it. Thick ear, cut lip, black eye ...'

Jeffery pauses then goes on. 'It was a very personal thing. In Malcolm's eyes and I think most people's eyes, if indeed that was what had happened, you would fucking do the same thing, I think. Absolutely. I don't think saying what it was will embellish it any more. But if it happened to me or you we'd have probably done the same thing. It didn't help it was at a time when everything was not in the gear it was supposed to be in. Another early-night finish and hit the sauce a bit, then go back in and another phone call comes in, and Malcolm's like, "Right, that's fucking it! I've just been told something, that's it!" Whatever's been festering, and it's after a few large whiskies have been consumed, and listening to tracks at 2000 decibels and everything else, then a phone call coming ... "Right, that's it! That's it! That's it!"

'It was the wrong time at the wrong moment, at the back end of being isolated on an island. Malcolm plied full of booze and that's it, you know? It was a huge fucking fight. We're all running over there, "What's going on?" And Phil's in there with a black eye and Malcolm's just standing around as if nothing's happened, just looking for another drink. So we're trying to make sense of Phil and he's going, "I don't know. I don't know. I don't know what he's talking about." So he's in denial as well, right? Then Malcolm comes back in. "Fucking get him on the plane now!" The whole thing. "I don't wanna fucking see his face any more! Get him out of here!" I was shaken by all this now. And then Phil becomes aggressive. "Fuck 'em. Okay, I'll go. Let 'em see if they can do it without me." So I went down to the hotel with him and had to put him on a plane first thing the next morning. Then he was gone. Bye, Phil, see ya, mate ...'

Utterly unrepentant, on the outside at least, Malcolm instructed Ian to begin searching for a new drummer straight away – almost as if he wanted it done before he could change his mind. What Brian Johnson or Cliff Williams had to say about it, no one thought to ask. Who cared what they thought about anything anyway? Even Angus had to simply grin and bear it.

Everyone began to pitch in ideas for who might replace Phil Rudd. Jeffrey recalls: 'In the end someone says, "The drummer with Procol Harum is fucking superb." B. J. Wilson. Malcolm's like, "What the fuck's this guy talking about? They're older than my dad, that lot!"' In fact, Wilson, a brilliant drummer who had been Jimmy Page's first choice when he formed Led Zeppelin in 1968, but who turned the guitarist down as Procul Harum were then doing so well, was just coming up to his 36th birthday, making him the same age as Brian Johnson and just six years older than Malcolm Young. When the guitarist had calmed down long enough to be apprised of these facts, he ordered Jeffery to try and track Wilson down. When Ian found him, though, he was living in Portland, Oregon, more or less out of the business, foresting and playing occasionally with Joe Cocker, whose giant hit version of 'Little Help From My Friends' he had drummed on. Not that the veteran player seemed remotely fazed by his changed circumstances when Jeffery finally got him on the phone and invited him out to Nassau.

'He was like, "Okay, and who the fuck are you anyway?" I told him I couldn't tell him the name of the band. He said, "I'm not getting on the plane unless you tell me who they are." I said, "I promise. It's an international band. It will be worth your while."' The following Friday night, Jeffery drove out to the airport to meet him. 'But I can't see any-body. I thought he must have missed the plane. In the end, out come these two stewardesses helping this guy off the plane – sozzled, com-pletely fucking sozzled. I thought, just what I fucking need! A Friday night, eleven o'clock at night, we're taking him back to the studio cos Malcolm wanted to see him straight away, cos that was one of his things, they wanted to put him in the studio straight away. There was gonna be no slacking for this guy ...' He breaks off, laughing.

Jeffery took him to the studio, sat him down in the control room. Malcolm, mildly amused, offered Wilson a brandy. 'Then they put the record on and BJ starts playing along with his hands on his knees. The brandy's flowing so suddenly it's like, soul-mates. We never get round to getting anywhere near a drum kit cos it's impossible. We get to the end of the record and Malcolm's like, "He's brilliant! He likes a bevy as well, he's brilliant!"'

The album was more or less finished and the tour was being booked. Realising BJ was not the man in the cold light of day, a sober Malcolm told Ian to get rid of him – hard to do on a remote island. Nevertheless, Jeffery once again managed the impossible and no one from AC/DC ever saw B. J. Wilson again. 'After that they decided they would audition drummers in New York, where they would be mixing the album, cos that way at least you could get rid of the drummers you didn't want without any hassle.'

Of those that were invited to audition in New York, one of the clos-est calls was Denny Carmassi, formerly of the influential Montrose, then of Heart, who he'd just finished recording the *Passionworks* album with. 'Denny flew in from Seattle and he was a fantastic drummer,' Jeffery recalls. 'He came in, I said, "Whatever you do, don't hit the tom-toms, keep it dead straight. Don't go wanking around with drum rolls or you'll not get the gig." And they loved him – but he was tall and he had a fucking poofy hairstyle. So he was out.'

Next to come under serious consideration was former Roxy Music drummer Paul Thompson, like Johnson from Newcastle upon Tyne, and who Jeffery also remembers as being 'Fantastic! What a drummer! We kept him for a week. I put him on per diems, and then Malcolm turned round and said, "Great. He can go home again." So I'm taking him out to JFK and saying, "I'll probably be in touch in a few days." He said, "Yeah, everything seemed fine and thanks for the PDs and for paying my hotel. We had a great time, the lads are great." I said, "It looks like they like you as well. I'm sure we'll be talking." Got back to the hotel, Malcolm says, "He's fucking history." No explanation, nothing ...'

Things were starting to boil over again. Even though George Young and Harry Vanda had flown to New York to try and rescue the album with the mix, early indications from Atlantic were not encouraging. There were mumblings again about the cover too – a simple line drawing by Angus. 'Because *For Those About To Rock* hadn't been as big [as *BIB*], when the band wanted an embossed cover, Atlantic refused to pay for it. They said to me, "We can't spend twelve cents on a cover, Ian. It's got to be four."'

With both George and Malcolm wilting under the heat of Atlantic's breath down their necks, the band decamped to London to finish the mix and begin anew their search for a drummer. 'By now they're shouting at me about everything,' says Jeffery. 'They started to hate me. It's all my fault now. There was a strange feeling coming up. I felt like I was Mensch all of a sudden, or in that category. So I'm in New York trying to sort through this. Malcolm was like, "You fucking stay there and if we need you we'll get you over."'

Discreet ads were taken in *Sounds* and *Melody Maker*: 'Wanted, Drummer for Top Band. If You Don't Hit Hard Don't Apply'. Two rehearsal rooms were rented at the Nomis studio complex in Baron's Court: one upstairs with just a kit and some recording equipment set up in it; the other, larger room downstairs with the band's full rig. The band's drum tech, Dickie Jones, would routine all prospective drummers in the small upper room, asking them to play along to three songs: 'Shoot To Thrill', Zeppelin's 'Black Dog' and ZZ Top's 'Tush'. Any that impressed Dickie would then get a full shot at auditioning for the band in the downstairs room.

One of the few who got that far was a 19-year-old unknown from Oldham named Simon Wright. Wright had begun 'hitting the drums' at 13, inspired by the likes of Rainbow drummer Cozy Powell, Zeppelin's John Bonham and, a little later, Ozzy Osbourne's drummer, Tommy Aldridge – all players known for their power and finesse. Like them, Wright saw himself as more than just a hitter. There had been the usual local school-age groups – notably A II Z, who released a live album – before Wright moved to London at the end of 1982 to join New Wave of British Heavy Metal act, Tytan. Formed by ex-members of NWOBHM stalwarts Angel Witch and occasionally featuring ex-members of Judas Priest and Rock Goddess, expectations had briefly been high for Tytan's debut album, *Rough Justice*. But when Kamaflage, the indie label it was to be released on, folded, the band followed suit shortly after. Which is how Wright came to be scouring the 'musicians wanted' pages in *Sounds* in the summer of 1983.

'They didn't tell me who the band was but I guessed it must be somebody with a name because the audition was at Nomis. Dickie was a nice guy, I played through three or four songs, just playing along to a tape, then he thanked me and I left thinking that was that. Then later that day Dickie phoned me and asked me if I could come back.' When Dickie told Simon to take a cab and that they would pay for it, 'I thought, what? They must be interested then. But he still didn't say who it was.' Walking down the corridor to the much bigger live room they would be playing in, he couldn't help noticing the flight cases with the AC/DC imprimatur plastered over them. 'Dickie's sort of smiling at me and I'm going, "Oh, no! You're *joking* ..."'

When Wright walked in the room the two Young brothers were already there waiting for him with Cliff. No Brian. He had 'some business to attend to', they told him. They didn't bother explaining he had nothing to do with the decision-making process anyway. Wright was 'in complete and utter shock' and hadn't noticed anyway. They ran through a few numbers, some AC/DC, some others, and decided there and then. The gig was his – if he wanted it? He laughs now, saying he doesn't remember saying yes, he was still in too much shock. He just did what he was told. 'I mean, it's AC/DC – what's not to like? I knew a lot of their stuff – kind of. 'Back In Black' and the usual stuff … It all started coming back to me as I started playing.'

The only thing he had to be conscious of as drummer, he says, was Phil Rudd's unique style of playing – using it as his template. 'He carved his own niche. It was so straight-ahead, you know, heavy and solid. Sometimes it was hard to believe how much he held back.' Specifically, he would have to restrain his own natural inclination as a drummer to, as he puts it, 'fire off' – especially when it came to the older material. 'If you start playing fills everywhere where Phil didn't do them, it's gonna sound a bit silly, cos Phil's playing with AC/DC is an integral part of their sound. So I had enough sense to realise if I started adding to that it wouldn't work. It can be a difficult, strenuous way to play. It sounds simple but it's not. Cos you wanna go for it, you wanna fire off, but you've got to ease back. You've really got to make those songs swing.'

Simon Wright's appointment to the drum stool meant there were no longer any members of AC/DC – the antipodean punk band – actually born in Australia. As the newest and youngest member, Wright admits he felt overwhelmed for a long time. 'They're very straight-forward, down to earth. They don't put on airs and graces. And that was a big, big help to me because there was a lot of times it was like being inside of a washing machine. Just like this total … stuff going on all the time, just massive things, a massive big stage to play on all the time, massive crowds of fans. But backstage it was very much a family atmosphere. There was not a hell of a lot of craziness that went on. So that was a good grounding too.'

Joining such a tight circle had its pros and cons too. 'I can only surmise it's from their upbringing. Family was very, very important to those guys. And I think it may have stemmed also from the experience that they had over the years with different situations, managers and people trying to take advantage of them maybe. So I think they'd learned over the years it was best to stick like brothers, and keep things in-house. It seemed that way anyway, when I first joined.' Though he was accepted into the circle there was still a zone into which only Malcolm and Angus were allowed. Things they sorted out on their own. 'They never made me feel left out. But there were certain situations where I just used to mind my own business, really. They were the leaders of the band and it would be taken care of by them, and rightly so it's their band.' On a personal level, he says his relationship with Malcolm and Angus was 'a fairly easy one. I didn't find it a problem. They were all a lot older than I was. That did leave sometimes a little bit of a gap in some instances. I was thrown in at the deep end. But they always treated me fine. Malcolm is obviously the leader of the whole thing. At the end of the day, when the big decisions come down, he's the guy who really thinks about things and gets the results.'

Wright had other distractions to keep his mind occupied. 'I went from having no money to having a little bit of money. Some cash where I could help out my family and stuff, be able to do a few things that I really couldn't do before. So that was a big thing, obviously. There were so many learning experiences on so many levels that didn't hit me immediately, but then you think back and go, oh yeah, that's how I should have dealt with that. It was quite a life-changing experience. They took me on a whirlwind trip and I'll thank them for ever for that.'

On 5 August 1983, Atlantic Records released a press release announcing the departure of Phil Rudd and his replacement by Simon Wright. Any blowback related to this unexplained switch would soon be eclipsed, however, by the muted reception of *Flick Of The Switch* a couple of weeks later. 'It was a big deal because they knew there would be a press scrum to meet the new guy,' says Ian

Jeffery, 'and be told why Phil had "left by mutual consent", and when the new album was due etc. But they wanted it done quickly, didn't want to talk about it really. It was very, very hard, because everything was starting to dysfunction and go off the rails. They had always been my priority. They were my bosses but they were my friends, growing up from almost day one. Been through the tragedy of Bon, through everything, you know? But now things were changing ...'

Malcolm, though he would never dream of showing it, knew his unilateral decision to fire Phil had bordered on the catastrophic. But that would blow over as long as the band continued to deliver. The problem was that *Flick Of The Switch* wasn't in the same league as its three Mutt Lange-produced predecessors. There was a palpable difference between workmanlike new tracks like 'Rising Power' and 'This House Is On Fire' – standouts in this lowly context – and true masterpieces like 'Highway To Hell' and 'Back In Black'. What had already begun to sound re-purposed on *For Those About To Rock* now had the reek of generic rock mulch; the sort of songs where the riffs arrive like fast food, instant gratification followed by a nauseous hollow feeling; songs where lyrically the titles come first and the verses feel typed by chimpanzees looking to get lucky. It says something when one-dimensional puns like 'Deep In The Hole' (geddit?) actually work better than uninspired dross like 'Bedlam In Belgium' – seriously? – and 'Nervous Shakedown'. Occasionally, as with parts of 'Landslide', 'Brain Shake' and the title track, the riffs look like they'll carry the weight but it's a forlorn hope. Lyrically, it is the band's most literal album, teeming with clichéd bravado and more tedious artillery metaphors; never had the gulf between Johnson and Scott appeared wider. The sly wink and mischievous grin that coloured Bon's lyrics had invested AC/DC with a sense of danger and mystery. Brian's lyrics reflected his physical presence, with his bulging biceps and cap pulled down over his face, pushing ahead with brute force and ill-temper. Even his metaphors felt literal. Certainly, there is nothing here that stands repeat listens. Worse still than being unable to match the peerless heights of the three albums with Lange, is that there is nothing worthy of the albums they built their reputation on with Bon. Not even when they were churning them out twice a year. At particularly desperate moments, they sound like they are regurgitating their own songs – not least on 'Nervous Shakedown' and 'Deep In The Hole', both of which sound like off-cuts from 'Back In Black'.

There were some legitimately catchy tracks ('Flick Of The Switch', 'Guns For Hire', 'Brain Shake'), but they lack the edge and bombast of the band's better and more recent output. Without Mutt there to guide them, *Flick Of The Switch* felt underdeveloped, unfocused and flat. A view borne out when, in subsequent decades, the band opened the floodgates of their archives, releasing a tsunami of live and studio rarities across a panoply of compilations. That the three unused songs from the *Flick Of The Switch* sessions (a cover of Junior Wells's 'Messin' With The Kid', plus two rejected originals 'Out Of Bounds' and 'Tightrope', appear on none of these, speaks to the band's assessment of their work during this period. Reviews of the new album, which were uniformly bad, reflected the general disappointment among fans, too. But bad reviews were not what stuck in Malcolm Young's throat. It was the fact that, as Ian Jeffery says now, 'It was negative energy from everywhere about the album. Nobody wanted it, nobody. Not radio, not concert promoters ... Everything had been on the up. All of a sudden it was a complete train wreck. Then when we got to LA for rehearsals there was so much anger within them, even to the crew guys. When Angus's guitar would go wrong he'd rip Plug a fucking new arsehole. Or if Malcolm's thing was out of tune he'd fucking get into Evo – guys that had been with them for ever. You could just feel these bad vibes everywhere. Malcolm was just antagonistic towards me all the time, for no reason. Instead of coming in and saying, "What can we do here?" it was like, "Mate, you've caused this, what are you gonna do?" I felt like, hey, mate, aren't we supposed to be a fucking team here, you know?'

Atlantic Records, viewing the album as single-free, prioritised it accordingly, to the band's tremendous offence, but Atlantic had read the writing on the wall – in three years, AC/DC's frontman had drunk himself to death, they had sacked their manager, dropped their hit-making producer, kicked out their drummer, then recorded a collection of songs that on a good day aspired to mediocrity. All Jeffery's foreboding was borne out when *Flick Of The Switch*, although burning up the UK and Australian charts with its usual haste, before vanishing again without trace, became AC/DC's first flop in America for five years, barely scraping the Top 20. Sales in the US initially reached 500,000, although the RIAA eventually certified the album as platinum. For most bands, these were career numbers but for AC/DC they were a disaster. As if to rub it in, the new Def Leppard album, *Pyromania* – the album Mutt Lange produced instead of *Flick Of The Switch* – sat at No. 2 in the US chart, on its way to selling more than ten million copies.

The ill-fated *Flick Of The Switch* tour kicked off in Vancouver on 11 October 1983 and, for Malcolm and the boys, it couldn't end fast enough. First, in several cities, the band had only one date scheduled where on previous tours these same cities had hosted multiple nights. Worse, many of these shows fell far short of a sell-out, and while AC/DC would play every show as if it were the main stage at Donington, they privately seethed when they would stare into half-full venues like Nassau Coliseum. Someone, as usual, was going to have to carry the can. That someone, as usual, was to be their manager. Or in this case, their old friend: Ian Jeffery.

'It came when they were back in Australia and me and Marsha [Vlasic at ICM] are in New York trying to book the FOTS dates. Cos the record wasn't happening. Radio didn't want it and radio was so local back then. You could play Cleveland, Columbus and Cincinnati, and play an arena, a stadium and a club. Sixty miles apart, it all depended on radio. And radio all over America didn't want [FOTS]. Promoters weren't interested. They were being forced to take it because it was AC/DC. Tickets were not selling. I'm on the phone down there to Alberts. You know, George and Harry are there and Malcolm's there. And sometimes Fifa [Riccobono] was there. And they were blaming me for everything, and I was just telling them the truth. They were like, "You're just listening to [the wrong] fucking people." I said, "The record is not happening at radio. Promoters are saying: 'Not at that price.' We're fighting a war. We should delay or not even [tour]." We pushed it [the US tour] back anyway. It was time not to tour. But it was their first record [without Mutt, or Mensch] and George was there going, "The record will turn itself around. We'll write a single, or we'll do something. We'll do whatever we've got to do." So I'm like, "Okay, great ..."

'Then they blamed me for sounding like the record company and everybody else. So it was a real struggle for me. I remember Malcolm slamming the phone down on a Friday night. He said, "Listen, we want forty-two shows. We're gonna play this, play there. Monday morning tell us it's booked, or you're fucking history" – or words to that effect. Slammed the phone down. Marsha came over to me and gave me a hug and says, "I'm so sorry to hear them speak to you like that, Ian. You know it's not you." I said, "They think it is and that's all that matters, Marsha. We've got to get this done." So we stayed the whole weekend in the office so we could get to them on the Monday and give them the whole date list. Then of course when the [tickets] went on sale, it stiffed! We're talking about the early promoters who want to get it put back. But of course that's something you can't say to them. You can't even suggest that to them. So now I've become the enemy. My whole life, my whole energy was 24/7 to those guys, you know? So we went through the tour and it was disastrous. Some [shows] were okay, some were not.

'Then we were getting near the end. It was Hartford, and the Meadowlands and Madison Square Garden to go, just a few weeks before Christmas. I was in my room at the Parker Meridian and I'm just booking up the cars cos it's like an eighty-mile drive. I was booking a couple extra cars so we could separate a bit so there wasn't fucking six or seven trying to squeeze into a car for that drive. There was a knock at the door ...'

It was Malcolm. Ian told him to hang on a moment while he finished on the phone call. 'I'd just brought the leaving time forward from four o'clock to three, to make sure we had plenty of travel time. I put the phone down and said, "What do you think – three o'clock?"

He says, "Don't matter to me. We don't need you any more." That was it – don't need you any more. I asked what he meant. He said, "We don't need you any more. We're done" – and walked out the door. That was it. He did say to me, "You can stay in the hotel a couple days and clean up all this fucking shit you gotta do. Then he went out and I stayed there a couple of days. I had to go to meetings with Alvin and John Clarke. They were very uncomfortable meetings for me, cos they were saying this and that … just the whole thing. It was just surreal for me because AC/DC were my whole life.'

What twisted the knife further for Jeffery was that nobody from the band came to say goodbye. Not even Angus. 'The two days I was in the hotel – nobody. None of the others. I've seen Simon a couple of times. But he was new. He said, "Fuck 'em. It was weird, Ian." Yet the day [I was fired] that was the darkest day of my life. My whole everything collapsed. I called my wife, she was crying, saying are you coming home? I said, "I'll be home in a couple of days, I've just got to sort this stuff out."'

He recalls being at John Clarke's office and Clarke shouting, 'We've gotta get this done, Ian!' Ian said: 'John, I'm trying.' There was an issue over a car Jeffery had purchased for the band, a £15,000 Rover, 'Cos Malcolm wanted a car available in England. So he said, "Go buy one and keep it as yours, so if we're [in London] and we need it we don't have to fuck around." John Clarke said, "By the way, you can either keep the car and we'll deduct £7,500 out of your wages, or give us the car back." I'm like, what car? It was the last thing in my thoughts, you know …'

That same week they also fired Marsha Vlasick. That meant that in the past two years alone, AC/DC had rid themselves of Peter Mensch, Mutt Lange, Phil Rudd, Ian Jeffery and Marsha Vlasick. 'Everything that had built that pyramid for them, they just decided to pull the rug out, for whatever reason, I don't know. Whether it was like, again, the input of the brothers down there. George would be like, "Fuck them. You're bigger than any of them." I don't know if that went on. It stinks to me of all that sort of thing. But the saddest thing for me was [losing] the creative magic of Bon. It was always going to be a slog after that, trying to make sure the integrity of AC/DC's music was still there, and find a way to keep that magic of the lyrics going, which they tried to do.' But AC/DC now seemed to have given up on that, convinced the band could run on its own fumes.

In their commentary on the *Live At Donington* DVD, the band insist they are proud of *Flick Of The Switch*, but their set lists in the following 20 years suggest otherwise. In fact, so discouraged were they after the US leg of the *Flick Of The Switch* tour that rather than hit Europe, they headed straight into the songwriting process for the next album. In July 1984, that painful songwriting process was nearing completion, with the band taking a break to take on eight headlining slots for the Monsters Of Rock tour, including their second headlining appearance at Donington, alongside the likes of Van Halen, Ozzy Osbourne and an up-and-coming Los Angeles outfit known as Mötley Crüe. Rather than redeem an otherwise horrid stretch, however, this mini-tour threw gasoline on the fires licking at the feet of AC/DC. As bad as Bon or Phil's substance abuse problems had become, Malcolm was faring equally poorly in his battle with John Barleycorn. At the Italian stop on the Monsters Of Rock tour, Malcolm, who bitterly eviscerated Phil for being too drunk to play, himself became so inebriated that he crashed into Simon's drum kit; yet he was still a long way from hitting his bottom. Meanwhile, AC/DC added some French dates after the Monsters Of Rock tour, and on their final night in Paris they played to an 18,000-seat arena, 12,000 of which were empty.

That October, they released *'74 Jailbreak* in North America and Japan. The five-song EP contained Bon Scott-era tracks that had previously been available only on Australian versions of previous albums ('Jailbreak' was on the Australian version of *Dirty Deeds* and the rest of the songs were on the Aussie version of *High Voltage*). Capturing the band at a creative highpoint, the release cut as a double-edged sword by reminding fans of AC/DC's declining prowess, while at the same time underscoring just how great they had sounded with Bon.

If the definition of insanity is doing the same thing and expecting different results, then AC/DC should have been committed during the *Fly On The Wall* sessions. AC/DC began the sessions in Montreux, Switzerland, again producing the album themselves, and again seeking to get back to basics. Mark Dearnley, who had been the house engineer on *Highway*, and the last-minute replacement for Platt in Paris, was there this time to fulfil the poor man's Mutt role. But as Trevor Rabin says, 'I know Mutt uses different guys [Dearnley, Platt] but it always sounds like Mutt because Mutt's sound is created by Mutt, not by engineers.'

Recording halfway to the sky at Mountain Studios, AC/DC's first album without Phil Rudd, *Fly On The Wall*, proved to be as forgettable as *Flick Of The Switch*, with a handful of marginally catchy rockers mixed in with a gang of duds. Simon Wright, making his first AC/DC album, inadvertently describes how lax the creative process had become for the band in the immediate post-Mutt era, when he remembers how 'We just started jamming away in rehearsals and the songs just started coming along. We just really started playing. There wasn't that much thought given ... cos that's not the way they work. They just play, you know? They don't really analyse a lot of stuff, ask if this is working. They just moved on, kept playing and it came out the way it did.'

Lyrically, the album swings 180 degrees from *Flick Of The Switch*, this time full of crude, ham-fisted double-entendres that are entirely devoid of creativity or cleverness. Songs like 'Sink The Pink' might elicit mirthful giggles from schoolboys but would find little purchase in the minds of serious rock fans. Like its forebear, *Fly On The Wall* boasts a handful of decent songs that, with more expansive production, might have pushed the record to a higher stature, although at least the sequencing was more intuitive. But if the performance of *Flick Of The Switch* was cause for concern, then the reception of *Fly On The Wall* was a veritable five-alarm fire, peaking at No. 32 in the US and 7 in the UK. Unintentionally, the band's juvenile lyrics were dovetailing perfectly into the glam metal scene then exploding on Hollywood's Sunset Strip, but those bands provided a far more entertaining and attractive version of the same puerile cock rock of *Fly On The Wall*.

AC/DC did take a stab at a different type of video promotion, releasing a five-song video for the new album, filmed at the World's End club in New York City. The film's loose conceit was that in this dirty little club full of beggars and thieves, the then-unknown AC/DC would show up, play some songs from their new album and, in doing so, transform the club into a massive dance party. The cheesiness of the video underlined just how desperately low-rent the music had become.

Positive news arrived in August 1985, when *Fly On The Wall* was certified as gold in the US, but whatever flimsy hope this might have offered was soon obliterated with the arrest of Richard Ramirez later that month. Dubbed the 'Night Stalker' by the local media, Ramirez had killed a jaw-dropping 16 people, viciously beating, raping, slashing and defiling his victims before and after killing them. On some he drew pentagrams with lipstick, others he required to swear allegiance to Satan before raping and killing them. The grisly murder spree commanded the attention of the United States until his arrest in southern California at the end of August. The subsequent investigation revealed that Ramirez was a devout AC/DC fan, particularly enthusiastic over the *Highway To Hell* song, 'Night Prowler', with its chilling lyric, ' ...*and you don't feel the steel, 'til it's hanging out your back ...*'

The band was immediately thrown into a PR nightmare, compounded by the discovery that Ramirez was wearing an AC/DC T-shirt at the time of his arrest and that he had left an AC/DC cap at one of the crime scenes. During his trial, Ramirez yelled, 'Hail, Satan', and proudly displayed a pentagram carved into his palm – a pentagram not unlike the one worn by Bon on the cover of *Highway To Hell*, which also portrayed Angus as a horned devil with a serpent's tail. The noose had never been tighter around the collective neck of AC/DC. Efforts to distance themselves from Ramirez proved futile, given the lyrics of 'Night Prowler' and the killer's public adoration of the band's music. Show cancellations, protests, and restrictions on the band's live show followed during the *Fly On The Wall* tour, and in September 1985, when another killer was caught in possession of

AC/DC gear, what little radio support they were receiving in California quickly dried-up.

The ship was rudderless and had been seemingly since the brothers battened down the hatches and took affairs into their own hands. David Krebs had been dispensed with in the wake of FOTW's abject failure. Even old familiar faces like Phil Carson at Atlantic were no longer around. 'Well, look, I always had a belief that Malcolm and Angus really could save the day, musically,' says Carson today. 'But I really had no connection with them after I left Atlantic. Doug [Morris] was handling it and because there was no manager other than an accountant that knew nothing about music running it, that was a problem. At least Peter Mensch knew if they weren't making the right record, and he would tell them. They had nobody there taking care of them. There was nobody in there at the record company that could communicate with the band.'

Crispin Dye, a young buck from the Alberts office, had been assigned the day-to-day role but Ian Jeffery, with his vast experience, was an impossible act to follow. Whether they were prepared to discuss it or not, AC/DC badly needed help. It arrived in the shape of a suave middle-aged Londoner named Stewart Young. Young had been the manager of Emerson, Lake & Palmer through their peak years in the Seventies, working alongside Phil Carson at Atlantic – who he had once been flatmates with. He had also managed Billy Squire through his successful period with the American hit albums *Don't Say No* (No. 5, 1981), *Emotions In Motion* (No. 5, 1982), and *Signs Of Life* (No. 11, 1984). More recently, he had overseen the American success of British pop-rockers Tears For Fears, whose album, *Songs From The Chair*, had been one of the biggest-selling hits of the year, reaching No. 1 in the US, as well as spawning two No. 1 singles in 'Shout' and 'Everyone Wants To Rule The World'. Stewart had just finished that cycle and was enjoying some down-time with his wife Gillian at the Parker Meridian hotel in New York when he bumped into Alvin Handwerker in the lobby. Handwerker was also Stewart's accountant; they had known each other for over 10 years. When he asked if Stewart would like to meet Malcolm and Angus Young, he said, 'Why not?' They sat and had tea and had a chat and, 'didn't talk anything about music'. At the time, Young was interested in Australian gold-mining shares. 'We just talked a bit like that and then I went. About fifteen minutes later, Alvin called me and he said, "Would you like to meet Malcolm and Angus?" I said, well, I've just met them. He said, "No, no. Would you like to *properly* meet them?" So I went down to their room and we had a business meeting.'

A pleasingly understated character with a so-dry-as-to-be-almost-charred sense of humour, Young claims he 'can't remember anything about' his time working with AC/DC. But he doesn't disagree when I suggest he has always enjoyed a reputation in the music business as a shrewd operator. If he wasn't in possession of all the facts about AC/DC when he went to meet them 'properly' he knew enough to know they were in trouble. He knew their latest album, *Fly On The Wall*, 'was out and hadn't been hugely successful, by their standards. They were on tour, which wasn't doing great, by their standards. I think they'd just had a European tour cancelled ...' He adds: 'At that stage I also understood that they were probably suspicious of any kind of managers, as most artists are. And I'm always suspicious of working with artists. Not because of anything other than, for it to work for me it has to be a relationship where you don't feel ill at ease if you go out for a cup of tea. I don't like it to be just a plain business situation.'

When, finally, amid the chitchat, Handwerker popped the question: 'Would you like to be involved?' Young replied: 'I would love to be.' However, his love was not as yet unconditional. 'I said, "You don't know me and I don't know you. Why don't we try and just experiment. Work together for two or three months, get to know each other, and see." And Alvin or one of them said, "What would that cost?" I said, "I don't care. Let me know what you wanna do. It doesn't matter to me. It's three months and the way I look upon it is, if you don't like me for any reason, there's no harm done. And vice versa. But if you like me, it's a way of doing it. You come up with [an offer] and whatever you come up with I'll accept."'

Young recalls ruefully how the brothers looked at him 'a little surprised'. But when Handwerker called Stewart again later that night, he told him: 'They wanna do it.' Still amusingly evasive, Young says he 'can't remember what he said about money but he said something and I said, "Fine." And he said, "They want you to start tomorrow."'

Stewart had been about to return home to London the following day, but Alvin said the band was insistent. Offering to pay for Stewart to stay on in the hotel for the next few weeks while he got used to being the new manager of AC/DC. Shrewdly, Young realised from the start that his own previous successes with other artists would count for nothing. 'From AC/DC's point of view, none of that mattered. What happened was we had a good, down to earth meeting and they were struggling at that time. They knew they needed help, and the fact that I was able to say I don't need a contract, let's see if we like each other after three months, they loved that. After about two months we knew we were gonna work together, and we did almost for ten years or so.'

What attracted the veteran manager to what on paper to many looked like an act now in steep decline, he says, was the fact that 'they are one of the greatest acts – or were when I met them – that's been there. Business can go up and business can go down but if you're great you're always gonna be great. For me it was a no-brainer. In fact Atlantic Records tried to stop me doing it, telling me they were finished. Doug Morris said to me, "I can introduce you to Paul Rodgers. You can work with Paul." I said, "It's very kind of you. I know Paul; I took him to Japan in '73 [as support act] with ELP. So I could call him myself. But, no, no, I like this band." The band was great, no doubt about it. They may have lost their confidence at that time because tickets were less, record sales were less. But there was something about them I just loved, and I thought: they'll bounce back.'

With four Youngs now playing a lead role in revitalising the career of AC/DC, the first project they took on together was an offer, in January 1986, to provide the soundtrack for the new Stephen King movie, *Maximum Overdrive*, based on his story 'Trucks', from the *Nightshift* story collection. 'Stephen King was a huge AC/DC fan.

But Atlantic tried to sell him on some of their other acts. Like, oh, AC/DC don't do that. But somebody knew me, gave me a call and I had a word with the boys. So we went and had a meeting with Stephen.' The result was their most successful album since their commercial heyday.

The lead song, 'Who Made Who', generated a fair amount of publicity, reaching a number of year-end Top 10 lists. Born from a riff Malcolm had demoed alone at home, the only stumbling block was the pounding drum intro – which became, ironically, the most memorable thing about the song. Recalls Simon Wright: 'There were a couple of ideas about how it should start. Then it got stripped down to just me and Cliff. That was when Harry and George came in and they were sort of steering the ship quite a lot.'

Something that had been arranged at the request of their new manager, Stewart Young: 'I listened to *Flick Of The Switch* and *Fly On The Wall* and there was something wrong with the way they sounded, especially the vocals. And they had produced those records themselves. But I said, "Do you still speak to George …"' The brothers said they weren't sure he'd do it. There were matters of pride involved. But when Stewart called George in Oz, 'He said, "For my brothers, no problem."' That's when he came in and they did 'Who Made Who'.

Using the extravagant movie budget to fly them out to the Bahamas, back in fact to the studio of their greatest triumph, *Back In Black*, but somewhere where neither George nor Harry had worked before, Young cleverly got the best out of his new charges. There were also two other instrumental tracks, 'Chase The Ace' and 'DT', which when added to the new title song and choice selections from *Back In Black*, *For Those About To Rock*, *Fly On The Wall* and the underappreciated Bon Scott classic, 'Ride On', became the album *Who Made Who*, released in May. It didn't crack the US Top 30, but would go on to sell five million copies over time. It was, without the band acknowledging it, even to themselves, essentially the kind of best-of collection they had always railed against releasing, going all the way back to the aborted *12 Of The Best* nearly a decade before.

There was also their first serious foray into video. With the MTV video revolution then in full swing, but with AC/DC's participation up until then having been of the lowly as-live variety, this was to be their first big-production MTV video. Shot at Brixton Academy in London, where hundreds of fan club members dressed as Angus were marshalled into choreographical shape by Arlene Phillips, and directed, at Stewart Young's inspired suggestion, by no lesser figure than David Mallet, whose groundbreaking work on David Bowie's 1980 'Ashes To Ashes' promo virtually invented the language of video in the Eighties, 'Who Made Who' introduced AC/DC to a whole new generation of rock and metal fans that barely knew who Bon Scott was or had been. Only that this cool new band had a far-out school guy wailing away on the guitar for them.

Stewart Young also earned kudos from the band by forcing the film's producer, the legendary Italian cineaste Dino De Laurentiis, to finance it. 'I had a lot of fights with Dino, but ended up becoming great friends with him.' When De Laurentiis said he wanted the song publishing, Stewart told him: 'Are you crazy? He said, "That's what we do in this business." Really? I got up to walk out, cos I didn't give a fuck. He was like, "No, wait, have a cigar ..." So then I wound him up for this video, got him to pay a huge budget. For me it was vintage,' he goes on, 'having George and Harry to produce it. And I used [the soundtrack] album as an opportunity to put some of the great songs on it. There had never been a best-of AC/DC album before and there hasn't been one since, to my knowledge. So it was a clever ruse.'

When they went out on tour in America to capitalise on this new-found success – 41 arena shows in just 51 days throughout August and September – 'I convinced them that we should tart up the show a bit. At first they thought it was a bit tacky. I said, "No, no, no. We're just gonna put a little bit of polish on it. It'll be cool." Because obviously they are very rootsy, but that's how we got Angus into wearing a velvet [schoolboy] suit. Before that it was always those scruffy things. Not that there was anything wrong with that.' But it was now the Eighties, the game had changed, stage shows had moved on. 'I just felt that I needed to make them look bigger. So we came up with a much more modern stage set.'

The show would start each night with 'Who Made Who'. The week before each show the local radio station would have a contest for Angus lookalikes. An event would take place, broadcast by radio, and the 10 best, who could look and dance and mime like Angus, would get to stand onstage and start the show each night, miming along, dressed as Angus, to 'Who Made Who'. It was the 1976 Lock Up Your Daughters tour brought back to life bigger than ever a decade on.

'All the radio stations went crazy. They always did competitions where you could win records or tickets or even get to meet the band. But how many do you get where the winner actually gets to play onstage with AC/DC – dressed as Angus? The first Angus would come on and the crowd would go wild because they thought it really was Angus. Then the second guy would come on and now they're confused. Followed by a third guy and a fourth … like, what the fuck's going on? It was a great competition and it really fired up [ticket sales]. We were starting to kick serious arse. But it was a nightmare for the crew, who hated me for it. Some of these competition winners, they were getting drunk, we couldn't get them off the stage. We'd have to chase them off! It was great. But I think that actually put [AC/DC] back.'

Not wanting to spoil the rekindled magic, Stewart Young arranged for George and Harry to come in and produce what would be the band's next major album, to be titled *Blow Up Your Video*, in mock rebellion against the prevailing orthodoxy that bands could only make it now on MTV. It was true and AC/DC would do everything they could to fit in with that, bringing David Mallet back for all three promo videos that would ensue from the album. But it was a neat marketing gimmick and something for local radio stations, who all abhorred the waning of their influence in the face of the colossus that was now music video television.

Recorded at Miraval Studios in the south of France, they set out to right the ship that had blown so far off course. Nevertheless, it would prove to be an album of lasts: it would be the last record where Brian would write the band's lyrics and their last time recording with Simon Wright. While *Blow Up Your Video* will never be regarded as one of their better outings, it nonetheless delivered what they needed: a powerful anthem in the form of 'Heatseeker', on which George and Harry re-created a sense of unchecked fury not seen since *For Those About To Rock*. The aptly named 'That's The Way I Wanna Rock 'N' Roll' was a groovy, booty-shaking counterpoint to 'Heatseeker' that created a commercially potent one-two punch. Like all AC/DC albums of this post-Mutt period, however, the hits on *Blow Up Your Video* were couched in yawn-inducing filler, although the two singles proved more than enough to push the boys back into the spotlight. Indeed, the album earned them a Grammy nomination, although they lost out to the giant-slaying Jethro Tull that year, for Tull's *Crest Of A Knave*. Not that anyone from AC/DC went to the Grammys. 'The thing is,' says Simon Wright, 'it's like a working man's band. It's like a job. Their attitude is, well, we've finished one song, we'd better start another one up. They didn't seem overwhelmed by anything. It was just their work ethic. Okay, we finished another show, let's do another one tomorrow. I don't think they were affected by a hell of a lot of other things outside of that. They weren't bowled over by nominations, it was just simple, pure, working-class kind of attitude.'

Released in July 1987, 'Maybe it wasn't the best album they did,' Stewart Young concedes, but it did the trick and suddenly they were heading back up the US charts for the first time since *For Those About To Rock* seven years of bad luck before. 'The problem with a band like that is you're always competing with your past. When you've got so many unbelievable songs, how can you have a [new] song that's gonna stand up with that?' *Blow Up Your Video* was eventually certified platinum in the US, where it peaked at No. 12, topping off at 4 in the UK. Interestingly, the band would play only six UK shows in support of the album, followed in March by 20 European dates. Whatever reassurances their commercial successes offered were muted by Malcolm's realisation that he was powerless over alcohol and that he could no longer function adequately within AC/DC.

The signs had been there for years. Unlike his teetotal younger brother, Malcolm had always been fond of 'the hooch'. Like most musicians of his generation he had sampled drugs along the way, but never really taken a shine to anything stronger than weed and dope. But booze – beer and wine and whisky and, latterly, vodka – had played a longer-lasting role in his life as the years swept by and he became able to afford the best that money could buy. That had all been – or seemed – fine when AC/DC were on a roll, their career towering to ever greater heights. But as the slump years of the late Eighties took hold, his drinking became more of a consolation at first, then merely fuel to feed his anger and frustration at the band's stalled career in America. Now with a six-month US tour looming, Malcolm finally threw in the towel and announced that he needed a break. Official cause given: 'nervous exhaustion'. Unofficially, behind the scenes, insiders now claim he was putting away a bottle of vodka a day and that the turning point came when his doctor told him he would be dead in a year if he continued. According to Malcolm though, he was just 'shagged out [and] getting really stale, not interested – a low point in my life'. It wasn't the amount he was drinking that was the problem, he insisted in 2004, it was that he 'drank consistently and it caught right up on me and I lost the plot. Angus was going, "I'm your brother; I don't want to see you dead here. Remember Bon?" So I took that break and cleaned myself up.'

Says Stewart Young now: 'Malcolm definitely had a drinking problem and so he decides he has to take a year out of the band.' Things had grown so bad between Malcolm and Angus before the break, Young recalls them fighting. 'There was definitely an argument because of his drinking. Angus had a go at him. Because Angus was teetotal.' He remembers seeing Angus at breakfast the next morning with a black eye. He asked him what happened and Angus told him he'd had a go at his brother Mal because of his drinking. 'I said, "Well, he beat the shit out of you, didn't he, fucking hell!" And Angus looked all sheepish. At that moment Malcolm comes down and he's got two black eyes! But they sit down talking because they're brothers, you know, they love each other. And I can't help thinking that may have contributed to Mal's decision. He didn't give up the smoking but he did give up the drinking.'

In the past decade, AC/DC had survived all manner of rock'n'roll destruction; they would transcend the absence of Malcolm as well. Calling in their nephew Stevie Young, formerly of the Starfighters, to take over from his uncle on the US tour, they rehearsed for 10 days in Boston, then set out that May to conquer the United States. With his strong resemblance to his uncle, and his agreed unobtrusiveness onstage, the band was relieved to discover very few fans even realised Malcolm wasn't onstage. Many critics also failed to notice, reviewing the shows without mention of the loss of the member the band itself regarded as its most important. Indeed, the band disingenuously kept details of Stevie's joining them for the tour to a bare minimum. If you didn't ask or know already, they were not about to spell it out. After many of the shows, Stevie was asked by fans to autograph their shirts 'Malcolm'. The subsequent tour of the US netted them a cool $20 million for the 110 shows they played in just over a hundred cities. Still, though, with the end of another decade, came the feeling that perhaps AC/DC's best days were behind them. Privately, Brian Johnson admitted to friends he had lost some of his enthusiasm, especially for songwriting. All out of double-entendres, overloaded already with reams of songs about cops firing guns, women burning up and pinks being repeatedly sunk, the 42-year-old singer wondered aloud – when others weren't listening – how much longer he could keep going for.

For 26-year-old Simon Wright, however, the novelty had definitely worn off. 'Things had changed a bit in the band. Things I wasn't privy to but slowly became aware of. It kind of was a weird time. I was just doing my thing, kind of going along with things.' As he says, 'If I'd questioned what was actually going on with the workings of the band I'd have been a fool. I was pretty dumb and full of come and all that but I wasn't stupid. It was made apparent how things were run there and that's the way they wanted to run it and it was fine by me.'

When, though, at the end of 1989, he was presented with an opportunity to play with another band, former Rainbow and Black Sabbath singer Ronnie James Dio's own eponymously named outfit, Wright jumped at it. He admits it was partly through boredom. 'Being a drummer [in AC/DC], it can be a bit of a challenge with the drumming that you sort of leave out. I think I'd moved on a little. I wanted to expand my horizons, as a musician, as a drummer. That's basically it. I think I'd become a little bit complacent with the whole thing.' Feelings that had not gone unnoticed by the brothers, either. 'They started to see this in me as well and it was ... I'd been in rehearsals [with Dio] and they heard about it ...'

Was there a part of him that was rebelling against the way AC/DC did things? 'I think there might have been, yeah. There was that, too. The way Phil plays ... it's really solid and it's really tight and it works in that band a treat. And I tried to do my best to make sure that things were rocking and keep them to the standard of the way Phil played. But after a while I just started to play a little bit more. It's just a natural thing, it just kind of happened. I just needed to do more on the drums and experiment a bit more and spread my wings. I had this stuff that was bottled up inside of me that I needed to do, that I needed to play. Just kind of get it out and play.'

He joined Dio, he says, because 'He let you be yourself. He let you take over the drum chair. He had total faith in me and I never forgot that. Because he gave me the chance to show a different side of me and let a bunch of stuff out that I could do, musically.' Compared to playing in AC/DC for all those years, 'It was a breath of fresh air, really, at that point. I don't want to take anything away from AC/DC but I was very pleased with the outcome of [the album he recorded with Dio] Lock Up The Wolves.'

Who left who? 'It wasn't very clear-cut at all. It was more of a feeling between both parties. It wasn't really talked about. There wasn't that time in the morning or afternoon when I called them or they called me. It just kind of became apparent that they were gonna be around and I wasn't gonna be around.' It all came to a head with a phone call from Stewart Young. 'I'd already established myself in a situation with Ronnie that I felt really comfortable with, and it didn't come as a surprise.' He admits, surprisingly, however, that he never spoke with Young directly. That in fact, it was his wife that Young spoke to on the phone. 'He talked to my wife at the time.' And he told her? 'Yeah. I said I was busy or something, I can't remember. And, yeah, that's just basically the way it went down.'

Any regrets now? 'No ... I really don't have any regrets. It was just one of those things, I think both parties felt they should part ways. And it just happened like that. There is a need for that phone call because you have to put a final full-stop at the end of the sentence, so to speak. But it's like I already had stuff going on, and was moving on and moving forward and so ... you know ...'

CHAPTER SIXTEEN

Last Chance To See

There is no happy ending to the AC/DC story. There is no ending at all. Like their music, sublime in its molecular surety that there is only one way to do things, AC/DC go on for ever, the great white shark of the music world, its eyes never blinking, its hungry snout pushing ever forwards, whether you like it or not, mate. Even as the Young brothers approach old age and inevitable infirmity the image of the ever-youthful schoolboy duck-walking his too-large guitar across that big stage in the pixelated sky grows more embedded in the popular consciousness with every YouTube click or CD flick we make.

Ted Albert died of cancer in 1990, just as the first signs of AC/DC's imminent ubiquity were occurring. Having somehow survived the self-harming years that followed the death of Bon Scott and the utterly unplanned for, unrepeatable and ultimately insurmountable success of *Back In Black*, the name AC/DC began to mean something new to whoever used it.

Newsweek reported in 1989 that when the Berlin wall came down in November that year and the newly liberated East Germans poured across the former border to gobble up consumer goods, their top music purchase was not The Beatles, nor Bob Dylan, nor even Mozart and Beethoven. It was AC/DC. When just weeks later, the murdering, drug-trafficking, money-laundering General Manuel Noriega fled the invasion of Panama by United States military forces, he was discovered hiding out at the Apostolic Nunciature, having claimed refuge at the Holy See's diplomatic mission. Unable to simply go in and get him, US forces drew up their tanks on the lawns and waved their guns, sending explosions around the compound. When that didn't work, they came up with a more cunning idea. They placed giant hi-fi speakers atop the tanks and aimed them at the embassy's windows. Then began to play *Highway To Hell* and *Back In Black*, among others, very, very, very loud. It was New Year's Day, 1990. Within 48 hours the mad, bad old general had surrendered.

Meanwhile, back on planet Earth, second-wavers of rock like The Cult and the Beastie Boys – led by a Young brothers disciple named Rick Rubin – began simply to absorb and regurgitate the Bon years: the stabbing riff from 'Rock'n'Roll Singer' used for 'Wild Flower'; the jab it in your eye lick from 'High Voltage' used for 'Fight For Your Right To Party'. 'I was in the studio in New York one time and Rubin was in the next studio, sitting there with all these AC/DC albums on the desk in front of him, using them to make sure he'd got the drums and guitar right,' remembers Tony Platt, with astonishment. 'They were like his template for the future.' When in the early Nineties the grunge generation took rock back to ground zero, levelling everybody from Guns N' Roses to Def Leppard in their wake, their leading lights still spoke in hushed tones of AC/DC and their evil ways: Nirvana's Kurt Cobain explaining the first song he ever learned to play on guitar was 'Back In Black'; Alice In Chains' heavy-lidded leader Jerry Cantrell describing Angus Young as 'the absolute god of real rock guitar'.

Of course, being AC/DC, a band lost in its own sightless cosmology almost from the day it was born, nobody in the band, with the occasional exception of Angus, seemed to notice any of this. At least, not at first ...

Fortunately, they now had people around them that had taken notice of all these things and more. There was Stewart Young, giving them their most proactive day-to-day manager since the Peter Mensch years; and at record company level, they were about to stumble upon a replacement, finally, for the long-departed Phil Carson; that is, someone who actually gave a damn. His name was Derek Shulman, a former singer and multi-instrumentalist for the British progressive rock group Gentle Giant, and latterly one of the fast-rising executives in the American record industry, responsible for signing superstar American acts like Bon Jovi, Kingdom Come and Cinderella. That had been for Polygram. When Steve Ross, newly installed god of Time Warner, owners of Atlantic Records and their various imprints, offered Shulman the opportunity to reactivate its ailing Atco label by becoming its new president and CEO, he took it.

One of Shulman's first meetings in his new post was with his opposite number at Atlantic, Doug Morris. Aware of Shulman's successes in the Eighties with rock giants like Bon Jovi, Morris came straight to the point: would he be interested in swapping some of the artists on Atco for some of the Atlantic roster? Shulman was intrigued, who did Morris mean exactly? 'Doug said he felt close to Stevie Nicks, and was interested in working with her again,' Shulman recalls now from his New York home. 'He offered me Bad Company, as an internal trade, for Stevie Nicks.' With Paul Rodgers no longer fronting the British supergroup, Morris was happy to see them go. Shulman, however, rated the potential of their new singer, Brian Howe, and agreed to the trade. It was a shrewd move; their first album on Atco, *Holy Water*, would go platinum. The other act Morris didn't feel had a shot any more, he told Shulman, was AC/DC. 'I said, "AC/DC are great." He said, "Well, they're not so great, I'm thinking of dropping them."' *Blow Up Your Video* may have been their best-selling album for years but as Shulman explains, 'The deal was pretty expensive and the implication was they didn't really have a future at Atlantic.'

Aware that Stewart Young and his business partner, Steve Barnett, had now come into the picture as managers, Shulman considered it a gamble worth taking. Where Morris saw an ageing band past its sales peak, Shulman saw a challenge. 'I knew that the band didn't really get on with the Atlantic people, that no one from Atlantic during that period – literally no one – was allowed in the studio at all at any time. Malcolm and Angus just did not want them there any more.'

So out of touch had Atlantic become with the group Phil Carson had signed all those years before, they had recently called Stewart Young in for a meeting where it was suggested AC/DC might like to make their own 'power ballad', in an attempt to further stall their own commercial mudslide: *Blow Up Your Video* had returned AC/DC to the upper reaches of the world's charts, but they hadn't cracked the US Top 10 for a decade. Stewart Young recalls: 'This was when there were all these bands on MTV with blond hair singing ballads. I mentioned it to Ang. He said, "You know, a ballad, Stewart, they're for people that are in pain. Forget about ballads, we do rock records." Mal said, "We'll do things that are true and if they're successful it's good. If we're not successful, I'm not gonna feel like a fucking idiot for doing that stupid song that I've got to live with for the next twenty years." They had very clear views.'

When, not long after, an exasperated Doug Morris asked Derek Shulman if he'd be willing to trade Pete Townshend for AC/DC, 'I said I'd be happy to. Much as I like Pete, AC/DC were for me the quintessential punk-slash-rock band. I mean, they're it. I loved the band.' Shrewdly, Shulman had decided he could make it work because 'the fan-base hadn't eroded, it was just the records hadn't been as good as they used to be. I knew there could have been a way to make their record and their branding much, much better than they had done on their own.'

Shulman also had another ace in his hand: like the Young family, he was from Glasgow. The same age as George, what's more, he'd known him in The Easybeats, who his first group, Simon Dupree and the Big Sound, had played shows with, in the Sixties. 'Stewart is a curmudgeon but he understood that I could break through the dynamic of these very, very insular, very private people because I knew the players involved and because I was a musician. They could trust me – that's the word. They're extremely clannish. You're either totally in or you're totally out. The inner circle is very tight, extremely close-knit, very family-oriented, and you have to have their trust, and they have to believe you're not bullshitting because they can see through that stuff.' Shulman also understood something else: 'They loved money. Their bank accounts are very, very fat. And I admire that Glaswegian trait in their character.'

Sessions for the next AC/DC album had already begun in Ireland – another tax haven – at Dublin's Windmill Lane Studios, with George

Young again at the controls. There was a new drummer in place, too. The 44-year-old Welsh-born Chris Slade had cut his teeth as a sideman for Tom Jones in the Sixties; his very first live appearance backing Jones while supporting the Rolling Stones. Slade played with his countryman for seven years, before quitting to briefly join Tomorrow, fronted by Olivia Newton-John. Slade went on to co-found Manfred Mann's Earth Band, where he stayed for six years and three UK Top 10 hits ('Joybringer', 'Blinded By The Light', 'Davy's On The Road Again'), before bouncing around medium-profile gigs, studio work, tours (with Pink Floyd's David Gilmour) and a particularly juicy opportunity to play with Jimmy Page's The Firm, which went on to soar comfortably beneath all expectations. It was while Slade was on tour with Gary Moore – then managed by Stewart Young's business partner, Steve Barnett – that Malcolm caught their set live, and from that moment Slade was the leading candidate for the AC/DC drumming vacancy, eventually skating through the audition and into the role on a part-time basis at first, though ultimately becoming a full-timer.

The band spent five weeks in Dublin before throwing in the towel. With Brian Johnson mired in a gruelling divorce, Malcolm and Angus took up the slack and wrote the lyrics themselves: a job they would retain through subsequent releases. Much harder to deal with was the fact that George was not working out. As Stewart Young recalls, 'George was having a personal problem with his daughter and he kind of wasn't there. He wasn't one hundred per cent. He was very worried about his daughter, and it was going terribly, really terribly. I had to sit down with the boys and say, "I'm not sure what's happened here."' They weren't sure either. Stewart said he would talk to George. 'I went out for a drink with George and I told him. It was a relief for him because he could go and deal with his family thing. He found it very, very difficult. He was happy to be fired.'

Derek approached a producer he'd recently had great success with: Bruce Fairbairn. Canadian Fairbairn had earned a reputation as a Midas-fingered studio titan after polishing Bon Jovi's 1986 breakthrough album *Slippery When Wet* into a commercial juggernaut, ultimately moving well in excess of 20 million copies. Bon Jovi returned the favour by bringing him back for their 1988 follow-up, *New Jersey*, which yielded five US Top 10 singles and skipped straight into multi-platinum status. Fairbairn's work with Aerosmith throughout the same period revealed a canny intuition for coaxing new tricks out of tired old dogs. It was this latter quality that appeared to make him uniquely qualified for the task of recording AC/DC at this late stage. Aerosmith's 1989 Fairbairn-produced album, *Pump*, had been their first Top 10 hit in America since their Seventies heyday and with accumulative worldwide sales of over eight million, the biggest of their career. When Shulman called Fairbairn about doing the same for AC/DC it was a no-brainer. 'Bruce said he wanted to do it, would love to do it, so I put them together.'

Says Stewart Young: 'They liked him because he was organised. Bit nine-to-five but a nice guy. It took a bit of time and then the atmosphere was great and things suddenly kind of lifted off.' They started again from the beginning, with the Ireland sessions forgotten. They loved Fairbairn's engineer, Mike Fraser, too, so much they have continued to work with him ever since. 'Bruce was very cognisant of who they were and how they were and he was able to allow them to be themselves and do what they wanted until it got to something he wasn't sure about, then he would suggest they try something a little different. Because he was a musician himself that helped enormously I think.' Bruce was also a Scotsman. 'All the clans and the tartans in the studio together,' Stewart chuckles. 'They're Glaswegian kids that went to Australia but they're not Australian, they're Scotsmen. That background in Scotland is very, very strong – in their music too, actually.'

The result was *The Razors Edge*: the best AC/DC album since *For Those About To Rock*. Released in January 1991, it also became their best-selling for a decade. Dante Bonutto was the band's record company product manager in London at the time. He remembers being invited over to Stewart Young's King's Road office to hear the album for the first time. 'He told me to go downstairs and sit in his Lexus and listen to the tape of *The Razors Edge*,' Bonutto recalls. 'As soon as I heard "Thunderstruck" I knew it was a big return for them. The Lexus was literally shaking as I played it. I thought they should have called the album *Thunderstruck*, actually. I believe it was discussed at one point but they didn't go with it in the end. But we all knew that "Thunderstruck" was the key track.'

Stewart Young felt the same way, identifying 'Thunderstruck' as the crucial jumping-off point for the album from the first time he heard the demo. 'That opening riff, once you hear that, you're in.' But when the label wanted to rush-release the album in time for Christmas, so they could get their end-of-year bonuses, Stewart put his foot down. 'I said, "I'm sorry, but this album's got to be set up properly. It's a worldwide record. This record's going to bring them back. I can't rush this album just because you want to get the money in your bin." They were like, "It's got nothing to do with that, Stewart!" Anyway I said, "No, no, no ..."'

The Razors Edge marauded onto the world's charts behind explosive sales and torrents of mainstream radio spins. While the album would never threaten *Highway To Hell* or *Back In Black* as an all-time classic, it was a blistering set of dirty rockers, with plenty of mountain-sized hooks, serpentine solos and four-on-the-floor rhythms; although as is the case with every album of the Brian era, it was not without its misses: 'Mistress For Christmas' – 'written about Donald Trump', according to Stewart Young – being the lowlight.

Most notable is 'Rock Your Heart Out', which features a drum and bass pattern so funky that were it not for Brian Johnson's wheezing vocals, you wouldn't imagine that you were listening to AC/DC: the most adventurous, and thus most un-AC/DC, part of the album. Tracks like 'Fire Your Guns' and 'Shot Of Love' cemented the album as above-average, and taken with the first two singles countered any criticism that their songs all sounded the same. In fact, these five songs establish that while their tone might not change, AC/DC remained as good as any band at shifting tempos and building momentum to craft very different rhythmic patterns from the same sonic cloth.

There was a second hit single in the track 'Moneytalks': the vapid tale of a wealthy guy dangling his 'wallet' in front of a young vixen, the sing-along chorus and bouncing rhythm putting AC/DC firmly back in touch with its populist mainstream sensibilities, and becoming the last major hit single they would have. As a result, *The Razors Edge* peaked at No. 2 in the US charts (bested only by M.C. Hammer's *Please Hammer Don't Hurt 'Em*) and No. 4 in the UK. With global sales now well in excess of 11 million copies it ranks as the fourth highest-selling in the group's catalogue (behind *Back In Black*, *Highway To Hell* and *Dirty Deeds*).

The resulting world tour was their biggest money-spinner yet, dwarfing the $20 million gross for the previous *Blow Up Your Video* jaunt. Not everything ran to plan, though. Tickets for the 18 January 1991 AC/DC show at Salt Lake City's Salt Palace sold out quickly, with fans queuing overnight for a shot at one of the $18 tickets. The venue held just north of 13,000, including 4,400 general admission tickets. However, for three of these fans, their General Admission tickets proved fatal. Like the 1979 Who concert in Cincinnati, where 11 fans were trampled to death early in the show, as the crowd pushed towards the front to connect with the band, three teenagers – Jimmie Boyd Jr, 14, Curtis White Child, 14, and Elizabeth Glausi, 19 – were felled and then trampled to death, while the band played on. In a country as litigious as the United States, that they would find themselves in court was a certainty, but ultimately they were dropped from a wrongful-death suit and settled the remainder of the cases out of court.

As the year moved on, the tour regained momentum and by August they were headlining the Monsters Of Rock tour, again headlining the festival at Castle Donington in England in front of over 70,000 raging punters. Filmed in 35mm by David Mallet, using 22 cameras, front, side and back, the resulting live video remains an unqualified masterpiece. Along with the live double album that accompanied it, simply titled *AC/DC: Live*, it gave AC/DC their second huge success of the Nineties. 'It brought them back everywhere,' says Stewart Young. '*The Razors Edge* started the process, and the live album and video completed it.' This, he says, despite the fact that Angus was so distraught about the way his guitar was feeding back throughout the Castle Donington appearance. 'I went to see him afterwards and he was in tears. He was so upset. I said, "Ang, it was great!" He wouldn't buy it at all …'

Amazingly, this legendary show was simply a starter for what lay before them at Tushino Airfield, just outside of Moscow, on 28 September 1991, when they played to over 500,000 fans at a free concert that also included Metallica, Pantera and The Black Crowes. Some reports place attendance in excess of one million, but verifying such numbers is a logistical and historical impossibility. Stewart recalls worrying whether it would rain on the day. The weather that week had been unpredictable. He was assured, on the eve of the show, however, by a Russian official he says he is still not sure was being serious or not: 'Fear not. There will be no rain. We are doing something about the clouds now.' The implication: Moscow had the technology to somehow stall the rain – for 24 hours at least.

Elsewhere on the Monsters festival dates, the band ran into an old friend. Now working as the tour manager for Metallica, Ian Jeffery was left in no doubt where he now stood in Malcolm Young's estimation. 'After Metallica had finished, I'd sit outside the dressing room to make sure nobody went in. Malcolm sent messages through AC/DC's security, "Throw him out the venue. Don't want to see his fucking face." They would come down to me, "Ian, don't know what to say here, mate, but you gotta go." I said, "I'm doing my job. I don't care about AC/DC, I work for Metallica now. I'm not going anywhere." It was horrible. So it was really uncomfortable that whole tour. Then Brian, one time, when we were walking onto the stage, he came out of the dressing room and sort of put his hand out and said, "Hey, how you doing there, lad?" I just walked past him, didn't even fucking answer him. I felt like, there was a time those years ago when you could have popped down [and said something] on any one of those two days after I was fired without anybody knowing. When it would have meant something …'

In New Zealand, during two shows marred by rain and near riots, during which two fans and a policeman were stabbed, another old friend put in an appearance: Phil Rudd. Unlike Ian, Phil was invited into the dressing room. Rudd had spent the preceding 10 years running a helicopter business in New Zealand. He made no secret, though, that should the band ever need a drummer …

With the unexpected large-scale success of *The Razors Edge*, from the outside looking in it seemed AC/DC would only need to keep their hands on the wheel to continue that upward trajectory. Instead, there would be only one more AC/DC studio album released in the Nineties and that – in a strange echo of the fall-out that occurred around *For Those About To Rock*, their last attempt at a follow-up to a significant hit – would be more memorable for events surrounding the album than anything recorded for it.

Arguably the most famous rock producer in the world by then, Rick Rubin had long let his passion for AC/DC be known. The studio guru who oversaw a stunning range of recent classics such as Slayer's *Reign In Blood*, Run DMC's *Raising Hell* and the Beastie Boys' *License to Ill*, told me in 1990 that he had two fantasies as a producer: working with AC/DC and Black Sabbath. In both cases, he dreamed of taking them back to their Seventies peaks. In AC/DC's case, specifically back to the Bon-era sound. Rubin finally got his shot at AC/DC just three years later, collaborating with them on the single 'Big Gun' for the soundtrack of *The Last Action Hero*, the abysmal box office flop starring a pre-governor Arnold Schwarzenegger.

Stewart Young tells an amusing story of how the future gubernator agreed to appear in the accompanying video. 'David Mallet was at a restaurant in London and he gets told that Arnold Schwarzenegger is on the phone for him. David hadn't told anybody to his knowledge that he was in this restaurant so how the guy got hold of him he doesn't know. Anyway he takes the call and the voice goes, "Hello!" It's Arnie. He says, "What's the idea then?" David tells him. "You're gonna be wearing a schoolboy suit, you're gonna have a guitar, an SG like Angus plays, and you're gonna be dancing across the stage and you're generally gonna make a cunt of yourself. But it's gonna be very, very cool." There's momentary silence followed by Arnold in that voice going, "I'll do it!"'

With Bruce Fairbairn already booked to make the next Van Halen album, AC/DC needed a new producer. Stewart Young suggested Brendan O'Brien, the former Georgia Satellites guitarist now turned producer *du jour* for grunge giants such as Pearl Jam and the Stone Temple Pilots. Angus, though, wanted to bring Rubin in again. Like everyone else, he had long noted Rubin's very public AC/DC love-in, and that he was now the producer of choice for so many stellar American acts. After his work on 'Big Gun', Rubin seemed a shoo-in for the gig. Hot off the back of his multi-platinum success with the Red Hot Chili Peppers' *BloodSugarSexMagick* album, and newly baptised critics' favourite after his work revitalising Johnny Cash's career with the first *American Recordings* album, Rubin was outspoken about his passion for all things AC/DC. 'When I was in junior high in 1979,' he told *Rolling Stone*, 'my classmates all liked Led Zeppelin. But I loved AC/DC. When I'm producing a rock band, I try to create albums that sound as powerful as *Highway To Hell*. Whether it's The Cult or the Red Hot Chili Peppers, I apply the same basic formula: keep it sparse. Make the guitar parts more rhythmic. It sounds simple, but what AC/DC did is almost impossible to duplicate. A great band like Metallica can play an AC/DC song note for note and they still wouldn't capture the tension and release that drives the music. There's nothing like it.'

When news broke that Phil Rudd would also be taking part in the album, it seemed the pieces were in place for a truly classic AC/DC album. Not that Chris Slade saw it like that. For, while there is no evidence that Slade got on poorly with the band, as they entered the writing process for the new album, Rudd's Auckland entreaty began to gnaw at Malcolm. His own feelings stirred by the thought that working with Rubin might provide some sort of musical time tunnel back to the place where it all began, he phoned Phil out of the blue and put it to him straight: would he like to fly to Malcolm's home in London and see if they still had the old chemistry? When, to nobody's surprise, they had lost zero in the way of chemistry, a unique situation arose – AC/DC had two drummers. Unwilling to make a decision, Malcolm apprised Chris of Phil's return and promised that his fate would be decided soon, although according to Chris 'soon' equated to weeks and then months, after which he finally resigned, disenchanted by the entire experience, later telling *Rock Hard* magazine in France: 'I was so disappointed, disgusted, that I didn't touch my drum kit for three years.' Despite several requests, Slade declined to be interviewed for this book. In August 1993, Phil officially rejoined the band. 'He just seemed just like the old Phil,' Malcolm later chirruped in *Mojo*. In New Zealand, 'He said, "Any time, you know, I'm ready ..." A couple of years later when we started on the album, me and Angus said, "Let's bring him down and have a jam and see how it goes, and it was just like the old days."'

Yet even with the old line-up back together, things started to go wrong for AC/DC almost immediately Rubin officially became involved – the name of the new album, *Ballbreaker*, growing more freakishly apt by the day. Malcolm had recently become enamoured of a funky New York studio named Pye, run by a friend, Perry Margouleff, who sometimes helped him chase down collectible guitars he wished to own. Pye had a vibe that strongly reminded Malcolm of the band's earliest days recording in the small room at Alberts' Kings Street studio. If Rubin's idea was to get them back to that kind of sound, what more perfect setting? He booked it with Perry. But when Rubin found out, he freaked and told them no way. 'I thought, what a shit. This guy really fucked me over,' says Margouleff. 'They booked my studio and he just told them that he wouldn't even show up.' For Rubin, there was only one place to record: his favoured crib at Ocean Way Studios, in LA. Instead, a compromise was reached that suited neither side: the band would record in New York, but at the Power Station.

Instead of recapturing their glory days in Australia, the band suddenly felt like they were back in Paris in 1981. Engineer Mike Fraser remembers: 'We could not get a drum sound. We tried a ton of different things to try to tame the room down. We put up baffles around the drums, nothing worked.' At one point they even hired a blue and yellow striped circus tent to set up around the drum kit. 'That was pretty funny – I wish we had a photo of it! We even tried bringing in a ton of burlap sacks that we had the studio staff staple onto all the walls. But no matter what, we just couldn't deaden the room enough.'

After 10 weeks of fruitless work, during which they still managed more than 50 hours of tape, none of which was eventually used on the album, Rubin finally got his way and the whole shebang moved to LA – 'which is where Rick wanted to record in the first place', according to Margouleff.

But while work at last started to progress at Ocean Way, new problems presented themselves. With Rubin now working concurrently on the next Red Hot Chili Peppers album – a clash of schedules occasioned, he reasoned, by the months wasted in New York – Fraser recalls how the producer would not arrive at Ocean Way until after 6pm most evenings. 'Quite often during the day we'd be sitting there, bored, and it would be like, "Why don't we just lay this song down and when Rick comes in he can check it out?" And they really didn't want to work that way. They said, "No, Rick's the producer ..." They're the kind of band they like to shoot off the hip. They didn't want to do something then have him come in and say they had to do it again.'

This continued until they had all the basic tracks done. Then Mike would sit there with Angus while he did the solos and with Brian while he did the vocals. 'We didn't worry about waiting for Rick too much at that point. But when it came to the band playing together, they wanted their producer there.' Behind the producer's back Malcolm called him Rasputin, complaining later: 'Working with [Rubin] was a mistake.'

Ballbreaker was released in September 1995 and while the band's sound is essentially the same, there are both subtle and obvious differences from its predecessor. Overtly, lyricists Malcolm and Angus tackle social commentary on songs like 'Burnin' Alive', about the incineration of the Branch Davidian complex in Waco, Texas, and 'Hail Caesar' takes on fire-and-brimstone religious fundamentalists with a thinly veiled parallel to Adolph Hitler. Not surprisingly, a number of people unencumbered by the gift of irony accused the band of promoting Nazism, which proved to be more of a passing headache than any lingering PR nightmare for the band. In fact, the lyrics are so simplistic that when one first hears the chorus, it can be difficult not to laugh at the song's unintentionally clumsy chorus:

'*I'm your furor baby*' Opener 'Hard As A Rock', with its snub-nosed groove, was more like it but that track alone couldn't save the album from being a disappointment. Never mind that *Ballbreaker* reached the Top 10 in both the British and American charts, Malcolm Young, thwarted in the studio he wished to work in, agitated no doubt by the fact Rubin had been Angus's first choice, not his, and deeply un-impressed by the way Rubin handled things in LA, decided the responsibility for these frustrations, as always, lay with the manager. Stewart Young was fired in February 1996, at the end of the first leg of the US tour, just as the band were about to fly down for sold-out shows in Mexico.

He got the phone call from Alvin. 'I was told that my presence wasn't required. He said to me, basically, they don't want you any more. So we're gonna split.' Did he say why? 'No. No.' Do you have any theories? 'I'm not into theories.' Did you see it coming? Long pause. 'Not really. There were a few things that had occurred, maybe misinterpretations or misunderstandings. But the bottom line was: if somebody doesn't wanna work with me, I don't wanna work with them. I couldn't see the point in discussing it. Of course, I wasn't happy to hear it, I'd always enjoyed working with them, and Alvin's a friend of mine, so it was a shock. But at the end of the day, you can't force somebody to work with you if they don't wanna work with you. Of course I've thought of it, but there's nothing I would wanna tell you, because if I was really honest with myself, I've no idea.'

In common with every other former AC/DC manager, Stewart Young has had next to no contact with anyone from the band since. He has never been to see them play, because he doesn't want to 'make them uncomfortable'. He spoke to Angus by accident once since. His wife Ellen had called to wish Stewart and his family a happy Christmas, but Stewart missed the call, and when he called back Angus answered the phone – by mistake. 'We spoke for a few moments which was nice, very friendly, like the old days. And I bumped into Mal's wife a few times because they used to live near her, always very friendly. But no, no real contact …'

Does that make you sad? Another long pause. 'Ah … it would be nice to see them. I wouldn't say I was sad about it though. Sad might be the wrong word ...'

In the nearly two decades that have passed since Rick Rubin promised and failed to bring AC/DC back to their glorious past, there have been but two 'new' AC/DC albums. The inverted commas invoked here because, as Angus Young once jokingly admitted, 'we put out the same album every year with a different cover'. More precisely, AC/DC stopped doing anything new with their music the day they stopped working with Mutt Lange – which was also, coincidentally, the last time they put out a new album every year.

Instead they have found their own, much more reliable way of rekindling past glories: they put out compilations, live DVDs, soundtracks, video albums and box sets. The band that once baulked at the suggestion of putting out a compilation album called *12 Of The Best* have put out nearly a dozen such collections since *Ballbreaker* failed to do what it said on the tin in 1995. Let's be clear: there is nothing wrong with this. Indeed, it is the modern way. We live in the classic rock era, a pan-generational phenomenon that means we don't actually care about new albums. Why should we when what we really crave more than anything in this post-internet, mobile-device-driven future-now are pathways to the most sought after yet hard to find commodity of the 21st century: authenticity. More than the limited pleasures of pushing the boat out and making new albums, AC/DC now offer us access to the golden-haloed past, when rock was young and larrikins like Bon Scott ran around with a shark's tooth earring and a coke spoon round his neck.

Of course, appearances have to be kept up and like their nearest cousins, the Rolling Stones, AC/DC will deign to record a 'new' album every once in a lifetime. In 2000 there was *Stiff Upper Lip*. Like their previous releases, they would release three singles from it – the title track, 'Safe In New York City' (which one year later would ring tragically ironic) and 'Satellite Blues'. Its real USP, though, was that once again it was produced by George Young – more than ably assisted, in small print, by the trusty Mike Fraser, which explains why the handful of tracks worth hearing sounded okay to listen to in the car. The days of George taking the controls while Harry sat at his shoulder whispering in his ear were over. It was Mike flying those faders now, while George sat there smoking, giving the yay or nay, depending on Malcolm's body language. The trouble was, as soon as you took it off you never put it back on again. If you fancied blasting the road to bits with some AC/DC, you reached for *Highway To Hell* or *Back In Black*.

It didn't matter, not to any of the brothers. Least of all, George. Nick Mallinson, who worked as a young gofer at the office Alberts opened in London in the Nineties, recalls 'at least two or three, sometimes more faxes coming in practically every week I worked there from some company in the world wanting to use "Love Is In The Air" – either for a TV advert, a film scene, a jingle, you name it. We reckoned that one song was enough to make George independently wealthy for the rest of his days.' Not that George shoved it down your throat. 'I don't know what he was like when he was young but by the time I met him he was just this really chilled-out older guy.'

Mallinson says all the brothers were like that. 'They never gave it the big "I am". I was sitting in reception one day and I could see what looked like this tramp hanging around Malcolm's car outside. I think he had a new Merc or something, I can't remember. But I do remember this funny-looking guy sort of peering through the windows. Next thing he comes through the door and goes straight past me towards the studio. I called after him, "Oi, mate, where do you think you're going!" It was Angus. I hadn't recognised him. He was like, "Er, just going in here, like. Any chance of a cup of tea?"'

Mallinson has another curious memory of talking to Malcolm one day about, of all things, music. 'I was still a kid, in my early twenties, and I knew they'd been on tour a little while before with Metallica. And I was a fan so I'm asking like, "What did you think of Metallica?" Malcolm looked puzzled. Like he'd never heard of them. He scratched his head. "Yeah, I think I've heard of them. They're supposed to be good, are they?" I thought maybe he was joking but then I realised he wasn't, he was just struggling to picture the band, even though they'd been on tour with them and Metallica was about the biggest metal band on the planet at that point. But these guys, Malcolm and George and Angus, it was like they're from another world.'

They were. One in which you kept your head down, ignored everyone outside your immediate blood brothers, and did your business to whoever stood in your road. The way of the clan, always.

In 2008, there was the much-trumpeted – at the time – *Black Ice* album. The first AC/DC album Brian Johnson had managed to scribble some lyrics for – or that the brothers had let him get in on – for 20 years, it wasn't until you'd sat through 'Rock'n'Roll Train', 'She Likes Rock'n'Roll', 'Rock'n'Roll Dream' and 'Rocking All The Way' that you realised this wasn't so much a return to form as simply business as usual. The only thing that had changed was the generation of critics that had grown up with the *idea* of AC/DC, more than the patchwork, shadow reality. An appropriate situation, given it is the *idea* of AC/DC that we all now cling to, even as we 'like' them on Facebook or download 'Rock'n'Roll Train' as a ringtone. When they finally won a Grammy for the admittedly superior 'War Machine', the feeling of awards-for-the-boys was unmistakeable. The Grammys have a history of doling out such awards. AC/DC, showered in all kinds of awards these past 10 years, now have a history of accepting them. When I went to see them play on the *Black Ice* tour, I went with a group of music business veterans who spent the evening waffling about how they were the best band in the world and how amazing it was to see Angus still in his school uniform, duck-walking across the stage while Brian Johnson, his cindered vocals properly aided by the best modern touring technology can offer, closed his eyes and pointed at the crowd. We talked about it so much as we sat having dinner at the Gaucho restaurant in the O2 arena's hospitality section that by the time we got to our private box we were just happy for them to come on and lower the big bell and fire the cannons. This ain't rock'n'roll, as David Bowie once memorably exclaimed, but it wasn't genocide either. It was simply ... pleasant. Like taking the kids to the circus. Fun and don't forget the T-shirt and tour programme. The ice-cream and Coke. Roll up, roll up. Last chance to see the ferocious lion put a man's head into his toothless, whiskery old mouth.

When Stewart Young was shown the door, interestingly the man who took over was his former partner, Steve Barnett. As Barnett once told an American journalist, he is 'not a music guy' but an extremely able and shrewd music businessman whose primary function is to make as much money for the artists and/or record labels he represents as possible. Hence the release two years later of *Bonfire*: the premium-priced four-CD Bon Scott-themed box set which sold a million copies in the US alone and cost the band virtually nothing to make. And when *Stiff Upper Lip* failed to crack the UK Top 10 and barely crawled to platinum in America, it became a side issue as Sony Music – now being run by Steve Barnett – announced a multimillion-dollar deal to re-release the entire AC/DC back catalogue on specially 'digitally remastered' CDs. Or put another way: all those AC/DC albums already out there on CD on the Atlantic and/or Atco labels would now be superseded by shiny new CD versions, with nothing whatsoever added to them other than new packaging, a new sound – if anyone can actually spot the difference – and a shiny new price tag to go with them. So spectacular was the success of these re-releases that, at time of writing, AC/DC's back-catalogue sales stand at around five million for the international version of *High Voltage*; nine million for the international version of *Dirty Deeds*; four million for the international version of *Let There Be Rock*; three million for *Powerage*; over ten million for *Highway To Hell*; over 40 million for *Back In Black*; and nearly six million for *For Those About To Rock*. That's just the big guns. Factor in another ten million for *The Razors Edge*, and approximately 12 million for all the albums no one really cares about, plus millions more in expensive compilations etc., and you don't have to be a mathematician to grasp that the game for AC/DC is no longer about listen to the quality of my new album, but feel the width of my catalogue sales, cobber. By the end of the decade, AC/DC had overtaken The Beatles for claiming the number-one-selling catalogue in the US.

Confirmation of AC/DC's royalty arrived in the form of a Rolling

Stones concert in Sydney in February 2003, where Malcolm and Angus were invited to jam with the Stones on an encore of the old BB King chestnut, 'Rock Me Baby'. The moment, an instant YouTube sensation, captured the Young brothers doing what they do best: Malcolm hung back next to Charlie Watts while Angus gave the people what they wanted, darting about the stage while Jagger wisely stayed out in front to give the little bruiser room to move. Ronnie Wood is seen trying to copy Angus's duck-walk at one point, and Keith is just having it, a goofy grin on his face as he stands toe-to-toe with Malcolm, the two bad-men of their respective groups, showing each other just how good they can really be.

If the brothers enjoyed themselves, the Stones must have as well because they subsequently invited AC/DC to open for them in June as special guests for three outdoor shows in Munich, for a reported $4 million. The romance would continue even beyond this, with the Stones inviting AC/DC to join them for a benefit concert in July 2003, for the city of Toronto, whose tourism business and good name had been devastated by the SARS outbreak. That concert was, of course, filmed, with two AC/DC songs appearing in the final cut – available now on DVD.

When the Rock and Roll Hall of Fame nominated and then inducted AC/DC into its hallowed roster in March 2003, along with The Clash, The Police, Elvis Costello and The Righteous Brothers, it came as no big surprise. The current line-up of Malcolm, Angus, Brian, Phil and Cliff, along with Bon, were inducted, with Aerosmith's Steven Tyler delivering the induction speech and Brian accepting on behalf of the band with Bon's two nephews standing in for him, introduced by Brian. There were some notable absentees from the band's official guest list, of course. No Michael Browning; no Ian Jeffery; no Mutt Lange. David Krebs, Peter Mensch and Stewart Young weren't there either but they wouldn't have gone anyway. Nor were any of the other musicians who have appeared on AC/DC albums, including Simon Wright, Chris Slade and, most put out of all, Mark Evans. When asked why they hadn't invited Evans by *Classic Rock*, Malcolm was typically brusque in his reply. 'Mark actually got picked by our manager. We never wanted him. We didn't think he could play properly. We could all hold our own, and so could Rob Bailey. What we thought was that when we'd kicked on a bit more we could override the manager and get in a good bass player.'

The release of *Black Ice* in 2008 was simply the latest leg on a long victory lap. In the US alone, on the day of its release *Black Ice* moved 193,000 units, with 110,000 selling in the UK. Within the week, it debuted at No. 1 on the album charts for not just the US and UK, but for a total of 29 countries, and was Columbia Records' (in the eight years since *Stiff Upper Lip*, the band had moved from Epic to Columbia) biggest debut since SoundScan started keeping track of such things in 1991. Like other releases, *Black Ice* hit the shelves in an array of editions, deluxe editions, limited editions, etc. Only Coldplay's *Viva La Vida* outpaced it as the biggest release of 2008 and the album went on to claim scores of year-end 'Best of' nominations and awards in the US, Europe and, of course, Australia.

While it did tremendously well over the counter, their biggest seller since *The Razors Edge*, this was thanks in no small part to the brilliant business decision not to make it available for download. Not to make it available anywhere in America, in fact, outside the giant supermarket chain Wal-Mart – or direct from their own official website. No iTunes or downloads for the new AC/DC album. As a PR stunt, it was worth more than a hundred good reviews. It also ensured physical sales at a time when CD sales elsewhere were stagnant and LPs were now the purview of elitist audiophiles. None of which prevented AC/DC from leasing the song 'Let There Be Rock' for the video game sensation of the year, *Rock Band 2*, later releasing the entire '91 Donington show for the video game as an *AC/DC Rock Band Track Pack*, again available exclusively through Wal-Mart.

It had nothing to do with the music. Ably produced by Brendan O'Brien – Stewart Young's astute but ignored suggestion from over a decade before – if you have never owned or heard an AC/DC album *Black Ice* is not a bad place to start; certainly in the lower reaches of their Top 10 best. But as Dante Bonutto says, 'I think what *Black Ice* showed was that there was a *need* for an AC/DC album. The fact that they actually made one that was better than some of the latter-day AC/DC albums was enough. There was also quite a gap since their previous album. They'd left it long enough that there was a demand for what AC/DC did. "Rock'n'Roll Train" gave a lot of encouragement that it might be a classic [album]. It didn't quite meet that criteria but it didn't *need* to be a classic at that point, put it that way. It just needed to be an AC/DC record that wasn't *Fly On The Wall* or *Flick Of The Switch*. As long as it wasn't that they were on safe territory.'

The *Black Ice* tour began in October 2008 in Wilkes Barre, Pennsylvania, and by the spring of 2010 the band had traipsed through North America, Europe, South America, Asia and, of course, down under. Their 20-song set list was split equally between the band's two eras, although offering no material from *Flick Of The Switch*, *Who Made Who*, *Ballbreaker*, *Fly On The Wall* or *Stiff Upper Lip*. All told, the band ticked off 160 shows, entertaining just under five million fans, raking in a cool $141 million, trailing only the Rolling Stones' *A Bigger Bang* tour and U2's *360°* tour.

Finding another new way to serve up old songs, the band signed on to contribute the soundtrack to the movie *Iron Man 2*, donating 15 songs from ten of their albums, all remixed by Mike Fraser. Unlike their contribution to the *Maximum Overdrive* soundtrack 25 years before, however, *Iron Man 2* would contain only AC/DC songs, but no new material – not even an outtake from *Black Ice*. The compilation (not a greatest hits album, but a compilation), debuted at No. 1 in Britain and No. 1 in the US, where it eventually claimed the No. 1 spot on the Mainstream Rock chart for five weeks. In the UK, it became their third best-selling album, behind *Back In Black* and *Black Ice*. When Malcolm and Angus were invited to attend the world premiere of the movie in Los Angeles, in April 2010, however, they walked out in disgust that their music was used so little in the actual film, leaving behind an array of famous but puzzled faces, like the movie's star, Robert Downey Junior, and pantomime villain – and AC/DC fan – Mickey Rourke.

The band headlined the first night of the UK's Download festival – the modern name for the old Castle Donington Monsters Of

Rock show – in June 2010; their first festival appearance for 15 years. At the band's insistence, Download set up a special AC/DC stage that allowed them to bring their full stadium show to the festival. How could the festival's subsequent headliners (Rage Against The Machine and Aerosmith) come close to competing on the Saturday and Sunday evenings? Who cared?

The man behind getting AC/DC to Download was Andy Copping, who'd been a fully-fledged AC/DC fan since his teens, and had long dreamed of working with them as a promoter. 'I defy anyone to find me a better-loved concert DVD than that one from Donington in 1991. From the minute that starts with "Thunderstruck" and the camera looks out over the crowd and you see all these Angus looka-likes, it was just phenomenal.'

Copping had pitched for the *Black Ice* tour, wanted to be the band's promoter in the UK, and had to fly to New York to make his pitch personally to Alvin Handwerker, 'who's a very soft-spoken, New York guy, deep thinker ... and eventually they agreed'. Co-promoting with Simon Moran at SJM, 'The minute we put them on sale they sold out within seconds. They could have done ten times the amount of dates in the UK. They were so hot that we knew we needed to bring them back in 2009. Which we did, then that sold out in seconds too.'

It was now that Copping decided to pitch them the idea of a Download headline. All the major festival promoters throughout the world wanted AC/DC to do their festivals. But AC/DC didn't do festi-vals any more. They were big enough to do their own outdoor shows. 'They are up with U2, Madonna, the Rolling Stones ... there's only a handful of acts that are consistently stadium-filling acts across the world, and AC/DC are one of them. Why would they do a UK festival then?'

Reading and Leeds had chased them for years. Coachella wanted them, Rock Am Ring, Rock Am Park, in Europe ... Glastonbury ... Copping chased them for four years for Download. But 2010 would be the 30th anniversary of Donington Park and Copping couldn't stop thinking about it. He had already pitched them twice but they had turned him down. 'I just wanted to have one last go.' He worked all night on his pitch, emailed it to their US agent, then sat there until the early hours of the morning, 'playing my AC/DC albums. It was like I was building a shrine to them in my mind, willing it to work.'

It did. But you know what they say: be careful what you wish for. 'They're definitely one of the hardest bands to work with,' he smiles, but it was still one of the greatest days of his life and career. 'Malcolm wants it this way and the rest of the guys follow. Brian Johnson is an outspoken guy. He gives his views. It's been rumoured in the past that Brian's gone against the grain a little bit because he believes things should be a certain way. But it always comes back to the godfather. Malcolm is like the Marlon Brando of that band. It's his vision.'

These days the Young brothers have a new guy running the day-to-day shop for them. A Scotsman by the name of Robbie McIntosh, a former head of marketing at Sony that Steve Barnett put them on to. 'He's a straight-talking guy,' says Andy Copping, 'and knows the industry really well. He suddenly became part of their entourage, and he's their go-to guy now. Anything that comes along, it's 'Well, what does Robbie think?' He's great for them because he's this independent ear that totally has the band's interests at heart.'

And the band's interests keep on expanding. As Copping says, 'Remember you can't get them on iTunes yet. I mean, even the fucking Beatles caved in, in the end! Can you imagine when AC/DC go on iTunes? It's just gonna be bonkers. I'm sure they'll do it one day. I mean, you're talking about a band that even when they're not working their catalogue continually sells in its millions. Not hundreds of thousands – millions. And their merchandise sales are through the ceiling! Even on the tour, I remember saying to Alvin, "How's merchandise been on the tour?" He just looked at me and said, "Beyond our wildest dreams." And that's probably as emotive as Alvin gets. They *are* a phenomenon and you just see them going on and on and on ...'

In the meantime, the band have released a range of wines in Australia, which are soon to be available in the United States, once again showing that if you can fit the AC/DC logo onto it, they'll find a way to sell it.

Being a good Scotsman, however, Angus is still careful with money. A friend tells a story of how his wife Ellen was pestering him that the BMW she drove was now 13 years old. She came home the next day and a smiling Angus told her: 'I've got a surprise for you.' A delighted Ellen skipped outside to find waiting for her ... a five-year-old BMW.

The question is, how much longer can the band members themselves physically go on? How much longer will they even want to? Brian Johnson has already tried to retire once, after the *Stiff Upper Lip* world tour ended. One of the more persistent rumours surrounding the five-year sabbatical the band appeared to take between the end of that tour and the start of the *Black Ice* tour was that the brothers, stubborn to the bitter end, were simply waiting Brian out. Others whispered they had actually sacked him but were keeping it quiet until a replacement was found. But, as Bon might say, you ain't forced to swallow all the bullshit. There was, however, no mistaking the wistfulness behind Johnson's 'joke' about the band having to talk him out of retiring in a 2009 interview with *Classic Rock*. Then there is the singer's physical health to consider. Brian Johnson is 65 now. Mick Jagger may be older but Mick doesn't smoke tabs and wet his whistle, let alone wear an old man's cloth cap. Brian was born old. Surely it's unrealistic to expect to see him still out there, wheezing into the mike when he's 70? In February 2009, a show in Antwerp was cancelled after the singer fell ill, and six additional shows were cancelled or postponed when it was revealed that he had been diagnosed with Barrett's Syndrome, a condition that affects the oesophagus and which, if left untreated, can lead to cancer and subsequent removal of the voice box. At the time the shows were postponed, this reason was not offered; only some months later did Brian come clean regarding the drastic extent of his condition.

One also has to wonder at what point does Johnson finally become sick and tired of playing the reverential second fiddle to Bon Scott's burning ever-brighter legacy, having to constantly proclaim Bon's greatness, sing his songs (generally half of every set list is from Bon's era) and, by implication, remind everybody that the only reason

Brian's not working on cars in Newcastle for a living is because of an accidental death.

When, in another interview in February 2010, it was brought to his attention that a large number of fans had put together a petition for the band to change the set list, their complaint being that by focusing on the hits the band were catering to the casual fans and that the *Black Ice* tour offered AC/DC and their fans a unique opportunity to celebrate some of the lesser-known gems from the classic albums, Johnson erupted, spitting, 'Fuck them.' Then weakly protesting that these fans were expecting far too much and that adding a song mid-set was the technical equivalent of landing a space shuttle, seeming to suggest that given the number of sound and light personnel on hand, 85 people would need to be consulted before the band even considered attempting to play something outside of the set. That after nearly 40 years, one of the self-proclaimed greatest rock bands in the world couldn't figure out how to improvise one of their own songs during a show. Yet when you see him onstage now, glancing at the lyrics scrolling on strategically placed teleprompters, one can't help but wonder if perhaps his alarmingly emotional response was rooted in a growing inability to stay sharp during shows.

One gets the impression that Brian is feeling the pressure of keeping up with his younger band-mates and that, given the chance, he would happily retire to his home in Florida, where he could play the odd gig with local bands and drive race cars all day long. To be fair to Brian he has always been loyal to Bon in public, but it would be reasonable for him to have a whisper of resentment – that, after 30 years, he still feels like the new guy.

As for the others, they'll keep going as long as Malcolm and Angus will have them. How long that will be will almost certainly depend on their health, too. Andy Copping told me while being interviewed for this book that there were strong whispers of a new AC/DC album and world tour being planned for 2013. Just weeks later, however, rumours began to circulate that one of AC/DC was seriously ill, though no names were mentioned. As Brian Johnson said in an interview with internet radio programme, the Cowhead show, in December 2011, press interview in 2012, 'One of the boys is a little sick. I can't say anything but he's getting better. He's doing wonderful. Full recovery expected.' Sometime after that, as this book was closing, someone else, unwilling to be named here, suggested it was Malcolm that was ill. That the condition had been deemed serious enough to call a halt to all plans but that the assumption now was that things had 'stabilised' and that the band would be back with an album and tour sometime in 2013. As if to prove the point, as I write these final words an announcement has now gone out that in just a few weeks time, on November 20, 2012 the first-live AC/DC album for 20 years is to be released. Titled *Live At Riverplate*, it was recorded during their mammoth outdoor show at the Argentinian Football Stadium before almost 200,000 people in 2009. It will be available as either a 3disc red vinyl edition, or as a 2CD edition. Never mind that it has already been available in DVD version since last year.

Like it really matters, either way, any more. As Dante Bonutto says, 'They can tour anytime they like, with or without an album. I think also there's a feeling that they might be coming to the end. So whatever they do now, people are gonna think, I better go and do this because it may be the last thing they ever do. All these classic rock bands are now thinking about their legacies. *Black Ice* would be an *okay* way to end. It wouldn't be classic. But you've got to ask: is there another record in them as good as *Back In Black*? I don't know ...'

Whether we like it or not, death stalks all of us that have passed the half-century mark, even AC/DC. And, of course, one of them is already dead.

'One thing Bon never had a chance to see,' says Ian Jeffery now, from his home in Japan, where he resides between tours with U2, 'is everything that he built, this complete pillar, this monolith that he built, he never had a chance to actually see it. That is very, very, very sad.

'I saw him at 10.30 in the morning performing to 70,000 people that didn't give a rat's arse about him, but he dealt with them like everybody was there to see him. Can you imagine what it would have been like if they had been? Just his body, his movements onstage, his interaction, the way he knew just when to dance, when to stand still, when to just fucking look at the ground, when to wrap the mike around one wrist and just pull it tight above his head and just stand there, looking up into the heavens ... there was just a magic about him cos he just knew everything, you know? You could see he just knew when to go, what to do, what not to do. I look back at the old videos now and think: what a picture! There is no frontman like Bon. You can talk about Daltrey swinging his mike around. You can talk about Ozzy walking round swearing and throwing buckets of water. But just the magic of that guy, in his little fucking cut-off denim jacket, his jeans, his bare chest, and when he was finished that's the way he walked around, you know? He didn't even change his fucking jeans, he was out there, you know? That was his persona and that was him to the hilt. No pretences ...'

Meanwhile, back in Oz, where AC/DC last toured in 2010, the band bumped into yet another old friend. Her name was Rosie. She had lost a lot of weight since they'd last seen her and was now living in Tasmania. She was said to be quite proud of the song they had written about her.

EPILOGUE

When Bon awoke, God was at the wheel and they were moving fast. Loud rock music blared from the car radio.

Bon had a headache. 'Jeez, turn it down, will ya?' he groaned.

God did as he was told and turned it down.

'Where we goin'?' Bon, still hazy, asked.

'Home,' said God.

Bon sat there in silence, taking it all in.

Puzzled, he asked, 'Was it a car crash?'

'Sort of,' said God, always with the elliptical answers.

'Am I... dead?'

'Sort of,' said God again.

'And the other fella?'

'Much worse, he's still alive.'

'I don't get you.'

'Yeah, you do,' said God. 'You always did, that's why I like you.'

They both sat in silence for a while, the car misting through the dark, rainy streets.

'That's it for me then, is it? End of story?'

'Oh, Bon,' said God, sympathetically. 'For you, the story's only just begun. You'll see.'

'What about the others?' he said, still worrying about the band.

'They'll see too, whether they believe it or not, trust me.'

And with that Bon was gone. Home, at last.

NOTES AND SOURCES

The foundations of this book, in terms of quotes and the facts of the story so far as I have gleaned them, are based on my own original investigations, and those of my invaluable researchers Malcolm Dome, Harry Paterson, Joe Matera and Joe Daly. Although none of the present line-up of AC/DC spoke to me directly for the book – their official management offices did not return calls or emails – I had occasion over the years to meet and/or interview Bon Scott, Malcolm and Angus Young, and Brian Johnson. Those who did agree to be interviewed specifically for this book include Michael Browning, Chris Gilbey, Mark Evans, Phil Carson, Ian Jeffery, Clinton Walker, Gordon 'Buzz' Bidstrup, John Swan, Ian 'Molly' Meldrum, Barry Bergman, David Krebs, Doug Thaler, Bob Daisley, Gary Moore, Dave Evans, Eddie Kramer, Tony Platt, Mark Dearnley, Trevor Rabin, Kevin Shirley, Stewart Young, Mike Fraser, Derek Shulman, Perry Margouleff, David Meniketti, Bernie Marsden, Simon Wright, Alan Niven, Nick Mallinson, Xavier Russell, Tony Wilson, Geoff Banks, Malcolm Dome, Dante Bonutto, Jerry Ewing, Pete Way, Andy Copping and a handful of others that wish to remain anonymous.

There were others who declined to be interviewed for the book but were helpful in their email exchanges, including Peter Mensch and Vince Lovegrove. And others still not interviewed specifically for this book but who shed light on important aspects of the AC/DC story for me in other interviews over the years, including John Kalodner, Joe Elliott, Ozzy Osbourne, Lemmy, Lars Ulrich, Slash and Rick Rubin.

I am also indebted to Jon Wiederhorn and Kathy Turman, for kind permission to utilise their excellent 2011 Brian Johnson interview, which can be read in full in their forthcoming collection: *Louder Than Hell: The Uncensored, Unflinching Saga Of Forty Years Of Metal Mayhem* (It Books, 2013).

I have also spent a great deal of time over the years compiling as much background material as possible from as much published – and, in a few cases, unpublished – material as there is available, including books, magazine and newspaper articles, fanzines, websites, TV and radio shows, DVDs, demo-tapes, bootleg CDs and any other form of media that contained useful information, the most important of which I have listed here.

However, extra special mention should also go to a handful of books and articles that proved especially helpful, in terms of adding to my own insights and investigations. First and foremost to Clinton Walker's wonderfully insightful *Highway To Hell: The Life & Times of AC/DC Legend Bon Scott* (Pan Macmillan Australia, 1994), and of course to the thoroughly well-researched *AC/DC: Maximum Rock & Roll* by Murray Engleheart and Arnaud Durieux (HarperCollins Australia, 2006). Also, Mark Evans's funny and touching *Dirty Deeds: My Life Inside/Outside AC/DC* (Bazillion US, 2011); Jane Albert's *House of Hits: The Great Untold Story of Australia's First Family Of Music* (Hardie Grant Australia, 2010); and Bob Geldof's *Is That It?* (Sidgwick & Jackson, 1986).

Also the always first-class David Fricke for his various articles in *Rolling Stone*; the equally superb Sylvie Simmons in *Mojo*, and various top-drawer pieces by *Mojo*'s editor-in-chief, Phil Alexander; as well as brilliant pieces in *Classic Rock* by Dave Ling and Philip Wilding.

There were many others, too, that I have endeavoured to list below, all of whom deserve praise and acknowledgement for the role they played in helping shape the direction of this book, and to all of whom I extend my thanks and whom I would urge readers to seek out. Most of these articles I purchased either when they were first published or via a back-catalogue resource. Many, however, I now discover are available via the internet. If you can get hold of the originals though, I would recommend it for there is nothing quite like holding – feeling and smelling – the real, now yellowing thing. Again, my utmost thanks to one and all.

MAGAZINES AND NEWSPAPERS

Go-Set, 14 June 1969
Anthony O'Grady, *RAM*, April 1975
RAM, 19 April 1975
Juke, 13 March 1976
Melody Maker, May 1976
Sounds, May 1976
RAM, 30 July 1976
RAM, 27 August 1976
Sounds, 28 August 1976
Beat Instrumental, August 1976
Spunky, 6 September 1976
New Musical Express, 16 October 1976
New Musical Express, November 1976
Observer, November 1976
The Times, November 1976
RAM, December 1976
Rolling Stone, 16 December 1976
Melody Maker, April 1977
Record Mirror, 1979
Circus Weekly, January 1979
Sounds, March 1980
Rolling Stone, October 1980
NME, 25 August, 1984
Kerrang!, 1980s
Martin Aston, *Auckland Star*, 1990
David Horowitz, *Juke*, 23 February 1991
Vic Garbarini, *Australian Playboy*, 1992
Stuart Coupe, *In Press Magazine*, 16 October 1996
Michael Smith, *Drum Media*, 28 January 1997
Philip Wilding, *Classic Rock*, summer 2000
Le Monde, October 2000
Rolling Stone, February 2003
Dave Ling, *Classic Rock*, 2003

Sylvie Simmons, AC/DC feature, *Mojo*, December 2004

Vince article, *RAM?*, 21 November 2008

David Fricke, AC/DC feature, *Rolling Stone*, November 2008

Carol Clerk, *Classic Rock*, June 2009

Herald Sun, February 2010

Mojo, June 2010

TV, RADIO AND FILM

Countdown appearances, various 1975–8

2SM Radio, 1975

John Peel sessions, BBC Radio One, 1976

2JJ in November 1976

WABX, July 1979

Let There Be Rock, film, 1980

German TV documentary, 1992

Bernie Bonvoisin, RTL radio, November 1997

And Then There Was Rock, DVD, 2005

Australian TV documentary, Perth, 2 October 2006

Silver, 891 ABC Radio, Adelaide, February 2010

Cliff Williams, YouTube interview

Behind the Music, VH1

INTERNET SOURCES

BBC Online News

Mongrels Of Passion, MySpace

www.ac-dc.net

www.acdcbackinblack.net

www.blabbermouth.net

www.MTV.com

www.rollingstone.com

www.thenervousbreakdown.com

www.williamsonmgt.com

www.youtube.com

INDEX

A II Z, 369
Abba, 162
Abbey Road Studios, 41, 46
ABC TV, 73, 94–5
Accept, 192
AC/DC
  back catalogue sales, 408
  band name, 56–7, 106–7
  band pub, 357
  Bon Scott joins, 103–5, 107–13, 119–20
  compilation albums, 405, 408, 411
  costumes, 62–4, 91
  decision-making, 65–6, 106, 119, 187, 200, 214, 220, 227, 358–61, 363, 370–1, 413
  early success, 89–98
  earnings, 161–2, 166, 171, 275–6, 394
  first British tour, 174–94
  first gig, 56, 380–2
  formation, 52–8
  label trade, 393–4
  lightning-flash logo, 93–4, 123
  line-up changes, 61–2, 65–6, 106–11, 130–3, 141, 142–5, 210–14, 364–70, 395
  live albums, 231, 242–3, 252–4, 398
  managers, 55, 97–8, 115–22, 272–4, 347–9, 358–60, 404
  Nazism accusations, 403
  promotional film, 94–5
  resistance to downloads, 410, 413
  return to Australia, 197–200
  return to Britain, 206–8
  row with Black Sabbath, 209–10
  sales plateau, 342–3, 352–3
  Satanism accusations, 355–6, 379–80
  Seedies nickname, 130, 217
  siege mentality, 145, 201–2, 358–9
  sign to Atlantic, 162–7
  stadium rock band, 356–7, 411–12
  tensions in band, 179, 199–200, 211, 233, 249, 373, 387
  unpopularity in America, 196–7
  US tours, 215–25, 231–3, 244–51, 287–8, 374–5, 388
AC/DC albums and videos, see individual titles
AC/DC tracks
  'Ain't No Fun Waiting Round To Be A Millionaire', 169
  'Baby, Please Don't Go', 65, 125, 127, 140, 145, 173, 178, 243
  'Back In Black', 323, 328–30, 332–4, 370, 372–3, 392
  'Backseat Confidential', 169, 268
  'Bad Boy Boogie', 203–4, 237
  'Beating Around The Bush', 170, 268
  'Bedlam In Belgium', 372
  'Big Balls', 169, 208
  'Big Gun', 400–1
  'Brain Shake', 372–3
  'Burnin' Alive', 403
  'Can I Sit Next To You, Girl', 60, 92–4, 98, 110, 133, 152, 169, 182, 187
  'Carry Me Home', 190–1
  'Chase The Ace', 383
  'Cold Hearted Man', 238
  'Crabsody In Blue', 205
  'Deep In The Hole', 372–3
  'Dirty Deeds Done Cheap', 168, 207, 243, 335
  'Dirty Eyes', 190, 204
  'Dog Eat Dog', 203, 207, 209, 243
  'Down Payment Blues', 236
  'DT', 383
  'Evil Walks', 352, 356

AC/DC tracks—*contd*
'Fell In Love', 127
'Fire Your Guns', 397
'Flick Of The Switch', 372–3
'Fling Thing', 170
'For Those About To Rock, 352
'Get It Hot', 267
'Gimme A Bullet', 237
'Girl's Got Rhythm', 268
'Givin' The Dog A Bone', 331
'Go Down', 151, 202
'Gone Shootin'', 236
'Gonorrhea', 199
'Guns For Hire', 373
'Hail Caesar', 403–4
'Hard As A Rock', 404
'Have A Drink On Me', 295, 330
'Heatseeker', 386
'Hell Ain't A Bad Place To Be', 203, 230–1
'Hell's Bells', 328–9, 334, 337
'High Voltage', 149–50, 152, 182, 192, 230, 243, 335, 392
'Highway To Hell', 259, 266–9, 271, 277, 280, 287, 292, 319, 323, 333, 372
'I'm A Rebel', 192
'If You Want Blood (You've Got It)', 267, 280
'Inject The Venom', 352
'It's A Long Way To The Top', 154, 160–1, 168, 170, 175, 196, 243, 335
'Jailbreak', 168–9, 172, 183, 189, 195, 243, 377
'Kicked In The Teeth', 216, 237
'Landslide', 372
'Let Me Put My Love Into You', 295, 330
'Let There Be Rock', 13, 202–3, 216–17, 230, 243, 253, 268–9, 410
'Let's Get It Up', 352
'Little Lover', 125, 181–2
'Live Wire', 155–6, 182, 187, 214, 231
'Love At First Feel', 190, 195, 229
'Love Hungry Man', 259, 267
'Love Song (Oh Jene)', 127–8, 140, 145
'Midnight Rock', 59
'Mistress For Christmas', 397
'Moneytalks', 397–8
'Nervous Shakedown', 372–3
'Night Prowler', 268, 355, 379
'Out Of Bounds', 373
'Overdose', 203
'Problem Child', 169, 230, 243
'Ride On', 169, 205, 268, 296, 383

'Riff Raff', 236
'RIP (Rock In Peace)', 169, 195
'Rising Power', 372
'Rock'n'Roll Singer', 61, 127, 133, 155, 392
'Rock And Roll Ain't Noise Pollution', 328
'Rock Your Heart Out', 397
'Rock'n'Roll Damnation', 241–2
'Rock'n'Roll Dream', 407
'Rock'n'Roll Train', 407, 411
'Rocker', 156, 171, 181, 195, 230, 253, 282
'Rockin' In The Parlour', 60, 92
'Rocking All The Way', 407
'Safe In New York City', 405
'Shake A Leg', 329
'She Likes Rock'n'Roll', 407
'She's Got Balls', 112, 114, 124–5, 153, 181, 243
'Shoot To Thrill', 328, 369
'Shot Down In Flames', 268, 280
'Shot Of Love', 397
'Show Business', 60, 127–8
'Sin City', 237, 268
'Sink The Pink', 378
'Soul Stripper', 61, 92, 126
'Squealer', 169
'Stick Around', 127
'Stiff Upper Lip', 405
'Sunset Strip', 60, 127
'That's The Way I Wanna Rock And Roll', 386
'The Jack', 152–3, 199, 205, 208, 231, 243, 253, 319
'The Old Bay Road', 59
'There's Gonna Be Some Rockin'', 169
'This House Is On Fire', 372
'Thunderstruck', 13, 397, 412
'Tightrope', 373
'TNT', 155, 168, 171, 243
'Touch Too Much', 216, 267, 293
'Up To My Neck In You', 216, 237
'Walk All Over You', 268, 280
'War Machine', 407
'What Do You Do For The Money Honey', 331
'What's Next To The Moon', 236
'Who Made Who', 383, 385
'Whole Lotta Rosie', 10, 190, 202, 204, 221, 230–1, 243, 246, 253, 282, 309, 319, 322, 335, 417
'You Ain't Got A Hold On Me', 127

'You Shook Me All Night Long', 327–8, 330–1
AC/DC: Let There Be Rock, 290–1
AC/DC Live, 398, 412
AC/DC Rock Band Track Pack, 410
Aerosmith, 208–9, 232–5, 238, 244–5, 252, 273, 275–8, 348, 396, 409, 412
Albert, Jane, 44–5, 53
Albert, Ted, 9–10, 41, 43–5, 122–3, 150, 152, 166, 201, 243, 336
  and Bon Scott's death, 313–14
  his death, 391
Albert Productions
  and Atlantic deal, 165–6
  and Easybeats, 9, 55
  greatest hits project, 243–4
  recording sessions, 122–4, 149–50, 153–4, 168–71, 202–4
  royalties deal, 120–1
  signs AC/DC, 92–3, 112, 132
  US agreements, 219, 223–4
  Vanda–Young productions and signings, 43–5, 52, 59, 108, 198, 224, 257
  working arrangements, 122–3
Aldridge, Tommy, 369
Alexander, Arthur, 37
Alexander, Phil, 281, 304
Alice In Chains, 392
American Talent International (ATI), 219–20, 274, 309
Amon Duul II, 87
Anderson, Gary 'Angry', 102, 126, 131–2, 239, 317
Andersson, Benny, 162
Angel Witch, 369
Angels, 59, 124, 203, 257, 336
Animals, 18, 256
Anna 'Baba', 293–7, 302, 308–10
Appice, Carmine, 51
Archer, Robyn, 99
Arden, Don, 270
Argent, 50
Arista Records, 222
Armageddon, 141
Armstrong, Louis, 19
Armstrong, Steve, 12
Arnold, Ray, 55, 65–6
Ashdown, Doug, 75
Ashfield High School, 12, 65
Atco label, 393–4
Atlantic Records, 170, 174–6, 180, 183–4, 189, 365, 371, 380
Atco label trades, 393–4

and Back in Black, 334–5
difficulties with AC/DC, 200–2, 208, 216, 219, 222–3, 238, 240–2, 382–3, 393
and Flick Of The Switch, 368, 374
and greatest hits project, 243–4
and Highway to Hell, 271–2
and replacement producer, 255–9, 265
and replacement singer, 254–5
signs AC/DC, 162–7
US release of Dirty Deeds, 342–3, 347
and US tours, 224, 227, 231
Atlantics, 13
Ayers, Kevin, 163

Babe Ruth, 228
Back in Black, 346, 351, 353, 363, 368, 383, 391, 397, 406, 416
  album cover, 334
  album title, 334
  and Panama invasion, 392
  recording and release, 325–38, 340–3
  sales, 333, 398, 408, 411
  songwriting, 330–2
Back Street Crawler, 162–5, 175–6, 182–3, 318
Bad Company, 287, 393
Bailey, Rob, 65, 96, 106, 124, 410
Bain, Jimmy, 249
Baker Gurvitz Army, 318
Ballbreaker, 401–5, 411
Band, The, 76
Bandit, 213
Bangs, Lester, 207
Banks, Geoff, 92
Bannister, Freddy, 208
Barnes, Jimmy, 102, 316
Barnett, Steve, 393, 395, 408, 413
Barrie, J. M., 21–2
Barrie, Jack, 188
Barsalona, Frank, 219
Baton, Geoff, 181, 195
Bay City Rollers, 119, 158
Be Bop Deluxe, 218–19
Beach Boys, 14
Beastie Boys, 392, 400
Beatles, 5, 27, 32–3, 55–6, 130, 211, 219, 256, 408
  Apple company, 14, 42
  Australian tour, 9, 90
  'Come Together', 16–17
  and downloads, 413
  and Easybeats, 9–10
  long-term career, 120–1

Beatles—*contd*
  and merchandising, 244
  Sgt Pepper album, 46
Beck, Jeff, 18
Bee Gees, 73
Beelzebub Blues, 16, 47, 53
bell and cannons, 353, 407
Bennett, Clive, 195
Bergman, Barry, 223–5, 227, 231, 233, 247,
  255, 271
Berlin Wall, fall of, 391
Berry, Chuck, 5, 12, 15, 18, 27, 55, 60, 92,
  104, 128, 135, 176
  'School Days', 92, 133, 152, 181
Berry, Jake, 302, 309
Bidstrup, Gordon 'Buzz', 59, 82, 89, 124,
  179, 203
Big Swifty, 217
bisexuality, 57–8
Bisset, John (JB), 75–8, 80–1, 84–6
Black, Jet, 281
Black Crowes, 399
Black Ice, 407, 410–12, 414–16
Black Oak Arkansas, 183
Black Sabbath, 16, 79, 90, 128, 209–10,
  218, 284, 356, 389
Blackfeather, 78, 82–3
Blackmore, Ritchie, 134
Blackwell, Chris, 295
Blodwyn Pig, 16
Bloomfield, Mike, 15
Blow Up Your Video, 385–6, 393–4, 398
Blue Oyster Cult, 235
Bogert, Tim, 51
Bolan, Marc, 55, 91, 187–8, 214
Bolton, Michael, 278
Bon Jovi, 393, 395–6
Bonfire, 408
Bonham, John, 369
Bonutto, Dante, 396, 410, 416
Bonvoisin, Bernard, 229–30, 291, 296
Boomtown Rats, 261, 265–6, 271
Boston, 235, 254, 276
Bowie, David, 55, 91, 384, 407
Boyd, Jimmy, Jr, 398
Braithwaite, Daryl, 156, 159
Branson, Richard, 162
Brel, Jacques, 153
Brisbane Festival Hall, 10–11, 95
Brockum, 279
Brown, Bruce, 122
Brown, Ray, and the Whispers, 38
Browning, Coral, 163–4, 167, 174, 176,
  180, 186–8, 228

  and Bon Scott's death, 297, 311
Browning, Michael, 123, 128–30, 132–6,
  139–40, 146, 150, 154–5, 159, 161
  and America, 208–9, 216, 221–3, 234
  and Atlantic deal, 162, 164–6, 180,
    201–2
  and band relationships, 205–6
  and band's return to Australia, 197–8,
    200
  and band's return to Britain, 208
  and Bon Scott's death, 310–11
  and British tour, 171–5, 177, 184–6,
    188–9, 191–2
  fired as manager, 272–5, 337, 409
  and management deal, 115–22, 157
  and *Powerage*, 235–6, 240–1
  and replacement bassist, 212–14
  and replacement producer, 257–61,
    266, 271–2
  and replacement singer, 254–5
Buettel, Tony, 75
Buffalo, 215
Bundrick, John 'Rabbit', 163–5
Burgess, Colin, 53, 55, 59, 61–2, 148, 210
Burnstein, Cliff, 278–9
Burwood school, 11–12
Buster Brown, 102, 131–3, 143
Butler, Geezer, 210, 356
Byrne, Brian, 44

Cactus, 50–2
Cadd, Brian, 68, 70
Calder, Clive, 259–62, 264, 272
Cannon, Bernie, 94–5
Cantrell, Jerry, 392
Capaldi, Jim, 163
Capiral Radio, 156
Carlotta (Richard Byron), 105–6
Carmassi, Denny, 368
Carson, Phil, 180–1, 183, 186, 188, 191,
  196, 253, 265, 281, 287, 363, 392–3
  arguments with Atlantic bosses, 200–1,
    215–16, 342–3, 380
  and Bon Scott's death, 309
  and punk bands, 226–7
  and sales plateau, 342–3, 352–3
  signs AC/DC, 162–7
Carter, Helen, 151
Cash, Johnny, 401
Castle Donington festival, 347, 349, 354,
  377, 398–9, 411–12
CBGB's, 226
Chandler, Chas, 45, 256
Charlemagne, 131

Charles, Prince of Wales, 353
Charley Daniels Band, 225
Cheap Trick, 232, 246, 277
Child, Curtis White, 398
Cinderella, 393
City Boy, 261, 264
Clack, Peter, 65, 94, 96, 106, 124
Clapton, Eric, 15–16, 297
Clapton, Richard, 48
Clarion Records, 37
Clarke, John, 274, 350, 360, 376
Clarke, Martin, 37
Clarke, Stanley, 212
Clash, 180, 190, 206, 317, 409
Classic Rock magazine, 147, 330, 409, 414
Clefs, 75
Cleminson, Zal, 126
Clerk, Carol, 152
Clover, 264
Cobain, Kurt, 392
cocaine, 229, 249–50, 285–6, 288–9, 299
Cochran, Eddie, 55, 90
Cocker, Joe, 47, 256, 262, 367
Cocks, Mick, 296
Cold Chisel, 102, 316
Coldplay, 410
Coleman, Russell, 132
Collins, John, 33
Colodny, Michael, 225
Colosseum, 213
Coloured Balls, 131
Conan The Barbarian, 176
Contemporary Communications
     Corporation, 208–9
Cook, Mick, 213
Cooper, Alice, 91, 234–5, 244, 268
Cooper, Perry, 222–4, 231, 274
Copping, Andy, 412–13, 415
Costello, Elvis, 409
Countdown, 145–7, 150, 156–8, 161, 170–2,
     197, 209, 227, 241, 280, 294, 316
Coverdale, David, 228, 317
Cowbell agency, 191
Cranhill, 3–4, 6, 19
Cream, 16
Creem magazine, 343
Cult, 155, 298, 392, 401
Cureton, Jeff, 12
Current, Tony, 124

Daddy Cool, 79, 117
Daily Planet, 117
Daisley, Bob, 91, 228
Daltrey, Roger, 320, 416

Damned, 193, 206, 228
Darcy, John, 137
datura, 85–6
Davies, Roger, 117
Davis, Miles, 325
Dayman, Ivan, 69–70
De Laurentiis, Dino, 384
Deaf School, 271
Dean, James, 29
Dearnley, Mark, 266, 345–6, 350, 378
Dee, Dave, 264
Deep Purple, 17, 48, 50, 76, 80, 90, 130,
     228
     and Sunbury festival, 134–5, 218
Def Leppard, 289–90, 333, 335, 345, 348,
     374, 392
Delroy Williams Soul Show, 212
Deltones, 13
Denny, Sandy, 163
Derek & The Dominoes, 256
Diamonde, Dick, 7–8
Diana, Princess of Wales, 353
Dictators, 180, 226, 233
Dio, Ronnie James, 218, 249, 389–90
Dio, 389
Dionysius, Eric, 290
Dire Straits, 219
Dirty Deeds Done Cheap, 190, 201, 219,
     238, 268, 353, 377
     album cover, 195–6
     international version, 181, 195–6, 200,
     408
     recording and release, 168–71, 195–6,
     198–9
     sales, 398, 408
     US release, 342–3
Disc magazine, 213
Doctor Feelgood, 180
Doherty, Harry, 207
Dome, Malcolm, 178–9, 181, 208, 228,
     269, 316, 330
Domino, Fats, 5
Donnelly, Albie, 264–5
Doobie Brothers, 260
Doors, 47
Do-Re-Mi, 151
Doug Parkinson In Focus, 116
Douglas, Greg, 110
Downbeat magazine, 19
Downey, Robert, Junior, 411
Download festival, 411–12
Drayson, Mike, 157
Duffy, Billy, 298
Dupree, Simon, and the Big Sound, 394

Dye, Crispin, 380
Dylan, Bob, 15, 76, 161

Eagles, 200, 235, 254, 333
Easybeats, 9–11, 13–15, 17, 52, 55, 70, 90,
    93, 266, 394
    fail to follow up success, 41–3, 56–7,
        89, 107, 120
    'Friday On My Mind', 37, 41–2, 56, 73,
        218
    and Valentines, 37–8, 73
EB Marks publishers, 223–4
Eddie, Jason, and his Rock And Roll Show,
    212
Eddie and the Hot Rods, 177, 180, 193,
    211, 228
Ekland, Britt, 198
Electric Elves, 218
Elliott, Joe, 289, 335
ELO, 235, 270
Elsen, Bill, 219–20
Emerson, Lake & Palmer, 162, 380, 382
Emmet, Rik, 276
Engleheart, Murray, 16, 217, 292
Ertegun, Ahmet, 162, 175, 222–3, 342, 350
Ertegun, Neshui, 201
Evans, Dave, 14, 115, 118, 140–1, 148, 155,
    179–80, 315
    with AC/DC, 51–4, 57, 59–63, 65–6,
        92–6
    and Bon Scott's death, 311
    and Bon Scott's replacement, 254–5
    and High Voltage, 126–7
    quits band, 98, 103–7, 109–13, 210
Evans, Judy, 143
Evans, Mark, 56, 148–9, 151, 154–5, 158,
    160, 206
    and Back in Black celebration, 336
    and band's return to Australia, 198–9
    and Bon Scott's death, 315–16
    and British tour, 173–5, 177, 179, 182,
        184, 186, 189, 193
    and Dirty Deeds, 201–2
    fired from band, 210–14, 409–10
    joins band, 142–5
    and Let There Be Rock, 202–4, 206
Evening Standard, 303
Everly Brothers, 28
Ewing, Jerry, 147, 158, 236
Exorcist, The, 162
Eyers, 'Uncle' John, 77, 80–1

Faces, 55, 83, 90, 213
Fairbairn, Bruce, 395–6, 401

Fang, 86–7
Firm, 395
Flake, 65
Fleet, Gordon 'Snowy', 8
Fleetwood Mac, 15, 200, 235, 254, 260,
    264
Flick Of The Switch, 363–4, 371–3, 377–8,
    383, 411
    album cover, 368
Fly On The Wall, 378–81, 383, 411
For Those About To Rock, 356, 358, 360,
    363, 368, 372, 383, 386, 396, 400
    acetates, 349–50
    recording and release, 341, 343–7,
        349–53
    sales, 353, 408
Foreigner, 215, 235, 245, 345
Frampton, Peter, 235
Fraser, Andy, 318
Fraser, Mike, 396, 402–3, 405, 411
Fraternity, 75–87, 98, 104–5, 109, 119, 127,
    139, 145, 179, 291–2, 316
    and groupies, 77–8
    London sojourn, 84–7, 173, 176,
        184–5
    name change, 86–7
Frazer, Phillip, 75
Free, 49–50, 55, 80, 83, 86, 92, 130–1,
    163, 267
Freedom's Children, 262
Freeman, John, 75, 104
French, Peter, 51
Fresh, 321
Frieke, David, 232
Fryer, Allan, 316–17
Furey, Joe, 239–40, 284, 294

Gaines, Steve, 222
Gallagher, Rory, 143–4
Gannon, Brian, 33
Geldof, Bob, 262, 266
Gentle Giant, 392
Geordie, 86, 318–19, 321–4
Georgia Satellites, 401
Gett, Steve, 253
Giant Dose Of Rock 'n' Roll tour, 197
Gilbey, Chris, 93, 122–3, 140, 150, 156–7,
    161, 164, 197–8
Gilmour, David, 395
Girl Can't Help It, The, 28
glam metal, 378
glam rock, 58, 63, 86, 91, 128
Glamis Castle, 21
Glasgow Rangers FC, 5

Glausi, Elizabeth, 398
Glitter, Gary, 111
Glitter Band, 94
Gobi Desert Canoe Club, 321
Golab, Ed, 16–17
Go-Set magazine, 39, 67, 71–2, 74–5, 117, 145
Graham, Bill, 223, 245
Grammy Awards, 407
Grant, Peter, 167
Grapefruit, 42
Gray, Paul, 211
Green, Peter, 15
Green, Wayne, 65
Greenberg, Jerry, 166–7, 200–1, 219, 222, 224, 227, 254–5, 272, 287, 342
Griffiths, Richard, 177
Groop, 38–9, 68
groupies, 114, 130, 138, 148, 151–2, 160, 202, 204–5, 210, 250–1, 354
Gudinski, Michael, 117, 131
guitars
   Epiphone Caballero, 184
   Gibson SG, 18, 400
Guns N' Roses, 171, 179, 392
Guy, Buddy, 19

Hair!, 321
Hall, Les, 47
Hammer, M.C., 398
Hammersmith Odeon, 193, 195, 228, 252–3, 289, 294, 299
Handwerker, Alvin, 360, 376, 380–2, 404, 412–13
Harris, Rolf, 181
Harrison, George, 48, 150
Harvey, Alex, 126, 229, 238
Hawkwind, 119
Haynes, Jayne, 184
Haze, Leonard, 245, 355
Head, Peter, 79–80, 99–100, 108, 292
Headband, 79, 99
Headline Artists, 177
Heart, 235, 276, 368
Heartbreakers, 182, 208
Heaven, 316
heavy metal, 333
Heavy Metal Kids, 175, 318
Heavy Publicity, 284
Henderson, Maureen, 28–9, 31
Henderson, Terry, 27–30
Hendrix, Jimi, 16, 18, 45, 50, 62
   Eddie Kramer and, 256–8
Henry, Hamish, 78–80, 82, 84–5, 120

heroin, 138–40, 185, 229, 239, 284–6, 297–301, 304–7, 311
   and alcohol, 300, 307
   use in seventies, 284–5
High Voltage, 61, 132, 144, 147–8, 150, 157, 219, 243, 377
   album cover, 140
   credits, 124
   Dave Evans songs, 126–7
   international edition, 180–1, 183, 188, 190–1, 195–6, 200, 408
   recording and release, 122–8, 140
   reviews, 181
   sales, 161, 171, 201, 271
Highway To Hell, 286–8, 290, 314, 326, 332, 345, 348, 351, 378, 397, 401, 406
   album cover, 272, 355, 379
   album title, 271–2
   and Mutt Lange, 260–73, 286–7
   and Panama invasion, 392
   recording and release, 266–71, 276–7, 279–80
   reviews, 286
   sales, 293, 295, 398, 408
   and Satanism accusations, 355, 379
Hipgnosis, 196
Hoadley Battle of the Bands, 38, 80
Hocus, 263
Holder, Noddy, 94, 319
Holloway, Ted, 74
Holly, Buddy, 28
Holton, Gary, 175, 318
Home, 213
Hooker, John Lee, 267
Horne, Nicky, 156
Horsburgh, Sam, 65
Howe, Brian, 393
Howe, Bruce, 75–6, 78, 80, 104
Howlin' Wolf, 143
Human League, 353
Humble Pie, 131
Humphreys, Kim, 50, 53–4
Humphries, Gerry, 67

If You Want Blood, 252–4, 271, 293
   album cover, 356
Ifield, Frank, 181
Imlah, Andy, 47–9
Iron Maiden, 244, 263, 333, 362
Iron Man 2, 411
Isle of Man, 362
iTunes, 410, 413

Jackson, John, 191

Jackson, Michael, 312, 333
Jackson, Python Lee, 116
Jacobsen, Philip, 117
Jagger, Mick, 180, 409
Jailbreak, 61, 377
Jailhouse Rock, 28
Jam, 206
James, Clive, 190
James, Dennis, 65
James, Trevor, 50, 52–3
Jasper, 62
Jasper Hart Band, 321
jazz, 49, 55, 59, 148
Jeffery, Ian, 6, 16, 199, 206, 217, 241, 282, 286, 295, 416
    and Atlantic difficulties, 341–2
    and *Back in Black*, 334–6
    and *Back in Black* lyrics, 308, 331–2
    and Bon Scott's death, 293–4, 296, 298–9, 302, 304–5, 308–10, 314–15
    and Bon Scott's replacement, 317–20, 322, 324
    and Brian Johnson's position, 337–8
    fired as manager, 374–6, 380, 399, 409
    and *Flick Of The Switch*, 373–4
    and *For Those About To Rock*, 343, 347, 349–50, 353
    and *Highway to Hell*, 266, 268–9, 272
    joins as tour manager, 182–3, 186–7
    manages band, 358–68
    and Mensch firing, 348–9
    and Mutt Lange firing, 351
    and replacement bassist, 211–12, 214
    and replacement drummer, 366–8, 372
    and replacement manager, 272–9
    and US tours, 218, 221, 223, 246–8, 287
Jeffrey, Emma, 294
Jeffrey, Suzie, 293–4, 296–7, 310
Jesus Christ Superstar, 108
Jethro Tull, 386
John Mayall's Bluesbreakers, 15–16
John, Elton, 90, 200
Johns, Neale, 83
Johnson, Alan, 321
Johnson, Brian, 335–9, 341–4, 346–7, 352, 354–8, 366, 370, 395, 397, 403, 407
    his contract, 337
    with Geordie, 86–7
    and groupies, 354
    his houses, 339, 344

    and Ian Jeffery, 399
    illness, 414
    joins band, 318–32
    outspokenness, 413
    and retirement, 388, 414–15
    and Satanism accusations, 355–6
    songwriting, 325, 327–8, 372, 385, 388, 397, 407
Johnson, Carol, 322
Johnson, Esther, 321
Jolson, Al, 217
Jones, Brian, 256
Jones, Dickie, 369–70
Jones, Kenney, 130
Jones, Tom, 395
Joseph, Bill, 122
Journey, 244, 276
Jovan agency, 102
Judas Priest, 219, 290, 333, 369
Juke magazine, 56, 161, 172
Jurd, Mick, 75

Kakoulli, Koulla, 298
Kakoulli, Zena, 298
Kalodner, John David, 215–16
Kamaflage label, 369
Kelly, Ned, 173
Kentuckee, 49–51, 53
Kids, 175
King, BB, 363, 409
King, Bruce, 84
King, Freddy, 143
King, Stephen, 382–3
Kingdom Come, 393
Kinks, 33, 41
Kinnear, Alistair, 297–301, 303–7, 310
Kinnear, Daniel, 307
Kirke, Simon, 130
Kirriemuir, 21–4, 309
Kiss, 219, 222, 231–2, 234–5, 242, 254, 256–7, 259
Kissick, Allan, 55, 62, 66
Kleffner, Michael, 222–4, 226, 241, 245
    and Eddie Kramer, 255–8, 272
Knight, Arthur, 116
Korner, Alexis, 212
Kossoff, Paul, 50, 55, 162–3, 175–6
Kovac, Herm, 18, 47–50
Kramer, Eddie, 256–9, 261, 265–6, 272–3
Krayne, 130
Krebs, David, 208–9, 275–9, 297, 316, 324, 349, 360–1, 380, 409
Kushner, Cedric, 259–60, 272–4

Laing, Corky, 130
Lange, Mutt, 290, 295, 358, 363, 372–4, 378, 405, 409
  and *Back in Black*, 325, 327–9, 332, 334–5
  and Bon Scott's replacement, 317, 319, 321
  fired as producer, 351–2, 376
  and *For Those About To Rock*, 344–7, 349–51
  and *Highway to Hell*, 260–73, 286–7
Last Action Hero, The, 400
Laughlin, Dennis, 97–8, 103–6, 118
Leach, Geordie, 131–2
Leber, Steve, 208, 275–7, 279
Leber–Krebs agency, 208, 275–9, 290, 334–5, 348
Led Zeppelin, 64, 83, 188, 213, 219, 238, 401
  album covers, 196
  and Atlantic Records, 162
  Australian tours, 90
  'Black Dog', 369
  breakup, 340
  covers, 71, 73, 130
  'dinosaur' rockers, 190, 206
  Eddie Kramer and, 256–7
  formation, 366
  and groupies, 354
  Kevin Shirley and, 263
  Knebworth shows, 280–1
  Led Zeppelin IV, 117, 333
  pretentiousness, 17, 76, 208
  'Rock And Roll', 18–19, 322
  'Whole Lotta Love', 73, 125, 204
Lennon, John, 42, 82, 297
Les Girls cabaret, 105–6
Let There Be Rock, 243, 281
  album cover, 215
  recording and release, 202–6, 208–9, 215–16, 224, 226–7
  reviews, 206, 227
  sales, 215, 242, 271, 408
Levin, Louis, 278
Levine, Sir Montague, 303, 314
Lewis, Alan, 281
Lewis, Dave, 228, 286, 304
Lewis, Huey, 264
Lewis, Jeanie, 84
Lewis, Jerry Lee, 27, 77–8, 115, 156
Ling, Dave, 110
Litherland, Jamie, 213
Little Richard, 5, 15, 18, 27–8, 60, 90, 92, 318

Little River Band, 75, 99
live album techniques, 252
Live At Donington DVD, 377
Loads, Leslie, 301
Lock Up Your Daughters tour, 162, 168, 183, 385
Lonesome No More, 298
Love 200 musical, 84
Loved Ones, 18, 67
Lovegrove, Helen, 102
Lovegrove, Vince, 75–6, 78, 98, 100, 250–1
  and Bon Scott's accident, 101–2
  and Bon Scott's death, 308, 311
  and Bon Scott's joining AC/DC, 103–4, 109
  and Valentines, 34–6, 38–40, 67–75
Lovin' Spoonful, 218
Loyde, Lobby, 131, 133
LSD, 76–7, 81
Ludwig, Bob, 350
Lush, Richard, 46
Lynott, Phil, 238, 253, 284
Lynyrd Skynyrd, 221–2, 229, 237

McAvoy, Gerry, 144
McCartney, Paul, 42
McCoys, 37
McGlynn, Bob, 50–1
McGrath, Steve, 143
McIntosh, Robbie, 413
McNeil, Phil, 193
Madonna, 412
Mahogany Rush, 277
Makoul, Tom, 233
Makowski, Peter, 58
Mallet, David, 384–5, 398, 400
Mallinson, Nick, 406
Manfred Mann's Earth Band, 212, 395
Manzarek, Ray, 47
Marbles, 226
Marcus Hook Roll Band, 46–7, 60, 124
Margouleff, Perry, 402–3
Marley, Bob, & The Wailers, 163
Marquee, the, 188–9, 192
Marriott, Steve, 42
Marsden, Bernie, 228–9, 289, 356–7
Martin, George, 10
Martyn, John, 163, 177
Masters Apprentices, 53, 55, 59, 75
Matlock, Glenn, 211
Matters, Paul, 141
Maximum Overdrive, 382, 411
Meat Loaf, 224

Melbourne Festival Hall, 95, 150, 159, 164
Melbourne Gaol, 173
Melbourne *Herald*, 253
Melbourne Symphony Orchestra, 84
Meldrum, Ian 'Molly', 39, 145–7, 160, 197, 227, 316
Melody Maker, 181, 189, 207, 213, 253, 369
Meniketti, Dave, 245, 354
Mensch, Peter, 209, 274, 277–9, 287, 289–90, 295, 358, 368, 380, 392
  and *Back in Black*, 334–7
  and Bon Scott's death, 302–3, 308–11, 314–15
  and Bon Scott's replacement, 315–16, 324
  fired as manager, 347–9, 376, 409
merchandising, 243–4, 413
Mercury Records, 278
Metallica, 399, 401, 406–7
Michael Stanley Band, 226
Miller, Steve, 235, 254
Milncroft school, 5
Milson, Wyn, 33, 35, 72
Missing Links, 18
Mistler, Eric, 290
Mojo, 281, 304, 346, 364, 402
Molly Hatchet, 246, 288
Montalbano, Maggie, 306
Montgomery, Mike, 163
Montrose, 368
Moore, Gary, 247, 249, 395
Moran, Simon, 41
Morris, Doug, 342–3, 350, 382, 393–4
Most, Mickie, 117
Mötley Crüe, 289, 377
Motörhead, 244, 333
Motors, 265
Mount Lofty Rangers, 99, 101, 108
Mountain, 50–2, 130
Move, James Taylor, 75
Move, 321
Moxy, 217, 317
MTV, 383–5, 394
Muddy Waters, 19
Mulry, Ted, 49, 123
Mushroom Records, 117, 131
Music Machine, 179, 298–9, 303–4
Myer department store, 157
Myponga festival, 79

Nash, Johnny, 163
New Musical Express, 181, 193, 195, 207, 227, 286
New York Dolls, 208

Newsweek, 391
Newton-John, Olivia, 395
Nicks, Stevie, 264, 393
Night, 261
Nirvana, 392
Niven, Alan, 171
Noriega, General Manuel, 391–2
North Miami, Florida, 225
Nugent, Ted, 208, 234, 275–8

O'Brien, Brendan, 401, 410
O'Grady, Anthony, 147, 159, 172, 184
O'Keefe, Johnny, 27
Oldfield, Mike (*Melody Maker*), 181
Oldfield, Mike (*Tubular Bells*), 162, 167
101ers, 180
Only Ones, 298
Ono, Yoko, 42
O'Reilly, Oonagh, 264
Osbourne, Ozzy, 91, 128, 209–10, 325, 356, 369, 377, 416
Oxford Polytechnic, 192

Page, Jimmy, 54, 64, 256, 366, 395
Palmer, Robert, 326
Pantera, 399
Parker, Fess, 217
Parker, Graham, 264–5, 271
Parsons, Gram, 99
Pat Travers Band, 219
Pattenden, Colin, 212, 214
Paul Butterfield Blues Band, 15
Pavel, Louis, 213
Pearl Jam, 401
Peel, John, 180–3, 189, 191, 208, 212
Perrett, Peter, 298
Perry, Joe, 232
Peters, Frank, 172
Phillips, Arlene, 384
Phillipson, Steve, 47
Pickett, Pat, 157, 160, 176, 204
Pickett, Wilson, 35
Pickford-Hopkins, Gary, 318–19
Pink, 117
Pink Fairies, 87
Pink Floyd, 55, 84, 196
pipe bands, 23–4, 26, 154
Pitney, Gene, 218
Plant, Robert, 83, 190, 254, 281
Platt, Tony, 267, 294–5, 326, 329, 331, 344–5, 351, 378, 392
  and Bon Scott's replacement, 317–18, 321
  produces *Flick Of The Switch*, 363–4

Polar Music, 162
Police, 335, 409
Polygram, 393
Pop, Iggy, 27
Powell, Cozy, 369
Powerage, 216, 271, 331
    recording and release, 235–43
    sales, 242, 271, 408
Premier Talent, 219–20
Presley, Elvis, 10, 27–8, 92, 133, 176,
    262
Pretty Things, 47
Priscilla, Queen Of The Desert, 105
Proby, P. J., 37
Procol Harum, 321, 366
progressive rock, 45, 83, 148, 205
Proud, John, 124
Pryor, Don, 67
Punk magazine, 226
punk rock, 180, 189–91, 198–9, 206–7,
    226–8

Q-Prime, 278
Queen, 134, 235, 353

Rabbit, 110
Rabbitt, 262
Rabin, Trevor, 262–3, 266, 344, 351, 378
Radio Luxembourg, 175
Radio One, 180, 182, 191, 208, 229
Rage Against The Machine, 412
Rainbow, 91, 191–2, 218, 228, 244–5, 249,
    369, 389
RAM magazine, 138, 142, 147, 170, 172,
    176, 195, 250
Ramirez, Richard, 355, 379
Ramones, 180–1, 226
Razors Edge, The, 394–8, 400, 408
Reading Festival, 189–90
Rebel Without a Cause, 29
Record Mirror, 171, 181
Red Cow, Hammersmith, 177–9
Red Hot Chili Peppers, 401, 403
Reed, Lou, 27, 58, 95–6
Regal Zonophone label, 321
REO Speedwagon, 221
Riccabono, Fifa, 111, 293, 314, 375
Richards, Keith, 54, 180, 229, 285, 317,
    409
Righteous Brothers, 409
Riverbank prison, 31–2
Robert the Bruce, 21
Robertson, Brian, 228, 284
Robertson, Malcolm, 4

Robinson, Alan, 35, 37–8
Robinson, John, 83
Rock And Roll Hall Of Fame, 409
Rock Band 2, 410
Rock Goddess, 369
Rock Hard magazine, 402
Rocky Horror Picture Show, The, 163
Rodgers, Paul, 55, 163, 254, 382, 393
Rofe, Stan 'The Man', 39
Rolling Stone, 64, 172, 196, 207, 232, 245,
    308, 316, 356, 401
Rolling Stones, 16, 33, 56, 90, 143, 181,
    312, 395
    AC/DC turn down support slot, 358
    and Atlantic Records, 183
    'Brown Sugar', 170, 203, 267
    covers, 33, 50, 59, 68, 71, 92, 133
    'dinosaur' rockers, 190, 206–7
    drug use, 229, 237
    Eddie Kramer and, 256
    Exile on Main Street, 56, 117
    and groupies, 354
    'Honky Tonk Women', 16, 92, 267
    jam with AC/DC, 408–9
    'Jumpin' Jack Flash', 16, 59, 92
    long-term career, 121
    new albums, 405
    stadium tours, 411–12
    'Stray Cat Blues', 125
Rose Tattoo, 102, 126, 131–2, 239, 257,
    296, 336
Rosie, 202, 204–5, 417
Ross, Steve, 393
Rotten, Johnny, 190, 207, 211
Rourke, Mickey, 411
Rowe, Normie, 69
Roxy Music, 368
royalties, 120–1, 161, 165–6, 171, 314
Rubin, Rick, 392, 400–5
Rudd, Phil, 130–3, 143, 148, 150–1, 158,
    160, 199, 212, 280
    alcohol abuse, 365, 377
    and Bon Scott's death, 315
    drum style, 130, 295, 357, 370, 389
    fired from band, 364–6, 371–2, 376
    and first British tour, 174, 179, 186
    and *Highway to Hell*, 272
    joins band, 130–3
    and *Let There Be Rock*, 204
    marriage, 344
    rejoins band, 400–2
    Scalextric rider, 287–8
    starts to crack, 249–50, 252
Run DMC, 400

Rush, 230, 244

Salt Lake City, 398
Sam and Dave, 35
Santana, 17, 83
Savoy Brown, 16
Sayer, Leo, 209
schoolboys and girls competition, 183–4
Schwarznegger, Arnold, 400
Scott, Alexander (Alec), 22–3, 31
Scott, Bon (Ronald Bedford Scott)
    attraction to big women, 204–5
    author meets, 284–6
    and Back in Black, 330–2
    and bagpipes, 154, 160, 193
    becomes heavy metal icon, 333–4
    bike accident, 101–2
    and Blackfeather sessions, 78, 82–3
    contracts VD, 152
    drinking, 77, 88, 101–2, 135, 159, 191,
        205, 215, 228, 239–40, 247, 249–50,
        253, 258, 282–3, 288–9, 291–2, 294,
        297, 299
    and Coral Browning, 186–7, 311
    death and funeral, 296–314
    early years, 20–1, 24–34
    and first British tour, 173–4, 176,
        184–6, 193
    and Fraternity, 75–87
    and Fraternity's London sojourn, 84–7,
        173, 176, 184–5
    friendship with Bernie Marsden,
        228–9, 289
    friendship with Doug Thaler, 238–40
    friendship with Ian Jeffrey, 199–200
    friendship with Ozzy Osbourne, 128,
        209–10
    hears 'Can I Sit Next To You, Girl', 98
    and heroin, 138–40, 185, 297–301,
        304–7
    and High Voltage, 124–7
    and Highway To Hell, 269
    joins band, 103–5, 107–13, 119–20
    likeability, 115, 179, 228, 248–9
    marriage, 85, 100–2, 114
    nicknames, 26, 115
    pornography charge, 138
    prison sentence, 30–2
    relationship with Anna, 293–8, 309–10
    relationship with Maria Van Vlijman,
        33–4, 39–40, 68–9
    relationship with Silver, 184–6, 205–6,
        214, 229, 237, 239–40, 286, 297,
        304, 307–9

and Rosie, 202, 204–5
    singing voice, 36, 83, 254–5
    songwriting, 99–100, 115, 125–8, 152–3,
        155, 191, 205, 236–8, 268, 296–7,
        372
    stage act, 136–7, 145–7, 149, 158
    starts to crack, 251–2, 289–92
    tattoos, 29, 174, 198
    and US tours, 220–2, 232, 245–7,
        249–51, 258, 276, 288–9
    and the Valentines, 35–40, 67–75
    violence and criminality, 27–32
    visit to Paris, 229–30
Scott, Charles 'Chick', 21–6, 29–31, 33,
    87, 292
    and Bon's death, 302, 308, 313–16
Scott, Derek, 24, 114
Scott, George, 22–3
Scott, Graeme, 24, 26–7, 114, 240
Scott, Isa, 23–7, 30–1, 34, 87, 292
    and Bon's death, 296, 302, 308,
        313–15
Scott, Jayne, 23, 31
Scott, Sandy, 23
Scott-Heron, Gil, 163
Sculthorpe, Peter, 84
See, Sam, 80, 86
Seger, Bob, 235, 260
Sensational Alex Harvey Band, 125–6,
    229, 238
Serelis, Vytas, 80, 99
Sex Pistols, 180, 189–90, 193, 199, 211,
    228
Shakespeare, William (John Stanley Cave),
    62, 107
Sharks, 318
Shearman, Buzz, 317
Sherbert, 97, 147, 156, 159, 198
Sheridan, Tony, 5
Shirley, Kevin, 261, 263, 325, 335
Shorrock, Glenn, 75, 99
Shulman, Derek, 3, 392–6
Sight and Sound, 229
Silver, see Smith, Margaret 'Silver'
Simmons, Gene, 222
Simmons, Sylvie, 109, 207
Simon, Ralph, 260, 264
Simon and Garfunkel, 262
69ers, 124
Skiathitis, Jim, 13
Skyhooks, 91, 102, 128, 134, 146–7,
    200
Slade, Chris, 395, 401–2, 409
Slade, 63, 86, 90, 94, 319, 321, 324

Slayer, 400
Sleath, Billy, 4
Slesser, Terry, 175, 182, 318–19
Smack, 131
Small Faces, 37, 42, 90, 130, 270
Smith, Barry, 99
Smith, Levi, 75
Smith, Margaret 'Silver', *see* Silver
Smith, Neil, 62, 65
Smith, Richard Jon, 263
Smith, Margaret 'Silver', 31, 184–6, 191,
    193, 205–6, 229, 237, 239–40, 249,
    284–6, 293–4
Sneddon, Mark, 51–3
Snips (Steve Parsons), 318
So It Goes, 190
Soft Machine, 70
Sounds, 58, 181, 183, 186, 193, 195, 227–8,
    281, 286, 304, 369
South Africa, 260–3
South Australian News, 75
Spector, Phil, 33
Spectrum, 117
Spektors, 33–6, 101
Spencer, Jeremy, 15
Spencer Davis Group, 72, 259
Spooky Tooth, 48
Springfield, Dusty, 37, 162
Squire, Billy, 380
Starfighters, 388
Starr, Ringo, 130
Status Quo, 84, 86
Stephen, 264
Steppenwolf, 260
Stevens, Cat, 79
Stevens, John, 303
Stewart, Al, 213
Stewart, Rod, 55, 63, 90–1, 107, 116, 190,
    200, 219, 235, 254
Stiff Upper Lip, 405, 408, 410–11,
    414
Stone Temple Pilots, 401
Stranglers, 206, 280–1
Strawbs, 218–19
Strummer, Joe, 180
Stubbs, Mick, 213
Sugar, 213
Summer, Donna, 171
Sun, The, 188
Sunbury festival, 133–5, 147–8, 218
Sunshine Records, 69
Supercharge, 264
Sutcliffe, Phil, 183, 193
Swanee, 336

Swann, John, 317
Sweden, 187, 210
Sweet, 321
Sweet Peach label, 78, 82–3
Swingle Singers, 42
Sydney Opera House, 93

T. Rex, 47, 55, 90, 187, 321
Talmy, Shel, 41
Tantrum, 52–3
Taylor, Noel, 62–3, 65
Tears For Fears, 380
Ted Mulry Gang, 49, 336
Thaler, Doug, 218–20, 223, 226, 233,
    238–40, 244–5, 274–5, 288–9,
    297
Them, 33, 59, 168
Thin Lizzy, 228, 238, 247, 249, 284
Thompson, Paul, 368
Thornton, Faye, 114
Thornton, Irene, 85, 87, 98, 100–3, 114,
    125, 297, 308
Thorpe, Billy, & The Aztecs, 9, 38, 71–2,
    79, 116–17, 134, 164, 173
Thunders, Johnny, 182, 298
Tilbrook, Peter, 75
Times, The, 195
TNT, 180–1, 195, 198, 243, 335
    recording and release, 152–7
    sales, 161, 171
Tomorrow, 395
Top of the Pops, 241, 293–4
Tosh, Peter, 163
Townshend, Pete, 91, 281–3, 394
Trans-Pacific Artists, 122
Travers, Pat, 245, 265, 284
Triumph, 276
Trump, Donald, 397
Trust, 229, 291, 296
Tubes, 208
Turner, Chris, 215
Turner, Ike and Tina, 37, 322
Turner, Tina, 117
Tushino Airfield, 399
TV Week, 158, 197
12 Of The Best, 243–4, 383, 405
Twilights, 75
Tyler, Steve, 409
Tytan, 369

U2, 411–12, 416
UFO, 228, 230, 273, 276, 284, 294,
    312
Ulvaeus, Bjorn, 162

Valentines, 35–40, 43, 67–76, 80, 82, 112, 117, 145, 168
    band uniforms, 70–1
    drugs charge, 72–3
Van Halen, 245, 273, 377, 401
Van Kriedt, Larry, 19, 53, 59, 62
Van Vlijman, Maria, 34, 39–40, 68–9
Van Zant, Ronnie, 221–2
Vanda, Harry, 7–10, 13, 38, 90, 93, 112, 161, 244, 314, 364, 406
    and *Back in Black*, 336
    and *Blow Up Your Video*, 385–6
    and *Dirty Deeds*, 168
    and Doug Thaler, 218–19, 238
    fired as producer, 255–9, 269
    and *Flick Of The Switch*, 374
    and formation of AC/DC, 58, 60
    and *High Voltage*, 123–4, 126–7
    and *If You Want Blood* , 252
    and *Let There Be Rock*, 203
    and *Powerage*, 235
    and Reading Festival gig, 189–90
    songwriting and production, 41–7, 49, 52, 59, 62, 70–1, 93, 103, 107–8, 112, 150, 198
    and videos, 384
    and *Who Made Who*, 383
Vanilla Fudge, 76
Vann, Stevie, 261, 263–4
Vaughan, Mike, 9, 120
Velvet Underground (Australia), 47–9, 51–2, 54
Velvet Underground (New York), 47, 231
venereal diseases, 152–3
Vibrants, 75
Victoria Park, Sydney, 156–7
video games, 410
videos, 383–5, 398
Vietnam War, 32
Village People, 63
Villawood Migrant Hostel, 7
Vincent, Gene, 90
Virgin Records, 162
Vlasic, Marsha, 374–6

W. G. Berg, 79
Wakeman, Rick, 186, 318
Walker, Clinton, 23–4, 31, 40, 69, 72, 97, 124, 151, 249, 293, 296, 301, 307–8
Waller, Alan 'Wally', 46
Wal-Mart, 410
Walton, Mary, 137–8, 308
Watts, Charlie, 409
Way, Pete, 228, 230, 294, 297, 311–12

Webb, Al, 172
Wells, Junior, 373
West, Leslie, 50
West Side Story, 199
White, Trevor, 52
Whitehorn, Geoff, 176
Whitesnake, 228, 289, 356
Whitman, Slim, 261
Who, 16, 41, 47, 50, 68, 90–1, 280–2, 398
Who Made Who, 382–3, 411
Wild Horses, 284
Wild Turkey, 318
Wilding, Philip, 330–1, 351
Williams, Cliff, 221, 234–6, 245, 280, 315, 344, 354, 366, 370, 383, 388
    joins band, 212–14, 216–17
Williams, Georgiana, 280
Williams, Hank, 261
Wilson, B. J., 366–7
Winter, Johnny, 143, 221, 363
Winztons, 34–5
Wisefield, Laurie, 213
Wishbone Ash, 213
Wolfman Jack, 197
Wood, Ronnie, 185, 229, 409
Wright, Gary, 48
Wright, Simon, 369–71, 376–8, 383, 385–6, 409
    leaves band, 388–90
Wright, Stevie, 8–10, 14, 35, 37–8, 42, 44–5, 47, 73, 103, 107, 132
    'Evie', 44–5, 52, 93, 107, 127
    heroin addiction, 107, 140, 316
    at Melbourne Festival Hall, 150

Yardbirds, 18, 90
Yes, 162, 186, 262
Yesterday and Today (Y&T), 245, 354
Young, Alex, 5–6, 12, 14, 42, 192
Young, Angus
    and aggression in band, 96–7, 387
    'Angus!' chants, 246, 253
    and birth of Malcolm's daughter's, 329
    and Bon Scott's death, 302, 304, 314–17
    and Bon Scott's replacement, 316–20, 323
    and Dave Evans's departure, 110–11
    early years, 3–6, 11–19
    first bands, 46–7, 49–53
    first sees Bon Scott on TV, 83
    and *For Those About To Rock*, 352–3
    and formation of AC/DC, 52–66
    friendship with Pete Way, 230–1
    guitar playing, 50, 58–9

lookalike contests, 385
marriage, 280, 293, 336, 344
mooning, 173, 192–3, 198, 221
relationship with Bon Scott, 115,
205–6, 233, 255
and Satanism accusations, 356
school uniform, 63–4, 91, 94, 135, 144,
147, 158, 190, 221, 340, 384, 407
stage act, 135–6
taught by Mutt Lange, 269
teetotal diet, 97, 118, 124, 135, 173, 231,
247, 336, 354, 387
Young, Cara, 329
Young, Ellen, 280, 336, 404, 414
Young, George
and Back in Black, 331, 336
bass playing, 15, 93, 124, 132–6, 142,
150, 210, 216
and Blow Up Your Video, 385–6
and Bon Scott's death, 314, 316
and Bon Scott's joining band, 112–13
and Dirty Deeds, 168, 170
and Doug Thaler, 218–19, 238
early years, 9–11, 19
early years of AC/DC, 93–5, 106–7,
118–20
and Easybeats, 9–11, 14–15, 38, 89–90
fired as producer, 255–9, 265, 269,
274, 288
and Flick Of The Switch, 374–5, 377
and formation of AC/DC, 52–7, 59–61,
66
and 'High Voltage', 149–51
and High Voltage, 122–7
and If You Want Blood, 252
and Let There Be Rock, 202–4
and Powerage, 235
and The Razors Edge, 394–5
and Reading Festival gig, 189–90
songwriting and production, 35, 41–7,
49, 52, 59, 62, 70–1, 93, 103, 107–8,
112, 150, 198
and Stiff Upper Lip, 405–6
and TNT, 154–5
and videos, 384
and Who Made Who, 383
Young, Gillian, 380
Young, John, 5, 11

Young, John Paul, 47, 108, 150, 198, 257
Young, Johnny, 10, 31, 35, 37–8, 67
Young, Linda, 293, 329
Young, Malcolm
alcoholism and absence, 377, 386–8
argument with Atlantic, 343–4, 347
and Back in Black, 330–1, 335
and bad gigs, 149, 189
and Bon Scott's death, 302, 304, 307,
310, 316–17
and Bon Scott's replacement, 288,
316–20, 323–4, 337–8
contracts VD, 152
daughter's birth, 329
and Dave Evans's departure, 109–11
desire for US success, 234–5, 288
early years, 3–6, 11–19
fires Ian Jeffery, 376, 399
fires Mutt Lange, 351–2
fires Peter Mensch, 347–9
fires Phil Rudd, 364–6, 372
first bands, 16–17, 46–9, 51–3
and For Those About To Rock, 349–52
formation of AC/DC, 52–66
guitar playing, 16, 58–9
illness rumour, 415–16
love of jazz, 49, 55, 59
marriage, 293–4, 344
and Phil Rudd's return, 401–2
relationship with Bon Scott, 115,
205–6, 233, 255, 288
row with Black Sabbath, 210
Young, Margaret (mother), 4–5, 7, 12, 18,
49
Young, Margaret (sister), 5, 12, 19, 57
and school uniform, 63–4
Young, Neil, 219
Young, Sandra, 45, 57
Young, Steven, 5
Young, Stevie, 388
Young, Stewart, 380–5, 387, 390, 392–8,
400–1, 404, 408–10
Young, Trevor, 131–2
Young, William (brother), 5
Young, William (father), 4–5, 7, 14
Young, Yvette, 45

ZZ Top, 369